CREATIVITY ACROSS DOMAINS

Faces of the Muse

CREATIVITY ACROSS DOMAINS

Faces of the Muse

Edited by

James C. Kaufman
California State University at San Bernardino

John Baer
Rider University

LAWRENCE ERLBAUM ASSOCIATES, PUBLISHERS
2005   Mahwah, New Jersey   London

Copyright © 2005 by Lawrence Erlbaum Associates, Inc.
All rights reserved. No part of this book may be reproduced in
any form, by photostat, microform, retrieval system, or any other
means, without the prior written permission of the publisher.

Lawrence Erlbaum Associates, Inc., Publishers
10 Industrial Avenue
Mahwah, New Jersey 07430

Cover design by Sean Trane Sciarrone

Library of Congress Cataloging-in-Publication Data

Creativity Across Domains: Faces of the Muse
    edited by James C. Kaufman and John Baer

ISBN 0-8058-4657-3 (cloth : alk. paper).

Includes bibliographical references and index.

Copyright information for this volume can be obtained by contacting the Library of Congress.

Books published by Lawrence Erlbaum Associates are printed on acid-free paper,
and their bindings are chosen for strength and durability.

Printed in the United States of America
10 9 8 7 6 5 4 3 2 1

This little book is for
Allison Kaufman
My wife and best friend
And the girl I adore
I'll love you forever
And ever and ever
And ever and ever
And fifteen days more
　　—JCK

To SKB, who makes everything possible,
and HASB, who sees possibility everywhere.
　　—JB

Contents

Acknowledgments   xi

Introduction: How People Think, Work, and Act
Creatively in Diverse Domains   xiii
James C. Kaufman and John Baer

1   The Creative Process in Poets   1
Jane Piirto

2   Flow and the Art of Fiction   23
Susan K. Perry

3   Acting   41
R. Keith Sawyer

4   Should Creativity Be a Visual Arts Orphan?   59
Enid Zimmerman

5   Creativity and Dance—A Call for Balance   81
John I. Morris

6   Musical Creativity Research   103
Marc Leman

7	Domain-Specific Creativity in the Physical Sciences *Gregory J. Feist*	123
8	Creativity in Psychology: On Becoming and Being a Great Psychologist *Dean Keith Simonton*	139
9	Creativity in Computer Science *Daniel Saunders and Paul Thagard*	153
10	Engineering Creativity: A Systems Concept of Functional Creativity *David Cropley and Arthur Cropley*	169
11	Creativity as a General and a Domain-Specific Ability: The Domain of Mathematics as an Exemplar *Roberta M. Milgram and Nava L. Livne*	187
12	Creative Problem-Solving Skills in Leadership: Direction, Actions, and Reactions *Michael D. Mumford, Jill M. Strange, Gina Marie Scott, and Blaine P. Gaddis*	205
13	Emotions as Mediators and as Products of Creative Activity *James R. Averill*	225
14	Selective Retention Processes That Create Tensions Between Novelty and Value in Business Domains *Cameron M. Ford and Diane M. Sullivan*	245
15	Management: Synchronizing Different Kinds of Creativity *Min Basadur*	261
16	Creativity in Teaching: Essential Knowledge, Skills, and Dispositions *Don Ambrose*	281
17	The Domain Generality Versus Specificity Debate: How Should It Be Posed? *Robert J. Sternberg*	299

18	The (Relatively) Generalist View of Creativity *Jonathan A. Plucker*	307
19	Whence Creativity? Overlapping and Dual-Aspect Skills and Traits *John Baer and James C. Kaufman*	313
20	The Amusement Park Theory of Creativity *James C. Kaufman and John Baer*	321

Author Index 329

Subject Index 343

Acknowledgments

Editing a book can be a daunting task, but it is made so much easier when both the contributors and the publishers are such great colleagues. In particular, we would like to thank Bill Webber at Lawrence Erlbaum Associates for his help, support, and encouragement—it has truly been a pleasure. We also thank Kristin Duch for her assistance.

As many theories discuss, it takes a supportive and nurturing environment to be creative. We have been particularly lucky in having such tremendous colleagues at California State University at San Bernardino (CSUSB) and Rider University.

At CSUSB, James' work on creativity has been enhanced by discussions with Mark Agars, Faith McClure, and Janel Sexton, among other professors. He has been given wonderful support by Stu Ellins, his chair, and John Conley, his dean, both in his research and in his work as director of the Learning Research Institute. James also has a dedicated team of students who work with him; he would like to single out Candace Andrews, Suzanne Grundy, Alicia Hunter, Michael Lucas, Erica Mitchell, and Terrence Robertson for their help, and anticipates adding many more names to this list. Erica, in particular, has served as an unpaid teaching and research assistant and will be an outstanding professor in the near future. James would like to especially thank Candace Andrews for help in preparing this manuscript; he has also been greatly helped by Roja Dilmore-Rios, his assistant at the Institute.

At Rider, John's work has benefited from discussions about creativity (and so many other things) with many colleagues present and past. The names of those who have helped shape his thinking—often by means of very earnest and thoughtful disagreement—are far too numerous to mention individually. His thinking has also been influenced by the ideas of many talented students over the years, whose inspiration continues to motivate his work.

James has benefited greatly from his friendship with his past and future mentor, Robert Sternberg. He would also like to thank his wife Allison Kaufman, his parents Alan and Nadeen Kaufman, his sister Jennie Kaufman Singer, and his friend David Hecht for putting up with him as he was working on this project.

John wishes especially to thank his wife Sylvia, whose creativity is far greater and more mysterious than any theory he has encountered.

Introduction: How People Think, Work, and Act Creatively in Diverse Domains

James C. Kaufman
John Baer

Picture a scientist who has creative insights about the human body, or a businessperson with a creative way of running a company, or a writer with a creative idea for a novel. Are they more similar or different? What are the particular features that distinguish them? The question of whether creativity is a general ability or whether it is domain specific is an important one that has yet to be resolved in creativity research. In the only point–counterpoint, debate-style pair of articles in its history, 5 years ago the *Creativity Research Journal* asked two leading proponents of these competing positions to square off and argue the cases for domain specificity and generality (Baer, 1998; Plucker, 1998). Differences of opinion remain, and evidence continues to be gathered and debated. Yet, whether or not general creative thinking abilities exist, there is no doubt that domain-specific abilities exist—and that such abilities matter very much in creative performance in diverse domains. Even those who argue for the existence of domain-general creative thinking skills recognize that domain-specific thinking skills also play an important role in creative thinking (e.g., Amabile, 1996; Anderson, Reder, & Simon, 1996; Conti, Coon, & Amabile, 1996).

The message that content matters is not unique to creativity research and theory. For example, the situated learning and situated cognition perspectives that have grown out of Vygotsky's work argue that thinking and learning are inherently social and imbedded in a particular cultural setting (Cobb & Bowers, 1999; Greeno, Collins, & Resnick, 1996). A similar message has been sent in education, where, for example, Hirsch (1996) has argued strongly for the importance of teaching specific content. As evidence of the responsive chord this work has struck, the *American School Board Journal* called Hirsch's book *The Schools We Need and Why We Don't Have Them* "the most important book of the past school year" (Harrington-Lueker, 1997, p. 31), and the American Federation of Teachers, which doesn't typically find itself in such complete agreement with boards of education, honored Hirsch with its QuEST Award.

The field of creativity is a natural one in which to explore issues of content and domain specificity. Although one can think of creativity as a construct in abstract, domain-transcending ways, all creative products come into being in some domain or field of endeavor (and they are ultimately judged by the current standards of the relevant field or domain). Creativity also has a much wider purview than it once did; no longer confined to just a few areas in the arts and sciences, creativity is now considered important in performances and products of all kinds. Indeed, interest in creativity has never been greater, with a special division within the American Psychological Association devoted to the empirical study of the arts, four different journals centered around the study of creativity, and several major annual awards given out to outstanding creativity researchers.

More and more work has focused on the domain-specific nature of creative thinking and creative performance. Even in domains that seem closely related, such as writing poetry and writing short stories (Baer, 1993, 1994a, 1994b, 1996; Kaufman, 2001) or creating different kinds of artwork (Runco, 1989), it appears that the underlying processes may be quite different. The important skills, attitudes, ways of working, guiding metaphors, and standards for assessing creative performance vary widely from domain to domain. There are many such domains—Karmiloff-Smith (1992) described them as micro domains because they are more narrowly defined than were the broad domains of earlier modularity theorists like Gardner (1983)—and psychologists are beginning to probe what the essential features of each are (Baer, 1993; Gardner, 1993; Gruber, 1981; Johnson-Laird, 1988; Piirto, 1998; Runco, 1987, 1989; Simonton, 1998; Sternberg & Lubart, 1995; Winner, 1996).

This volume joins and sorts through the sometimes confusing theoretical diversity that domain specificity has spawned. Our goal has been to bring together researchers who have looked at how creative thinkers in different arenas—such as the various arts (creativity in poetry, fiction, visual art, music, dance, acting), sciences (creativity in psychology, mathematics, physics, engineering, computer science), and communication/leadership (creativity in business, management, teaching, leadership, and emotional expression)—and ask each to explain what is known about the cognitive processes, ways of conceptualizing and solving problems, personality and motivational attributes, guiding metaphors, and work habits or styles common among creative people in the domain he or she has investigated. Their answers are exciting, and they comprise the bulk of this book.

There are six chapters in the creativity in the arts section. In chapter 2, Susan K. Perry writes about creativity in fiction writing, giving special attention to the nature of "flow" and suggesting many techniques that enable writers to enter a state of "flow." In chapter 3, R. Keith Sawyer looks at creativity in acting, which is a relatively new topic for creativity research but, he argues, one that has "potential implications for studies of creativity in all domains" because of the unique, real-time constraints of acting. In chapter 1, Jane Piirto discusses creativity in the writing of poetry and relates what is known about creativity in poetry to her Pyramid of Talent Development. Enid Zimmerman, in chapter 4, points out that creativity in the visual arts, although of great importance in the world of art and the work of artists, has been neglected in art education in recent years. She also discusses such topics as the relationship between intelligence and creativity and the effects of formal art instruction on creativity. In chapter 5, John I. Morris considers how the field of creativity research intersects the domain of dance, with special attention to movement performance, improvisation, and dance making. And Marc Leman, in chapter 6, discusses research on musical creativity in relation to societal and cultural developments.

The creativity in science section consists of five chapters. In chapter 9, Daniel Saunders and Paul Thagard look at creativity in the relatively new field of computer science, comparing and contrasting it to creativity in such related fields as engineering and mathematics. They also consider two very different modes of creative work, which they term "intense" and "casual." In chapter 10, David Cropley and Arthur Cropley note that although "there are common elements to creativity in all domains, creativity in engineering clearly differs from creativity in, for instance, fine arts," and their chapter on creativity in engineering discusses the very different constraints that influence creativity when one is designing something that must have a functional purpose as well as an aesthetic one. As part of their chapter on creativity in mathematics, in chapter 11 Roberta M. Milgram and Nava L. Livne argue that mathematics is both a general and a domain-specific ability, and that an emphasis on a distinction between intelligence and creativity has led to the neglect of important ways in which intelligence and creativity are similar. In chapter 7, Gregory J. Feist considers evolutionary and developmental pressures influencing creativity in the physical sciences. He argues that "the disposition to be interested in and have a talent for understanding the physical and inanimate world has been shaped by evolutionary pressures" and as a result humans have a specific cognitive domain devoted to solving physical science problems. In chapter 8, Dean Keith Simonton discusses how creativity in psychology is both similar to and very unlike creativity in other domains, and suggests that even among creative psychologists there is great diversity. In fact, Simonton shows that most great psychologists have personality traits that cluster at one of two very distinct poles, with experimental psychologists tending to be similar to creators in the natural sciences and correlational/humanistic psychologists tending to have personality profiles that are similar to creators in artistic fields.

The section on creativity in communication/leadership also contains five chapters. In chapter 16, Don Ambrose probes what it means to be creative in teaching, arguing that teaching is a highly complex endeavor that is influenced by a wide range of contexts and constraints, and requires a broad array of skills and dispositions. In chapter 12, Michael D. Mumford, Jill M. Strange, Gina Marie Scott, and Blaine P. Gaddis discuss the importance of creative problem solving in creative leadership, with special emphasis on three key aspects of leadership: setting direction, guiding action, and managing others' reactions. James R. Averill, in chapter 13, addresses emotions as mediators and as products of creative activity, and emotional syndromes as potentially creative products in their own right. In their discussion of business creativity, in chapter 14 Cameron Ford and Diane Sullivan suggest that creativity can be best understood through the lens of the theory of evolution. They show why they believe that "the tensions between novelty and ascribed value present challenges that are unique, or at least substantially more salient, in business domains" than in most other domains. In chapter 15, Min Basadur argues that there are different kinds of creativity within the domain of management, presents a four-part model of creativity in management (generation, conceptualization, optimization, and implementation), and shows how this model relates to other models of creativity.

The conclusions section of the book includes three very different chapters that look at creativity more globally. In chapter 17, Robert Sternberg considers how we might most profitably think about domain specificity. In chapter 18, Jonathan Plucker reviews the earlier chapters of this volume from what he calls a "(relatively) generalist view of creativity." In chapter 19, we ask (and try to answer) the question "Whence creativity?" based on our review of what our many expert contributors have written about creativity in their respective domains.

Following this, in chapter 20, we present a new theory of creativity that is the product of a large and ongoing research project that has been deeply influenced and enriched by the views of the contributors to this book.

REFERENCES

Amabile, T. M. (1996). *Creativity in context: Update to the social psychology of creativity*. Boulder, CO: Westview.

Anderson, J. R., Reder, L. M., & Simon, H. A. (1996). Situated learning and education. *Educational Researcher*, *25*(4), 5–11.
Baer, J. (1993). *Creativity and divergent thinking: A task-specific approach*. Hillsdale, NJ: Lawrence Erlbaum Associates.
Baer, J. (1994a). Divergent thinking is not a general trait: A multi-domain training experiment. *Creativity Research Journal*, *7*, 35–46.
Baer, J. (1994b). Generality of creativity across performance domains: A replication. *Perceptual and Motor Skills*, *79*, 1217–1218.
Baer, J. (1996). The effects of task-specific divergent-thinking training. *Journal of Creative Behavior*, *30*, 183–187.
Baer, J. (1998). The case for domain specificity in creativity. *Creativity Research Journal*, *11*, 173–177.
Cobb, P., & Bowers, J. (1999). Cognitive and situated learning: Perspectives in theory and practice. *Educational Researcher*, *28*(2), 4–15.
Conti, R., Coon, H., & Amabile, T. M. (1996). Evidence to support the componential model of creativity: Secondary analyses of three studies. *Creativity Research Journal*, *9*, 385–389.
Gardner, H. (1983). *Frames of mind: The theory of multiple intelligences*. New York: Basic Books.
Gardner, H. (1993). *Creating minds: An anatomy of creativity seen through the lives of Freud, Einstein, Picasso, Stravinsky, Eliot, Graham, & Gandhi*. New York: Basic Books.
Greeno, J. G., Collins, A. M., & Resnick, L. B. (1996). Cognition and learning. In D. Berliner & R. Calfee (Eds.), *Handbook of educational psychology* (pp. 15–46). New York: Macmillan.
Gruber, H. E. (1981). *Darwin on man: A psychological study of scientific creativity* (2nd ed.). Chicago: University of Chicago Press.
Harrington-Lueker, D. (1987). The year's best books. *American School Board Journal*, *184*(8), 31–34.
Hirsch, E. D., Jr. (1996). *The schools we need and why we don't have them*. New York: Doubleday.
Johnson-Laird, P. N. (1988). Freedom and constraint in creativity. In R. J. Sternberg (Ed.), *The nature of creativity* (pp. 202–219). New York: Cambridge University Press.
Karmiloff-Smith, A. (1992). *Beyond modularity: A developmental perspective on cognitive science*. Cambridge, MA: MIT Press.
Kaufman, J. C. (2001). The Sylvia Plath effect. Mental illness in eminent creative writers. *Journal of Creative Behavior*, *35*(1), 37–50.
Piirto, J. (1998). *Understanding those who create*. Scottsdale, AZ: Gifted Psychology Press.
Plucker, J. A. (1998). Beware of simple conclusions: The case for the content generality of creativity. *Creativity Research Journal*, *11*, 179–182.
Runco, M. A. (1987). The generality of creative performance in gifted and nongifted children. *Gifted Child Quarterly*, *31*, 121–125.
Runco, M. A. (1989). The creativity of children's art. *Child Study Journal*, *19*, 177–190.
Simonton, D. K. (1988). *Scientific genius: A psychology of science*. New York: Cambridge University Press.
Simonton, D. K. (1994). *Greatness: Who makes history and why*. New York: Guilford.
Sternberg, R. J., & Lubart, T. I. (1995). *Defying the crowd*. New York: Free Press.
Winner, E. (1996). *Gifted children*. New York: Basic Books.

Chapter 1

The Creative Process in Poets

Jane Piirto
Ashland University

What makes up the specific talent of the poet? What skills are shown, or acquired on the way to expertise? There is the musical sense of making rhythm and rhyme, consonance and dissonance in conscious or unconscious patterns. There is the interest in inner probing of the self. There is the need to see life more deeply than most, and if so, to tell about it in formal patterns of language. The poet can make an image that relates metaphorically to what is being discussed so that the thing itself breaks open and is illuminated through the choices or analogies that the writer has made. The poet often stubbornly insists on these metaphors, which at first may seem strange but then become commonplace to the observers. Ultimately, although the impetus for writing may stem from emotion, the poet is inspired by language and its implications. As Nobel laureate for poetry Joseph Brodsky said, "If there is any deity to me, it's language" (Plimpton, 1988, p. 399).

From where does poetry stem? Poetry's connection with divinity goes back even farther than the Greeks, who called poetry "divine madness" (Plato, 1952, p. 134). The events of September 11, 2001, caused the nation to turn to poetry as solace, as comfort (personal communication, Caroline Kennedy on the *Diane Rheem Show*, July 5, 2002, WCPN Cleveland). Our souls need poetry in ways we do not need other forms of literature except perhaps drama, which also has divine roots in sacred rituals played out in places of worship (Piirto, 1999b). Poet Ted Hughes (Heinz, 1995) said that poetry exists on a deep, bottom level: "We all live on two levels—a top level where we scramble to respond . . . to . . . impressions, demands, opportunities. And a bottom level where our last-ditch human values live . . . poetry is one of the voices of the bottom level" (p. 90).

Whereas Freud (1908/1976) thought these visionary works stemmed from personal experience, Jung thought they stemmed from the primordial. Jung (1933) maintained that the artist was a vehicle, "one who allows art to realize its purposes through him" (p. 171). The life of the poet cannot explain the work of the poet: "It is his art that explains the artist, and not the insufficiencies and conflicts of his personal life" (p. 171). My point of view is similar—although the life of the artist (person) is interesting, the work of art stands on its own; through somewhat mysterious channels it speaks for all people who find a relationship to it. This is perhaps best explained in people's bonding to popular songs, which are the society's rune songs, or poetry.

However universal the impulse to write poetry may be, this chapter uses examples from only those poets who have met a certain standard of peer review by virtue of publication in recognized literary venues. The standard for being cited or discussed in this chapter is that the poets discussed here would have or have met the criteria in their nations or countries for being listed in the U.S. *Directory of Poets and Writers.* In order to qualify, a writer must have 12 points of accumulated credit, with the following as means of qualification: one published poem counts as 1 point; a published novel counts as 12 points, a published book of poetry counts as 12 points, and having received an established literary award counts as 4 points. In 1999–2000, there were 4,050 poets and 1,850 fiction writers. Performance writers numbered 71 people, and those who are listed as both poets and fiction writers numbered 1,225. (I am among the 1,225. See Piirto, 1985, 1995a, 1996a, 1996b.) Many of the studies done on poets have not used such a high standard; in this article, I try to focus on studies in which this publication and peer review standard has clearly been met.

Each field defines its "experts" through peers. The idea of individual, domain, and field is pertinent here (Feldman, Csikszentmihalyi, & Gardner, 1994). A domain is "a formally organized body of knowledge that is associated with a given field" (p. 20). Mathematics is a field, but algebra, geometry, number theory, are domains. Literature is a field, but poetry is a domain. Feldman et al. noted, "Domains have representational techniques that uniquely capture the knowledge that is in the domain" (p. 22). This is done through symbol systems unique to the domain, a special vocabulary, and special technologies used only within that domain. A field is transformed by individual creators pushing the boundaries of their domains. In order to transform a field, the creator must have mastery of the theory, the rules, the ways of knowing of that field, and also of the domain that is being used to transform it.

1. CREATIVE PROCESS IN POETS

Creative people, no matter what their field, have certain characteristics in common. Although this chapter is about poets, most other creative producers also possess these characteristics. Among these are certain *core attitudes*: *risk taking*, or taking chances in their field; *self-discipline*, an ability to constantly work with their talent, to practice and practice; *motivation*, both to do the work and to promote the work; a sense of *naiveté*, or openness, that constitutes the ability and willingness to see the old in new ways; and *unconventionality*, or the ability to inure oneself against pressures to conform. I have constructed a model called the Piirto Pyramid of Talent Development that illustrates this (Fig. 1.1). This model has guided my work on talent in domains (Piirto, 1994/1999, 1992/1998, 2002). It is a contextual framework that considers person, process, and product, as well as environmental factors.

THE PIIRTO PYRAMID OF TALENT DEVELOPMENT

1. The Genetic Aspect

At the base of the pyramid is the level of genes—the DNA combination of one's father and one's mother and their ancestors. Writing ability sometimes runs in families, but most writers do not come from families in which writing was the family profession. Whether talent is inherited or environmental is currently at issue. Much is inherited, but the environment also has an important place in working with what is inherited (Piirto, 1992/1998, 1994/1999, 2002).

2. The Emotional Aspect: Personality

Many studies have emphasized that successful creators in all domains have certain *personality attributes* in common. These make up the base of the model. Among the personality attributes are *androgyny* (Barron, 1969; Csikszentmihalyi, Rathunde, & Whalen, 1993; Piirto, 1992/1998; Piirto & Fraas, 1995); creativity[1]; *imagination* (Dewey, 1934; Langer, 1957; Plato, 1952; Rugg, 1963; Santayana, 1896); *insight* (Davidson, 1992; Sternberg & Davidson, 1995); *intuition* (Myers & McCaulley, 1985); the presence of *overexcitabilities*, or intensity (Dabrowski, 1965; Dabrowski & Piechowski, 1977; Piechowski, 1979; Silverman, 1993); *passion for work in a domain* (Amabile, 1983, 1989, 2001; Benbow, 1992; Bloom, 1985; Piirto, 1992, 1994, 1998a,

---

[1] Along with some other thinkers (e.g., Cattell, 1971; Renzulli, 1978; Tannenbaum, 1983), I concur that creativity is mostly an attribute of personality—with a hat doffed to the cognitive psychologists.

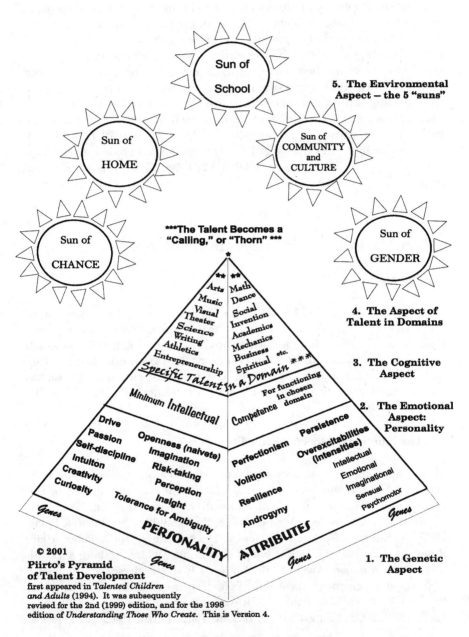

FIG. 1.1. Pyramid of talent development.

1998b, 1999a, 1999c, 2002); *perceptiveness* (Myers & McCaulley, 1985; Piirto, 1998a, 1999d); *perfectionism* (Adderholdt-Elliot, 1991; Silverman, 1993); *persistence* (Renzulli, 1978); *resilience* (Block & Kremen, 1996; Jenkins-Friedman & Tollefson, 1992); *risk taking* (Barron, 1969; MacKinnon, 1978; Renzulli, 1978); *self-efficacy* (Sternberg & Lubart, 1992; Zimmerman, Bandura, & Martinez-Pons, 1992); *tolerance for ambiguity* (Barron, 1968, 1995); and *volition, or will* (Corno & Kanfer, 1993).

This list is by no means discrete or complete, but it does demonstrate some of the work that has been done on the personalities of creative people and indicates that this work has converged to show that such adults have achieved much by force of personality. The consolidation of personality traits into the Big Five Personality Attributes of neuroticism, extroversion, openness, agreeableness, and conscientiousness (McCrae & Costa, 1999) are noted here, but earlier work on creative people has noted that these other traits as listed, and so I include them here. Talented writers and other creative adults who achieve success possess many of these attributes. One could call these the foundation, and one could go further and say that aspects of these attributes may be innate but other aspects can also be developed. Elsewhere (Piirto, 2002) I have discussed and given examples of how writers' personalities display the attributes listed here. I also discussed elsewhere other personality attributes that seem to be present in creative writers, including poets: ambition/envy, concern with philosophical matters, frankness often expressed in political or social activism, psychopathology, depression, empathy, and a sense of humor. Space does not permit discussion here.

3. The Cognitive Aspect

Writers seem to have IQs in the 120s and above (Simonton, 1994). IQ tests measure verbal ability as well as spatial and quantitative ability, and writers seem not to score as high in spatial or in quantitative areas as they do in verbal areas. That may cause lower IQ scores. For example, world-class writers given the Terman Concept Mastery Test at the University of California at Berkeley's IPAR study scored highest (about 156) on this test of all the creative groups studied (Barron, 1968). I (Piirto, 2002) found that although no IQ tests were available for the creative writers I studied, they were still high academic achievers who attended prestigious colleges.

4. The Aspect of Talent in Domains

The *talent* itself—inborn, innate, mysterious—is usually a skill to do certain tasks in specific areas, or domains. Talent is the apex of the Piirto Pyramid. Many writers tell of being accused, during their early school years, of cheating on a writing assignment because what they produced sounded so adult (Piirto, 2002). For example, take the first woman poet to win the Pulitzer prize, Edna St. Vincent Millay. Entering a new school at age 12, she was kept after school so that the teacher could find out if someone helped her write her first composition for the class. Millay said, "Excuse me, Mrs. Harrington . . . but I can tell that you think I didn't write that composition. Well, I did! But the only way I can prove it will be to write the next one you assign right here, in front of you. And I promise it will be as good as this one, and maybe better" (Milford, 2001, p. 5).

Most talents are recognized through certain *predictive behaviors*; for example, voracious reading for linguistically talented students (Piirto, 1994, 1999, 2002). The most salient predictive behavior for writers was the constant reading they did from a very early age. Writing is a talent that serves well in all professions and occupations, but poets, novelists, playwrights, songwriters, writers of creative nonfiction—creative writers—write with levels of talent that are astounding. Often their abilities move and delight people.

The Thorn: The Notion of a "Calling." On the Pyramid is a metaphorical thorn. The thorn pricks and pains, impels. The writer can't *not* write. Poet Sam Hamill described his thorn, the thorn of poetry:

> Streetwise and tough, on the run, I read, memorized, recited, and wrote poetry in exactly the same way a decent young musician practices scales. . . . Poets in America don't have "careers" in poetry but I have a life in it. So I have no career, only a deep avocation and a will to practice . . . I am a scholar without students, a student whose teachers have mostly been dead for centuries. (*Contemporary Authors, 161,* p. 112)

The presence of the thorn gives a person an idea of what his or her call, or vocation, might be. The notion of the call, or the vocation, has a religious connotation, because the poet is impelled much as the priest is.

The personality attribute of *volition*, or will, comes into play here. Hillman (1996), Jung (1933), and Plato (1952) said that a *daimon* pursues each person, and that person cannot rest until their *daimon* is answered. Nobel Prize winner Derek Walcott described being a poet as "a religious vocation. I have never separated the writing of poetry from prayer" (Plimpton, 1988, p. 272). Poetry writing, like other forms of art, becomes a form of autotherapy as well as a form of inquiry about the world. Poet Emily Dickinson, for example, spent years in her room working out her own psychological problems through what Habegger (2001) called "self-therapy" (p. 480) and a "drive to expression" (p. 481).

1. CREATIVE PROCESS IN POETS

The Environmental Aspect: The 5 "Suns"

In addition, everyone is influenced by five "suns." These suns may be likened to certain factors in the environment. The three major suns are the "sun of home," the "sun of community and culture," and the "sun of school." Other, smaller suns are the "sun of chance" and the "sun of gender." The presence or absence of all or several of these make the difference between whether a talent is developed or whether it atrophies. In a lengthy study of themes in the lives of 160 contemporary U.S. writers (Piirto, 1999, 2002), 16 themes emerged. These have been arranged in terms of the environmental suns in the Piirto Pyramid.

The Sun of Home

Theme 1: Unconventional families and family traumas.
Theme 2: Predictive behavior of extensive early reading.
Theme 3: Predictive behavior of early publication and interest in writing.
Theme 4: Incidence of depression and/or acts such as use of alcohol, drugs, or the like.
Theme 5: Being in an occupation different from those of their parents.

The Sun of Community and Culture

Theme 6: Feeling of marginalization or being an outsider, and a resulting need to have their group's story told (e.g. minorities, lesbians, regional writers, writers from lower socioeconomic class, writers of different immigration groups).
Theme 7: Late career recognition.

The Sun of School

Theme 8: High academic achievement and many writing awards.
Theme 9: Nurturing of talents by both male and female teachers and mentors.
Theme 10: Attendance at prestigious colleges, majoring in English literature but not attaining a Ph.D.

The Sun of Chance

Theme 11: Residence in New York City at some point, especially among the most prominent creative writers.

Theme 12: The accident of place of birth and of ethnicity.

The Sun of Gender

Theme 13: Conflict when combining parenthood and careers in writing.
Theme 14: Societal gender expectations incongruent with their essential personalities.
Theme 15: History of divorce more prevalent in women.
Theme 16: History of military service more prevalent in men.

I found that poets and fiction writers are similar, except that poets seem to exhibit more symptoms of psychopathology (Andreason, 1987; Andreason & Canter, 1974; Jamison, 1989, 1993). (The studies that show this to be true have been questioned. See Nettle, 2000; Schlesinger, 2002.) I have been asked to write this chapter about poets, and thus I have focused on examples from poets, although to my mind there is little difference among creative writers in most attributes.

In discussing creativity, it is common to refer to the person, product, process, and press. The Pyramid previously addressed the person and press. The product is what has been reviewed and admired by peer review. The next section looks at the creative process in poets (Piirto, 1992/1998, 2002).

THE CREATIVE PROCESS IN POETS

Current Psychological Theories of the Creative Process

In other writings I (Piirto 1992/1998, 1994/1999, 1999e) have discussed several psychological approaches to understanding the creative process: developmental, social, cognitive, educational, and humanistic. I also classified psychoanalytic, philosophical, and religious approaches. However, creative writers themselves never seem to refer to psychologists' theories as they talk about the creative process. One might say that their descriptions of the creative process verge on the mystical (Sternberg & Lubart, 1999). Poet Robert Bly acknowledged two people within: "I think writing poetry is a matter of agreeing that you have these two people inside: every day you set aside time to be with the subtle person, who has funny little ideas, who is probably in touch with retarded children, and who can say surprising things" (Moyers, 1995, p. 63). The "subtle person" is the one who is susceptible to the inspiration discussed here, and could perhaps be also called the unconscious.

Thirteen aspects of the creative process seem to impel writers and poets: They seem to have prewriting rituals—for example, they like to walk; they crave silence; they seek inspiration from the muse, from nature, through substances, from dreams, from travel, and from others' works of art and music; they use imagination; they seek solitude so that they may go into a state of reverie (or flow); they fast; and they meditate. In looking at these themes, one could say that poets, at least, seem to be people of the dream rather than people who consciously follow a given step-by-step process such as that commonly discussed by those who advocate creative problem solving. This might have to do with their almost universal preference for intuition over sensing (Myers & McCaulley, 1985). The term *transliminality* has been used to describe this aspect of the creative process (Thalbourne, 2000).

Rituals

Rituals abound. Rituals of exercise before and while writing seem to be common. Some poets like to walk: Coleridge said he liked to think about writing while walking on uneven ground, climbing over rocks, or breaking through the woods. Wordsworth liked to walk back and forth on a straight gravel sidewalk. Tennyson walked with his son, saying his latest poem out loud in rhythm, adding new lines as they seemed necessary. Hodges (1992), who collected these anecdotes, called such acts "ritualistic pacing" (p. 39). Such physical activities perhaps enhance seratonin and endorphins and let the pacers reach a state of creative fecundity.

The Quest for Silence

Some writers are extremely susceptible to noise and distraction, and seek to isolate themselves in a quiet place. In order to concentrate—in order to hear the inner voice—many writers must retire from sound. The appeal of writers' retreats and colonies is that of peace and quiet away from the melee, so that the creative spirit can descend. At Yaddo, a writers' retreat, lunch is delivered in baskets to the writers hard at work in their cottages. Advertisements for such retreats promise remoteness, stillness, and solitude.

Inspiration

All creators talk about inspiration. Literally, inspiration is a taking in of breath. In terms of creativity, inspiration provides the motivation to write. When one takes in breath, one fills the lungs with air, with environment, with the stuff of life; after the intake comes the necessary release. For poets, this release is in the writing of the poem. Various kinds of inspiration are discussed next: the visitation of the muse, the inspiration of nature, inspiration through substances, inspiration from dreams (discussed at greater length later in the chap.), inspiration of novel surroundings, and inspiration by works of art and music.

Inspiration of the Muse. Writers often speak as if what they write was sent from something within but afar. Poems "come"—British Poet Laureate Ted Hughes said, "Poems get to the point where they are stronger than you are. They come up from some other depth and they find a place on the page" (Heinz, 1995, p. 67). Pulitzer Prize-winning poet Anne Sexton said, "Now I tend to become dissatisfied with the fact that I write poems so slowly, that they come to me so slowly. When they come, I write them; when they don't come, I don't" (Kevles, 1968, p. 281).

Some writers feel as if they are go-betweens, mediums. Some mysterious force impels them, works through their hands, wiggles through their fingers on the keyboard, and shoots to the page or the virtual page on the screen in front of the eyes. Nobel Prize winner Octavio Paz said that his poem "Sun Stone" was written as if someone were "silently dictating," "from far off and from nearby, from within my own chest." He referred to this inspiration as "the current" (MacAdam, 1991, pp. 113–114). Many others have called it "the muse."

Inspiration comes in response to a feeling for someone, quite possibly a sexual feeling, certainly an emotional identification. Everyone has written a secret love poem to a beloved, requited or unrequited. The longing lyrics of the Brownings show that the place of erotic desire and longing for sexual union cannot be underestimated in considering the products of any artist. Poets write love poems. Choreographers make ballets. Visual artists paint nudes. Many of these works are efforts to express eroticism within the boundaries of the medium in which the artists are working.

It is surprising how many poets, writers, musicians, and visual artists refer to the inspiration of the muse. Here are some examples from poets. Pulitzer Prize-winning poet Carolyn Kizer (1990) wrote an essay called, appropriately, "A Muse." The muse was her mother. Poet Molly Peacock (1996) said that her muse was her own inner child. Poet Anne Waldman (1991) noted that her Muse was sometimes "an androgynous shape-shifter" (p. 315).

The quintessential homage to and historical explanation of the power of the muse is Robert Graves' long, complicated, involved, and fascinating tome, *The White Goddess* (1948). Here, the inspiration of the muse was transmogrified from the Greek daughters to the female moon. The thesis was that the poetic mythical language of Europe "was a magical language bound up with popular religious ceremonies in honour of the Moon-goddess, or Muse" (p. 9). During his long career as a writer Graves himself was often inspired by beautiful young women, and at times he asked his two wives to live in a kind of *menage á trois* relationship with the current muse (Seymour, 1995).

May Sarton said she could only write poetry when she was inspired by a muse, "a woman who focuses the world for me" (Saum, 1983, p. 94). Poet James Tipton's muse, novelist and memoirist Isabel Allende, wrote an introduction to the collection of poems that won him the award of Colorado Poet of the Year (Tipton, 1998). In that introduction, Allende (1998) detailed the circumstances of their long and passionate correspondence.

The inspiration of the muse is also spoken of by poets of rock and roll. Songwriter Tori Amos addressed the visitation of the muse: "You can begin to feel a presence when she comes. I call it a she, like it's a bath product. I would start to know when she's coming. And when that happens, I know I have to remember it. I'll write on my hand or something" ("Two for the Road," 1998, p. 56).

Inspiration of Nature. The inspiration of nature, of trees, brooks, skies, birds, animals, and weather is well known. The scene for the poem that speaks of the vagaries of life is often set in nature. The English romantics used nature as inspiration; Wordsworth's cry against the Industrial revolution—"Little we see in nature that is ours"—still resonates with writers (Wordsworth, cited in Woods, 1950, p. 328).

Inspiration Through Substances. The use of substances—alcohol, drugs, herbs—has a long and respectable reputation within the literature on the creative process in writers, artists, and others. Aldous Huxley wrote about the influence of mescaline; Samuel Taylor Coleridge about the influence of opium; Jack Kerouac about amphetamines; Edgar Allan Poe about absinthe; 7th-century Chinese Zen poet Li Po about wine; Fyodor Dostoevsky about whiskey; Allen Ginsberg about LSD; and Michael McClure on mushrooms—peyote—and also about heroin and cocaine (McClure, 1966).

The list of substances used could go on and on. The altered mental state brought about by substances has been thought to enhance creativity—to a certain extent. The partaker must not only retain enough wits to descend (or ascend) into the abyss to reap what is learned there, but also to be able to return and put that learning down (Bold, 1982; Leonard, 1989). The danger of turning from creative messenger to addicted body is great, and many writers have succumbed, especially to the siren song of alcohol. The poet Charles Baudelaire used alcohol to enhance imagination: "Always be drunk. That is all: it is the question. You want to stop Time crushing your shoulders, bending you double, so get drunk—militantly. How? Use wine, poetry, or virtue, use your imagination. Just get drunk" (Bold, 1982, pp. 87–88).

Today such talk is not politically correct, because the dangers of addiction and the climate of recovery and codependency groups have led most people to be cautious about substance use. However, the use of substances has often taken on a mystical, spiritual aspect in the creative process of writers. For example, Allen Ginsberg had a vision of William Blake. While reading Blake, he experienced enhanced visual and auditory perception that lasted for several days. This experience led Ginsberg, who had previously used alcohol and marijuana, to experiment with mind-altering drugs, such as laughing gas, mescaline, heroin, ether, hashish, ayahuasca, and LSD. Ginsberg viewed the initial vision as "the only really genuine experience I feel I've had" (Miles, 1989, p. 245).

More than half of the U.S. writers who have won the Nobel Prize for Literature had alcohol difficulties (Rothenberg, 1990). Rothenberg theorized that writers use alcohol after writing "to cope with the anxiety that is generated by the creative process itself" (p. 92). Pulitzer Prize-winning novelist Robert Olen Butler also noted that the abuse of alcohol comes after writing as a way of coping with the intensity the writer has uncovered while writing (personal communication, Art & Soul Conference, Baylor University, February 2002).

Inspiration of Novel Surroundings: Travel. Travel seems to facilitate the creative process of writers, perhaps because the novelty of sensory experience is inspirational and a sense of naiveté is easy to maintain. Riding in a car or on a train into a new geographical location is often a sure way to fire the creative urges. Let me give a personal example from my life as a poet. When I visited the Himalayas, I felt able to write about them because I had actually stood by the side of a road in upper Pakistan being cajoled by an old goatherd in a turban, next to a rushing aqua-limestone-water river, among the piles of pale brown rocks where nothing green could grow. I didn't have a dupatta on my head and he cluck-clucked, deeply offended at my nakedness, although I was wearing a full-length jumpsuit with long sleeves and a high neck. I still remember that bright blue sky, that high sun, his white shalwar chemise and dirty turban, his white beard, my red jumpsuit, and his pointing finger, all on a dusty tan dirt road lined with high cliffs of unstable rock a few miles from a valley resort called "Shangri-La." Far up above there was another goatherd, shooing his charges along a high narrow path that paralleled the rock-banked road. That weekend, Easter weekend, I wrote a postcard poem to my friends. I remember sitting in a chair in the clear air, next to a quiet pond reflecting the sharp peaks, copying this poem over and over as if it were a mantra. When the United States sent Cruise missiles to Afghanistan terrorist hideouts in 1998, I was easily able to picture the terrain targeted.

1. CREATIVE PROCESS IN POETS 13

Inspiration by Works of Art and Music. Many writers are inspired by works of art produced by other artists. Art inspires, and some writers work from images. Many are also good at other arts, working across genres. Nobel Prize-winning novelist Günter Grass said, "Invariably the first drafts of my poems combine drawings and verse, sometimes taking off from an image, sometimes from words" (Gaffney & Simon, 1991, p. 213). Poet John Brandi's books are also illustrated, and his published journals also indicate that he works from drawings. Nobel Prize winner Derek Walcott started out as a painter, and then became a writer, and then went back to painting. He likes the sensuality of painting, but he feels more driven to create quality in writing: "I'm content to be a moderately good watercolorist. But I'm not content to be a moderately good poet. That's a very different thing" (Hirsch, 1988, p. 275).

Music also inspires, and some writers are talented musicians. Pulitzer Prize winner and National Poet Laureate Rita Dove said, "I have a very personal connection to music." She has played the cello since she was a child: "I think that my musical bent has spilled over into my writing. I love to experiment with the motion of words, and to me, language that doesn't sing in some way isn't valid" (Smith, 1994, p. 34). Many writers have studied music. Poet and novelist Robert Fox is a professional blues musician, playing both the guitar and piano in public gigs. When I was on the Ohio Arts Council Literature Panel, we writers on the panel used to meet in someone's hotel room, and pickup bands would play until the wee hours. How can the rhythms and rhymes of music not influence our writing?

On another note, friendships between artists of different genres abound in biographical literature. Dan Wakefield (1995) described the cross-fertilization in the 1950s among artists in Greenwich Village, New York. Centered in the White Horse Tavern (where the writers gathered) and the Cedar Tavern (where the abstract expressionist visual artists gathered), the avant-garde met, discussed, and appreciated each others' work, often marrying each other or having affairs with one another. The Village scene in the 1960s put into proximity such artists as playwright Sam Shepard, songwriters Bob Dylan, Joan Baez, Joni Mitchell, and Patti Smith, photographer Robert Mapplethorpe, visual artist Andy Warhol, and many others.

Many poems inspired by paintings, photographs, and symphonies exist; many writers quote lines of popular songs in their novels. Besides being inspired by works of art, many writers are also talented in other domains. For example, one cannot read Michelangelo's journals or Van Gogh's letters to his brother Theo without noticing how eloquent they were. In fact, the writer/artist combination is well known: A very partial list of writers who were also visual artists includes William Carlos Williams (who was also a medical doctor), e.e. cummings, Kenneth Patchen, Kenneth Rexroth, Lawrence Ferlinghetti, Philip Lamantia, Aldous Huxley, and Henri Michaux.

Imagination

In the *Oxford English Dictionary* (1971), imagination is called "the creative faculty of the mind in its highest aspect; the power of framing new and striking intellectual conceptions; poetic genius" (p. 1377). To imagine is to make an image. Poet W. S. Merwin noted that "Real image is a kind of fusion of all aspects of perception and of being in one tiny focus. . . . You can steal almost anything, but you can't steal images" (*Contemporary Authors New Revised 15*, p. 325).

Aristotle considered works of the imagination such as poetry, drama, and fiction as being more true than history, because the poet can fabricate truth from the elements of history rather than exhaustively tell the facts. The poet is able to tell the truth on a deep level, being able to see the patterns, and the overarching themes. Aristotle said, "Poetry is something more philosophic and of graver import than history, since its statements are of the nature rather of universals, whereas those of history are singulars" (Aristotle, *On Poetics*, p. 626).

Visual imagination is not the only kind of imagination (making of images) that writers use. Poets, of course, must use their aural sense, but so too must prose writers. W. S. Merwin talked about how a line must sound: "I think there is no intellectual way of saying that a line or a poem is okay or complete or anything like that; you can hear if it's complete, and then you want to let it alone" (*CANR 15*, 1985, p. 325).

Poet Tess Gallagher described the imagination as being magical and dark. She said, "Events of the imagination precede and sometimes outdo the events of life. We're all islands—inaccessible, drifting apart, thirsting to be explored, magical. . . . The landscape of the imagination is the darkest of all" (Gallagher, 1983, pp. 137, 147). Some writers connect imagination and dreaming. Poet Denise Levertov (1973) related how, in a dream, she went to the mirror and saw the dream character, a woman with hair wet with a spidery net of diamondlike water drops from misty fields, and said that the very detail of the woman in the mirror was evidence for the "total imagination," which is different from the intellect. She called it the "creative unconscious" (p. 72).

One fascinating explanation for the simultaneous interiorness and explosiveness of the writer's creative process was postulated by Prescott (1920), who noted that the poet sees with the eye of the mind, and the eye of the mind is "the characteristic organ of the poet and visionary. . . . The true poet is gifted with a kind of 'second sight,' higher and freer than the ordinary sense, and with this gift he becomes a 'seer' " (p. 139).

Flow

The state of reverie common to people engaged in the creative process has recently come to be called *flow*, a term fortuitously coined by Csikszentmihalyi (1990). Flow happens when a person is engaged in an activity that is challenging and rewarding at the same time. The person enjoys the activity and seeks to repeat it. This activity produces a positive feeling. While doing the activity, the person experiences deep concentration, a sense of being removed from present worries and cares, a sense of control over the activity, and an altered sense of time. In fact, time flies by. This state is most often experienced in solitude or in working in a group with whom one has little conflict, or creative conflict together.

Of course, *flow* is the word of the moment, but the feeling has been called other names. Poet Brewster Ghiselin (1952) called it "oceanic consciousness." A trancelike state, it has been called the "visitation of the Muse" by the Greeks; mystics, creators, athletes, long-distance drivers, and computer hackers have all entered this state willingly and with a sense of purpose and direction. It has been induced by fasting (remember, Jesus went into the wilderness for 40 days before the triumphal entry into Jerusalem, and he fasted and prayed before he committed his ultimate creativity). It has been induced by chemicals (Jack Kerouac typed the entire text of *On the Road* on a roll of butcher paper in the kitchen, while high on amphetamines). It has been induced by aerobic exercise and called the "runner's high."

Fasting

Some writers and creators alter their creative consciousness through diet. Poet Tess Gallagher (1983) talked about how fasting helps her creative process. Fasting brings her to a state of "out-of-body consciousness" that transfers to her poems. "During these periods I don't do much. I don't write . . . I try to stay alone during the fasting." She begins to stand on "an island of calm," where she can gain some clarity about her life. "It is a time to adjust my vision about what matters, what I should give my energy to. Time during fasting takes on a slower dimension." Of course, fasting can become anorexia, as described in a memoir by poet Louise Glück (1993).

Meditation

The numbers of writers who embrace Buddhism or aspects of Buddhism is nothing short of astonishing. One suspects this is because of the attention paid to meditation, to solitude, to going within that religious faith. Here is a partial list of such writers, many from an anthology (Johnson & Paulenich, 1992): Allen Ginsberg, Robert Bly, W. S. Merwin, Anselm Hollo, Anne

Waldman, Gary Snyder, Jane Augustine, Stephen Berg, Olga Broumas, John Cage, Diane di Prima, Norman Fischer, Dan Gerber, Susan Griffin, Sam Hamill, Jim Harrison, William Heyen, Jane Hirshfield, Robert Kelly, Jackson MacLow, Anthony Piccione, Jed Rasula, Larry Smith, Lucien Stryk, and Philip Whalen. Others have embraced the contemplative life of the Christian monastery; for example, the poets Kathleen Norris and Daniel Berrigan. The Naropa Institute in Boulder, Colorado, called the Jack Kerouac School of Disembodied Poetics, taught Tibetan Buddhism to many poets and others.

In fact, many writers, such as poet Gerald Stern, consider writing itself a form of meditation: "For whatever else it is, writing for me is also meditation." Stern, as other writers, views poetry as akin to religion: "My poetry is a kind of religion for me. It's a way of seeking redemption for myself, but just on the page. It is, finally, a way of understanding things so that they can be reconciled, explained, justified, redeemed" (Moyers, 1995, p. 383). The idea that the practice of writing itself is meditation is not a new one. The connection of writing to the spiritual has resounded since the time of the Greeks.

Descriptions of the creative process among writers often takes on language that is spiritual, mystical. Take this comment by poet Dick Allen: "A sense of mysticism, a complete dissolving into wonder and beauty has been with me through my life. I remember always feeling nearly ecstatic in childhood. I had known I would be a writer since the third grade" (*Contemporary Authors Autobiography Series, 11*, p. 4).

Wonder. Beauty. Dissolving. Disintegrating. Ecstasy. What "unscientific" words these are! What language used by those who treasure precision in language. In more prosaic terms, the experimental research psychologists seeking to justify creativity studies as "science" have categorized such responses and examples as the "mystical" approach, an approach that has hampered the study of creativity (Sternberg & Lubart, 1999). However, such examples exist and pervade the discussions of creativity in other domains, such as literature. Perhaps experimental psychologists would do well to pay a little more attention to these accounts rather than to dismiss them as "mystical" and therefore not scientific.

IMPROVISATION

Improvisation seems to be a key part of the creative process in writers. Poet Hayden Carruth stated that his writing process was like playing jazz. He asked, "What happens, subjectively and spiritually, when a musician improvises freely? He transcends the objective world, including the objectively conditioned ego, and becomes a free, undetermined sensibility in communion with others equally free and undetermined." Carruth, a fervent jazz aficionado, said that "my best poems have all been written in states of transcendent concentration and with great speed.... I have interfused thematic improvisation and ... metrical predictability" (Carruth, 1983, pp. 30–32).

Automatic writing is also part of the improvisational creative process. The poet James Merrill (1992) used automatic writing as an improvisational technique: "Writing down whatever came into one's head, giving oneself over to every impulse—reasonable and unreasonable—concrete and abstract ... a means of granting oneself permission to speak from the heart, the depths of one's unconscious" (p. 89). Other writers have worked similarly. William Butler Yeats used both his own and his wife's automatic writing as inspiration for work. Poet Octavio Paz also engaged in the practice.

DREAMS AND THE CREATIVE PROCESS

Many creative writers trust their dreams. Like other artists and musicians, they realize that the other side—the dark side, the night side—is very important to the creative process. Poet Linda Hogan (2001) stated it thus:

> Dreams are the creative store that is true wealth. They reside at the human edge of the holy. From the unknown, from eternity, into the restless minds of sleepers, their light is given off. In the human body, worlds are charted, wounds healed, illnesses reversed. In our vulnerable sleep, those hours when anything could happen. Like dark matter in the universe, dreams have mass and presence, even when not remembered. (pp. 130–131)

Dreams have inspired many poems, stories, and novels. Tennyson said he dreamed his poetry, which came to him whole, in long passages. Poet and novelist Jim Harrison noted that one third of one's life is spent in sleep and thus should not be dismissed. He said that humans have been noticing their dreams since the Pleistocene period, but for the past 20 years we have been paying more attention to the global economy than to our dreams: "But the global economy is supposed to be relevant, right? Well, fuck the global economy. Why should we discard a third of our lives?" (Miles, 1998).

Poet Philip Levine said he had a dream about snubbing an African American man he had worked with in an auto factory in Detroit. "I had had a dream and that dream was a warning of what might happen to me if I rejected what I'd been and who I was." Levine went back to bed "with my yellow legal pad and my pen. I was in that magical state in which nothing could hurt me or sidetrack me; I had achieved that extraordinary level of concentration we call inspiration." Levine stayed in bed for a week. "The poems were coming" (Levine, 1995, pp. 91–92).

THE NEED FOR SOLITUDE

The core of the creative process is solitude. Creative people often live lives in which their work is the most important thing.

Poet and novelist Jim Harrison (1991a) wrote that he requires a few months of near solitude every year: "I have learned . . . that I must spend several months a year, mostly alone, in the woods and the desert in order to cope with contemporary life, to function in the place in culture I have chosen." He walks and loses his "lesser self" in the "intricacies of the natural world." In nature, he is able to imagine himself back to 1945, and "the coyotes, loons, bear, deer, bobcats, crows, ravens, heron and other birds that helped heal me then, are still with me now" (p. 317).

Some evidence exists that these writers were solitary children, as well. Poet Amy Clampitt said, "I think the happiest times in my childhood were spent in solitude—reading. . . . Socially, I was a misfit" (Hosmer, 1993, p. 80). Whether this feeling of not fitting in is more true for writers than for the general population is not known. The feeling of being a misfit—an outsider—has occurred in many writers' lives (Piirto, 2002). A state of reverie seems induced by solitude, and in this solitude many ideas are generated. This state is between sleeping and waking, and the subject is relaxed, allowing images and ideas to come so that attention can be paid. What is important is a state of passivity and receptivity (Storr, 1983).

In his *Autobiography* (1953), Nobel Prize-winning poet William Butler Yeats commented that when one is alone, the world is apprehended more vividly and intensely: "My passions, my loves, and my despairs . . . became so beautiful that I had to be constantly alone to give them my whole attentions. . . . [W]hat I saw when alone is more vivid in my memory than what I saw in company" (p. 38).

DIFFERENCES BETWEEN NOVELISTS' AND POETS' CREATIVE PROCESSES

The novelist Norman Mailer, in his student days at Harvard when he was learning how to write, made a vow to write 3,000 words a day, every day. His first wife said of his writing habits a few years later: "There was never a question of waiting for the muse to descend" (Mills, 1982, p. 82). Mailer worked through the whole outlines of the books he was writing: how many chapters, how each chapter would move the plot forward. He had 3"-by-5" cards on which he kept track of the structure and the personalities of the characters. He would shuffle these to make sure he was on track. He wrote about 25 pages a week on the first draft of a 750-page manuscript.

Poets and prose writers work differently. The poet Louis Simpson (1972) commented about how prose writers just don't understand how a poet works: "Descriptions of poetry by men who are not poets are usually ridiculous, for they describe rational thought processes" (p. 198).

REFERENCES

Adderholdt-Elliott, M. (1991). Perfectionism and the gifted adolescent. In J. Genshaft & M. Bireley (Eds.), *Understanding the gifted adolescent* (pp. 65–75). New York: Teachers College Press.
Amabile, T. M. (1983). *The social psychology of creativity.* New York: Springer-Verlag.
Amabile, T. M. (1989). *Growing up creative.* New York: Crown.
Amabile, T. M. (2001). Beyond talent: John Irving and the passionate craft of creativity. *American Psychologist, 56,* 333–336.
Andreason, N. (1987). Creativity and mental illness: Prevalence rates in writers and their first-degree relatives. *American Journal of Psychiatry, 144,* 1288–1292.
Andreason, N., & Canter, A. (1974). The creative writer: Psychiatric symptoms and family history. *Comprehensive Psychiatry, 15,* 123–131.
Aristotle. (1952). On poetics. In R. Hutchins (Ed.), *Great books of the western world, 9* (pp. 681–699). (Ingram Bywater, Trans.). Chicago: University of Chicago Press.
Barron, F. (1968). *Creativity and personal freedom.* Princeton, NJ: Van Nostrand.
Barron, F. (1969). The psychology of the creative writer. *Explorations in Creativity, 43*(12), 69–74.
Barron, F. (1995). *No rootless flower: An ecology of creativity.* Cresskill, NJ: Hampton.
Benbow, C. P. (1992). Mathematical talent: Its nature and consequences. In N. Colangelo, S. G. Assouline, & D. L. Ambroson (Eds.), *Talent development: Proceedings from the 1991 Henry B. and Jocelyn Wallace National Research Symposium on Talent Development* (pp. 95–123). Unionville, NY: Trillium.
Block, J., & Kremen, A. M. (1996). IQ and ego-resiliency: Conceptual and empirical connections and separateness. *Journal of Personality and Social Psychology, 70*(2), 349–361.
Bold, A. (Ed.). (1982). *Drink to me only: The prose (and cons) of drinking.* London: Robin Clark.
Carruth, H. (1983). The formal idea of jazz. In S. Berg (Ed.), *In praise of what persists* (pp. 33–44). New York: Harper & Row.
Cattell, R. B. (1971). The process of creative thought. In R. Cattell (Ed.), *Abilities: Their structure, growth, and action* (pp. 407–417). Boston: Houghton Mifflin.
Corno, L., & Kanfer, R. (1993). The role of volition in learning and performance. In L. Darling-Hammond (Ed.), *Review of research in education* (Vol. 19, pp. 301–342). Washington, DC: American Educational Research Association.
Csikszentmihalyi, M. M. (1990). *Flow.* New York: Cambridge University Press.
Csikszentmihalyi, M. M., Rathunde, K., & Whalen, S. (1993). *Talented teens.* New York: Cambridge University Press.
Dabrowski, K. (1965). *Personality shaping through positive disintegration.* Boston: Little, Brown.
Dabrowski, K., & Piechowski, M. M. (1977). *Theory of levels of emotional development.* Oceanside, NY: Dabor.
Dewey, J. (1934). *Art and experience.* New York: Putnam.

Eisner, E. (1998). *The enlightened eye: Qualitative inquiry and the enhancement of educational practice.* Columbus, OH: Merrill/Prentice-Hall.
Feldman, D. H., Csikszentmihalyi, M., & Gardner, H. (1994). *Changing the world: A framework for the study of creativity.* Westport, CT: Praeger.
Freud, S. (1976). Creative writers and daydreaming. In A. Rothenberg & C. Hausman (Eds.), *The creativity question* (pp. 48–52). Durham, NC: Duke University Press. (Original work published 1908)
Gaffney, E., & Simon, J. (1991). Interview with Günter Grass: The art of fiction, CXXIV. *Paris Review, 119,* 208–240.
Gallagher, T. (1983). My father's love letters. In S. Berg (Ed.), *In praise of what persists* (pp. 109–124). New York: Harper & Row.
Ghiselin, B. (1952). *The creative process.* New York: Mentor.
Glück, L. (1991). The education of the poet. In E. Shelnutt (Ed.), *The confidence woman: 26 female writers at work* (pp. 133–148). Marietta, GA: Longstreet.
Graves, R. (1948). *The white goddess.* New York: Farrar, Straus, & Giroux.
Habegger, A. (2001). *The life of Emily Dickinson: My wars are laid away in books.* New York: Random House.
Harrison, J. (1991a). Everyday life. In K. Johnson & C. Paulenich (Eds.), *Beneath a single moon: Buddhism in contemporary American poetry* (pp. 124–132). Boston: Shambhala.
Harrison, J. (1991b). *Just before dark: Collected nonfiction.* New York: Houghton Mifflin.
Heinz, D. (1995). Interview with Ted Hughes: The art of poetry, LXXI. *Paris Review, 134,* 54–94.
Hillman, J. (1996). *The soul's code.* New York: Random House.
Hirsch, E. (1988). Interview with Derek Walcott. In G. Plimpton (Ed.), *Writers at work: The Paris Review interviews, 8th series* (pp. 265–298). New York: Penguin.
Hodges, J. (1992). *The genius of writers: A treasury of facts, anecdotes, and comparisons: The lives of English writers compared.* New York: St. Martin's Press.
Hogan, J. (2001). *The woman who watches over the world: A native memoir.* New York: Norton.
Hosmer, R. (1993). The art of poetry: Interview with Amy Clampitt. *The Paris Review, 126,* 76–109.
Jamison, K. R. (1989). Mood disorders and patterns of creativity in British writers and artists. *Psychiatry, 52,* 125–134.
Jamison, K. R. (1993). *Touched with fire: Manic-depressive illness and the artistic temperament.* New York: Free Press.
Jenkins-Friedman, R., & Tollefson, N. (1992). Resiliency in cognition and motivation: Its applicability to giftedness. In N. Colangelo, S. Assouline, & D. Ambroson (Eds.), *Talent development: Proceedings from the 1991 Henry B. And Jocelyn Wallace National Research Symposium on Talent Development* (pp. 325–333). Unionville, NY: Trillium.
Johnson, K., & Paulenich, C. (Eds.). (1992). *Beneath a single moon: Buddhism in contemporary American poetry.* Boston: Shambhala.
Jung, C. G. (1933). *Modern man in search of a soul.* New York: Bantam.
Kevles, B. (1968). Interview w/ Anne Sexton. In G. Plimpton (Ed.), *Women writers at work: The Paris Review interviews* (pp. 263–290). New York: Viking.
Kizer, C. (1990). A muse. In L. Lyfshin (Ed.), *Lips unsealed* (pp. 26–32). Santa Barbara, CA: Capra.
Langer, S. K. (1957). *Problems of art.* New York: Scribner's.
Leonard, L. (1989). *Witness to the fire: Creativity and the evil of addiction.* Boston: Shambhala.
Levertov, D. (1973). *The poet in the world.* New York: New Directions.
Levine, P. (1995). Entering poetry. In N. Baldwin & D. Osen (Eds.), *The writing life: A collection of essays and interviews with National Book Award winners* (pp. 85–96). New York: Random House.
MacAdam, A. (1991). Interview with Octavio Paz. *Paris Review, 119,* 82–123.

MacKinnon, D. (1978). *In search of human effectiveness: Identifying and developing creativity*. Buffalo, NY: Bearly.
McClure, M. (1966). *Meat science essays*. San Francisco: City Lights.
McCrae, R. R., & Costa, P. T. (1999). A five-factor theory of personality. In L. A. Pervin & O. P. John (Eds.), *Handbook of personality theory and research* (2nd ed., pp. 139–153). San Diego: Academic Press.
Merrill, J. (1992). Permission to speak. In E. Shelnutt (Ed.), *My poor elephant: 27 male writers at work* (pp. 83–100). Marietta, GA: Longstreet.
Miles, B. (1989). *Ginsberg*. New York: Simon & Schuster.
Miles, J. (1998, December 2). Interview with Jim Harrison. *Salon Magazine*. (Internet). Accessed January 24, 2004, from http://dir.salon.com/books/int/1998/12/cov_02intb.html
Milford, N. (2001). *Savage beauty: The life of Edna St. Vincent Millay*. New York: Random House.
Mills, H. (1982). *Mailer: A biography*. New York: McGraw-Hill.
Moyers, B. (1995). *The language of life: A festival of poets*. New York: Doubleday.
Myers, I., & McCaulley, M. (1985). *Manual: A guide to the development and use of the Myers-Briggs Type Indicator*. Palo Alto, CA: Consulting Psychologists Press.
Nettle, D. (2000). *Strong imagination: Madness, creativity and human nature*. London: Oxford University Press.
Patrick, C. (1935). Creative thought in poets. *Archives of Psychology, 26*, 1–74.
Patrick, C. (1941). Whole and part relationship in creative thought. *American Journal of Psychology, 54*, 128–131.
Peacock, M. (1996, August). The intense art. *Elle*, pp. 106–108.
Piechowski, M. M. (1979). Developmental potential. In N. Colangelo & R. Zaffer (Eds.), *New voices in counseling the gifted* (pp. 25–57). Dubuque, IA: Kendall-Hunt.
Piirto, J. (1985). *The three-week trance diet*. Columbus, OH: Carpenter Press.
Piirto, J. (1992). *Understanding those who create*. Dayton: Ohio Psychology Press.
Piirto, J. (1994). *Talented children and adults: Their development and education*. New York: Macmillan.
Piirto, J. (1995a). *A location in the Upper Peninsula: Essays, stories, poems*. New Brighton, MN: Sampo.
Piirto, J. (1995b, May). *Themes in the lives of contemporary women creative writers*. Invited speech presented at the Third Henry B. and Jocelyn Wallace National Research Symposium on Talent Development, Iowa City.
Piirto, J. (1996a). *Between the memory and the experience. Poetry chapbook*. Ashland, OH: Sisu Press.
Piirto, J. (1996b). Why does a writer write? Because. *Advanced Development, 7*, 13–30.
Piirto, J. (1998a). Themes in the lives of successful contemporary U.S. women creative writers. *Roeper Review, 21*(1), 60–70.
Piirto, J. (1998b). *Understanding those who create* (2nd ed.). Scottsdale, AZ: Gifted Psychology Press.
Piirto, J. (1999a). *Talented children and adults: Their development and education* (2nd ed.). Columbus, OH: Prentice-Hall.
Piirto, J. (1999b). Poetry. In M. Runco & S. Pritzer (Eds.), *Encyclopedia of creativity, 2* (pp. 409–416). San Diego: Academic Press.
Piirto, J. (1999c). Themes in the lives of successful contemporary U.S. women creative writers at midlife: A qualitative study. In N. Colangelo & S. G. Assouline (Eds.), *Talent development, III* (pp. 173–202). Scottsdale, AZ: Gifted Psychology Press.
Piirto, J. (1999d). Synchronicity. In M. Runco & S. Pritzer (Eds.), *Encyclopedia of creativity, 2* (pp. 591–596). San Diego: Academic Press.
Piirto, J. (1999e). A survey of psychological studies of creativity. In A. Fishkin, B. Cramond, & P. Olszewski-Kubilius (Eds.), *Investigating creativity in youth* (pp.). Cresskill, NJ: Hampton.
Piirto, J. (2002). *"My teeming brain": Understanding creative writers*. Cresskill, NJ: Hampton.
Piirto, J. (2004). *Understanding creativity*. Scottsdale, AZ: Great Potential Press.

Piirto, J., & Battison, S. (1994). Successful creative women writers at midlife. In N. Colangelo, S. G. Assouline, & D. Ambroson (Eds.), *Talent development, II. Proceedings from the 1993 Henry B. and Jocelyn Wallace National Research Symposium on Talent Development* (pp. 255–257). Iowa City: University of Iowa Press.

Piirto, J., & Fraas, J. (1995). Androgyny in the personalities of talented youth. *Journal of Secondary Gifted Education, 6*(1), 65–71.

Plato. (1952). Dialogues. In R. Hutchins (Ed.), *Great books of the western world* (Vol. 7, B. Jowett, Trans.). Chicago: University of Chicago Press.

Plimpton, G. (Ed.). (1988). *Writers at work: The Paris Review interviews* (8th series). New York: Penguin.

Plimpton, G. (Ed.). (1989). *Women writers at work.* New York: Penguin.

Prescott, F. C. (1920). *The poetic mind.* Ithaca, NY: Great Seal.

Renzulli, J. S. (1978). What makes giftedness? Reexamining a definition. *Phi Delta Kappan, 60,* 180–184, 261.

Richardson, J. (1986). *Wallace Stevens: The early years, 1879–1923.* New York: Morrow.

Rothenberg, A. (1990). *Creativity and madness.* Baltimore, MD: Johns Hopkins University Press.

Rugg, H. (1963). *Imagination.* New York: Harper & Row.

Santayana, G. (1896). *The sense of beauty: Being the outline of aesthetic theory.* New York: Dover.

Saum, K. (1983). Interview with May Sarton. The art of poetry XXXII. *The Paris Review, 89,* 80–130.

Schlesinger, J. (2002). Issues in creativity and madness part one: Ancient questions, modern answers. *Ethical Human Sciences and Services, 4*(1), 73–76.

Seymour, M. (1995). *Robert Graves: Life on the edge.* New York: Henry Holt.

Silverman, L. K. (Ed.). (1993). *Counseling the gifted and talented.* Denver, CO: Love Publishing.

Simonton, D. K. (1994). *Greatness: What makes history and why.* New York: Guilford.

Simpson, L. (1972). *North of Jamaica.* New York: Harper & Row.

Smith, S. I. (1994, March/April). Interview with Poet Laureate Rita Dove. *Poets & Writers Magazine,* pp. 28–35.

Sternberg, R., & Davidson, J. (Eds.). (1995). *The nature of insight.* Cambridge, MA: MIT Press.

Sternberg, R., Kaufman, J. C., & Pretz, J. *A propulsion model of kinds of creative contributions.* New Haven, CT: Yale University.

Sternberg, R., & Lubart, T. (1991). An investment theory of creativity and its development. *Human Development, 34,* 1–31.

Sternberg, R., & Lubart, T. (1999). The concept of creativity: Prospects and paradigms. In R. Sternberg (Ed.), *Handbook of creativity* (pp. 3–15). London, UK: Oxford University Press.

Storr, A. (1988). *Solitude: A return to the self.* New York: Free Press.

Tannenbaum, A. (1983). *Gifted children: Psychological and educational perspectives.* New York: Macmillan.

Thalbourne, M. A. (2000). Transliminality and creativity. *The Journal of Creative Behavior, 34*(3), 193–202.

Tipton, J. (1998). *Letters from a stranger.* Crested Butte, CO: Conundrum.

Two for the road. (1998, July 27). *Newsweek,* p. 56.

Wakefield, D. (1995). *New York in the 50s.* Boston: Houghton Mifflin.

Waldman, A. (1991). Gender and the wisdom body: Secular/sexual musings. In K. Johnson & C. Paulenich (Eds.), *Beneath a single moon: Buddhism in contemporary American poetry* (pp. 314–327). Boston: Shambhala.

Yeats, W. B. (1953). *The autobiography of William Butler Yeats: Consisting of reveries over childhood and youth, the trembling of the veil, and dramatis personae.* New York: Macmillan.

Zimmerman, B. J., Bandura, A., & Martinez-Pons, M. (1992). Self-motivation for academic attainment: The role of self-efficacy beliefs and personal goal setting. *American Educational Research Journal, 19*(3), 663–676.

Chapter 2

Flow and the Art of Fiction

Susan K. Perry

Novelists invent their imaginary worlds by tapping into some personal source of creativity. How they do this has been a matter for conjecture (among readers) and angst (among writers) throughout the ages: Where, oh where, is the muse to be found? In my interviews with 40 successful authors of fiction, I learned that many writers enter a state of flow that is highly conducive to creative accomplishment.

In *flow*, an altered state that is a universal human experience (Massimini, Csikszentmihalyi, & Fave, 1988), time seems to disappear. Theory mandates that a flow state is entered when the following requirements are in place: The activity has clear goals and offers feedback, you have the sense that your personal skills are suited to the challenges of the activity, you are intensely focused, you lose awareness of yourself, your sense of time is altered, and the experience becomes self-rewarding (Csikszentmihalyi, 1975/2000, 1990, 1996). Csikszentmihalyi found that "every flow activity . . . provided a sense of discovery, a creative feeling of transporting the person into a new reality. It pushed the person to higher levels of performance" (1990, p. 74).

THE BENEFITS OF WRITING IN FLOW

Although there is no scientific proof that flow necessarily produces top-quality writing, I have found that many writers are convinced they produce much of their best work while they are in such an altered state. As one writer told me, "I have to keep reminding myself that all I have to do is get into that place and the language will furnish itself."

Flow is significant to creative writers because it's been found that creators do not learn to increase the ratio of successful "hits" to overall output over a lifetime of work (Simonton, 1994). Therefore, entering flow easily and frequently should enable a writer to write more fluently and prolifically, and thus potentially to produce more distinguished and lasting fiction. Fiction writers typically have to motivate themselves to write, so that whatever state of consciousness is most motivating and effective for getting the work done is clearly a useful state into which to tap.

If flow is such a desirable state to be in while attempting to be creative (Amabile, 1996; Csikszentmihalyi, 1996), it's nonetheless a condition that's more often wished for by fiction writers than dependably achieved (e.g., Heffron, 1994, 1995; Plimpton, 1976, 1981, 1984, 1986, 1988, 1992; Sternburg, 1980, 1991). Common among writers at all levels is to experience a tiny flash of something like inspiration, sometimes followed by a resounding . . . nothing. Learning to induce flow is an effective way to access deeper levels of creativity, so that those initial bursts of inspiration may turn into lengthier and more productive writing sessions.

TRACKING DOWN WRITERS IN FLOW

I set out to examine creative writers and learn how flow fits into their process. I investigated a convenience sample of 40 short story writers and novelists (as well as 36 poets, to which I'll refer tangentially here) for whom writing is a major part of their lives (Perry, 1996, 1999). Each of the writers, including some with prize-winning literary books to their credit and others who have written best-selling novels in popular genres such as mystery or science fiction, was listed or qualified to be listed in *A Directory of American Poets and Fiction Writers* (1995–1996 ed.). Requirements for fiction writers to be listed are publication of three short stories, a novel, or a story collection. I knew a few respondents personally, and the rest (with whose work I was familiar) responded to my personal, telephone, or mail requests for interviews.

The writers' ages ranged from 34 to 86, with those in their 40s, 50s, and 60s predominating. The number of years they have been writing ranges from 16 years to "since childhood" or "all my life." There were 17 males and 23 females in the final sample of fiction writers.

Is this sample representative of all fiction writers? Some of those who chose not to participate indicated that they do not experience flow, and thus there's no way to be certain how many of those who never responded do indeed write in flow. Yet, the responses I obtained—and the patterns and themes underlying the specifics—were so consistent among all the writers (including those I talked to more than once, as well as numerous other writers I encountered and read about once the initial study was complete) that I'm convinced this discussion reflects a healthy level of accuracy about the writing-in-flow experience.

I began my investigations with the question "Have you ever had a fiction-writing experience in which you've lost track of time? Think about the most recent time you entered this state—which I'll call *flow*—and describe your experience of what led up to that shift in consciousness." I then followed up with a series of questions in order to determine if there are larger themes that connect the many personalized ways writers have found to induce flow, and how much control a creative writer can actually have over flow entry and thus, perhaps, over the so-called muse herself.

All the preparatory methods used by writers appear to fulfill certain common purposes. In the following discussion, when I say *many* writers tend to do such-and-such, I mean that such an activity was mentioned in at least half the interviews. I found little difference attributable to gender. Extent of writing experience and personality variance seemed to account for most of the individual differences. Where poets and fiction writers differed, I mention such minor divergences in the relevant sections. All uncited quotes in this chapter are from personal interviews or were heard during public talks made by the writers.

METAPHORS TO WRITE BY

Flow is a complex psychological process that is impossible to describe fully using literal language. Most authors spontaneously mentioned a metaphor, whether *flow* or another one, when discussing the state of consciousness in which the words seem to gush out of them. Even those who said they don't experience time seeming to disappear, agreed that something distinct is happening when their writing is going well.

Nearly twice as many poets as fiction writers offered metaphors. Poetry is typically a metaphor-intensive form of writing. Yet, when I compared the types of metaphors used by poets and by fiction writers, the differences were surprisingly small. Novelists used phrases such as "moving into the movie screen," "peeling layers," and "opening a faucet," and several volunteered multiple metaphors. Poets used such evocative phrases as "tapping into a vein," "diving underwater," "becoming part of some pulse," "surfing the wave of transformation," and "feeling my way into the skin of the poem."

Something stands out in the majority of the metaphors: a sense of active participation in making flow happen. The experience of entering flow includes a sense of travel, of having to perform a physical movement through space to get to the place of no time, no self, and, perhaps, no rationality. In the usual reality, space and time are thought of as two dissimilar concepts, which then collapse in the state of flow. Faye Moskowitz described removing one layer of memory at a time, going down deeper and deeper, as though on a dig. "At first," she added, "I am reasonably sure of what I will be charting, but at a certain depth, (I can never predict quite where), I uncover what I could not have predicted, and then, flow begins."

Ethan Canin described flow as a cave he can't purposely find a way into: "You spend so much of your conscious effort to approach this cave and looking at this dreamy, unapproachable mass of rock and there's no entrances, and you look and push there, and nothing is there, and then you give up and you leave, and on the way out, you see an opening. And that's so often how it starts."

FIVE KEYS TO FLOW ENTRY FOR FICTION

The way writers produce fiction is apparently at least partly under their control. After analyzing the data from the interviews, I divided what I call the *keys to flow entry* into five components. Two of these are preconditions related to motivation and personality or attitudes. The other three occur during the writing process itself: loosening up, focusing in, and balancing among several opposites.

Key 1: Have a Reason to Write

Novelists write for a range of reasons: something outside themselves may be urging them to do it, or they may have some deep, interior sense of the need to do it. Often, a combination of motivating factors comes into play. Some authors have numerous motives, such as best-selling novelist Amy Tan, who writes because her childhood disturbed her, because oftentimes she can't express herself any other way, to startle her mind, to churn her heart, "to knock the blinders off my eyes and allow me to see beyond the pale," because she's been in love with words since she was a child, and because it is how she hopes to discover what she means by truth (Tan, 1996, p. 9).

When writers are writing because something in the project is pulling them in, and not because it feels like they have to or because something outside themselves is pushing them, by definition they are intrinsically motivated and quite possibly in flow. Csikszentmihalyi and Rathunde commented, "Intrinsic motivation acts like a ratchet on the development of personal capacities. A person who has experienced flow will want to experience it again. But the only way to do so is by taking on new or greater challenges or by developing more skills" (1993, p. 76). It's likely that people are more creative when they are motivated by the enjoyment and challenge of the work itself (Hennessey & Amabile, 1988; Russ, 1993).

Feedback Loop. Feedback is another flow requirement, but writing is one of those creative activities that does not offer feedback from the outside, at least until the work is sent to an editor. Experienced writers are able to provide this feedback for themselves.

Sometimes the inability to match one's internal ideal can be highly troubling, and that frustration motivates the writer to keep trying to match that ideal. Many of the writers I interviewed weren't able to describe exactly how they manage to give themselves the requisite feedback. Novelist Margot Livesey told me that she provides feedback to herself by reading aloud whatever she writes, and "If a character is sitting in a room, or pruning a hedge or fixing a bicycle or sitting on a bus, I try to see that character both internally and externally as clearly as possible. I might begin writing a scene with three dozen details of the bus journey, then decide that only two of them really further the novel, and are therefore to my mind what is needed." Others told me that on some level, "something" is giving them permission to continue in the vein in which they've begun; if they lack that sense of rightness, they know something is wrong.

Writing Matters. One of the most powerful combinations of motivators is the sheer love of writing and the belief that it matters. Writing in flow is the way most writers feel they are their best selves: "I consider the gift of being absorbed into my work the greatest pleasure and the noblest privilege of my life" (Ursula K. Le Guin); "Sometimes I look up in the middle of writing and I think, 'I'm happy' " (Nancy Kress).

Barron, Montuori, and Barron—in summing up decades of research (1997), much of it with writers—pointed out that an intense desire to create is the most common aspect of creative people. In addition, they posited a "cosmological motive," that is, a drive to find order and make sense of everything, including this world. A good example of this is T. Coraghessan Boyle, who said he writes to counter existential despair: "Everything is chaos and we are so small and so meaningless—this world and universe—that we want to be individuals in some way, and art is great because it's an expression of me and me alone. So it's satisfying in that way because it issues some kind of a sense of order in a completely chaotic universe, which is terrifying."

This matter of "mattering," however, is not determined once and for all. At various stages of their careers, writers may feel deeply ambivalent—"Who cares?" (e.g., See, 2002, p. 48)—before finding their way back to a sense of commitment and meaningfulness that allows the work to proceed.

Mystery, Surprise, Challenge. Mystery and surprise were mentioned in a third of the interviews. The challenge that is so integral to flow is often supplied by these elements. Sometimes a writer knows the ending of a work before writing the first word, but if there are no unknowns along the way, there may not be enough interest to finish. Only a few of the writers I interviewed use outlines, and those who do find that their work never ends up following the outline completely. Some writers design alternatives to outlines, such as "a written conversation with myself . . . that stimulates my imagination" (Morrell, 2002, p. 25).

Some writers set themselves specific and concrete challenges to raise their motivation level. When a writer feels the need to beat boredom (Hamilton, 1981), he or she often tries to achieve new writing feats. Novelist David Gerrold told me that all his "lesser" books were experiments: "One was written in present tense, one was written with no passive tenses at all, one was written with a kind of metric prose that had its own lyrical rhythm, and those were all the books where the story wasn't as important as the exercise. So that way when I go back to the book that's important, those muscles have been trained and they just click in when necessary."

Another writer said that rather than write in a new genre, she has tried, for example, adding surreal elements to a realistic story. Another writer complexifies the dialogue, such as writing a mob scene, or delves into a challenging emotional scene.

Fullness and Other Motivators. Sometimes an overflowing mind allows words to cascade onto the paper. Writers don't always know how they "fill up," but they do know that when they're "full" it's time to write. Isabel Allende said, "Books don't happen in my mind, they happen somewhere in my belly. It's like a long elephant pregnancy that can last two years. And then, when I'm ready to give birth, I sit down and begin the book that has been growing inside me" (Epel, 1993, p. 8).

Nora Okja Keller, author of *Comfort Woman*—a novel about the Korean women who were kept as slaves by the Japanese during World War II—heard a former comfort woman give a talk. Keller explained, "It was like that story somehow penetrated me to such a degree that I started dreaming about comfort women, a lot of vivid images with no real story line. One night I got up after dreaming and started taking down notes to kind of exorcize it from my body."

Sheer fun is another motivator. Phyllis Gebauer noted, "Thought processes beforehand and after sitting down: Yippee! Now I can work on my book, get out of here, 'play' with my people."

Another reason authors write is a sense of duty, whether to oneself, to one's goals, or to one's art. Cees Nooteboom said that what gets him started is a sense of duty and knowing it would not be "good" if he put off the writing, for example, until after the weekend. It's not a matter of guilt, he explained, but rather of the arithmetic he follows: "It's the idea that you must finish the thing. And I have this idea that you have to do a certain amount of words a day."

David Gerrold motivates himself by using a spreadsheet to tally how many hours a day he writes. He stops every quarter hour or so to do a word count. He sets himself a target of about 2,000 words a day, and tries to beat his own average. Gerrold also finds that the break to count words "is an opportunity for a pat on the back so that every time that I stop, instead of acknowledging failure, which makes it harder to get back to the work, I'm acknowledging my success at moving forward."

Deadlines and Rewards: Good or Evil? Researchers have found again and again that work feels like play when you're motivated intrinsically—that an intense involvement in an activity for its own sake, with little or no thought of future rewards, leads to positive feelings, persistence, creativity, and flow. It's also been found, however, that when extrinsic rewards or motivators (e.g., competition or the pressure of being evaluated) are thrown into the mix, the desire to do the thing for its own sake may be undermined (Hill & Amabile, 1993). All rewards—even verbal feedback ("Good writing!") or something as simple as a pat on the back—provide information regarding competence. However, such remarks and rewards often tend to have a controlling aspect: They shift the focus, the locus of causality, from internal to external. This shift, in turn, tends to reduce the inner urge to do the thing for its own sake, at least in the long run (Deci, 1975; Ryan, 1993).

Some writers are able to ignore deadlines when they become inhibiting. Best-selling author Diana Gabaldon claimed, "Let's put it this way: We have deadlines in my contracts because there's a space for them. I've never met one. They get the book when I'm finished with it. They scream and tear their hair a lot. . . . But I have a much higher loyalty to my book than I do to any of them."

Extrinsic motivators may combine with intrinsic ones to make flow even more likely, as long as the extrinsic push doesn't come to feel like an effort at control by someone else (Hennessey & Amabile, 1988). It seems likely that those who are eminent in and knowledgeable about a domain have learned how to deal with the potentially negative effects of extrinsic rewards. Just as people need to find some internal rewards for uninteresting tasks even when they feel constrained to do them (Sansone, Weir, Harpster, & Morgan, 1992), experienced writers apparently are often able to transform their task by either concentrating on some previously overlooked portion of the environment or of the writing, or by putting variety into the way they write.

Key 2: Think Like a Writer

Is there a creative writer's personality? Given my limited data, this was impossible to ascertain with any degree of confidence, but I was able to develop some ideas about how an effective writer thinks. Rather than focusing on fixed traits, much of this discussion emphasizes attitudes, which tend to be more malleable.

The Natural Writer. About a quarter of those writers I studied (including both novelists and poets) are what I call "natural writers"—those who, more than most, live in an extended daylong flow. Prolific romance novelist Phoebe Conn explained, "I sit down and turn on my computer and work. I wouldn't even notice [moving into a flow state]. There's not a shift." A few spend most of their lives in a parallel world of their own imagining, always in a mild flow around their characters' lives. It's as though there's a valve (the prosaic concerns of reality) holding them back from flow. They just have to open it and let themselves go through. Novelist Madison Smartt Bell, for instance, told me that he thinks he has a natural facility for living in a dreamworld, and that's probably why he became a fiction writer. Faye Kellerman reported that she was always a spacey child who lived inside her head.

Open to Experience. Openness to experience, for a writer, is a combination of being curious, feeling sensitive to what's going on in the world, and having a certain liberal attitude about life (McCrae, 1987). When researchers looked at the relationship among openness to experience, creative ability, and creative accomplishment, they determined that openness moderates the relation between creative ability and creative accomplishments (King, Walker, & Broyles, 1996).

In my research, I often found examples of an openness to experience and a blurring of boundaries. This was sometimes accompanied by a fascination with Zen/Buddhist/mystical/occult thought. Such an openness to crossing boundaries may directly relate to ease of flow entry.

Award-winning science fiction author Ursula K. Le Guin commented, "Fiction is made out of experience, your whole life from infancy on. . . . But experience isn't something you go and *get*—it's a gift, and the only prerequisite for receiving it is that you be open to it. When you're open, you're also more readily inspired by everyday events—you don't need something extraordinary to happen before you feel the urge to write."

Willing to Take a Risk. A delight in intellectual risk taking was prevalent among my interviewees, who felt that it increases the odds they may create something novel. Playwright Edward Albee has been quoted as saying, "If you're willing to fail interestingly, you tend to succeed interestingly" (quoted in Joyner, 1998, p. B6). Many authors take extreme risks in their writing, whether emotionally, psychologically, or aesthetically. In an interview in which Anne Rice described writing one of her books, she said that as she surrendered to the process, she kept asking herself, "How *dare* you write these things!" (Gilmore, 1995, p. 94).

Fully Absorbed. As a personality trait, absorption reflects the degree of an individual's tendency to become deeply engaged in movies, nature, past events, fantasy, or anything else. It's also been argued that high-absorption people are motivated intrinsically, by their own experiences, whereas low-absorption people tend to be more motivated by outside events (Tellegen, 1981).

Interesting connections have been shown to exist among absorption, openness to experience, and hypnotizability (Glisky, Tataryn, Tobias, Kihlstrom, & McConkey, 1991; Tellegen & Atkinson, 1974), the last of which has analogues to a flow state. It seems that absorption involves a tendency to process information in unusual ways, which is what creative writers do. Absorption and a propensity to fantasize may also be related (Roche & McConkey, 1990). Again, this calls to mind the abilities of creative writers.

High-absorption types are better able to screen out distractions (Davidson, Schwartz, & Rothman, 1976), which is helpful to flow entry and creative production. Pulitzer Prize-winner Robert Olen Butler told me he "applies absolute absorption and concentration in things." A few writers insist they're not good at getting deeply absorbed, but when Jane Smiley described her writing process to me, I suspected that she gets more absorbed than she realizes: "I can write while talking on the phone. One chapter of the book I'm writing now, I wrote while feeling very distracted. My bookkeeper was here, my kids were walking through, the cleaning ladies were walking through, the dogs were barking, I had to get up every several minutes to do something, and when I came back to that chapter later, it was great."

Growing Confident. The writers I interviewed didn't started out naturally resilient and optimistic. Rather, they have all to some degree mastered their weaknesses and anxieties while traversing their career paths. Confidence, in the realm of fiction writing, relates to a sense that one's skills are suited to the task one has set oneself.

It's necessary to distinguish between a writer's confidence that he or she can produce work, and an assurance that the work will, at any particular session, be up to his or her standards. Ethan Canin revealed, "I still have a great fear after three, four books, I have no idea if it's utterly horrendous or great." Michael Connelly told me that knowing he is his own toughest critic has built his confidence to the point that, once he gets past his own demands on himself, he has confidence in the work. Some writers, after a long career, have learned to be confident of the results too, even if they cannot always depend on an even output.

Some productive writers tend to reframe anxiety as excitement about the work. Few writers, of course, are completely predictable in their psychological tenor. Time spent creating can be, as novelist Hilma Wolitzer said, a "sickening joy." However, anxiety typically does not intrude once a writer negotiates the transition into flow.

Key 3: Loosen Up

Creativity has been related to looseness of thinking and its accompanying lessening of inhibition that broadens the concept of relevance (Eysenck, 1994). Writers whose personalities are at the looser end of the continuum (Ornstein, 1993) are more likely to leap boundaries in separate parts of the mind, leading to better communication among brain segments. Thus, a fresher series of associations can be evoked.

Looseness may be encouraged by bringing a sense of play into the work. Another way is to stop *trying* and wait for looseness to occur. In addition, writers typically evolve certain individualized routines and rituals that, due to their habitual nature, ease the shift into an alternate consciousness and flow. Multiple specific techniques for loosening are discussed later in this chapter.

Key 4: Focus In

The process of narrowly focusing attention to the writing is another precursor for accessing creativity in flow. Writers make flow more likely by *deciding* to direct their awareness to a limited stimulus field. Some individuals seem to have the knack for directing their attention from inside (Goleman, 1988; Massimini et al., 1988). Those who performed well on tests of attentional regulation were also able to become absorbed in activities and enjoy them intrinsically, "a state wherein our experience seems to 'flow' " (Hamilton, 1981, p. 282).

Wanting to create fiction, highly focused writers begin writing, and some combination of their focusing ability and the writing process itself shifts them into a flow state. Writers may seek out a particularly engaging part of the task in order to ease the shift. Alternatively, they may structure the environment around their writing task in a particular way, such as by entering the study, turning on the computer, and having a cup of coffee within reach. For some writers, having a clear desk and a clear mind are essential.

Part of focusing in to write involves carving out a sense of solitude, whether that entails strict aloneness or merely psychically cutting oneself off from surrounding activity. Many of the routines to which writers become attached serve the purpose of centering attention on the work (as well as of loosening up, which has to happen virtually simultaneously). The very fact of automating one's working habits helps eliminate the distraction of the outside world and its expected judgments.

Once accustomed to a stimulus or situation (e.g., a chapter of a novel), attention may begin to wander again. Boredom is often both the cause and the result of such mental distractibility. Here's where a strong-enough motivation comes into play: When a writer genuinely wants to finish a narrative, he or she struggles to find ways to stay focused on it. Staying focused is a form of mindfulness. Those with the ability to be "mindful" are open to novelty, alert to distinction, sensitive to contexts, aware of multiple perspectives, and oriented in the present (Langer, 1997). Some of these traits coincide with the requirements of flow.

At times, this focusing in is done consciously: Diana Gabaldon related, "While I am actually working on a piece, I do have that feeling of needing to concentrate very hard to listen. It's not that they talk to you and you write it down. It's that you're actually working with them." Sue Grafton explained that she can't work if she thinks of reviewers. She tells herself to lower her sights and to quit looking at the end product: "My only responsibility is to write the next sentence well. And so I pull my focus down to as small and tiny as I can get it."

Key 5: Balance Among Opposites

Contradictions exist not only among writers, but coexist within the same writer. I found that writers' personal working methods place them somewhere along a number of continua, as they find their own ways of balancing among several opposing concepts or processes. With emotional states, too, writers balance among pairs of opposites in order to find what they need in the tension between two poles of feeling: "Writers seem to draw strength from emotional antitheses. . . . Writing often seems propelled by a collision, a tug-of-war between positive and negative feelings, agony and ecstasy" (Brand, 1989, p. 15).

Will Versus Inspiration? How much control do fiction writers have as they progress from images and ideas to completed works? It's the out-of-control state that many notable writers find produces their most intense and original work (e.g., Kolodny, 2000). Writers vary in how much they give up or let go of control, and in how much they depend on inspiration versus some process of will.

For the most part, writers express more of a sense of control during revision and editing than in first draft writing. A few writers are adamant about the necessity of maintaining some control at all times, whereas others cannot write without feeling they have totally let go. Such surrendering is one way to move into a more relaxed, open, and creative place. For instance, Chitra Banerjee Divakaruni compared writing to driving through fog: "You only see a little bit ahead." And Merrill Joan Gerber believes that flow "seems to come out of a state of partially 'idle' concentration (at least a willingness to work), whereupon, at some point, the imagined idea, thought, scene, invention takes on a sensual reality that overpowers the everyday demand on the senses."

Moving from will to what I see as its opposite, inspiration, I found that writers operate with a variety of belief systems. Whereas some writers experience whatever it is that goes into making their art as being the result of inspiration that comes from outside, other writers are equally certain that their creativity comes from their own subconscious minds. Numerous writers believe they can facilitate their own inspiration by sitting down to write and willing the process to begin.

Which Audience? If a writer is sharply aware too early of who is going to read the work when it is finished, the free flow of ideas may be inhibited (Roen & Willey, 1988). Yet, in order to access the necessary internal feedback (is this line or scene working?), some writers specifically ask themselves what their actual future audience might make of it.

It's more typical to consider the eventual audience during the revision process, but, even then, successful writers often claim to do so only in the interests of clarity. For some, knowledge of an audience's potential reaction is integral to the work. Writers work out the duality by manipulating the way they think about their readers. For example, the term *audience* is a frightening one to Susan Taylor Chehak, because it implies the scariness of strangers. She tries to divide herself in half, both writing for the audience and "just writing, rather than thinking of some objective person with glasses in a chair sitting in front of the fire reading my book."

Some writers have supportive spouses or friends with whom they regularly share their work. Those who don't have such friendly audiences often invent one to hold in their minds.

TECHNIQUES FOR LURING FLOW

The majority of the writers I interviewed have discovered how to get themselves into flow, although the shift is never guaranteed. Ritualizing one's behavior loosens the writer and enhances focus. Gore Vidal succinctly wrote,

"First coffee, then a bowel movement. Then the muse joins me" (Clarke, 1981, p. 311).

Almost anything can become routine and become an aid to flow. Robert Olen Butler commented, "I wrote every one of my first four published novels longhand on legal pads on a masonite lap board, using a certain kind of thick lead drafting pencil, on the Long Island Railroad. I would write 400 polished words going in and 400 polished words coming out. As soon as I was in that place and engaged those objects, I was in flow."

There's the deeply held belief by many writers that whatever worked once will work every time, and that one dare not deviate. It appears that many of these fetishlike behaviors actually do help shift consciousness and make creative output more likely. A writer's chosen set of rituals are habits that may cause processes to occur on a biological level. They may be similar to the instant arousal a person might experience when looking at something he or she thinks of as sensual.

Timing, Eating, Drinking

About three times as many of my interviewees write in the morning as at night. Mornings are conducive to creative flow because the morning mind is fresh out of the dream state and more easily moves into an alternate reality, and procrastination never has a chance to take hold. Night writers mention the lack of concentrated time earlier in the day, the lack of expected interruptions, and the atmosphere late at night that is so unlike that of the daylight world.

Some writers repeatedly eat the same foods while working on a particular project. Liquids can be vital to the flowing writer, from keeping a glass of water nearby to the ubiquitous cup of coffee. Few of the writers I talked to mentioned imbibing alcohol in relation to their writing. Perhaps this is related to the fact that so many more writers prefer to work in the morning, and alcohol, when it is imbibed, is typically done so in the evening to shrug off the anxieties of the day. As many writers were quite free in describing their writing-related sexual habits and their ingestion of antidepressants, I tend to believe them about their liquor habits as well.

Sensory Input

Writers often refer to "hearing" something that causes them to begin entering flow. A screenwriter told me that her characters mumble to her, but later, after she's compiled an outline, they scream.

For some, the visual sense is pivotal. Playwright Willard Simms said that when he was working on a historical play about Leonardo Da Vinci, he would get out a book of Da Vinci's paintings, as well as books containing other paintings he loved. Then he would try to get "involved in the paintings" to heighten his visual senses as a way to jumpstart his writing.

Diana Gabaldon's system for constructing a novel begins with picking up some bit of resonance that she calls a *kernel*: "It's a very vivid image or line of dialogue or an emotional ambiance that I can put on paper easily. And then you've got something to stand on when you're working backwards and forwards."

Music is often mentioned by writers talking about flow. This may be because the senses generally tend to operate from a different part or combination of parts of the brain from the logical, linguistic part. Flip on the music, smell the incense, taste the tea—these simple sensory acts help make the switch from active thinking to "letting it come." Carolyn See wrote three recent novels accompanied by Van Morrison. She plays the same album over and over, and the music works so well for her that she doesn't dare play the same tunes while she's driving, because "it zonks me right out into like a real profound daydream."

Some writers are no longer aware on a conscious level that they depend on these sensory rituals. Novelist Susan Taylor Chehak, for example, didn't mention her routine use of music until late in our interview, at which point she elaborated: "I actually even on Fridays go out and buy music for this purpose. I listen to the radio in the car purposely for songs that I think will be right."

On the other hand, silence is a prerequisite for some writers. Telephones come in for an amazing amount of verbal abuse by writers, because the phones' ringing is one of the more common and infuriating interrupters of flow in progress. Those writers who talk about having a strong sense of the importance of rhythm and sound in their work (more typically poets but a few novelists as well) are much less likely to listen to music while they work.

To ease into writing, some writers regulate their internal states by using meditation, because the essence of all meditative disciplines is to exclude distracting stimuli, focus attention, and move yourself away from your regular habits of thinking (Goleman, 1988). Self-hypnosis is another possible option, although only a few writers mentioned such rituals in our interviews.

Starting and Stopping

Numerous authors reread what they've written up to that point in order to get themselves writing again. Going over previous work helps return writers to the same mental states they were in the last time they were in flow. The characters start moving again, their speech rhythms resume, and environmental and internal distractions begin to fade. Some writers revise the previous day's work as well, as a way to segue into new material.

Some writers take advantage of psychological momentum by leaving their work while it feels incomplete. Then—and this makes sense in the context of some of the metaphors writers use—they don't have to "gear up" all over again each time they write. Instead, they're already "rolling."

The Best Tools

Writers describe their attachment to their preferred tool with terms varying from the prosaic "It's just what I'm used to," to the impassioned, along the lines of "I couldn't work without it." It was uncommon to have a writer tell me about his or her writing implement without including the words "always" and "never."

It sometimes happens that the requirements of a particular writing tool may take on special properties that contribute to the creative process, as Madison Smartt Bell explained: "I write with a pen, a Kohinoor rapidograph which I use for fiction only, or almost only. It requires a certain amount of futzing around, cleaning, coaxing, etc., . . . writer's block can be displaced onto these procedures" (Bell, 1996, p. 14). It's typical for advocates of handwritten work to experience that as somehow more "organic," although for some it depends on the kind of work, whether poetry or prose. Computer aficionados explain their choice by stating that the technology simplifies both writing and revising.

Reading to Write

Certain authors pick up a book by another author they like, read a few paragraphs, and feel instantly inspired to begin or resume their own writing. Reading is valuable for several reasons: When a writer reads for layers of meaning and patterns, the connection-seeking parts of the brain are getting stimulated; reading is a pleasure, so it relaxes the writer and begins the loosening up process; and reading fiction or poetry helps focus the mind on creative, imaginary linguistic activity and away from more mundane, linear thinking.

Walking or Running

The repetitive movement of walking or running puts the mind into somewhat of a meditative state, beginning the loosening process. It also begins the process of focusing inward, away from everyday reality. While walking or running, the writer may be precomposing or composing mentally. Sometimes a writer finds that a walk offers a stimulus that is missing, some nonverbal input needed to get the writing going again. Some authors get up and walk around the house, or pace back and forth, while trying to work out a creative task.

HOW LONG SPENT WRITING AND IN FLOW?

Flow doesn't necessarily begin at the start of a writing session, although once the writing has begun, flow may eventually follow. The range and variety of flow entry and writing routines is wide: "A lot of times I kind of ease in slowly. It takes an hour or two of struggle" (Aimee Liu); "I'm in the work right away, if it's going well, but it will be not a completely submersed flow state right away. It'll be more conscious in the beginning. If I'm lucky—it doesn't always happen—somewhere around, oh, I don't know, 20 minutes or a half hour I'll get really with it" (Nancy Kress).

The working writers I interviewed write on a regular or semiregular basis, whether daily, or several days a week when their other responsibilities allow. A few produce in cycles, binges, or spurts. For some, flow happens whenever they write, whereas for others, it is more elusive.

Length of writing sessions varied widely. Surprisingly, there weren't significant differences between poets and fiction writers. Poets told me they tend to spend anywhere from a half-hour a day to, very rarely, 40 hours at a sitting, but more commonly they write for a few hours (1 or 2) up to many hours (4 to 8). The length of time novelists say they work ranges from less than a half-hour a day (one respondent) to "all day" or 12 hours. More common responses range between 2 to 3 hours and 4 to 6 hours.

Flow can begin at any point in the entire creative process: during the preparation/thinking/dreaming/planning stage; the incubation stage when the writer is consciously doing something else (resting, tidying the drawers, playing racquetball) and waiting for the ideas to gel; the illumination/inspiration stage; or the rewriting and revising stage. When raw writing emerges from a deep flow state, authors later polish and revise to meet their own standards. In flow, critical faculties are put aside, for the most part, to allow for a more spontaneous outpouring. Later, say many writers, they can take what they get from flow and craft it into better work. Adding to the subjective flavor of flow is the fact that some writers believe editing is the hardest part of their work, regardless of whether they say they're in flow then or not, whereas others claim editing is the easiest, most emotionally thrilling part.

CONCLUSION

Flow is the antithesis of writer's block and, as such, is a highly desirable state for fiction writers. In the current research, it was found that entering a flow state to access creativity is common among writers, and that many of them actively seek out ways to make this process more dependable for themselves. Once such routes to flow are learned, writers tend to adhere to them habitually. Long experience in the domain appears to maximize writers' ability to shrug off everyday anxieties and distractions, enter flow, and create compelling fictional worlds.

Finally, unlike a great many amateur writers who procrastinate endlessly, these accomplished writers typically enjoy their abilities and look forward to losing themselves—whether they are able to do so rarely or regularly—in the joys of creation.

REFERENCES

Amabile, T. M. (1996). *Creativity in context (update to the social psychology of creativity)*. Boulder, CO: Westview.
Barron, F., Montuori, A., & Barron, A. (Eds.). (1997). *Creators on creating*. New York: Tarcher/Putnam.
Bell, M. S. (1996, May/Summer). Unconscious mind: The art & soul of fiction. *AWP Chronicle, 28*(6), 1–14.
Brand, A. G. (1989). *The psychology of writing: The affective experience*. New York: Greenwood.
Clarke, G. (1981). Gore Vidal. In G. Plimpton (Ed.), *Writers at work: The Paris Review interviews, Fifth Series* (pp. 283–311). New York: Penguin.
Csikszentmihalyi, M. (1975/2000). *Beyond boredom and anxiety*. San Francisco: Jossey-Bass.
Csikszentmihalyi, M. (1990). *Flow: The psychology of optimal experience*. New York: HarperCollins.
Csikszentmihalyi, M. (1996). *Creativity: Flow and the psychology of discovery and invention*. New York: HarperCollins.
Csikszentmihalyi, M., & Rathunde, K. (1993). The measurement of flow in everyday life: Toward a theory of emergent motivation. In J. E. Jacobs (Ed.), *Developmental perspectives on motivation* (pp. 57–97). Lincoln: University of Nebraska Press.
Davidson, R. J., Schwartz, G. E., & Rothman, L. P. (1976). Attentional style and the self-regulation of mode-specific attention: An electroencephalographic study. *Journal of Abnormal Psychology, 85*, 611–621.
Deci, E. L. (1975). *Intrinsic motivation*. New York: Plenum.
Directory of American poets and fiction writers (1995–1996 ed.). (1995). New York: Poets & Writers.
Epel, N. (1993). *Writers dreaming*. New York: Carol Southern.
Eysenck, H. J. (1994). The measurement of creativity. In M. A. Boden (Ed.), *Dimensions of creativity* (pp. 200–242). Cambridge, MA: MIT Press.
Gilmore, M. (1995, July 13–27). The devil and Anne Rice. *Rolling Stone*, pp. 92–98.
Glisky, M. L., Tataryn, D. J., Tobias, B. A., Kihlstrom, J. F., & McConkey, K. M. (1991). Absorption, openness to experience, and hypnotizability. *Journal of Personality and Social Psychology, 60*, 263–272.
Goleman, D. (1988). *The meditative mind: The varieties of meditative experience*. New York: Tarcher/Perigee.
Hamilton, J. A. (1981). Attention, personality, and the self-regulation of mood: Absorbing interest and boredom. *Progress in Experimental Personality Research, 10*, 281–315.
Heffron, J. (Ed.). (1994). *The best writing on writing*. Cincinnati: Story Press.
Heffron, J. (Ed.). (1995). *The best writing on writing* (Vol. 2). Cincinnati: Story Press.

Hennessey, B. A., & Amabile, T. M. (1988). The conditions of creativity. In R. J. Sternberg (Ed.), *The nature of creativity: Contemporary psychological perspectives* (pp. 11–38). Cambridge, UK: Cambridge University Press.

Hill, K. G., & Amabile, T. M. (1993). A social psychological perspective on creativity: Intrinsic motivation and creativity in the classroom and workplace. In S. G. Isaksen, M. C. Murdock, R. L. Firestien, & D. J. Treffinger (Eds.), *Understanding and recognizing creativity: The emergence of a discipline* (pp. 400–432). Norwood, NJ: Ablex.

Joyner, W. (1998, July 8). Television review: Sam Shepard, beyond the writing and acting. *The New York Times*, p. B6.

King, L. A., Walker, L. M., & Broyles, S. J. (1996). Creativity and the five-factor model. *Journal of Research in Personality, 30*, 189–203.

Kolodny, S. (2000). *The captive muse: On creativity and its inhibition*. Madison, CT: Psychosocial Press.

Langer, E. J. (1997). *The power of mindful learning*. Reading, MA: Addison-Wesley.

Massimini, F., Csikszentmihalyi, M., & Fave, A. D. (1988). Flow and biocultural evolution. In M. Csikszentmihalyi & I. S. Csikszentmihalyi (Eds.), *Optimal experience: Psychological studies of flow in consciousness* (pp. 60–81). New York: Cambridge University Press.

McCrae, R. R. (1987). Creativity, divergent thinking, and openness to experience. *Journal of Personality and Social Psychology, 52*, 1258–1265.

Morrell, D. (2002). *Lessons from a lifetime of writing: A novelist looks at his craft*. Cincinnati: Writer's Digest Books.

Ornstein, R. (1993). *The roots of the self*. New York: HarperCollins.

Perry, S. K. (1996). *When time stops: How creative writers experience entry into the flow state* (Doctoral dissertation, The Fielding Institute, 1996). *Dissertation Abstracts International, 58*(08), 4484.

Perry, S. K. (1999). *Writing in flow: Keys to enhanced creativity*. Cincinnati: Writer's Digest Books.

Plimpton, G. (Ed.). (1976/1981/1984/1986/1988/1992). *Writers at work: The Paris Review interviews* (fourth through ninth series). New York: Penguin.

Roche, S. M., & McConkey, K. M. (1990). Absorption: Nature, assessment, and correlates. *Journal of Personality and Social Psychology, 59*, 91–101.

Roen, D. H., & Willey, R. L. (1988). The effects of audience awareness in drafting and revising. *Research in the Teaching of English, 22*, 75–88.

Russ, S. W. (1993). *Affect and creativity: The role of affect and play in the creative process*. Hillsdale, NJ: Lawrence Erlbaum Associates.

Ryan, R. M. (1993). Agency and organization: Intrinsic motivation, autonomy, and the self in psychological development. In J. E. Jacobs (Ed.), *Developmental perspectives on motivation* (pp. 2–56). Lincoln: University of Nebraska Press.

Sansone, C., Weir, C., Harpster, L., & Morgan, C. (1992). *Journal of Personality and Social Psychology, 63*(3), 379–390.

See, C. (2002). *Making a literary life: Advice for writers and other dreamers*. New York: Random House.

Simonton, D. (1994). *Greatness: Who makes history and why*. New York: Guilford.

Sternburg, J. (Ed.). (1980). *The writer on her work*. New York: Norton.

Sternburg, J. (Ed.). (1991). *The writer on her work* (Vol. II). New York: Norton.

Tan, A. (1996, Fall). Required reading and other dangerous subjects. *The Threepenny Review*, pp. 5–9.

Tellegen, A. (1981). Practicing the two disciplines for relaxation and enlightenment. *Journal of Experimental Psychology: General, 110*, 217–226.

Tellegen, A., & Atkinson, G. (1974). Openness to absorbing and self-altering experiences ("absorption"), a trait related to hypnotic susceptibility. *Journal of Abnormal Psychology, 83*, 268–277.

Chapter 3

Acting

R. Keith Sawyer
Washington University, St. Louis

Since psychologists began to study creativity in the 1950s, they have focused on product creativity—domains of creative activity in which the creative process results in a finished, fixed product (Sawyer, 1995, 1996, 2003b). Creative products include ostensible physical artifacts, like paintings, sculptures, and musical scores, and also less tangible products, like a journal article outlining a new theory in particle physics. What these products share in common is that a creative process of essentially unlimited length generates the product; the creator works on the product in private, in a studio, laboratory, or office; and the creator has unlimited opportunities for revision. The created product does not appear until the creator makes a final decision that the process is complete and that the product is ready to be revealed to others working in the domain.

Acting is a relatively new topic for creativity research, only beginning to receive attention in the 1990s (Sawyer, 1997). When compared to product creativity, acting has three characteristics that make it uniquely valuable to creativity researchers: It emphasizes the creative process, rather than the created product; it is usually created by a collaborative ensemble; and it emphasizes spontaneity. Acting gives us an opportunity to observe a collaborative creative process in action, thereby providing insights about the creative process more generally. In creative domains that result in creative products—such as art and science—the creative process often takes place in isolation, in a studio or a laboratory, and it can take months or years before the final product is completed. This isolation and the long time period make the creative process difficult for researchers to study directly. But with acting, the creative process occurs on stage in front of the audience.

Creativity researchers have perhaps neglected acting as a result of a common distinction between "creation" and "execution"—the actor is thought to be nothing more than an executor of a work that is actually created by the playwright. The assumption that an actor is an uncreative interpreter is related to what has been called the *literary fallacy* (Alter, 1981): the reduction of theater to its text, and its analysis as a genre of literature. Yet the text is not autonomous from its performance, as those who study it as "literature" implicitly assume. The written script has to be transformed into a performance—a process technically known as *mise en scène*, literally "putting into the scene"—and this involves many creative decisions on the parts of the director and the actors: blocking movements, gestures, facial expressions, pacing, and timing. Some scripts more rigidly specify the eventual performance, thus yielding fewer variations across performances; other scripts are more open to interpretation, and allow the director and actors more creativity.

Improvisational theater is particularly interesting because there is no script and no playwright; all creativity rests with the actors. And although improvisation may seem radically different from scripted performance, actors themselves perceive a continuity between improvisation and conventional theater, and most professional improv actors also perform scripted theater. In this chapter, I identify those aspects of acting creativity that are most clearly revealed by improvisation, and I show that they are also important in scripted theater.

Acting is one of the oldest of human creative activities. Modern theater originated with the ancient Greeks. Long before recorded history, human societies performed rituals that most anthropologists believe are the source of all theater. For example, in many rituals the participants wear masks and enact otherworldly characters. The various techniques used by shamans are basic to many performing arts, including conjuring and illusion, ventriloquism, puppetry, and hypnotizing people on stage (Wilson, 1985). Acting is like shamanism in that the actor is partially possessed and yet also partially retains control of his or her actions. Many influential 20th-century directors (including Artaud, Beckett, Grotowski, & Beck) believed that modern theater is a sort of secular holy experience that helps us to liberate ourselves from the mundanity of daily life, by depicting a greater reality, and by making the invisible visible.

The process of creating a character on stage is a complex interaction among actor, director, and the playwright's script, and it is difficult to consider the actor's creativity apart from these other factors. In this chapter, I attempt to keep the focus on acting creativity by emphasizing improvisational acting, in which the actors perform on stage without a script and without a director. When considering the performance of scripted plays, I focus on the improvisational dimensions of performance. I argue that studies of acting creativity have potential implications for studies of creativity in all domains, for three reasons: They allow us direct access to the creative process, they allow us to study collaboration and mutual influence during the creative process, and they allow us to study the role of spontaneity in creativity.

The guiding question of this volume is whether creativity is a domain-general ability, or whether creativity is specific to a given domain of activity. Discussions of domain generality and specificity first arose in Piagetian developmental psychology (Sawyer, 2003a). In this context, the question was whether children passed through Piaget's proposed stages of cognitive development in all domains simultaneously, or whether each domain might develop through the stages at its own rate. Many developmentalists were swayed away from Piaget's general conception of stages by experimental evidence that children seemed to perform at different levels of cognitive ability when tested in different domains.

From the beginning of this developmental debate in the 1970s, psychologists such as David Henry Feldman applied these same concepts to creativity (1980). In the early 1990s, Csikszentmihalyi's influential *systems view* (1988, 1990a) argued that creativity itself could not even be defined apart from a domain of activity. At about the same time, Gardner's equally influential "multiple intelligences" view (1983) began to influence educational theory and practice.

The first distinctive feature of acting creativity is how it highlights the creative process. There is no fixed object that is created and that remains as evidence of the prior creative process; instead, the creative process occurs onstage in front of the audience, and the creative process *is* the created product. In improvisation, there is no private period of creation in a laboratory or studio, and there are no opportunities for revision. In performing a script, there is an extended rehearsal period, but the final product is always a public performance that involves creativity in the moment, and this creative process is public and unrevisable. (I do not consider acting for film or television in this same context, because the goal is to create a fixed product, and there is opportunity for revision; I believe that much of what I say here is applicable to such acting, but I do not argue that in this chapter.)

In acting, and in improvisational acting in particular, the audience is exposed to the creative process as it unfolds. Because the performance is live, in front of an audience, there is no opportunity for reflection or revision in the creative process. The audience observes the creative process in action. With improvisation, the creative process *is* the creative product. This provides the creativity researcher with a unique opportunity—to observe and analyze the creative process in action.

Acting is different from product creativity in a second way: Almost all acting is done by an ensemble, and requires collaboration among all of the performers. For example, in an improv theater group, no single actor can control or direct the performance. During a scene, no actor takes on a director's role and guides the performance. Instead, the dialogue is collaboratively created from line to line, as the actors respond to each other's words on the spot.

Because collaboration is central to improvisational acting, improvisation can help creativity researchers understand how collaboration influences the creative process in all domains. For example, most modern scientific laboratories involve the efforts of many top scientists, Ph.D.-level researchers, and graduate assistants. Conducting a scientific experiment is a highly collaborative endeavor. In a broader sense, an entire scientific discipline evolves and grows as a result of collaborations—ideas and theories are published, rejected, and elaborated in the pages of journals; constant e-mails are sent across the country (and indeed the world) among leading researchers; grant proposals are accepted, edited, and revised by committees of experts in Washington. Although the collaborations of stage performers are obviously very different, some aspects of improvisational performance may be common to all collaborations.

A third difference between acting and product creativity is that acting takes the emphasis on spontaneity to an extreme. Again, this difference is exaggerated in improvisational theater. Twentieth-century post-World War II American culture placed a high value on spontaneity in the arts, and it's no surprise that improvisational theater was created in the 1950s as part of a broad cultural shift to spontaneity in all of the arts (Belgrad, 1998; Sawyer, 2003b). In improvisation, the actors are forced to respond quickly, with the first line of dialogue that comes into their head, because to think analytically and edit that line would result in too much delay in the performance. Only by speaking the first thought immediately can a natural-sounding dialogue be sustained.

The current predominance of scripted theater makes it hard to imagine a time when *all* acting was improvised. But, of course, this was the case at the beginning of human culture, when writing systems had not yet been developed. The idea that a playwright would write down a script for later performance is a relatively recent innovation in human history. Until at least the late medieval period, many European actors remained illiterate. Some scholars, for example, maintain that Shakespeare did not write scripts, but rather taught his actors their parts orally; the extant scripts were transcriptions of actual performances, or from memory by one of Shakespeare's entourage (Delbanco, 2002). In a society without widespread literacy, by necessity all acting has an improvisational element.

IMPROVISATION

All modern theater is rooted in ancient, prehistoric ritual performances. These performances, because they predated literacy, were essentially improvisational. A ritual can involve a regular sequence of semiscripted acts that involve many people, or it can be a semi-improvised performance of a trance-possessed shaman. Some rituals are more structured and repetitive than others; nonetheless, all rituals that are not scripted display variation from one performance to the next. Anthropologists study verbal ritual performance around the world, and they have documented variations even in the most sacred rituals. For example, in many performance traditions only experienced elders have acquired the skills required to speak at important rituals. But even after a lifetime of performing prayers, incantations, and sermons, an examination of different audiotapes always shows multiple, and frequently substantive, variation.

Stanislavsky revived interest in improvisation at the turn of the 20th century, although it was first used exclusively as a training method for actors, rather than performed live. Influenced by Freud's psychology of the unconscious, Stanislavsky taught his actors to emphasize the feelings, moods, and expressions of a character, so that the performance would seem more authentic. He called this new technique *psychological realism*. Stanislavsky's techniques have been influential in the United States for decades, leading to *method acting* and the *New York school* of actor training. But until the 1950s these improvisational techniques were used only in the privacy of rehearsal.

Modern improvisation originated with The Compass Players, a group that emerged from the University of Chicago theater community in 1955. The Compass later evolved into the well-known improv group, The Second City, the model for the popular TV show *Saturday Night Live*. Classic Chicago improv performances begin with the stage lights up and the ensemble standing on an empty stage. They ask for a suggestion from the audience—a location, a relationship, a problem. After repeating the suggestion to be used, the actors immediately begin improvising a dialogue based on the suggestion. Nothing is planned in advance—the actors develop characters, plot lines, and dramatic tension as they go along.

Since its origins in the 1950s, improvisational theater has grown dramatically in Chicago and in other urban centers. With this growth has come a remarkable variety of styles and approaches to improvisation, from short games with cute gimmicks to fully improvised 30-minute "long form" plays. These performances often are so good that many audience members assume a script is being followed, yet this is never the case with authentic improv groups. The actors work very hard to avoid repeating even brief segments of a performance from a prior night.

For most of human history, improvisation has been a necessary skill for any performer. With the onset of literacy and the increasing division of labor in European society generally, the roles of playwright, actor, and director became increasingly distinct, for the first time allowing actors to be successful even if they could not improvise. But since first Stanislavsky and then 1950s Chicago improv transformed modern theater, improvisation has once again become central to actor training and performance. The explanation of acting creativity must begin with improvisational creativity, and only then can we consider the unique demands of scripted acting.

SCRIPTED ACTING

In many ways, scripted acting seems the opposite from improvisation. In a scripted play, much of the creative power of interaction occurs in rehearsal, rather than on stage during the actual live performance. Some directors are notoriously controlling and know exactly every detail of what they want before the first rehearsal; however, this is considered to be the least creative kind of director (Brook, 1968). A more creative process results when the play grows over a series of rehearsals, with mutual communication between the actors and the director: "[The director] cannot fully understand a play by himself. Whatever ideas he brings on the first day must evolve continually, thanks to the process he is going through with the actors" (Brook, 1968, p. 106).

Even when acting from a script, improvisation is necessary to an effective performance, because a script underdetermines performance. Otherwise, as one scholar wrote, "performing works would be akin to minting coins" (Godlovitch, 1998, p. 85). Acting a scripted play can only work when the actors are closely attuned to each other; monitoring the other actors' actions at the same time that they continue their own performance, they are able to quickly hear or see what the other actors are doing, and then to respond by altering their own unfolding, ongoing activity. Performing a play demonstrates a form of interactional synchrony (Sawyer, 2003b). The term *interactional synchrony* was first coined and conceptualized by Condon and Ogston, who analyzed videotapes of speakers and hearers frame by frame and found that "the speaker and hearer look like puppets moved by the same set of strings" (Condon & Ogston, 1971, p. 158). People can synchronize an incredible number of verbal and nonverbal behaviors in as little as 1/20th of a second (Condon & Ogston, 1967). Scholars also emphasized the importance of focusing on the entire ensemble. As Scheflen (1982) wrote, "If we observe only one person or one person at a time, there is no way we will observe synchrony or co-action or interactional rhythm" (p. 15). In theater, actors maintain interactional synchrony through a myriad of subtle facial expressions and gestural movements (Caudle, 1991). In this way, the actor's interactions communicate information about interpersonal interactions to the audience.

This is why interaction with other actors is almost as important in scripted theater as in improvisation. Actors themselves are well aware of this: "So let's say your fellow actor has the flu that night and is giving you fifty percent, you have to adjust" (Nemiro, 1997, pp. 233–234). Interaction with the audience is also essential: "There are some audiences that will just give you so much. They'll be generous, and you'll feel it . . . and it feeds your performance" (Nemiro, 1997, p. 234).

Thus, even in scripted theater the creative process is a significant component of the product. Although much of the creative process occurs in the rehearsals that precede the performance, the creative process continues during the performance; the essence of acting creativity is what is done on stage, not what is done during rehearsal. In product creativity, the creative process ends when the created product is complete and fixed, whereas in acting, the creative process continues through performance and constitutes the creative product—it has no existence apart from the creative process of performance.

Conversation analysts have studied how interactional synchrony is maintained in conversation, and several conversation analysts have examined dramatic dialogue, applying techniques and concepts from conversational study to the scripted creations of playwrights (Burton, 1980; Herman, 1995; Issacharoff, 1989). Researchers in the tradition known as *everyday life performance* use the analytic techniques of conversation analysis to generate their scripts (Hopper, 1993; Stucky, 1993). These researchers draw on the detailed transcriptions of conversation analysts to show that the scripted dialogue of most plays is quite different from everyday conversation. For example, detailed transcripts of everyday talk show that speakers often overlap at turn transitions; that listeners often speak single-word encouragements or affirmations that overlap with a speaker's story; that each turn is typically quite short; that pauses between turns of dialogue vary in length; that rhythm and melody often play key roles in communicating meaning; and that speakers often hesitate, or stop in mid-sentence and restart their sentence to go in a different direction.

Scripts do not specify this sort of detail. For example, they rarely indicate overlaps between speakers, or the length of pauses between turns. These missing details result in the underdetermined nature of written scripts. Actors (sometimes with help from the director) must decide where to insert pauses, and how long each pause should be; they must decide whether there should be speaker overlap at various points in the dialogue; and they must decide how to deliver each line—which words to emphasize, and with what tone of voice. Many of these decisions will be made improvisationally, at the moment of performance, rather than planned, discussed, and premeditated.

There are only a few studies (Hafez, 1991; Stucky, 1994) that have transcribed the live performances of scripted theater groups for later conversational analysis. Although the script provides the words for the actors, the actors must perform the words so that they sound like natural human dialogue. For example, the actors must manage turn transitions between each other so that the turn transitions sound natural; doing this requires ensemble interaction and a form of interactional synchrony. Stucky (1994) focused on pauses between speaker turns. He transcribed live theater performances and compared the detailed transcripts and the scripted directions to pause provided by the playwright. Conversation analysts have demonstrated that turn transitions are collaboratively improvised, and emerge from the collective actions of the entire group (Sacks, Schegloff, & Jefferson, 1974). Stucky's analysis of staged theater dialogues also revealed that actors collectively improvise the length of these pauses. In some cases, actors improvisationally omit an authorial pause, or insert a pause not indicated in the script. These group improvisations implicitly communicate important meanings to the audience, and can significantly alter the meaning of the text.

Studies like these are rare, but they demonstrate that group creativity is required even in genres in which each performer performs from a score or script. Although conventional theater acting takes place in a highly structured context—actors must memorize their lines and follow patterns of blocking worked out in rehearsal (Noice & Noice, 1997)—actors' own subjective experience of acting is the need for spontaneity and responsive interaction (Nemiro, 1997).

THE PSYCHOLOGY OF ACTING

Psychological studies of acting are rare (Reciniello, 1991; Sawyer, 1997). This is partly due to the methodological difficulty of studying live performance: The actor cannot be examined in a controlled laboratory setting while acting, and acting is an ensemble art form, making it difficult to isolate the creative contribution of any one actor (Sawyer, 2003b). However, the scarcity of psychological studies of acting is also due to the all-too-common belief that performance is not creative, but is rather interpretive.

The Stages of the Creative Process

Acting creativity involves preparation, just as in the various genres of product creativity. Several researchers have proposed three sequential stages to the creative process of acting: general preparation, rehearsal, and performance (Nemiro, 1997). *Preparation* is the period during which the basics of acting are collected and assimilated by the actor. This is done through academic training, observing other actors in theater and in films, and watching people interacting in everyday life. *Rehearsal* involves five activities in addition to memorizing the script (Noice & Noice, 1997): identifying something in the character to which the actor can relate; using personal experiences as substitutes for the character's feelings; discovering the character's objectives; creating a physical persona for the character—how the character walks and moves; and studying the script to learn what the other characters think about the character. The third and final stage, *performance*, is the one I have emphasized in this chapter. Performance involves five activities: focusing on the moment—what has just happened and how the character would perceive the situation at that moment, with no knowledge of how the rest of the play unfolds; adjusting to other actors; interacting with the audience; keeping the concentration and energy level high; and improving the performance and keeping it fresh over repeated performances (Nemiro, 1997). Whereas much of the preparation and rehearsal stages occur in isolation, performance is fundamentally public and collaborative.

Emotion

Conceptions of good acting have changed historically and are different in different cultures; for example, I have already explained that our focus on the literal performance of scripted plays is culturally and historically unique. In the following discussion, I show that the role of emotion in performance has also varied historically and culturally. These different conceptions of acting make it difficult to examine acting creativity, because its study must incorporate the conceptions of creativity shared by the society of the creator and the audience. Judging good acting is difficult, even among members of the domain who have been well trained. One study asked four different expert observers to rate the performance quality of four amateur actors (Konijn, 1991) and found that their interrater reliability was quite low, even after a special training session in the rating method (Cohen's kappa under .20).

A particularly important ability in performing a script is the believable communication of emotion. Particularly in 20th-century realist theater, playwrights tended to portray a close focus on interpersonal relationships, and many of these involved strong emotions, such as dysfunctional families, alcoholism, or abusive relationships. The pioneering work of Stanislavsky is often associated with this emotionally expressive style of acting. Research on the facial expression of emotion has shown that people are incredibly sensitive to the difference between genuine emotion and the intentional communication of emotion (Ekman, 1985). Thus, effective acting—at least of 20th-century realist theater—requires the ability to make the performance seem to be a genuine expression of emotion.

In this context, it has often been observed that an actor cannot play an emotion that he or she has not experienced (Hammond & Edelmann, 1991b). The idea that acting is a reliving and reexpression of prior experienced emotional states is generally associated with Stanislavsky's psychological realism. Qualitative and quantitative studies have provided some evidence for this; actors who perform conventional scripted theater develop complex psychological relationships with their characters. In a series of studies in Romania, Neacsu (Marcus & Neacsu, 1972; Neacsu, 1972) found that actors who had a higher capacity for reliving affective states performed more effectively. Performing certain characters can be cathartic, allowing an actor to work out a personal dilemma through the character, or to get out certain feelings: "[I]n a show once . . . I cried for an hour and a half on stage. Well I was never more happy-go-lucky than during the run of that show 'cause I got it all out" (Nemiro, 1997, p. 235). However, this catharsis only works because of the identification with a character, and it can go too far; many actors fear taking on too much of a character's identity, and losing themselves in the character. During the run of a play, some actors find it hard to exclude the presence of their character from the rest of their life offstage. The character takes up mental, emotional, and even physical space within the actor (Bates, 1991). Actors often report losing control to the emotions of their character. In 1989, *The Guardian* reported the case of an established British actor who was removed from his role as Hamlet, after he began to talk of the "demons" in the role, and began to see his father in the ghost (published in the issue of September 16, 1989, described in Hammond & Edelmann, 1991b).

The actor's mental state while acting has been compared to shamanic trance and possession states (Bates, 1991). In drawing this comparison, Bates (1991) was aware that *possession* typically means that a person is totally out of control. Yet, even in traditional societies, when actors become possessed by spirits, they remain in control of the culturally specified requirements of the performance they are giving (Bates, 1991). One shaman was quoted as saying, "I am never absent, I always know what I am doing or saying" (Cole, 1975, p. 42). Performing actors and shamans alike have a "double consciousness," one part possessed and the other part observing and controlling.

This double consciousness raises questions about the Stanislavskian emphasis on reliving personal emotion. In fact, a contrary school of acting theory holds that the actor should be in complete control on stage and should not actually be emotional, but instead only convey emotionality. As director Peter Brook reported, "[T]he actor himself is hardly ever scarred by his efforts. Any actor in his dressing-room after playing a tremendous, horrifying role is relaxed and glowing" (1968, p. 136). This conception of acting predated Stanislavsky, and is often associated with Denis Diderot (1713–1784). Diderot (1936) stated in strong terms that emotionality or "sensibility" interfered with effective acting: "Extreme emotionality results in mediocre actors; mediocre emotionality results in most bad actors; and the absolute absence of emotionality results in sublime actors" (p. 259; author's translation). Diderot's argument was that if an actor had a high degree of emotionality, then he or she would be unpredictable from night to night. For example, the actor might be exceptional on opening night, but by the third night his or her inner inspiration would have dried up. In contrast, the more intellectual, in-control actor would improve from night to night, as he or she reflected on each night's performance, and progressively gained more insight into the character. The actor's "talent is not in feeling . . . but in rendering scrupulously the external signs of feeling" (p. 258; author's translation). This more detached conception of acting returned in the mid-20th century with Brecht's argument that the actor should play his or her character with distance. Debates about the merits of Stanislavskian training techniques became increasingly common in the New York theater community through the 1990s.

Anxiety and Flow

Several experimental laboratory studies of human performance have shown that the presence of an audience increases stress (Konijn, 1991). An audience will heighten the stress level only if the performance concerns a complex task, and an audience has facilitating effects on well-learned behaviors (Guerin, 1993). These studies suggest that effective actors are those who have mastered the task of acting—so that it is not too complex—and those who have rehearsed the play well (Konijn, 1991). In fact, many actors believe that their performance is better during public performance compared to rehearsal (Konijn, 1991); high stress levels seem to improve performance quality (Konijn, 1991; Wilson, 1985).

This pattern is consistent with Csikszentmihalyi's flow theory (1990b): Actors are faced with a relatively challenging task, but they have mastered the skills necessary to perform the task. Consequently, to experience flow, they seek out the experience of live performance. Konijn (1991) found that actors' heart rates were higher during public performance than during rehearsal, but that their performances were also rated more highly by the actors and by expert observers during the public stagings, suggesting that the increased stress level improves their performance. And following flow theory, even for professional actors there is often a point beyond which stress becomes too great and begins to interfere with the performance. This can happen in auditions, competitions, or particularly important public performances.

Personality

In the 1960s, personality psychologists discovered that performing artists score higher than do control groups on measures of creativity such as ideational fluency, suggesting that performers are not simply interpreters or "executors" with no creativity of their own (Lang & Ryba, 1976; Mackler & Shontz, 1965; Torrance & Khatena, 1969). Some psychoanalytically oriented studies found that actors lack a firm sense of self, they have poorly integrated or schizoid personalities, are exhibitionistic and narcissistic, and are more extroverted than average (Wilson, 1985). In a more recent study in the trait psychological tradition (Hammond & Edelmann, 1991a), actors compared to nonactors were found to be more privately self-conscious, less attentive to social comparison information, more honest, less socially anxious, less shy, more sociable, and more sensitive to the expressive behavior of other people. Although these are statistically significant, the effect sizes are rather small, and the standard deviations are large. Further research is necessary before firm conclusions can be drawn.

Cognitive Process

A tradition in creativity research (Campbell, 1960; Hadamard, 1945; Rothenberg, 1979; Simonton, 1988) holds that creativity occurs in (at least) two stages. Beginning with Guilford's (1968) seminal studies of creativity in the 1950s, creativity researchers have usually placed the source of novelty in *divergent thinking*, an "ideation stage" that often occurs below the level of consciousness. In this formulation, the conscious mind then filters or *evaluates* these many ideas, using *convergent* or *critical* thought processes. Novelty originates deep in the brain in an undirected, nonconscious fashion, and the conscious mind decides which of those novel ideas are coherent with the creative domain. The two-stage model of ideation followed by evaluation has a strong intuitive validity, and has repeatedly appeared in the history of thought about creativity.

The output of the ideation stage has been studied at length by psychologists, in part because they have often equated ideation or divergent thought with something like a "creativity quotient." Precisely how divergent processes generate novelty has been a source of much speculation among creativity researchers, but unfortunately the experimental method has not been successful at revealing these processes. In contrast, psychologists have had more success with the empirical study of evaluative processes, in part because those processes are often accessible to consciousness. Researchers take it for granted that divergent thought somehow drives the system by creating novelty; the research agenda then becomes an exploration of how evaluative thought processes select among these options.

Acting raises a fundamental issue for staged psychological models of creativity: Is it appropriate to represent creativity as occurring in sequential stages? In improvisation in particular, it is unclear whether there are distinct creative stages corresponding to ideation and evaluation. In improvisational performance new ideas emerge spontaneously during execution, without time for conscious evaluation.

Creativity theories also may need to be extended because, in improvisation, ideation and evaluation are collective and are accomplished by the group. When one actor introduces a new idea, the other actors evaluate it immediately, determining whether or not the performance will shift to incorporate the proposed new idea (Sawyer, 2003b). The eventual meaning of the new idea is thus determined retrospectively and collectively. Hence, the evaluative filtering of new plot or character ideas in improvisation is a collective group process; one could think of it by analogy as the individual's evaluation stage, but externalized into the social world and made into a group process. This social process of spontaneous evaluation has interesting parallels with Csikszentmihalyi's analysis of how an evaluation is performed by a field when an individual proposes a new creative product. For Csikszentmihalyi, after the individual has created a product, a social process of evaluation then takes effect as the members of the field select among new products to evaluate which are appropriate to enter the domain. Thus, changes to a product domain depend on both group-level evaluative processes and psychological processes. In this view, social groups play an essential role in evaluating creative products; after all, an individual's evaluative filter may be faulty, and he or she may propose creative products that the field determines are uninteresting, repetitive, or wrong.

Yet, unlike in product creativity, in improvisation there is no opportunity for the iterative evaluation and revision that are common in other forms of creativity. The social filtering occurs in parallel with the creative process of each performer, in the same way that each performer's evaluative processes must be operating in parallel with his or her internal psychological processes of ideation. Hence, not only must intrapsychic evaluation occur in parallel with ideation; interpsychic evaluation also occurs in parallel in a performance. How can the analyst separate the ideation and evaluation stages, when the time constraints of a performance do not allow conscious reflection and evaluation? If the ideation and evaluation stages are temporally indistinguishable during acting, then they may be indistinguishable in other forms of creativity as well.

Evaluation processes result from an internalization of the social processes of person-domain-field (Csikszentmihalyi & Sawyer, 1995). An evaluation is, in part, a judgment about whether or not the new insight will be acceptable to the field, and how it can be integrated with the domain (through an appropriately skillful elaboration). Thus, when an individual evaluates the new idea (whether during the ideation stage or during conscious evaluation), knowledge of the domain and field plays an important role. Because of the long period of professional socialization required by actors, there is ample time for this social process to be internalized by the actor. This social process knowledge can be internalized to such an extent that it can take effect at the preconscious level of ideation.

Group Interaction

There are many metaphors one can use to describe a talented ensemble when they are "on," in interactional synchrony, performing well. One might say that they have a *good chemistry*, or that things are *clicking* or *in sync*. For example, Jimerson (1999) wrote about a pickup basketball team, "[W]e played quietly and efficiently. We rarely spoke and played effortlessly and effectively. As teammates, we were 'in sync' with each other" (p. 13). For just about any sports team, one can speak of the *group spirit*, the *team spirit*, or the *esprit de corps*. These metaphors focus on the entire group and on their performance together as an ensemble. Even if the individual performers are prepared and focused, a good ensemble performance doesn't always emerge.

When a group is performing at its peak, I refer to the group as being in *group flow*, in the same way that an individual performing at his or her peak often experiences a subjective feeling of flow. The concept of group flow is related to Csikszentmihalyi's flow, but with a critical difference. Csikszentmihalyi intended flow to represent a state of consciousness within the individual performer, whereas group flow is a property of the entire ensemble as a collective unit. When studying group creativity we need a way of characterizing the collective experience of the entire group. Based on my observations of performing groups, I have developed the concept of group flow to characterize those groups that are collectively in a flow state (Sawyer, 2003b). Group flow has been neglected in studies of flow, which have focused on how individuals attain flow through their own actions (cf. Jimerson, 1999). In group flow, everything seems to come naturally; the performers are in interactional synchrony. In this state, each of the group members can even feel as if they are able to anticipate what their fellow performers will do before they actually do it.

Groups attain group flow by staying in the zone between complete predictability and going too far, between their shared knowledge about conventional situations, and doing something so inconsistent that it just doesn't make sense (Sawyer, 2003b). Actors become highly attuned to this zone, and they are always trying to attain group flow. Yet, acting's unpredictability makes it a risky way to attain flow; it doesn't always happen, even in a group of talented, well-trained performers. Many actors talk about both the high they get from a good performance and the terror they feel when a performance is not going well. The unpredictability of group creativity can be frightening because failure is public, unlike creative genres like writing or painting. If a painter fails, he or she can paint over the canvas or perhaps even throw it away.

SUMMARY

Acting is a unique creative domain. Although talented actors share many traits with other creative individuals, they are also different in many ways. Acting is of interest to all creativity researchers because it sheds light on the creative process, on collaboration, and on spontaneity. These features are present in all acting, but they are most salient in improvisation.

In a sense, improvisation is present in all creativity. For example, painters are constantly responding to their canvases and oils as they are painting. More importantly, each step of the painting changes the artist's conception of what he or she is doing—the first part of a painting often leads to a new insight about what to do next. Fiction writers are constantly interacting with the story as they write. A character or a plot line frequently emerges from the pen unexpectedly, and an experienced writer will respond and follow that new thread, in an essentially improvisational fashion.

Improvisation is essential in stage acting, because unlike the painter or the writer, actors do not have the opportunity to revise their work. Where the improvisations of the painter can be painted over or discarded, and the writer has the power of a word processor to generate the next draft, the improvisations that occur on stage are exposed to the audience. As a result, the audience sees the creative process in action—they share in every unexpected inspiration, but also in those disappointing attempts that fail. Even the most famous artists often destroy or paint over a significant number of their canvases, but these aborted attempts are generally lost to history and no longer available for study. Because acting is the creative process made visible, it can teach us about the creative process in general.

The collaborative nature of acting also makes it a promising field of study for creativity researchers. Collaboration is important in most creative domains. In modern scientific research, these collaborations range from the group work that goes on in the laboratory to informal conversations over late-night coffee. The creative interactions of a theater group are much easier to study, because the analyst can hear and transcribe how this interaction affects each actor's creative process. Studying acting can help creativity researchers better understand all group collaborations.

REFERENCES

Alter, J. (1981). From text to performance: Semiotics of theatrality. In R. Amossy (Ed.), *Drama, theater, performance: A semiotic perspective* (pp. 113–139). Cambridge, MA: Schenkman.
Bates, B. (1991). Performance and possession: The actor and our inner demons. In G. D. Wilson (Ed.), *Psychology and performing arts* (pp. 11–18). Amsterdam: Swets & Zeitlinger.
Belgrad, D. (1998). *The culture of spontaneity: Improvisation and the arts in postwar America.* Chicago: University of Chicago Press.
Brook, P. (1968). *The empty space.* New York: Atheneum.
Burton, D. (1980). *Dialogue and discourse: A sociolinguistic approach to modern drama dialogue and naturally occurring conversation.* London: Routledge & Kegan Paul.
Campbell, D. T. (1960). Blind variation and selective retention in scientific discovery. *Psychological Review, 67,* 380–400.
Caudle, F. M. (1991). An ecological view of social perception: Implications for theatrical performance. In G. D. Wilson (Ed.), *Psychology and performing arts* (pp. 45–57). Amsterdam: Swets & Zeitlinger.
Cole, D. (1975). *The theatrical event.* Middletown, CT: Wesleyan University Press.
Condon, W. S., & Ogston, W. D. (1967). A segmentation of behavior. *Journal of Psychiatric Research, 5,* 221–235.
Condon, W. S., & Ogston, W. D. (1971). Speech and body motion synchrony of the speaker-hearer. In D. L. Horton & J. J. Jenkins (Eds.), *Perception of language* (pp. 150–173). Columbus, OH: Merrill.
Csikszentmihalyi, M. (1988). Society, culture, and person: A systems view of creativity. In R. J. Sternberg (Ed.), *The nature of creativity* (pp. 325–339). New York: Cambridge University Press.
Csikszentmihalyi, M. (1990a). The domain of creativity. In M. A. Runco & R. S. Albert (Eds.), *Theories of creativity* (pp. 190–212). Newbury Park, CA: Sage.
Csikszentmihalyi, M. (1990b). *Flow: The psychology of optimal experience.* New York: HarperCollins.
Csikszentmihalyi, M., & Sawyer, R. K. (1995). Creative insight: The social dimension of a solitary moment. In R. J. Sternberg & J. E. Davidson (Eds.), *The nature of insight* (pp. 329–363). Cambridge, MA: MIT Press.
Delbanco, N. (2002, July). In praise of imitation. *Harper's Magazine,* pp. 57–63.
Diderot, D. (1936). Paradox sur le Comédien. In F. C. Green (Ed.), *Diderot's writings on the theatre* (pp. 249–317). New York: Cambridge University Press.
Ekman, P. (1985). *Telling lies: Clues to deceit in the marketplace, politics and marriage.* New York: Norton.
Feldman, D. H. (1980). *Beyond universals in cognitive development.* Norwood, NJ: Ablex.
Gardner, H. (1983). *Frames of mind: The theory of multiple intelligences.* New York: Basic Books.
Godlovitch, S. (1998). *Musical performance: A philosophical study.* New York: Routledge.
Guerin, B. (1993). *Social facilitation.* New York: Cambridge University Press.
Guilford, J. P. (1968). *Creativity, intelligence, and their educational implications.* San Diego: EDITS/Knapp.
Hadamard, J. (1945). *The psychology of invention in the mathematical field.* Princeton, NJ: Princeton University Press.
Hafez, O. M. (1991). Turn-taking in Egyptian Arabic: Spontaneous speech vs. drama dialogue. *Journal of Pragmatics, 15,* 59–81.
Hammond, J., & Edelmann, R. J. (1991a). The act of being: Personality characteristics of professional actors, amateur actors and non-actors. In G. D. Wilson (Ed.), *Psychology and performing arts* (pp. 123–131). Amsterdam: Swets & Zeitlinger.

Hammond, J., & Edelmann, R. J. (1991b). Double identity: The effect of the acting process on the self-perception of professional actors—two case illustrations. In G. D. Wilson (Ed.), *Psychology and performing arts* (pp. 24–44). Amsterdam: Swets & Zeitlinger.
Herman, V. (1995). *Dramatic discourse: Dialogue as interaction in plays.* New York: Routledge.
Hopper, R. (1993). Conversational dramatism and everyday life performance. *Text and Performance Quarterly, 13,* 181–183.
Issacharoff, M. (1989). *Discourse as performance.* Palo Alto, CA: Stanford University Press.
Jimerson, J. B. (1999). *Interpersonal flow in pickup basketball.* Unpublished manuscript, Indiana University at Bloomington.
Konijn, E. A. (1991). What's on between the actor and his audience? Empirical analysis of emotion processes in the theatre. In G. D. Wilson (Ed.), *Psychology and performing arts* (pp. 59–73). Amsterdam: Swets & Zeitlinger.
Lang, R. J., & Ryba, K. A. (1976). The identification of some creative thinking parameters common to the artistic and musical personality. *British Journal of Educational Psychology, 46,* 267–279.
Mackler, B., & Shontz, F. C. (1965). Life style and creativity: An empirical investigation. *Perceptual and Motor Skills, 20,* 873–896.
Marcus, S., & Neacsu, G. (1972). La structure psychologique du talent dramatique. *Revue Roumaine des Sciences Sociales, Série de Psychologie, 16*(2), 133–149.
Neacsu, G. (1972). L'Unité de la transposition et de l'expressivité: Indice fondamental du talent scénique. *Revue Roumaine des Sciences Sociales, Série de Psychologie, 16*(1), 3–15.
Nemiro, J. (1997). Interpretive artists: A qualitative exploration of the creative process of actors. *Creativity Research Journal, 10*(2 & 3), 229–239.
Noice, T., & Noice, H. (1997). *The nature of expertise in professional acting: A cognitive view.* Mahwah, NJ: Lawrence Erlbaum Associates.
Reciniello, S. (1991). Toward an understanding of the performing artist. In G. D. Wilson (Ed.), *Psychology and performing arts* (pp. 95–122). Amsterdam: Swets & Zeitlinger.
Rothenberg, A. (1979). *The emerging goddess: The creative process in art, science, and other fields.* Chicago: University of Chicago Press.
Sacks, H., Schegloff, E., & Jefferson, G. (1974). A simplest systematics for the organization of turn-taking in conversation. *Language, 50*(4), 696–735.
Sawyer, R. K. (1995). Creativity as mediated action: A comparison of improvisational performance and product creativity. *Mind, Culture, and Activity, 2,* 172–191.
Sawyer, R. K. (1996). The semiotics of improvisation: The pragmatics of musical and verbal performance. *Semiotica, 108*(3/4), 269–306.
Sawyer, R. K. (Ed.). (1997). *Creativity in performance.* Greenwich, CT: Ablex.
Sawyer, R. K. (2003a). Emergence in creativity and development. In R. K. Sawyer, V. John-Steiner, S. Moran, R. Sternberg, D. H. Feldman, M. Csikszentmihalyi, & J. Nakamura (Eds.), *Creativity and development* (pp. 12–60). New York: Oxford University Press.
Sawyer, R. K. (2003b). *Group creativity: Music, theater, collaboration.* Mahwah, NJ: Lawrence Erlbaum Associates.
Scheflen, A. E. (1982). Comments on the significance of interaction rhythms. In M. Davis (Ed.), *Interaction rhythms: Periodicity in communicative behavior* (pp. 13–22). New York: Human Sciences Press.
Simonton, D. K. (1988). *Scientific genius: A psychology of science.* New York: Cambridge University Press.
Stucky, N. (1993). Toward an aesthetics of natural performance. *Text and Performance Quarterly, 13,* 168–180.
Stucky, N. (1994). Interactional silence: Pauses in dramatic performance. *Journal of Pragmatics, 21,* 171–190.
Torrance, E. P., & Khatena, J. (1969). Originality of imagery in identifying creative talent in music. *Gifted Child Quarterly, 13,* 3–8.
Wilson, G. (1985). *The psychology of the performing arts.* London: Croom Helm.

Chapter 4

Should Creativity Be a Visual Arts Orphan?

Enid Zimmerman
Indiana University

In his 1950 American Psychological Association presidential address, Guilford (in Sternberg & Lubart, 1999) reported that until 1950 less than 0.2% of entries in *Psychological Abstracts* focused on creativity, and that it was a marginal topic. Sternberg and Lubart (1999) noted that from 1974 to 1994, 0.5% of entries in *Psychological Abstracts* concerned creativity. They concluded that "Creativity is important in society, but it traditionally has been one of psychology's orphans" (p. 4). One would expect that if creativity were orphaned in the field of psychology, it would have found a home in the visual arts and related educational pursuits that—in the mind of the general public—are synonymous with creativity. Unfortunately, this is not the case. The 2002 National Art Education Convention theme was "An Expanding Vision: Refocusing Content, Contexts, and Strategies." Of the over 590 sessions in the conference program, only 8 mentioned creativity in an abstract and only a single entry included creativity in its title. This was not always the case in visual arts education.

In the United States, the late 1930s and 1940s were greatly influenced by the writings of John Dewey and the progressive education movement. Emphasis was placed on interrelatedness of individuals, schools, and society, and the role of experience in education. Educators questioned the value of standardized tests and instruction that relied heavily on test results, and they often placed little focus on individual achievement and development. The time was ripe for the emergence of Viktor Lowenfeld's notions of self-expression and creativity applied to visual arts education, notions that

59

quickly became popular and dominated the art education scene for the next 5 decades. Most textbooks and articles written during this time frame included creativity in their titles; the most well known was Lowenfeld's *Creative and Mental Growth* (1947), which went through seven successive editions.

The late 1970s witnessed a waning of the civil rights movement, whereas interest in social equity and educational excellence was manifest in the back-to-basics mandate. By the 1980s, numerous public and private studies and reports were published about the status of public education the United States. Some educators and policymakers did not support arts programs at all, some acknowledged that arts should exist as a subject in schools, and some recognized the arts as "basic" subjects. The early 1980s also saw the establishment of the Getty Center for Education in the Arts, which emphasized attainment of skills and understandings in the four disciplines of art criticism, art history, aesthetics, and art making. Due to the influence of Getty Center initiatives within the past decade and a half, there has been a major shift in theory and practice in the field of visual arts education. This shift, popularly referred to first as *discipline-based art education* and now known as *comprehensive art education*, refers to fields of study emphasized by the Getty Center that are "marked by recognized communities of scholars or practitioners, established conceptual structures, and accepted methods of inquiry" (Clark, Day, & Greer, 1987, p. 131). Discipline-based art education (DBAE) differed significantly from creative self-expression, an approach to art education that had been dominant for over 45 years. The core of creative self-expression was to develop each student's inherent creative and expressive abilities. Creativity was represented as being innate and developing naturally without imposing adult conceptions on a learner's creative development. Curricula usually were composed idiosyncratically, without articulation or sequencing through the grades. The teacher's role in a creative self-expression, visual arts programs was to provide motivation, support, and resources and supplies, but not to interfere directly in any student's creative activities.

In discipline-based art education, creativity is viewed as "unconventional behavior that can occur as conventional art understandings are attained" (Clark et al., 1987, p. 134); untutored childhood expression is not necessarily regarded as creative. In a discipline-based approach to art education, students are taught directly through articulated and sequenced curricula in which art disciplines are emphasized and the work of adult art makers, from diverse cultural contexts, serve as motivators for students' creative development.

In visual arts education before the late 1980s, directive teaching, ability testing, and evaluation of student artwork—although commonly practiced in other school subjects—were considered detrimental to highly valued creativity and unfettered self-expression. In the 1980s and 1990s, the discipline-centered movement quickly became popular, and any mention of the term *creativity* was almost entirely erased from theory and practice in the field of visual art education. The term *creativity* rarely appears in visual arts education literature, and there is a scant amount of research being conducted in this area. It should be noted that many visual art programs emphasize creativity as an outcome, but do not have either valid means for identifying creativity or a research basis on which to assess creative outcomes.

DEFINITIONS OF GIFTEDNESS, TALENT, AND CREATIVITY

There are no agreed-on definitions of the terms *gifted* and *talent*. Hunsaker and Callahan (1995) described three ways that a relationship between creativity and talent development can be formulated: Giftedness and talent can be viewed as separate intellectual abilities, giftedness being associated with high intelligence and creativity being associated with novel or divergent thinking; creativity can be seen as a fundamental concept of giftedness; and creativity can be considered as a separate category or style of giftedness. In popular educational usage, the term *gifted* often refers to students who have superior academic abilities, whereas the term *talented* usually refers to students with superior abilities in the visual and performing arts. There is another view that the term *gifted* is a fixed concept, not amenable to the influence of education, whereas *talent* and *talent development* imply more active concepts by which students can be nurtured to grow and develop special abilities in diverse pursuits, and where educational intervention plays an important role. A new conception of the term *talent* was recommended by Feldhusen (1992), which focuses on talent development as viewed in direct relation to academic school subjects that students pursue in future careers as adults. Therefore, in many contexts the term *gifted and talented* has been replaced by the term *talent development*, driven by an emphasis on processes of nurturing talents, rather than on working with predetermined "gifts" (Feldhusen, 1992; Feldhusen & Hoover, 1986).

There also is no agreement among the terms *talent, giftedness,* and *creativity* themselves and the relationships among these terms. Sternberg and Lubart's (1999) definition of creativity as "the ability to produce work that is both novel ... and appropriate" (p. 3) is one that has been widely accepted. Many contemporary psychologists and educators also agree that creativity is a complex process that can be viewed as an interactive system in which relationships among people, process, products, and social and cultural contexts is of paramount importance (Csikszentmihalyi, 1996; Feldman, 1999; Gruber, 1989; Sternberg, 1999). All creative work, according to Sternberg (1999), happens in one or more domains; people are not creative in a general sense, they are creative in particular domains such as the visual arts. People, acts, or products cannot be creative alone; they need to be judged by a community of experts within a domain.

According to Csikszentmihalyi (1996), talent differs from creativity in that talent focuses on an innate ability to do something really well and many people achieve creative success without evidence of exceptional talent. Gardner (1996) categorized seven individuals as creative according to his intelligence types (Picasso was included in the spatial intelligence category). He explained that talented individuals fit well under a certain domain of knowledge that exists within their cultures. Then, members in a field relevant to their interests recognize these talented people as being highly competent. On the other hand, creative individuals often "lack fit" within a domain of knowledge and only after much time and effort establish a body of work that may come to be valued in a culture. As a result of case studies of adults who achieved success in the arts and sciences, Feist (1999) concluded that giftedness, as measured by high IQ scores, might be a poor indicator of adult creative achievement, and that there was not a significant relationship between IQ scores and creativity. Possessing certain personality traits may play a role in determining which gifted and talented children achieve their potentials in areas of art and science as adults.

Within various arts areas, many vastly different behaviors and abilities often are required for success. Students with superior drawing or painting abilities, for example, may have different sensibilities than those students who are talented at creating three-dimensional objects. Even within two-dimensional visual arts practices, different abilities and sensitivities are clearly needed in order to be successful in such diverse fields as photography, printmaking, painting, or political cartooning. Csikszentmihalyi and Getzels (1973) studied personalities of college-level visual arts students and concluded that their personalities and abilities differed substantially from those of advertising and industrial arts majors. Barron (1972) drew similar conclusions based on studies of students and professionals in acting, dance, writing, and the visual arts. Each domain required different abilities. Professionals in fields related to the arts—such as aestheticians, critics, and historians—demonstrate skills and abilities that differ greatly from those required for success by visual artists. Intelligence needed for success clearly cannot be defined as a single characteristic, but instead contains multiple ways of dealing with knowledge, skills, and understandings in the visual arts.

IQ, CREATIVITY, AND ACHIEVEMENT TESTS

A controversial issue is determining relationships among intelligence tests, creativity tests, and achievement tests, and how these relate to creativity in the visual arts. One contested claim is that above-average intelligence is a requirement for superior performance in the arts. Winner (1996) found little evidence that visually gifted children consistently have high IQs in academic areas. The arbitrary separation of intelligence and art performance, however, has been questioned for many years (Clark & Zimmerman, 1984). During the 1970s, a number of researchers demonstrated that many highly intelligent students also were highly able in the arts, and that most highly able arts students were also highly intelligent in a traditional sense (although not all highly intelligent students possess art talent). A high degree of intelligence has been described as necessary for acquiring the kinds of advanced techniques and skills required for superior arts performance (Luca & Allen, 1974; Schubert, 1973; Vernon, Adamson, & Vernon, 1977).

During the 1980s, many educators and researchers challenged the use of IQ tests in determining giftedness and talent (Feldhusen & Hoover, 1986; Gagné, 1985; Gardner, 1983; Sternberg, 1984, 1985, 1986; Treffinger & Renzulli, 1986). At the same time, despite such challenges, other educators and researchers continued to advocate the use of IQ tests for identification of gifted and talented students, although always in conjunction with other measures (Borland, 1986; Kaufman & Harrison, 1986; Robinson & Chamrad, 1986). Sternberg (2001) differentiated between intelligence and creativity. He considered intelligence in a dialectical relationship to creativity, in which intelligence is viewed as advancing societal norms and creativity as opposing societal norms and proposing new norms. A person needs intelligence to be creative, therefore, but not all intelligent people are creative. From this point of view, creativity is a characteristic of an individual as he or she reacts with one or more systems within a particular social context. Sternberg (2001) used the example of Cubist paintings that were seen as highly creative in a particular time period, but may be viewed today as less creative because such an idea is no longer considered novel.

During the 1970s, Torrance's (1974) and others' creativity tests came into popular usage, and creativity became a by-word in gifted and talented education. When originally designed, creativity tests were used to measure general problem-solving skills and divergent thinking abilities that were applicable to various situations. Kulp and Tartar (1986) developed instruments to measure creativity in order to identify highly able visual arts students, and a number of authors endorsed using creativity tests to identify talented students for visual arts programs (Greenlaw & McIntosh, 1988; Hurwitz, 1983; Khatena, 1982, 1989; Parker, 1989). However, Torrance

(1962) reported that creative achievements in writing, science, medicine, and leadership were more easily predicted than were creative achievements in music, the visual arts, business, or industry.

Khatena (1982) and others asserted that visual and performing arts abilities are closely associated with creativity as a measurable construct. When Clark tested over 1,200 third graders in four ethnically diverse communities in the United States, he found a strong correlation between drawing ability (as measured by Clark's Drawing Abilities Test, or CDAT), creativity (as determined by Torrance Tests of Creative Thinking, or TTCT), and results of statewide achievement tests (Clark & Zimmerman, 2001b). This finding indicated that, for these populations, performance on the two tests is affected by one or more factors such as intelligence, problem-solving skills, or other abilities. The TTCT and the CDAT, however, appeared to measure different sets of abilities. The TTCT measured fluency, flexibility, and elaboration, traditionally associated with creativity and based on both verbal and visual responses. It also appeared to measure native, inherent abilities that are relatively unaffected by past experiences and skills. The CDAT measured both problem-solving skills and differentiated drawing abilities, and scores on the CDAT were sensitive to past experiences and previously learned skills and techniques. CDAT scores often accelerated with age, whereas scores on the TTCT remained relatively constant over time. There also was a positive correlation among scores on TTCT, CDAT, and state achievement test scores. Clark concluded that correlation among the CDAT, TTCT, and achievement test scores indicated performance on these measures to be affected by another factor, or set of factors, that may include intelligence and/or general problem-solving skills as well as specific skills required in the visual arts. Such findings may indicate that there is a positive correlation among high intelligence, high academic achievement, and high ability in the visual arts. It should be noted, however, that the TTCT was developed in the 1970s, and there is debate about its relevance, especially in respect to how creativity is nurtured and valued in different cultural contexts (Sternberg & Lubart, 1999).

CREATIVE ACTS OF CHILDREN AND ART STUDENTS

Although some scholars agree that creative achievement is reflected in production of useful new ideas or products that result from defining a problem and solving it in a novel way (Hunsaker & Callahan, 1995; McPherson, 1997; Mumford, Connely, Baughman, & Marks, 1994; Wakefield, 1992), others distinguish between expert, adult creative acts and those of novices. James (1999–2000) defined *artistic creativity* as a series of "decisions and actions that are both purposeful and not predictable . . . it is an individual and a social process during which materials, forms, and cultural conventions are fused with the artist's personal history and emotions. Something is created that has never before existed in exactly that form" (p. 115). Csikszentmihalyi (1988, 1990, 1996), Feldman (1982), Gardner (1999), and Winner and Martino (1993) all referred to creativity as inventiveness within a domain of knowledge, in which a creative individual's work is recognized as a significant addition to that domain, by persons or organizations in the field that monitor the domain. No talented children, Winner and Martino (1993) maintained, have "effected reorganization of a domain of knowledge" (p. 253). Children, according to Csikszentmihalyi (1996), can demonstrate talent in a number of areas, but they cannot be creative because creativity involves changing a domain and the ways of thinking within that domain. He felt that no child, no matter how precocious, is able to accomplish this achievement. Csikszentmihalyi (1996) and Sternberg (1999) made cases for differentiating creativity at an individual level (as a person solves problems in daily life) and at a societal level (where creativity can lead to new findings, movements, inventions, and programs).

If children and students cannot be viewed as creative, then it would not be possible or practical to teach them skills and understandings to help them think creatively, because few would ever be able to reach this goal. Some researchers, however, have supported the position that nearly everyone has some creative ability and that this potential should be supported in educational settings (Parkhurst, 1999). Creativity would then be viewed as what is creative for an individual rather than what is creative for the society in which that person resides.

As a subset of creativity, *artistic creativity* has been defined as a range of multidimensional processes that includes knowledge of art concepts and traditions in a culture, creative thinking skills, and intrinsic motivation (Amabile, 1983). Although examining art products for evidence of talent and creativity in the visual arts is common, it also is possible to observe behaviors that may indicate a predisposition to create art products or are manifest while students engage in art making. Dispositional factors also were found to differentiate creative art students from those less creative. Those considered less creative produced drawings that were realistic without much inventiveness, whereas creative students found problems and attempted to solve them, thus producing more novel solutions (Getzels & Csikszentmihalyi, 1976). Attributes such as problem finding, problem solving, being able to become emotionally involved, and focusing on finding a personal vision were found by Dudek and Cote (1994) to be relevant throughout students' successful creative engagement with an art project.

Winner (1996) concluded that children gifted in the visual arts produced large numbers of drawings, created imaginative worlds, were intensely involved in a specific domain, experimented with spatial and naturalistic renderings, and evidenced stylized approaches to representation and learning processes over time. Other characteristics, cited by Pariser (1997), include intensity of application and early mastery of cultural forms, production of a large volume of works over a sustained period of time, nurturance from family and teachers, and thematically specialized work. In her study of artistically talented children, Milbrath (1998) found that artistically talented children begin drawing representationally 1 to 2 years earlier than did other children, evidenced a high degree of creativity in respect to originality, demonstrated a deep commitment to a specific domain, and drew in qualitatively different ways than did their peers. However, Hurwitz and Day (2001) cautioned that behaviors of artistically talented students are not necessarily consistent with characteristics associated with creativity; success that is achieved after developing skills and techniques is not "easily relinquished in journeys into the unknown" (p. 94).

Pariser (1987, 1991, 1995) pointed out that collections of juvenilia exist for a number of world-class artists, and art educators and psychologists have examined these records to see what connections might exist between their childhood and adult artwork and their later creative achievements (e.g., Feldman & Goldsmith, 1986a; Golomb, 1995; Paine, 1987; Pariser, 1987, 1991, 1995; Rostan, Pariser, & Gruber, 2001; Winner, 1996; Zimmerman, 1992b, 1995). They attempted to draw conclusions about how graphic development of creative adult artists is similar to, or different from, graphic development of others. Pariser (1987, 1991)—in his research about Klee's, Lautrec's, and Picasso's juvenilia—observed that as young children these artists did not exhibit an outstanding capacity for spatial rendering; what they did show was inventiveness and a capacity to render their subjects with enthusiasm. Pariser explained that these artists were able to master, at an early age, norms of artistry found in Western culture. Their differences from others were not in their progression through basic developmental steps, but instead in their experimentation with many genres and conventions within a domain.

GENDER ISSUES RELATED TO CREATIVE ART STUDENTS

Zimmerman (1994–1995) interviewed artistically talented teenagers and found that although all the boys realized that they possessed special talents at an early age, only half the girls were aware of their capabilities in art. Artistically talented boys developed stronger senses of identity through their artwork than did girls, and artistically talented girls generally lacked self-esteem, which contributed to their lower levels of achievement. Zimmerman also found that almost all the girls had unrealistic notions about what artists must do to achieve success. Lack of realistic and practical planning for future careers was more apparent in girls' responses than in boys. Most girls in the Zimmerman study were model students, interested in getting good grades and gaining admiration from their teachers and peers; they demonstrated what Loeb and Jay (1987) described as a need for achievement through conformity. This conformity may have identified them as talented art students, but perhaps they were less likely to become creative visual artists who were able to make a difference in respect to changing concepts or ideas in their domain of interest. Boys were less interested in being well behaved or conscientious about their schoolwork, were more independent and self-reliant than were girls, and possessed traits that indicated they might become creative adult artists.

CREATIVE ACTS OF ADULTS

Feist (1999) conducted an extensive longitudinal literature review to determine if personality has an influence on adult creative achievement in art and science. He found that personality meaningfully covaries with artistic and scientific creativity. Both creative artists and scientists tended to be open to new experiences, self-confident, self-accepting, driven, ambitious, hostile, and impulsive, and less conventional and conscientious than others in the general population. Artists, however, were found to be more affective and emotionally unstable, as well as less socialized and accepting of group norms, than were scientists, who were found to be more conscientious. It also was determined that traits that distinguish creative children and adolescents tend to be ones that distinguish creative adults. Creative personalities, therefore, tend to be stable over time. Feist also conjectured that adolescents who are viewed as talented may experience adult success, but probably will not be considered creative in their overall accomplishments.

Individual creative adult traits also were described by Gardner (1999) in his study of many creative individuals from different domains who were seen as having high energy; being extremely demanding, self-promoting, and prone to deprecate others; evidencing childlike traits; ignoring convention; and being fascinated by their own childhood experiences. Gardner characterized five kinds of creative activity: (a) solving a well-defined problem, (b) devising an all-encompassing theory, (c) creating work that has distance in time from creation to when the work is evaluated, (d) performing a ritualized work, and (e) performing a series of actions that bring about some kind of political or social change. According to Gardner categories c and d are concerned with artistic creativity. The arts today, he conjectured, are ripe for creative change due to the lack of attention and agreement as to what constitutes creative behaviors, acts, or products in the arts.

Researchers such as Stokes (2001) challenged the notion that successful problem finding and problem solving are always a means for producing a body of work that can be considered creative. Getzels and Csikszentmihalyi (1976) studied young college art students and the relationship between their problem-finding behaviors and the originality of their artworks. The authors concluded that students' methods of discovery, their visualization techniques, and the ways in which they sought productive questions were often far better indicators of high ability than were their solutions to artistic problems. Stokes (2001) maintained that many creative individuals (Monet as a case in point), rather than adopting problem-finding strategies, instead imposed restrictive task constraints on their work; for example, they employed constraining motifs and had outcomes of high levels of variability.

Csikszentmihalyi (1996) and his colleagues interviewed over 90 exceptional, creative men and women from around the world, including artists, who were at least 60 years old and who had made a contribution in a major domain in their culture. Traits that Csikszentmihalyi and his colleagues found associated with creativity were often dichotomous and included displaying a great amount of physical energy and a need for quiet times, being wise and childish, being playful and disciplined, using imagination rooted in reality, being extroverted and introverted, being humble and proud, displaying a tendency toward being androgynous, being traditional and rebellious, being passionate yet objective about work, and displaying the ability to suffer and enjoy creation for its own sake.

CASE STUDIES OF CHILDREN AND ADULTS

The case study method has long been considered a productive avenue when considering the work of significantly creative adults and children. There have been a number of case studies about the work of talented young artists who evidenced precocious abilities in the visual arts (Gardner, 1980; Goldsmith, 1992; Golomb, 1992, 1995; Wilson & Wilson, 1980; Zimmerman, 1992b, 1995). All of these studies emphasized spontaneous artwork done by precocious youngsters, from early childhood through their adolescence, or emphasized separate time periods during the development of these young artists.

Gardner (1980) presented a case study of spontaneous drawings of a 16-year-old artistically talented adolescent and did not find formal art instruction to have much impact on this student's development. Robertson (1987) reported a case study in which she intimated that formal art instruction, rather than supporting art talent development, might have been an inhibiting factor. In case studies noted by Goldsmith (1992) and Golomb (1992), formal art lessons or directed art experiences were viewed as inhibiting the visual art development of artistically gifted and talented students. Bloom (1985) and his associates reported case studies of talented individuals who, before the age of 35, had reached extremely high levels of accomplishment in their respective fields. One of the case studies (Sloan & Sosniak, 1985) focused on 20 sculptors, and the researchers concluded that the absence of formal art education before college did not appear to have had a negative effect on the sculptors' art development and eventual success as practicing artists.

Few researchers have studied the positive effects of accelerated or enriched learning in art on a student with high visual arts abilities, although the impact of successful teaching experiences have been shown in a number of studies to have a great positive impact. Wilson and Wilson (1980) studied the graphic work of a talented 15-year-old and credited his art teacher with encouraging the student's talents by stressing the value of popular, narrative models rather than only emphasizing fine arts instruction. In Golomb's (1992) case studies, several art teachers encouraged students' art talent development.

In Zimmerman's (1992b, 1995) case study about Eric, an artistically talented student, Eric's body of work demonstrated a learned set of characteristics influenced by his home life, culture, and the educational opportunities that were available to him. To produce and be supported in maintaining his body of work, Eric spoke about development of both perceptual and conceptual qualities of his artwork through expression and skill with a variety of media. Issues about the process of his art-making activities included his use of themes, puns, paradoxes, and emotive qualities. He also discussed the influence on his artwork of popular culture such as comic books, magazines, and rock groups. Meta-level manipulation of drawing frames, changing points of view, spatial issues, competition with peers, plagiarism and interpretation of borrowed images, and pure pleasure from the act of creating all played important roles in the development of Eric's talent. Those teachers whom Eric viewed positively possessed important characteristics, such as their emphasis on art skills, general knowledge about art, empathy with students, ability to make classes challenging, readiness to help students become aware of the contexts in which they make art, and their expectations that students examine their reasons for creating art. Eric described a number of transformational experiences that allowed him to view himself as a young artist achieving his own predetermined goals. The accelerated and enriched art program options provided him with an impetus to continue to study art and, as an adult, to become a creative, successful, independent, interactive game designer. Zimmerman (1992b, 1995) concluded that creative, artistic development is not an automatic consequence of maturation. Instead, it is a learned set of complex abilities that, to a great extent, are influenced by culture and available educational opportunities within that culture.

Feldman (1980) and Feldman and Goldsmith (1986a, 1986b) studied children who were precocious in many different areas, including the arts, and became convinced that all progress in learning is the result of intensive and prolonged instruction. Feldman and Goldsmith contended that talent does not develop without an enormous amount of work, practice, and study, coupled with a great amount of directive assistance, guidance, and encouragement. Their conclusion was that an individual's talent within a culture involves the interplay of many forces, including education.

Recently, psychologists have used multiple, individual case studies to compare and contrast the influence of personality and patterns of development on adults who have achieved success in particular domains of knowledge, including the visual arts (Feist, 1999; Gardner, 1996). Csikszentmihalyi (1996), after 30 years of research and in nearly 100 interviews with creative people in many different fields including the arts, determined that creative individuals need support of culture and society. The most creative person will not be able to achieve anything of importance without a constellation of conditions provided by the field, including training, expectations, resources, recognition, hope, opportunity, and both intrinsic and extrinsic recognition.

ART TEACHERS, CREATIVITY, AND ART TALENT DEVELOPMENT

The role of the art teacher and his or her impact on creative students cannot be minimized. Talented and sensitive teachers challenge their creative students to have transformational experiences when involved in the process of art making, and influence their students to view themselves as having abilities to respond to artwork and produce artwork at a very high level. In some cases, however, when involved with students possessing high interest and abilities in the visual arts, teachers can be neutral factors or, in more isolated cases, can have a detrimental influence on a student's art talent development.

There is research demonstrating that problem-finding and problem-solving skills can be taught, and students' abilities to be productive thinkers and creative problem solvers can be nurtured (Treffinger, Sortore, & Cross, 1993). Talent development can be enhanced in a "supportive, flexible, but intellectually-demanding academic environment" (Mumford et al., 1994, p. 245) by encouraging students to work consistently and responsibly when confronted by frustration. According to Feldhusen (1992), students can be taught to find problems, clarify problems, and use certain skills when attempting to solve problems. They also can be taught to monitor their own learning activities and seek and test alternative solutions. As discussed in educational literature, problem finding, problem solving, divergent and convergent thinking, self-expression, and adaptability in new situations are all traits commonly associated with creativity (Csikszentmihalyi 1996; Mumford et al., 1994; Runco, 1993; Runco & Nemiro, 1993; Starko, 2001; Sternberg, 1988, 1997, 1999). In their study of visual artists, Rostan, Pariser, and Gruber (2000) found that successful teachers of highly able students were knowledgeable about their subject matter and able to communicate instructions effectively. They also selected important learning experiences that challenged their students to attain advanced levels of achievement. Roland (1991) suggested that art teachers have groups of students share processes that they experienced to create their artwork, and allow the students to make meaningful choices when creating these products so that art can become cognitively stimulating and important in their lives. The role of the teacher in preparing students for assessment and developing art students' creativity, and expectations of society in terms of producing art products, can create a dynamic tension among these variables. Brown and Thomas (1999) studied art students at the college level in Australia, and found that when the students were becoming ready to make a creative leap to individual self-expression, their teachers often expected them to produce outcomes that were conventional as determined by examination expectations instead of individual creative responses in either processes or products.

Csikszentmihalyi (1996) suggested that talented children be exposed and involved in a domain of interest early in life, even if it is not the domain they later pursue. Such students' interests may go beyond a single domain, and this breadth of interest often is not encouraged in current schooling. Student creativity also can be developed by adapting teaching strategies that balance generation of new ideas, critical thinking abilities, and abilities to translate theory into practice (Sternberg & Williams, 1996). Successful teachers of highly able students are knowledgeable about their subject matter, able to communicate instruction effectively, and select important learning experiences that lead their students to attain challenging and advanced levels of achievement.

Zimmerman (1991, 1992a) studied two teachers of artistically talented students. One teacher was knowledgeable about subject matter, understood and communicated effectively with his students, and was deeply involved in teaching. His success was due to his attention to all students, his ability to make classes challenging and interesting through humor and storytelling, and his encouragement of students to become engaged in art issues and think reflectively about the context in which they were creating art. The other teacher only met the students' needs for developing skills and techniques. It was suggested that teachers of artistically talented students go beyond teaching art skills and techniques and attempt to understand each student's sensibilities, teach proactively, instill feelings of competence, promote problem solving, encourage students' searches for novelty and complexity, and reflect critically about their teaching practices art. To develop art talent and creativity, therefore, it is important that art teachers be sensitive to the needs of artistically talented students and go beyond simply teaching skills to encouraging students' independent thought, spontaneity, and originality.

Rather than focusing teaching strategies on students who evidenced artistic creativity through producing works that were open ended, purposeful, and had multiple levels of meaning, James (1999–2000) put emphasis on students in an art class who were described as having blocks to creativity. These students had creativity blocks in a number of areas, including cultural blocks, in which they were not willing or able to understand art concepts and processes and the meaning and worth of art in a contemporary context; conceptual and personal blocks, in which they had difficulty interpreting meaning and metaphor in artworks; emotional and personal blocks, in which discomfort with expressing emotion in public and confronting ambiguity were evident; social blocks, which were evidenced in students' concerns about how their products would be viewed; and instructional and classroom environmental factors, such as unclear teacher expectations, and space to work in a quiet setting. James suggested that supportive climates be created where students can learn to recognize their blocks to creativity and find personal meaning. Such an environment would encourage risk taking, and instructors would focus on both differentiating curricula to meet individual students' needs and direct teaching of a repertoire of strategies for working creatively.

DIVERSITY, POSTMODERN, AND GLOBAL ISSUES

Of current concern to many researchers and educators is the issue of identifying and providing appropriate programs for students from diverse populations who possess superior talent, interest, and creative potential in the visual arts. Students from diverse backgrounds, including minority students and students from low socioeconomic groups, usually are underrepresented in one or more phases of programming for special educational opportunities for artistically talented students (Richert, 1987). In Clark and Zimmerman's (2001b) study of elementary students with interests and abilities in the visual arts, the authors found that students from "minority" groups, often economically challenged, could be identified as talented and creative through sensitive measures developed locally by teachers, students, parents, community members, and artists. According to Sternberg and Lubart (1999), "Cross-cultural comparisons . . . have demonstrated cultural variability in the expression of creativity. In cultures that are traditional and adhere to tradition, it takes much effort and time to achieve new ways of thinking" (p. 9). They explained that cultures differ simply in the amount in which they value creative enterprise. Culture also is learned and passed on from one generation to the next, and cultures are dynamic and changing (Lubart, 1999). From a Western perspective, creativity often is defined as constructing a product that is both novel and appropriate within a particular cultural context. Cognitive problem-finding and problem-solving initiatives are strategies that fit a product-oriented conception of creativity that emphasizes individuality, a strong work ethic, and belief that progress is always for the betterment of society. Creativity, according to Csikszentmihalyi (1996), is more likely to occur in places where new ideas take less time to enact and be accepted.

An Eastern view of creativity, according to Lubart (1999), is less focused on a final product than with the process of creativity and connection to a psychic realm; therefore, it is more personal than the view of creativity in product-oriented, Western cultures. In cultures that are less traditional than others, change and creativity are not only tolerated but encouraged. In other cultures, collaboration, cooperation, conformity, and traditions are valued more highly than are novel solutions to problems and circumstances within that culture.

In China, technical skill in art is viewed as fundamental for development of art ability and expression (Gardner, 1989). Most Chinese art teachers stress developing skills that are necessary before students can begin to demonstrate creativity. The case of Wang Yani—a precocious, artistically talented girl from China—is an example of how her culture rewarded her intricate, detailed brush drawings of animals (Andrews, 1989; Feldman & Goldsmith, 1989a). She also had, in common with many of her Western counterparts, support from her father (who was her teacher and mentor), her commitment to a specific domain, and a mastery of art forms judged as significant by art experts. Children and adults alike, therefore, can only be recognized as talented, gifted, and/or creative in areas that are valued within their own cultures (Feldman & Goldsmith, 1986a; Gallagher, 1985; Greenlaw & McIntosh, 1988; Sternberg & Lubart, 1999; Zimmerman, 1995).

In postmodernism, it is an accepted premise that recycled imagery and objects can be used to create artworks and confront a modernistic notion of a progressive art history (Efland, Freedman, & Stuhr, 1996). This means that contemporary notions about creativity and art talent development may need to be reconsidered if creativity is seen only as something new, novel, original within a particular cultural context, and produced by only a few individuals who make an impact and change paradigms with that culture. Peat (2000) suggested that renewing and revitalizing something that already exists might also be viewed as creative. In fact, he is of the opinion that innovation may disrupt the stability of society in traditional societies, where focus is not on novelty but rather on creative acts that may be seen as acts of transformation that arise out of respect for a particular art form. In postmodern times, artists are free to adapt any style from the past and employ it in modern use. Peat offered the example of contemporary icon painters, working from a book of patterns, who still create something "fresh and vibrant that arises out of a deep respect for the prototype" (p. 12).

Common characteristics associated with artistically talented students in the United States are well developed drawing skills, high cognitive abilities, interest, and motivation. It has been suggested that artistically talented students manifest their talents along a number of trajectories, not just the single track of realistic drawing, and that people need to reconsider "representational" skills and focus more on enthusiasm for visual ideas and the wide range of art talents and abilities within cultural traditions (Pariser, 1997). Ability to depict the world realistically should be considered only one among many indicators of talent in the visual arts. In contemporary art, depiction of abstract concepts and themes often becomes more important than demonstration of realistic graphic skills based on perception. Some artistically talented young people concentrate on realistic depiction of objects and are influenced by Western spatial conventions. Others may concentrate on using art to depict visual narratives creatively through use of themes and variations, humor, paradoxes, puns, metaphors, and deep emotional involvement (Zimmerman, 1992b, 1995).

Peer pressure and adult intervention during early adolescent years probably push most talented young people toward creating realistic images. During these early adolescent years, problems being solved are usually spatial-perceptual, rather than abstract-conceptual. Popular culture, postmodernism, and new conceptions about creativity and art talent development need to be addressed in programs for creative students with interest and abilities in the visual arts.

CONCLUSIONS AND RECOMMENDATIONS

It is clear that there are many ways to describe and categorize characteristics of creative students with talents in the visual arts, and no single set of characteristics has been developed to comprehensively describe all covert or overt manifestations of such talents. Some common understandings among researchers from various fields about relationships among creativity, art talent, and cognitive abilities should be further explored. Although *artistic creativity* does not have an agreed-on meaning in the education and psychology literature, its usage in schools should be expanded to include indicators other than solely depicting the world realistically through well-developed graphic skills. Productive and creative thinking in the visual arts also can be nurtured, and restrictive task constraints and visualization techniques may prove to be equally as effective as is developing problem-solving techniques. Use of a variety of procedures is recommended for developing art talent and creativity through educational interventions that result in enriched educational experiences for students with high interest and abilities in the visual arts.

The importance of developing enriched programs for artistically talented students who have creative potential cannot be underestimated. As we continue through the 21st century, it is apparent that students need to be prepared for a new information age. Those students who will later become practicing artists should be prepared to think creatively and develop appropriate skills and abilities for a rapidly changing world. Educational interventions and accelerated and enriched programs, for both academically talented and artistically talented students with interests and abilities in the arts, can foster leadership and creative thinking with the potential to generate solutions to real-life problems both now and in the future.

Teachers of artistically talented students can become powerful influences by being knowledgeable about subject matter, communicating effectively, making classes interesting and challenging, and helping students to be aware of why they create art and the contexts in which they work. It is recommended that teachers go beyond teaching skills and encourage in their artistically talented students independent thought, spontaneity, and originality through differentiated and enriched art curricula.

A model of creativity for the visual arts that is inclusive rather than exclusive and that views creativity as being possessed by all people is one that should be considered. This position would infer that all people have some ability to be creative. The quality of that creativity would differ from person to person and culture to culture—some people would evidence a small amount of creative abilities and dispositions, whereas others would possess greater amounts. Those who demonstrate potential to be highly creative as adults should be offered differentiated opportunities to develop their talents. Peat (2000) suggested that although artists need long apprenticeships to be able to hone their crafts, everyone can learn techniques to "disrupt persistent habits of thought and free us for new ways of thinking" (p. 24) so that blocks are eliminated and creativity can flow. In fact, Csikszentmihalyi (1996) stated that "each person has potentially all the psychic energy he or she needs to lead a creative life" (p. 344). For researchers in the fields of psychology and education, it will be necessary to focus on not only on grand narratives, but also on small narratives. Then, creativity in everyday lives and events could be studied and interpreted. Researchers and visual arts teachers would no longer view creativity as an "orphan"; instead, they could bring it home to be nurtured and embraced within many different local and global cultural contexts.

REFERENCES

Amabile, T. (1983). *The social psychology of creativity.* New York: Springer-Verlag.
Andrews, J. (1989). Wang Yani and contemporary Chinese painting. In H. W. Ching (Ed.), *Yani the brush of innocence* (pp. 39–50). New York: Hudson Hills.
Barron, F. (1972). *Artists in the making.* New York: Seminar.
Bloom, B. (1985). *Developing talent in young people.* New York: Ballantine.
Borland, J. H. (1986). IQ tests: Throwing out the bathwater, saving the baby. *Roeper Review, 8,* 163–167.
Brown, N., & Thomas, K. (1999, September). *Creativity as a collective misrecognition in the relationship between art students and their teachers.* Paper presented at the Annual World Congress of the International Society for Education Through Art, Brisbane, Australia. (Eric Document Reproduction Service No. ED 455 140)
Clark, G., Day, M., & Greer, W. D. (1987). Discipline-based art education: Becoming students of art. *Journal of Aesthetic Education, 24*(2), 129–193.
Clark, G., & Zimmerman, E. (1984). *Educating artistically talented students.* Syracuse, NY: Syracuse University Press.
Clark, G., & Zimmerman, E. (2001a). Art talent development, creativity, and enrichment in programs for artistically talented students in grades K–8. In M. D. Lynch & C. R. Harris (Eds.), *Fostering creativity in children, K–8: Theory and practice* (pp. 211–226). Boston: Allyn & Bacon.
Clark, G., & Zimmerman, E. (2001b). Identifying artistically talented students in four rural communities in the United States. *Gifted Child Quarterly, 45*(2), 104–144.
Csikszentmihalyi, M. (1988). Society, culture and person: A systems view of creativity. In R. J. Sternberg (Ed.), *The nature of creativity: Contemporary psychological perspectives* (pp. 325–339). New York: Cambridge University Press.
Csikszentmihalyi, M. (1990). *Flow: The psychology of optimal experience.* New York: Harper & Row.
Csikszentmihalyi, M. (1996). *Creativity: Flow and the psychology of discovery and invention.* New York: HarperCollins.
Csikszentmihalyi, M., & Getzels, J. W. (1973). The personality of young artists: An empirical and theoretical exploration. *British Journal of Psychology, 64*(1), 91–104.
Dudek, S. Z., & Cote, R. (1994). Problem finding revisited. In M. A. Runco (Ed.), *Problem finding, problem solving, and creativity* (pp. 130–150). Norwood, NJ: Ablex.
Efland, A., Freedman, K., & Stuhr, P. (1996). *Postmodern art education: An approach to curriculum.* Reston, VA: National Art Education Association.
Feist, J. (1999). The influence of personality on artistic and scientific creativity. In R. J. Sternberg (Ed.), *Handbook of creativity* (pp. 273–296). Cambridge, UK: Cambridge University Press.
Feldhusen, J. F. (1992). *Talent identification and development in Education (TIDE).* Sarasota, FL: Center for Creative Learning.
Feldhusen, J. F., & Hoover, S. M. (1986). A conception of giftedness: Intelligence, self-concept, and motivation. *Roeper Review, 8*(3), 140–143.
Feldman, D. H. (1980). *Beyond universals in cognitive development.* Norwood, NJ: Ablex.
Feldman, D. H. (1982). *Developmental approaches to giftedness and creativity.* San Francisco: Jossey-Bass.
Feldman, D. H. (1999). The development of creativity. In R. J. Sternberg (Ed.), *Handbook of creativity* (pp. 169–186). Cambridge, UK: Cambridge University Press.
Feldman, D. H., & Goldsmith, L. (1986a). *Nature's gambit: Child prodigies and the development of human potential.* New York: Basic Books.

4. SHOULD CREATIVITY BE A VISUAL ARTS ORPHAN?

Feldman, D. H., & Goldsmith, L. (1986b). Transgenerational influences on the development of early prodigious behavior: A case study approach. In W. Fowler (Ed.), *Early experience and the development of competencies* (pp. 83–97). San Francisco: Jossey-Bass.

Gagné, F. (1985). Giftedness and talent: Reexamining a reexamination of definitions. *Gifted Child Quarterly, 29*(3), 103–112.

Gallagher, J. J. (1985). *Teaching the gifted child* (2nd & 3rd eds.). Boston, MA: Allyn & Bacon.

Gardner, H. (1980). *Artful scribbles. The significance of children's drawings.* New York: Basic Books.

Gardner, H. (1983). *Frames of mind: The theory of multiple intelligences.* New York: Basic Books.

Gardner, H. (1989). *To open minds. Chinese clues to the dilemma of contemporary education.* New York: Basic Books.

Gardner, H. (1996). The creator's patterns. In M. A. Boden (Ed.), *Dimensions of creativity* (pp. 143–158). Cambridge, MA: MIT Press.

Gardner, H. (1999). *Intelligences reframed: Multiple intelligences for the 21st century.* New York: Basic Books.

Getzels, J. W., & Csikszentmihalyi, M. (1976). *The creative vision: A longitudinal study of problem finding in art.* New York: Wiley.

Goldsmith, L. T. (1992). Wang Yani: Stylistic development of a Chinese prodigy. *Creativity Research Journal, 5*(3), 281–293.

Goldsmith, L., & Feldman, D. (1989). Wang Yani: Gifts well given. In H. W. Ching (Ed.), *Yani: The brush of innocence* (pp. 51–65). New York: Hudson-Hills Press.

Golomb, C. (1992). *The child's creation of a pictorial world.* Berkeley: University of California Press.

Golomb, C. (Ed). (1995). *The development of artistically gifted children: Selected case studies.* Hillsdale, NJ: Lawrence Erlbaum Associates.

Greenlaw, M. J., & McIntosh, M. E. (1988). *Educating the gifted: A sourcebook.* Chicago: American Library Association.

Gruber, H. E. (1989). The evolving systems approach to creative work. In D. B. Wallace & H. Gruber (Eds.), *Creative people at work: Twelve cognitive case studies* (pp. 3–24). New York: Oxford University Press.

Hunsaker, S. L., & Callahan, C. (1995). Creativity and giftedness: Instrument uses and abuses. *Gifted Child Quarterly, 39*(2), 110–114.

Hurwitz, A. (1983). *The gifted and talented in art: A guide to program planning.* Worcester, MA: Davis.

Hurwitz, A., & Day, M. (2001). *Children and their art: Methods for the elementary school* (7th ed.). Orlando: Harcourt, Brace, Jovanovich.

James, P. (1999–2000). Blocks and bridges: Learning artistic creativity. *Arts and Learning Research Journal, 16*(1), 110–133.

Kaufman, A. S., & Harrison, P. L. (1986). Intelligence tests and gifted assessment: What are the positives? *Roeper Review, 8*(3), 154–159.

Khatena, J. (1982). *Educational psychology of the gifted.* New York: Wiley.

Khatena, J. (1989). Intelligence and creativity to multitalent. *Journal of Creative Behavior, 23*(2), 93–97.

Kulp, M., & Tartar, B. J. (1986). The Creative Process Rating Scale. *The Creative Child and Adult Quarterly, 11*(3), 166–176.

Loeb, R. C., & Jay, G. (1987). Self-concept in gifted children: Differentiated impact on boys and girls. *Gifted Child Quarterly, 31*(1), 9–14.

Lowenfeld, V. (1949). *Creative and mental growth.* New York: Wiley.

Lubart, T. I. (1999). Creativity across cultures. In R. J. Sternberg (Ed.), *Handbook of creativity* (pp. 339–350). Cambridge, UK: Cambridge University Press.

Luca, M., & Allen, B. (1974). *Teaching gifted children art in grades one through three.* Sacramento: California State Department of Education.

McPherson, G. E. (1997). Giftedness and talent in music. *Journal of Aesthetic Education, 31*(4), 65–77.
Milbrath, C. (1998). *Patterns of artistic development: Comparative studies of talent.* Cambridge, UK: Cambridge University Press.
Mumford, M. D., Connely, M. S., Baughman, W. A., & Marks, M. A. (1994). Creativity and problem solving: Cognition, adaptability, and wisdom. *Roeper Review, 16*(4), 241–246.
Paine, S. (1987). The childhood and adolescent drawings of Henri de Toulouse-Lautrec (1864–1901): Drawings from 6 to 18 years. *Journal of Art and Design Education, 6*(3), 297–312.
Pariser, D. (1984). Two methods of teaching drawing skills. In R. MacGregor (Ed.), *Readings in Canadian Art Education* (pp. 143–158). Vancouver: Wedge.
Pariser, D. (1987). The juvenile drawings of Klee, Toulouse-Lautrec and Picasso. *Visual Arts Research, 13*(2), 53–67.
Pariser, D. (1991). Normal and unusual aspects of juvenile artistic development in Klee, Lautrec and Picasso: A Review of findings and direction for future research. *Creativity Research Journal, 4*(1), 51–67.
Pariser, D. (1995). Lautrec: Gifted child-artist and artistic monument connections between juvenile and mature work. In C. Golomb (Ed.), *The development of gifted child artists: Selected case studies* (pp. 31–71). Hillsdale, NJ: Lawrence Erlbaum Associates.
Pariser, D. (1997). Conceptions of children's artistic giftedness from modern and postmodern perspectives. *The Journal of Aesthetic Education, 31*(4), 35–47.
Parker, J. P. (1989). *Instructional strategies for teaching the gifted.* Boston: Allyn & Bacon.
Parkhurst, H. B. (1999). Confusion, lack of consensus, and the definition of creativity as a construct. *Journal of Creative Behavior, 33*(1), 1–21.
Peat, F. D. (2000). *The black winged night: Creativity in nature and mind.* Cambridge, MA: Perseus.
Richert, E. S. (1987). Rampant problems and promising practices on the identification of disadvantaged gifted students. *Gifted Child Quarterly, 31*(4), 149–154.
Robertson, A. (1987). Borrowing and artistic behavior: A case study of Bruce's spontaneous drawings from six to sixteen. *Studies in Art Education, 29*(1), 37–51.
Robinson, N. M., & Chamrad, D. L. (1986). Intelligence tests with gifted children. *Roeper Review, 8*(3), 160–163.
Roland, C. (1991). *Creativity and art education: A new look at an old relationship* (NAEA advisory). Reston, VA: National Art Education Association.
Rostan, S., Pariser, D., & Gruber, H. (2000, November). *Across time and place: A cross-cultural study of early artistic development: Two young artists.* Paper presented at the Jean Piaget Society meeting, Montreal, Canada.
Rostan, S., Pariser, D., & Gruber, H. (2001). *Cross-cultural study of artistic talent and creativity.* American Psychological Association, paper presented at Division 10, San Francisco.
Runco, M. (1993). *Creativity as an educational objective for disadvantaged students.* Storrs, CT: National Center on the Gifted and Talented.
Runco, M., & Nemiro, J. (1993). Problem finding and problem solving. *Roeper Review, 16*(4), 235–241.
Schubert, D. S. P. (1973). Intelligence as necessary but not sufficient for creativity. *Journal of Genetic Psychology, 122,* 45–47.
Sloan, K. D., & Sosniak, L. A. (1985). The development of accomplished sculptors. In B. Bloom (Ed.), *Developing talent in young people* (pp. 90–138). New York: Ballantine.
Starko, A. J. (2001). *Creativity in the classroom: Schools of curious delight* (2nd ed.). Mahwah, NJ: Lawrence Erlbaum Associates.
Sternberg, R. J. (1984). How can we teach intelligence? *Educational Leadership, 42,* 38–48.
Sternberg, R. J. (1985). *Beyond IQ: A triarchic theory of human intelligence.* Cambridge, UK: Cambridge University Press.

Sternberg, R. J. (1986). Identifying the gifted through IQ: Why a little bit of knowledge is a dangerous thing. *Roeper Review, 8*(3), 143–150.
Sternberg, R. J. (Ed). (1988). *The nature of creativity. Contemporary psychological perspectives.* New York: Cambridge University Press.
Sternberg, R. J. (1997). *Successful intelligence: How practical and creative intelligence determine success in life.* New York: PLUME.
Sternberg, R. J. (Ed.). (1999). *Handbook of creativity.* Cambridge, UK: Cambridge University Press.
Sternberg, R. J. (2001). What is the common thread of creativity? *American Psychologist, 56*(4), 360–362.
Sternberg, R. J., & Lubart, T. I. (1999). Concept of creativity: Prospects and paradigms. In R. J. Sternberg (Ed.), *Handbook of creativity* (pp. 3–15). Cambridge, UK: Cambridge University Press.
Sternberg, R. J., & Williams, W. M. (1996). *How to develop student creativity.* Alexandria, VA: Association for Supervision and Curriculum Development.
Stokes, P. D. (2001). Variability, constraints, and creativity: Shedding light on Claude Monet. *American Psychologist, 56*(4), 355–359.
Torrance, E. P. (1962). *Education and the creative potential.* Minneapolis: University of Minnesota Press.
Torrance, E. P. (1974). *Torrance Tests of Creative Thinking: Norms-technical manual.* Lexington, MA: Personnel Press.
Treffinger, D. J., & Renzulli, J. (1986). Giftedness as potential for creative productivity: Transcending IQ issues. *Roeper Review, 8*(3), 150–163.
Treffinger, D. J., Sortore, M. R., & Cross, J. A. (1993). Programs and strategies for nurturing creativity. In K. A. Heller, F. J. Monk, & A. H. Passow (Eds.), *International handbook of research and development of giftedness and talent* (pp. 555–567). New York: Pergamon.
Vernon, P. E., Adamson, G., & Vernon, D. (1977). *The psychology and education of gifted children.* Boulder, CO: Viewpoint.
Wakefield, J. F. (1992). *Creative thinking: Problem solving skills and the arts orientation.* Norwood, NJ: Ablex.
Wilson, B., & Wilson, M. (1980). Beyond marvelous: Conventions and inventions in John Scott's Gemini. *School Arts, 80*(2), 19–26.
Winner, E. (1996). *Gifted children: Myths and realities.* New York: Basic Books.
Winner, E., & Martino, G. (1993). Giftedness in the visual arts and music. In K. A. Heller, E. J. Monks, & A. H. Passow (Eds.), *International handbook of research and development of giftedness and talent* (pp. 253–281). New York: Pergamon.
Zimmerman, E. (1991). Rembrandt to Rembrandt: A case study of a memorable painting teacher of artistically talented 13 to 16 year-old students. *Roeper Review, 13*(2), 76–81.
Zimmerman, E. (1992a). A comparative study of two painting teachers of talented adolescents. *Studies in Art Education, 33*(2), 174–185.
Zimmerman, E. (1992b). Factors influencing the graphic development of a talented young artist. *Creativity Research Journal, 5*(3), 295–311.
Zimmerman, E. (1994–1995). Factors influencing the art education of artistically talented girls. *The Journal of Secondary Gifted Education, 6*(2), 103–112.
Zimmerman, E. (1995). It was an incredible experience: The impact of educational opportunities on a talented student's art development. In C. Golomb (Ed.), *The development of artistically gifted children: Selected case studies* (pp. 135–170). Hillsdale, NJ: Lawrence Erlbaum Associates.

Chapter 5

Creativity and Dance—
A Call for Balance

John I. Morris
Educational Testing Service

INTRODUCTION

One day while working with my seventh grade students at a middle school in New York State, two students came forward to show a dance. One sprawled half on the floor, half against the cinder block of the front wall. The other student took a whirling, spinning path across the performing space, arms swinging freely from his torso. The first student waited a beat for the second student to exit, then made a single spasm with his entire body, and lay motionless. When asked the title of the dance, he looked up and said: "Toxic Waste in the Galaxy," upon which the entire class burst into spontaneous applause. However brief, we all felt we had seen something creative that day. (Morris, 1996, p. 121)

Dance is an activity dating to prehistoric times. Dance—as sacred ritual, as communication, as social activity, as art form—exists in every culture and follows many paths. How does "creativity" play out in a domain that is both universal and culture specific? And why did the dance described at the beginning of this chapter, made and performed in a classroom by students with little dance training, have such an impact on those who watched?

Dance, as an expressive art form, is often considered inherently creative—especially when compared with a "nonartistic" domain. But dance, along with its social functions and expressive capabilities, is also a domain with a body of knowledge. It is an academic subject in its own right that includes studies of history, criticism, aesthetics, and biomechanics. Dance embodies a rapidly growing tradition of scholarship. It is important to honor that tradition while also honoring the passion of dance as an art form.

This inquiry into creativity in dance focuses on 1900 to the present, a timeline roughly corresponding to the development of creativity research. Creativity—and the research that surrounds it—takes on many meanings in many different contexts. Often, people ask others to "be creative," either at work, at school or at home, or say of themselves, "Oh, I'm not creative." Even within the field of creativity research, there is still much disagreement on what creativity is, what it does, or where it can be found.

CREATIVITY—AN OVERVIEW

Since 1960, researchers have published over 10,000 articles on creativity, and over 600 books in the 1990s alone (Runco & Pritzker, 1999). Interest in creativity goes back at least as far as Plato, and the term *creativity* itself was used in the late Renaissance as an analogy between divine creation of the natural world and the artist's ability to bring forth new shapes or sounds (Csikszentmihalyi, 1994).

One early form of creativity theory stems from research done by Wallas (1926), who advocated a creative process defined by a series of specific stages occurring in a given order. Today, stage theories for the most part have given way to more fluid models, as further research has revealed greater complexity in the nature of creativity.

Psychoanalysts, along with behavioral and humanistic psychologists, have extensively explored creativity as a function of personality. Their viewpoints on the creative person are grounded in the framework of their larger theories. Cognitive psychologists have studied the relationship between creativity and brain functioning, looking at creativity in terms of how people process information. Other researchers have extended creativity theory by exploring the role of environment, context, and developmental factors. At least 50 or 60 theories and definitions of creativity flourished by the mid-1980s (Taylor, 1988).

The study of creativity has taken on life as an independent field. Creativity is more frequently discussed than ever before in fields not traditionally associated with the topic. In fact, it is now common to refer to one's entire life as a creative work. Anna Lee Walters (1992), a writer of Pawnee and Otoe-Missouria descent, said of creativity, "In the cultures by which I am most affected, creativity is understood to be inherent in being human and resourceful" (p. 100).

DANCE—AN OVERVIEW

When people experience dance or any art form, they experience choices the artist has made in creating a specific world. In dance, these choices include how, when, or whether particular movements should be performed. I focus here on three distinct areas of choice making in dance: movement performance, dance improvisation, and dance making. Movement performance, for this exploration, is not limited to an actual performance of dance on a stage, but instead refers to any context in which dance movement is done, whether on a stage, in a class, or in a social or spiritual context. Dance improvisation includes any situation in which a dance or dance movement is made as it is performed. Dance making refers to the pre-planned process of creating a finished dance.

Dance is a multifaceted domain, and separation of these activities facilitates a clear discussion of relevant creative skills or characteristics. A creative dance maker may not be creative as an improviser or as a movement performer. Creativity additionally plays out differently across different dance styles such as ballet, modern, jazz, hip-hop, tap, and folk dance. A "creative" modern dancer will not necessarily be a creative ballet dancer, and the creative characteristics of a butoh dance may not match those of a jazz dance.

In my own research on creativity in dance, I have found that creativity is both general and domain specific (Morris, 1996). For creativity to exist in any domain, the following overarching factors must be present, appearing in no particular sequence of stages: *attentiveness, engagement, intent,* and the *materials* of a discipline. *Attentiveness* involves paying attention on many different levels, whether to the details of one's life, sensory information, emotional states, or the characteristics of materials involved in one's domain. *Engagement* may include motivation, interest, or connection. Engagement leads to true discovery by the creator; it brings about genuine experience. *Intent* refers not to an intent to be creative per se, but instead to an intent to initiate, carry through, and conclude a process that manifests something where nothing existed before. *Materials* of a discipline must be involved for the creative process to be active. Materials can refer to paint, words, music, ideas, or, in this case, movement.

Transpersonal psychology provides a final but crucial component of this exploration of creativity in dance. Transpersonal psychology represents a growing domain of study and practice within Western psychology. This domain recognizes that, for millennia, wisdom traditions, indigenous cultures, and artists have viewed the "separate self identity" as only a partial version of what it means to be human (Boucouvalas, 2000). Boucouvalas stated that the transpersonal orientation is capable of accommodating many areas, including alternative methods of communicating, knowing, and healing. Rational and nonrational modes are accommodated, leading to a broader, deeper way of perceiving creativity that is particularly suitable for dance.

In the entry for *insight* in the *Encyclopedia of Creativity*, Sternberg and Davidson (1999) labeled what they called the "mystical approach" as the one method they rejected categorically because it can't be scientifically analyzed. Although such a rejection is perfectly suitable for particular research goals, this chapter calls for a more inclusive approach. Parallels with transpersonal inquiry, of which mysticism is only one aspect, appear currently in creativity research, from Csikszentmihalyi's (1993) description of a "flow" state when involved in creative activity to Gardner's (1999) potential inclusion of an "existential" intelligence to his framework of multiple intelligences (MI). I maintain that both rational and nonrational views are necessary for an accurate understanding of creativity in dance.

Ken Wilber, one of the current leading theorists in transpersonal psychology, has called for a marriage of science and religion. Wilber (1998) claimed that a significant barrier between the two is the attempt of science to know nonrational events through rational means. He pointed out that Zen meditation (as only one of many such traditions) represents a longstanding practice of contemplative inquiry, confirmed by hundreds of thousands of practitioners, as "Ph.D. training in the realm of spiritual data" (p. 172). The tradition provides reliable, verifiable experiential research. Dance, I contend, represents a similar practice. It is primarily an experiential form, thousands of years old, with reliable and verifiable accounting of spiritual and other nonrational components.

CULTURE, CREATIVITY, AND DANCE

Dance and culture are deeply intertwined. Adjusting a scholarly perspective to honor this complex relationship may be challenging. As Walters (1992) suggested, "Scholars or authorities from academia, from outside tribal societies, do not necessarily know tribal people best" (p. 86). And, without this knowing, the very essence of what we seek to honor by examining culture remains elusive. As evidence of this elusiveness, many Native American languages have no word to define art because it is so embedded in the daily practices of the cultures in question. We must, then, attempt to understand creativity as both a separate scheme that can be examined and as an element inexorably intertwined with the essence of daily living itself.

The Lakota Sioux traditional dances provide examples of the "daily living" aspect of dance creativity. Although the dances are complete artistic performances, they are always also social and cultural events. Dancers participate neither for themselves nor just to perform for an audience, but instead to support the gathering and the continuation of tribal culture (Huenemann, 1992). Many of the male dance forms, however, leave room for extensive individuality. Some forms, like the Stomp dance of several Southeastern tribes, feature infinite variation and are improvisational in nature (Heth, 1992).

In Tewa (Southwestern Pueblo) dance, creativity is expressed in unison dancing, and in choreography that is simple and repetitive. This style emphasizes the Tewa notion that the needs of the individual are secondary to the needs of the community (Sweet, 1992). Movements are contained; gestures are close to the body. Creativity is inherent in the sincerity of the participants. *Shadeh*, the Tewa word for dance, literally means "to be in the act of waking up" (Swentzell & Warren, 1992, p. 93). Hence, the authors claimed, to dance is to awaken in a heightened sense of awareness to the dance and its meaning. Creativity in this case, rather than possibly being judged as lacking by Western standards because of the dance's contained style or unvaried movement vocabulary, may instead be seen as transformative and affirming, and thus closer to transpersonal elements espoused by Wilbur and Boucouvalas. In this understanding, establishing a connection with one's historical and spiritual roots through deeply felt movement performance is a decidedly creative act. Because of this, one aspect of creativity must be defined as cultural creativity, the choice to uphold and transform the lives of a people in a fundamental way.

The merging of different cultural dance forms has often contributed to creative development in dance. Asian, West African, European, and Native American dance forms all contributed to 20th-century dance in the United States. Desmond (1997) noted that the influence always goes both ways, not just toward the dominant culture. Generally, both cultures' dance practices change when borrowing occurs. One of the most obvious examples of cultural influence is the infusion of dance movement from African slaves that led to social dance forms such as the Charleston and the Lindy. Other movement patterns, such as isolated movement of body parts, became the foundation of jazz dance. Vernacular dancing from the plantation setting merged with the Irish jig and English clog to create tap dance.

African movement characteristics also influenced the growing modern dance tradition. Along with direct contributions from African American dance pioneers, a common means of finding novelty in both dance choreography and movement vocabulary involved taking inspiration from the movement vocabulary, themes, and music of different cultures. At other times, appropriation of actual movement vocabulary contributed to change. This interplay of both movement and thematic sharing continues today, with newfound sensitivity for authentic cultural movement practices.

CREATIVITY RESEARCH IN DANCE

Creativity is not a new term or a new concept in dance. What *is* new in dance is a formal tradition of research focused solely on creativity. If we looked only at "creativity research" as it plays out in the field of dance, we would necessarily slight the history of writings about dance that address creativity without naming it specifically. For that reason, this section deals with dance researchers who claim a de facto, if unstated, relationship to creativity research.

Much of the scholarly research in dance today is driven by the area of dance education. Until recently, even some of the most current research on dance had been difficult to locate, either because it fell under a category other than dance, such as anthropology or physical education, or because it was uncatalogued. Fortunately, this situation is changing. The Research in Dance Education (RDE) project, run by the National Dance Education Organization (NDEO), is currently cataloging research in dance. Among the project's goals are a comprehensive identification and evaluation of existing research in the field of dance and movement education from 1926 onward. "Creative process" is one of the targeted educational research issues. Project outcomes include a comprehensive, web-based database documenting this existing research, and making available reference to specific research issues in dance, including the creative process (NDEO, 2003). An NDEO report to the nation, *Research Priorities in Dance Education*, is in publication as of this writing.

Much early information about creativity in dance must be culled from biographies and autobiographies of famous dancers and choreographers. Collections of interviews with dance artists about their creative products and processes, including works by Cohen (1965) and Kreemer (1987), allow a more comparative approach than does personal memoir. Dance criticism provides another form of early research. Copeland and Cohen (1984) anthologized significant writings of authors such as John Martin and Selma Jeanne Cohen. The editors provided insight still relevant today in suggesting that dance is the most resistant of the arts to theoretical consideration.

Perhaps in keeping with this observation, theoretical literature on dance is relatively new compared to the literature available for some of the other arts. For early writing in this category, one can turn to dance education at the K–12 level, as well as to writings for higher education. Dance educators—including Margaret H'Doubler (1998), Ruth Lovell Murray (1975), and Valerie Preston-Dunlop (1990)—discussed issues directly related to the performance of movement, including use of time, space, effort, and shape, as well as expression through movement.

The work of many of these educators paralleled and was often influenced by the scholarship of Hungarian-born Rudolph Von Laban. He experimented with the nature of movement beginning in the early 1900s, eventually developing Laban Movement Analysis, a sophisticated system for analyzing movement characteristics and capabilities, including the expressive aspects of movement. Additionally, Laban influenced creative development in modern dance as a teacher of many founders of the German Expressionist dance movement that evolved during the early to mid-1900s.

American modern dancer Doris Humphrey wrote a seminal dance theory text (1959) that reached both educational and popular audiences. She provided a systematic view of choreography as craft that was influential for many years. Significant later works on dance making include Blom and Chaplin (1982), and writing by Alma Hawkins, who specifically addressed creativity theory in dance. In her earlier work, she argued that "Comparatively little thought and time have been given to the phenomenon of creativity and its relationship to choreography" (1988, p. vii). In later writing (1991), after shifting from traditional teaching methods to a more student-centered and experiential approach to dance making that reflected the practices of earlier dance educators, she advocated a more complex view of the creative process.

Notable dancers writing about theory and creativity include Erick Hawkins (1992) and Murray Louis (1980). Daniel Nagrin, a prominent dance improviser, has written a series of books; a recent contribution is on dance making (2001). Jamake Highwater (1978) provided useful insight into dance as ritual art. Highwater referred to the artist as a modern incarnation of the shaman. He also pointed out that ritual is primal, not primitive, and produced by all people still connected with the ability to express themselves through metaphor. Writing in dance specifically on issues of culture, gender, age, and social context has expanded in recent years as represented by Desmond (1997).

Although limited, writings in fields other than dance further helped dance theory gain academic legitimacy. Suzanne Langer included dance in her writing on aesthetics, and noted, "No art suffers more misunderstanding, sentimental judgment and mystical interpretation than the art of dancing" (1953, p. 169).

The advent of film and video changed the nature of dance research. Because of dance's ephemeral nature, many early masterworks were lost. Today, we have available not only a growing video record of dances, but also documentaries focusing on the creative process of well-known dance makers (Diamond, 1998). Television has provided rich source material for inquiry with two PBS series, *Dance in America* and *Dancing*.

Specific references to dance in the main body of creativity research are few. A collection of writings by well-known creators (Ghiselin, 1952) included only one dancer, whereas a more recent, similarly structured work (Barron, Montouri, & Barron, 1997) included only two. Csikszentmihalyi, in *Creativity* (1996), interviewed 91 respondents from several domains about their creative practices; of the 38 representing the arts and humanities, none are dancers. It is fascinating to see how—even through the 1990s—dance as an art form has been overlooked by those researching creativity. Perhaps this lack reveals that Langer's observations about common misperceptions of dance still play out today.

On a more promising note, Howard Gardner, in a series of case studies on creativity entitled *Creating Minds* (1993), featured modern dance pioneer Martha Graham in his section on kinesthetic intelligence. Judith Alter (1999), in the *Encyclopedia of Creativity*, focused on creative historical innovations in dance. Mary Catherine Bateson (1990), although perhaps not considered a traditional creativity researcher, developed comparative biographies of five women, one of whom was trained as a dancer and dance educator. Significantly, the concept of improvisation was important to Bateson, who declared that the book was about life as an improvisatory art.

Scholarly dance research on creativity represents a quite recent contribution to the domain. Press (2002) looked at creativity in modern dance as it plays out in choreography. She focused on the work of self psychologist Heinz Kohut, analyzing his theories of self, the artist, and the creative encounter. Significant dissertations include Hanstein (1986) on the choreographic process, and Green (1994), who provided a postpositivist investigation into the relationship between somatics and the creative process.

Some research presented in journal articles focuses on how dancers perform on a variety of creativity tests, either alone or in comparison with the performance of nondance populations on the same tests (Alter, 1984; Brennan, 1983). Other studies measure the effect of teaching methods on motor creativity (Garaigordobil-Landazabal & Perez-Fernandez, 2001; O'Neill, 1982), or the effect of dance on a variety of physical, cognitive, or creative factors (Caf, Kroflic, & Tancig, 1997).

The Arts Education Partnership Critical Links report provided a compendium of seven studies, some with implications for creativity, offering directions for future dance researchers. Dr. Karen Bradley (2002), in her accompanying essay, contended that dance is in need of research that explains the interrelations of its specific dimensions as an arts experience and cognitive processes. She also expressed the need for clearly defined, discipline-embedded studies, as well as a need for a common language to describe and analyze dance and its effects.

This much-needed push by dance educators for greater uniformity and more rigorous practices in dance research mirrors a call in the early days of both psychology and creativity research for a more scientific approach. Scientific research must, however, work in partnership with and not replace experiential research. As Wilber (1998) pointed out in reference to nonrational ways of knowing, we cannot theoretically or rationally describe

Spirit other than to say, "If you want to know this, you must do this" (p. 173).

DANCE PERFORMANCE

The creativity of performing dance movement is grounded in movement itself. Human beings move constantly in daily life. More fundamentally, movement occurs constantly within the human body. This movement, far from being simple or predictable, is complex, intuitive—and creative. Dance educator H'Doubler (1998) reminded us that all movement depends on an interaction of anatomical mechanics, neurological functioning, and, beyond mechanics, the ability to think, feel, and will.

The body/mind system, then, is viewed by many in dance as consisting of more than the sum of its parts. Although this outlook may contradict a materialistic scientific view, the development of several body therapies in recent decades, such as Alexander Technique and Body-Mind Centering, indicates that the Cartesian split (Gardner, 1999) or what Desmond (1997) referred to as the "fictive separation of mental and physical production" (p. 30), is a thing of the past. "Mind" does not equate with the brain but instead extends beyond it into the body in complex ways. Eastern meditation forms, as well as healing systems based on the flow of energy through and around the body, are currently influencing Western medical practices and research. The Chinese movement system of Tai Chi (*Chi* meaning "life force") is based on energy flow, as is the practice of acupuncture, which has been successfully used as anesthesia for surgery. Diepold (2002) cited a variety of research into bioelectrical capabilities of the body, including the flow of electrical currents along the body meridians used in acupuncture. H'Doubler also wrote of "life force" (1998) and referred to relaxation as allowing energy to flow through an uninhibited body.

Creative performers of movement are those who maintain heightened awareness of and sensitivity to the creativity of the human body at rest and in motion, as well as the creativity of the interface of the body/mind. The more fully a dancer can feel his or her movement in class or rehearsal, whether it involves internal awareness of the pelvis in motion or a sensing of the skull's weight perched in alignment on top of the spine, the more appropriate choices he or she can make in performance. This is no easy task. Human beings are not conditioned to pay attention to muscular sensation. We often take our movement for granted unless we encounter difficulty or pain.

In a workshop taught by Robert Ellis Dunn, titled "Can Choreography Be Taught," Dunn constantly talked about trying to "hypermobilize" the students, or to short-circuit the conscious mind. He told us that our first duty was to *experience* our own movement (personal communication, June

1994). We can see that no matter what the activity—performance, improvisation, or choreography—this form of deep attending on the movement level is an important part of dance creativity.

How does a dancer access coordination with which conscious, intellectual thought would only interfere? A creative mover is able to make use of imagery—whether visual, auditory, or kinesthetic—that enables him or her to perform movement with exactly the quality intended. A visual image circumvents the intellect and holistically creates a muscular activation that would otherwise not be possible. Not limited to enhancing the physical response, imagery can also transform emotional and expressive qualities. Franklin (1996) referred to the perfect movement experience, often described in many ways—wholeness, oneness, connectedness, total freedom—and wrote of images as "inner teachers" that facilitate awareness throughout the body. Indeed, in traditional creativity research, the description by Csikszentmihalyi (1996) of a flow state during creative activity as an "almost automatic, effortless, yet highly focused state of consciousness" (p. 110) is certainly related to the awareness that Franklin hoped to create through the use of imagery.

Somatic disciplines were defined by Martha Eddy (2000) as "those systems of study that view physical reality and specific bodily or even cellular awareness as a source of knowledge, usually to be gained through touch, movement and imagery as processes of embodiment" (p. 144). Although beyond the scope of this chapter, the use of somatics, imagery, imitation, and other nonrational strategies to directly experience and creatively engage in movement may be referenced in many sources, including Dowd (1990).

What happens within the mover's body/mind is not yet the full picture of creativity in movement. All humans, as potentially graceful movers, act in and as an inseparable part of their environment. Creative dance movers are able to maintain a heightened awareness and sensitivity to movement potential while doing so. Thus, dancers attain a state of connectedness with their surroundings. They are able to tune out certain influences, such as noisy steam radiators (or use the sound if they desire), and hone in on others, such as distance from the edge of the stage, while simultaneously receiving and interpreting rich sensory stimulation in a continuous inward-outward flow. This ability ultimately allows creative movers to consider a greater variety of movement possibilities and to make more finely tuned and appropriate choices.

What does a dancer do, in terms of performing movement? He or she "fills" the movement with awareness and "just-so-ness," to borrow a term from Zen. Every movement receives the exact treatment it calls for and deserves. Dance choreographer and teacher Murray Louis offered an analogy in a workshop when he explained that a chef preparing a seven-course meal doesn't throw the food in one big pot. Each ingredient receives exactly the attention called for (personal communication, February 1983).

Attentiveness, engagement, and intent are manifested through the materials of dance. These materials include movements of the body and its parts in isolation, in different combinations or as a whole, as well as the creation of different shapes with the body; use of space, such as following different pathways (floor patterns), facing different directions, or moving on low, middle, or high levels; use of time, including fast or slow movement, acceleration and deceleration, or variation of rhythm; and variation of effort behind the movement, including strong or light force. This list is a sampling; the combinations are myriad, especially when factoring in emotional or dramatic possibilities and interaction with music, visual stimuli, or other dancers.

The previously mentioned dance materials call for attentiveness at the movement level. Attentiveness feeds and is fed by a dancer's engagement. Beth Hennesey and Teresa Amabile (1988) cited a strong positive link between a person's motivational state and creativity of performance. They found that "People will be most creative when they feel motivated primarily by the interest, enjoyment, satisfaction and challenge of the work itself—not by external pressures" (p. 11). Many movers, improvisers, and dance makers tend to make different and more informed choices when truly interested in their process than when pushing the process by force or will. It may be most accurate, however, to say that both internal and external motivations are involved at different points in a variety of dance contexts. Some dancers may require the imposition of an external motivation, such as a looming performance date, to plunge into an engaged state, whereas other dancers may lose their sense of engagement under the same conditions.

Along with engagement, a creative dancer has the intent to perform movement with awareness of a world larger than oneself moving. This world includes an audience—whether a traditional audience in a theater, a watchful teacher, an infant crawling nearby, or possibly only a "sense" of being seen if dancing alone—even if that audience is not directly acknowledged or engaged by the dancer. The audience presence creates a tension that, for better or worse, affects the mover's performance. Awareness of the larger world may also involve a specific dramatic intent, an abstract movement intent, awareness of other dancers in the space, relationship with fellow folk dancers moving in a circle around musicians in a band, or commitment to the world a choreographer hopes to create.

Ultimately, creative movers supply appropriateness of movement, no matter what the style or context of the dance. Whether performing a Tewa dance, an Irish step dance, hip-hop, or a classical ballet, creative movers have a sense of just so-ness, of context, indeed of past and future, even as they inhabit the present moment. They surpass mere movement technique in some way, even in dances purely about movement.

Different styles of dance often emphasize different qualities of movement (e.g., the contrast of sharp and angular jazz dance movement with the more smooth and flowing quality of the Hawkins modern dance style). Dancers, at any level of proficiency, may be drawn to one particular style of movement over another based on these movement qualities. In teaching dance, I have frequently observed not only students who have a proclivity for expression through movement rather than through writing or drawing, but also students who have affinity, comfort, and often greater creative facility with particular *styles* of movement, or with movement qualities that range *across* dance styles. Dancers who become accomplished performers may either be experts in one style of movement, or, as is more often the case currently in the professional and educational dance world, may take the route of exploring many movement forms to broaden their capabilities.

DANCE IMPROVISATION

Some dance styles are at least partly improvisational in nature, from tap dance and social dancing to flamenco and the Native American Stomp dance. For other styles, such as modern dance in which the movement most often is made before the performance, improvisation serves two general purposes. First, it is used as a tool for making dances, a tradition established in the early days of modern dance. This is the purpose most frequently found in higher education. A variation found in dance education for K–12 incorporates improvisation as a means for students to expand their movement skills through individual exploration.

As a second and more recent purpose, improvisation is engaged in as its own experience and is sometimes presented for performance. This tradition in modern dance stems from experimentation in the 1960s and 1970s, including dance improvisers such as Daniel Nagrin and Margaret Beals, Anna Halprin and the "Happenings" on the West Coast, and the Judson Dance Theatre in New York City. Steve Paxton, a member of the Judson group, later developed contact improvisation, a specific improvisational form in which the dancers maintain a point of physical contact between them as the focus and source of movement discovery.

The amount of structure imposed in dance improvisation for performance lies on a continuum from completely unstructured to heavily structured, and depends on the temperament of the individual dancer, the group, or the group director. Some groups may follow a problem-solving-based approach, and work with complex structures that include instructions dictating where in the space certain events occur, designated events that serve as chronological markers, and roles or tasks for particular dancers. Other groups may follow an open-ended approach and work with movement meditations on images, memories or evocative words, or determine beforehand only whether the musicians or the dancers begin the improvisation.

Improvisation is, perhaps, the artistic practice closest to everyday life—when does a day go by that any of us do not improvise, at some point, while striving to be authentic? Human beings are confronted with choices every day, and creativity in dance improvisation is all about making choices—appropriate, meaningful, internally felt choices. Ultimately, humans today still do not know where choices come from (at least, not the creative choices with which this chapter is concerned). We could say that these choices come from an inner voice that has been given many names by different cultures, traditions, and domains.

Many theories of the creative process address where creative ideas and choices originate. This source is given many different labels, not necessarily referring to the same "location," including *subconscious, unconscious, superconscious, preconscious, psyche,* or an internal-external source such as the *ground of being, higher self,* or *divine inspiration.* In another parallel between dance and creativity research, cognitive creativity researchers Finke, Ward, and Smith (1992) echoed improviser Nagrin (1988) in suggesting that the preconscious is an important source of creativity for artists, because the unconscious may produce the "same old thing." In dance improvisation, this means habitual movement. Habitual movement, although at times intriguing to work with for improvisers, often may not provide the most appropriate choice for a particular context. The improviser must be patient, willing to wait for a deeper impulse, and open to risking the unknown.

Choices based on this deeper awareness represent the essence of creativity. Such choices may or may not be novel: The simple act of sitting down may stun the audience, not because it is novel but because it is *called for.* It is intriguing that viewers, also on a deep level, recognize such choices when they see them. The shared experience is exciting, and at times viewers are left with the feeling that what they saw, for moments or for entire dances, could not have been choreographed.

Dance improvisers face the stereotype that they just go out and do anything that comes to them without practice. Most improvisers have solid technical training and, often, at least some dance making in their background. When preparing to perform improvisation, dancers practice opening to experience by improvising in different situations. They attempt to respond in movement without blocking or inhibiting their truest impulses, and to get beyond habitual movement unless deciding consciously to explore it. This ability may take years to develop to a high level. Thus, creativity in dance improvisation is, in one sense, more a matter of opening to creative potential than acquiring it. This process of paring away rather than building up relates more to nonrational approaches than to skill-building approaches.

What assists dancers in opening to creative choices? For one, familiarity with craft, so that concerns of technique and form have less need of engaging conscious thought. Craft can exist on a subterranean level, taking little energy, leaving the improviser free to spontaneously receive and act on inspiration. At times, however, the conscious mind of the improviser is very involved in the work. The resulting process is an interweaving of the known and the unknown, the conscious and the preconscious, the rational and the nonrational. At certain times, as Margaret Beals pointed out, the unknown takes over and the dancer rides it until catching up (personal communication, May 2003). Then conscious thinking becomes more involved. If the conscious is called on to do the job of the preconscious, however, it may create a lower energy movement choice than does opening to a wealth of choices guided by depth of feeling and intuitive affinity. The latter might just lead to magic.

Creative improvisation sometimes involves being connected in body/mind awareness with a partner or other members of a group. This connection is not achieved solely through visual cues, because improvisers may remain connected without being able to see each other. Such a link may be established through rhythmic cues (whether or not music is involved), touch, sound, or all that movement itself inspires and is inspired by—mood, timing, energy, use of space, and psychological and psychic awareness.

Improvisers may establish or maintain connection through unison movement, contrast, shadowing, accenting, mirroring, as well as through emotional or dramatic relationship. Improvisers may connect by placing themselves in the same world before the dance begins. They might do so by viewing the same painting or listening together to a few lines of poetry. What they experience might affect each of them in a number of ways, but they respond primarily in movement. One improviser might respond to use of line, color, or light in a painting, whereas another might focus on a mood, dramatic tension, or the depiction of literal action. If working with poetry, the dancers might respond to meter, pure sound, or the same dramatic or literal possibilities a painting would offer. Use of music, live or taped, is another common way for improvisers to maintain connection. More often than not, a group working in the same "world" dances with a common thread, a shared sense of consciousness.

Shared consciousness among dancers may be similar to the experience of close-knit sports teams, or any group that works closely together. Sheldrake (2003) cited several examples of sports figures, from ice dancers Torville and Dean to soccer star Pele to members of the New York Knicks, who recounted frequent experiences of altered consciousness, intuition, or even telepathic ability during sporting events. Sheldrake reported similar stories from musicians, actors, and dancers. Such accounts, although many, are admittedly anecdotal. Sheldrake, however, noted that tests for telepathic activity have indicated results above random chance. Tests conducted by Schlitz and Honorton (as cited in Sheldrake, 2003) of students at the Juilliard School in New York City revealed a 50% success rate, significantly higher than chance and higher than nonarts subjects. These results with students in the arts were replicated by Dalton (as cited in Sheldrake, 2003) at Edinburgh University.

Research into expanded consciousness, even though conducted rigorously and often replicated consistently in a variety of tests with both animal and human subjects, is controversial in some circles. I include this research to expand the range of possibilities for theories of group creative process. I maintain that the growing body of research exploring the possibility that mind is "nonlocal," or extends beyond both brain and body into a larger field of consciousness, is relevant to a true exploration of creativity.

Creative improvisers incorporate and at times transcend the awareness of the mind/body by working with the materials of dance. The descriptions of Nagrin, Beals, and Csikszentmihalyi indicate the presence of a transpersonal approach. It may be that the process involves an interplay of conscious and preconscious cognitive factors, as well as an informative awareness extending beyond the individual to connect with a universal creative state.

DANCE MAKING

A dance maker attends to life, and to what intrigues, motivates, or inspires him or her. Some dances are based on interpretation of or response to music, or an experience of nature. Others are based on literary works, autobiographical events, random chance, and the experience of gravity or use of breath. The creative process may vary greatly from one dance maker to another—even varying significantly from dance to dance for the same dance maker. Similarities in approach, if any, may be more likely to occur within dance styles.

Attention, engagement, intent, and materials—these elements flow together in complex ways, each taking prominence in the choreographic process at different points, or often acting simultaneously. The dance maker may have no idea when going into the studio what his or her inspiration will be—this time. He or she may start with the materials of movement, manipulating, playing—and then attending to what interests him or her. Dance makers create and resolve tension through use of form, guided by sensation, feeling, past experience, and personal knowledge. The dance maker creates a world that unfolds in time, moves in and through space, with specific energetic dynamics and an overarching intent. One or more of these aspects may be of greater interest or importance to the dance maker than the others, either for a single dance or over the course of many dances in a body of work.

The main focus of the choreographer, however, may not be the main focus of the viewer. The audience connection is an important aspect of creativity in dance making. Often, a dance is revised at least once, or many times, after the choreographer shows it. What happens when a dance is seen, and how is that a part of the creative process?

A dance is experienced by the audience visually, kinesthetically, aurally, and emotionally. We remember from the discussion of movement performance that engaged movement choices are often qualitatively different from unengaged choices. The audience senses engaged choreographic choices for their fullness, appropriateness, clarity, and originality. The dancers' engagement in performance mirrors and transmits the choreographer's engagement during the original creative act. Feedback on this audience experience is often crucial for the dance maker.

As with improvisation, choreographers try to find not just what is novel, but what is appropriate. This may lead them to reject vague or overly familiar movement options; hence, Dunn's attempt to "hypermobilize" the students in his choreography class as a preliminary step to choreographing. Twyla Tharp, Paul Taylor, and other modern dance makers achieved a certain amount of novelty by freeing the vocabulary of ballet from its traditional structure. They went beyond novelty for novelty's sake, however, and used the newfound novelty to make new meaning. The middle school students featured at the beginning of this chapter created an effective dance because the movement, although simple and novel to a minor degree, was appropriate for the theme of the dance.

Some dance makers think of their process as problem solving, whereas others do not. This view may depend in part on the choreographers' backgrounds and the dance genre within which they work. Problem solving may not be the most useful terminology to describe dances made in more improvisational genres, or genres in which the intent is to discover and make meaning in tangible form through individual exploration.

Postmodernism and contemporary dance have introduced many new possibilities for creative use of materials in dance making. With an increased emphasis on incorporating nonmovement elements such as spoken text, video, extensive use of props, and involvement of traditionally nonperforming spaces, such as the theater lobby—the creative emphasis must shift in part to how these elements work together to achieve a whole.

Movement may or may not be deemphasized. Even if the former is the case, movement must still be truthful (a feeling that it is not forced or imposed on the world created by the dance or the person performing it), and appropriate to the main focus of the dance.

Issues of age and gender also characterize postmodern and contemporary dance. Gender role reversal, such as women supporting and lifting men, as well as same-gender partnering, enhance creative options for dance making. A general shift toward older dancers in some genres, indeed a revaluing of the sensibilities that a mature dance artist offers, also has changed the picture of creativity in dance in recent years. The Liz Lerman Company regularly features dancers ranging in ages from their 20s to their 80s.

Along with age and gender, the role of community has been revised in contemporary dance making. With seeds in the experimentation of the Judson Theater Group era, improvisational collaboration as a method of dance making is much more common today. Instead of listing a choreographer, program notes may list the company director's name—in artistic collaboration with the dancers. As a cultural parallel, the Hopi Indians have no tradition of naming a choreographer for their dances, although they know within a society who makes certain innovations and why (Kealiinohomoku, 1983).

Contemporary dance makers go to local communities and make dances that integrate nondancers from the community as collaborators. Dance themes often address issues facing the community at large. This activity possibly reflects a cultural influence, reminiscent of the importance of communal creativity found in many of the Native American dances. Perhaps, too, this shift reflects a shift in dance creativity—for some genres—away from virtuosity or specialization to creativity claimed by all.

CONCLUSION

Margaret H'Doubler sought to develop dance as both a science and an art. Dance educators and artists alike have echoed this desire many times over the past hundred years, and their efforts are now coming to fruition. H'Doubler and other educators have spent hour after hour systematically mapping out principles and ideas included in this chapter, based on careful experimentation with students and extensive scholarship. The painstaking artistic process of countless choreographers, dancers, and improvisers represents an equally important aspect of this exploration. A new balance between scientific, artistic, and scholarly research in dance is emerging.

Accordingly, in conducting dance research, we need to be clear about the information we already have, how it relates to new discoveries we are making, and connections made among traditionally separate areas of inquiry. Bradley's call for rigorous methods in dance research and a common language among researchers is justified. By addressing creativity within different dance activities and, as a further subdivision, across a range of dance styles, we gain some of this clarity.

Creativity in dance must be looked at across cultures and social contexts, with the awareness that both similarities and differences may be found from culture to culture. Cultural creativity as a specific area within dance is worthy of further investigation. Dance improvisation is particularly suited for study of process and spontaneous choice making, whereas dance making is suited to studying the relationship of the dance maker to a variety of contextual influences.

The creativity of movement itself is also a rich area of study, and includes awareness of specific motor and cognitive issues, as well as how movement engages nonrational processes of communication and facilitates opening to expanded awareness. Eddy (2000) reminded us that somatics and other nonrational means of knowing are capable of systematic study. Although considering mind/body potential as creative may not be new to many within the domain, it is perhaps a shift in perspective for those outside of dance and related areas.

In many Eastern and indigenous worldviews, a unified approach to life such as the viewpoint accommodated by Boucouvalis, Walters, and others is maintained simultaneously with an awareness of dualism. In many Western philosophies, however, dualism exists as the sole guiding belief. Watts (1961) contended that dualism is at the heart of most forms of Western psychotherapy, a domain that generated much early creativity research. In discussing Zen, however, Watts referred specifically to artists as those who move between egocentric awareness and cosmic consciousness, or the feeling that one's identity is the whole field of the organism in its environment (Watts, 1961).

The disconnect between dance and creativity research is slowly changing, as the existence of this book and other works cited indicate. Dance, as a domain that is most fundamentally of, for, and about the body, facilitates an exploration of creativity that questions traditional boundaries among body, mind, and spirit. Creativity in dance is found partly within the individual, partly in the interconnections of an individual acting within multiple contexts, and, perhaps, as part of a larger, all-encompassing source. Possibilities for research into creativity in dance are myriad, and spill over into many areas of inquiry. Dance, thus, is a uniquely experiential domain offering a challenging opportunity for researchers interested in how transpersonal elements intersect with more traditionally measured aspects of creativity.

REFERENCES

Alter, J. (1984). Creativity profile of university and conservatory dance students. *Journal of Personality Assessment, 48*(2), 153–158.
Alter, J. (1999). Dance and creativity. In M. A. Runco & S. R. Pritzker (Eds.), *Encyclopedia of creativity* (pp. 469–481). London: Academic Press.
Barron, F., Montouri, A., & Barron, A. (Eds.). (1997). *Creators on creating: Awakening and cultivating the imaginative mind.* New York: Tarcher/Putnam.
Bateson, M. C. (1990). *Composing a life.* New York: Plume.
Blom, L. A., & Chaplin, L. T. (1982). *The intimate act of choreography.* Pittsburgh, PA: University of Pittsburgh Press.
Boucouvalas, M. (2000). The transpersonal orientation as a framework for understanding adult development and creative processes. In M. E. Miller & S. Cook-Greuter (Eds.), *Creativity, spirituality, and transcendence—paths to integrity and wisdom in the mature self* (pp. 208–229). Stamford, CT: Ablex.
Bradley, K. K. (2002). Informing and reforming dance education research. In R. J. Deasey (Ed.), *Critical links: Learning in the arts and student academic and social development.* Retrieved April 21, 2003, from http://aep-arts.org/PDF%20Files/CLdance.pdf
Brennan, M. A. (1983). Relationship between creative ability in dance and selected creative attributes. *Perceptual and Motor Skills, 55*(1), 47–56.
Caf, B., Kroflic, B., & Tancig, S. (1997). Activation of hypoactive children with creative movement and dance in primary school. *Arts in Psychotherapy, 24*(4), 355–365.
Cohen, S. J. (Ed.). (1965). *The modern dance: Seven statements of belief.* Middletown, CT: Wesleyan University Press.
Copeland, R., & Cohen, M. (Eds.). (1983). *What is dance?* New York: Oxford University Press.
Csikszentmihalyi, M. (1993). *The evolving self: A psychology for the third millennium.* New York: HarperCollins.
Csikszentmihalyi, M. (1994). Creativity. In R. J. Sternberg (Ed.), *Encyclopedia of human intelligence* (pp. 298–306). New York: Macmillan.
Csikszentmihalyi, M. (1996). *Creativity.* New York: HarperCollins.
Desmond, J. C. (1997). Embodying difference: Issues in dance and cultural studies. In J. C. Desmond, (Ed.), *Meaning in motion: New cultural studies of dance* (pp. 29–54). Durham, NC: Duke University Press.
Diamond, M. (Producer/Director). (1998). *Dancemaker* [Film Documentary]. United States: Artistic License Films.
Diepold, J. H., Jr. (2002). Thought field therapy: Advancements in theory and practice. In F. P. Gallo (Ed.), *Energy psychology in psychotherapy: A comprehensive source book* (pp. 3–34). New York: Norton.
Dowd, I. (1981/1990). *Taking root to fly: Ten articles on functional anatomy.* Northampton, MA: Contact.
Eddy, M. H. (2000). Access to somatic theory and applications: Socio-political concerns. In J. Crone-Willis (Compiler), *Conference proceedings: Dancing in the millennium, an international conference* (pp. 144–148). Washington, DC: Dancing in the Millenium.
Finke, R. A., Ward, T. B., & Smith, S. M. (1992). *Creative cognition: Theory, research and applications.* Cambridge, MA: MIT Press.
Franklin, E. (1996). *Dance imagery for technique and performance.* Champaign, IL: Human Kinetics.
Garaigordobil-Landazabal, M., & Perez-Fernandez, J. I. (2001). Impact of an art program in motor creativity, perceptual and motor skills, body image, and self-concept in children aged 6–7 yrs old. *Boletin de Psicologia Spain, 71,* 45–62.
Gardner, H. (1993). *Creating minds.* New York: Basic Books.

Gardner, H. (1999). *Intelligence reframed: Multiple intelligences for the 21st century.* New York: Basic Books.

Ghiselin, B. (Ed.). (1952). *The creative process.* New York: New American Library.

Green, J. (1994). Guiding choreography: A process-oriented, person-centered approach with contributions from psychoanalytic, cognitive and humanistic psychology. *Dissertation Abstracts International, 55*(4-A), 778.

Hanstein, P. (1986). *On the nature of art making in dance: An artistic process skills model for the teaching of choreography.* Doctoral dissertation, Ohio State University, Columbus.

Hawkins, A. (1988). *Creating through dance* (rev. ed.). Princeton, NJ: Princeton Book Company.

Hawkins, A. (1991). *Moving from within: A new method for dance making.* Princeton, NJ: a cappella books.

Hawkins, E. (1992). *The body is a clear place—and other statements on dance.* Princeton, NJ: Princeton Book Company.

H'Doubler, M. N. (1998). *Dance: A creative art experience* (rev. ed.). Madison: University of Wisconsin Press.

Hennesey, B. A., & Amabile, T. M. (1988). The conditions of creativity. In R. J. Sternberg (Ed.), *The nature of creativity: Contemporary psychological perspectives* (pp. 11–38). New York: Cambridge University Press.

Heth, C. (1992). American Indian dance: A celebration of survival and adaptation. In C. Heth (Ed.), *Native American dance: Ceremonies and social traditions* (pp. 1–17). Washington, DC: Smithsonian Institution.

Highwater, J. (1978). *Dance: Rituals of experience* (3rd ed.). New York: Oxford University Press.

Huenemann, L. F. (1992). Northern Plains dance. In C. Heth (Ed.), *Native American dance: Ceremonies and social traditions* (pp. 125–147). Washington, DC: Smithsonian Institution.

Humphrey, D. (1959). *The art of making dances.* New York: Grove.

Kealiinohomoku, J. (1983). An anthropologist looks at ballet as a form of ethnic dance. In R. Copeland & M. Cohen (Eds.), *What is dance?* (pp. 533–549). New York: Oxford University Press.

Kreemer, C. (Ed.). (1987). *Further steps: Fifteen choreographers on modern dance.* New York: Harper & Row.

Langer, S. K. (1953). *Feeling and form.* New York: Scribner's.

Louis, M. (1980). *Inside dance—essays by Murray Louis.* New York: St. Martin's Press.

Morris, J. (1996). *Inside the creative process with dance: A learning unit for adolescents.* Unpublished master's thesis, Teachers College, New York.

Murray, R. L. (1975). *Dance in elementary education: A program for boys and girls* (3rd ed.). New York: Harper & Row.

Nagrin, D. (1988). *How to dance forever—surviving against the odds.* New York: Quill—William Morrow.

Nagrin, D. (2001). *Choreography and the specific image.* Pittsburgh, PA: University of Pittsburgh Press.

National Dance Education Organization (NDEO). (2003). *Research in dance education project summary.* Retrieved April 21, 2003, from http://www.ndeo.org/grant.pdf

O'Neill, D. V. (1982). The development of a refined movement analysis and its relationship to motor creativity among grade two children. *Dissertation Abstracts International, 43*(2-A), 396.

Press, C. (2002). *The dancing self: Creativity, modern dance, self psychology and transformative education.* Cresskill, NJ: Hampton.

Preston-Dunlop, V. (1990). *Modern educational dance* (rev. ed.). Boston: Plays, Inc.

Runco, M. A., & Pritzker, S. R. (Eds.). (1999). *Encyclopedia of creativity.* London: Academic Press.

Sheldrake, R. (2003). *The sense of being stared at and other aspects of the extended mind.* New York: Crown.

Sternberg, R. A., & Davidson, J. E. (1999). Insight. In M. A. Runco & S. R. Pritzker (Eds.), *Encyclopedia of creativity* (pp. 57–69). London: Academic Press.

Sweet, J. D. (1992). The beauty, humor and power of Tewa pueblo dance. In C. Heth (Ed.), *Native American dance: Ceremonies and social traditions* (pp. 83–103). Washington, DC: Smithsonian Institution.

Swentzell, R., & Warren, D. (1992). Shadeh. In C. Heth (Ed.), *Native American dance: Ceremonies and social traditions* (pp. 92, 93). Washington, DC: Smithsonian Institution.

Taylor, C. W. (1988). Various approaches to and definitions of creativity. In R. J. Sternberg (Ed.), *The nature of creativity: Contemporary psychological perspectives* (pp. 99–121). New York: Cambridge University Press.

Wallas, G. (1926). *The art of thought.* Great Britain: Butler & Tanner.

Walters, A. L. (1992). *Talking Indian: Reflections on survival and writing.* Ithaca, NY: Firebrand.

Watts, A. (1961). *Psychotherapy east and west.* New York: Vintage.

Wilber, K. (1998). *The marriage of sense and soul—integrating science and religion.* New York: Broadway.

Chapter 6

Musical Creativity Research

Marc Leman
Ghent University

INTRODUCTION

Creativity is steered by historical, social, and economical conditions. When these conditions change over time, both creativity and our conception of it seem to follow a similar pace. Hence, the complexity of understanding creativity: Research on creativity should take into account historical aspects and it should aim at clarifying a broad set of background factors, including physical processes and mental processes, and social interactions.

Musical creativity research has evolved along two parallel roads. One road leads to the artistic exploitation of creative processes using tools that allow flexible control and manipulation of musical materials. Another road contributes to the understanding of the creation process through analysis of the creative context, observation of behavioral and neurophysiological processes, and the knowledge-based construction of tools for creative exploration. The latter, moreover, often traverses borderlines between scientific investigation and artistic exploration: Better understanding of the different phases in a creation process is indeed helpful in developing better tools for creative explorations, whereas explorative uses of such tools provide insights in the process. As a result, musical creativity research is characterized by a mutual fertilization between explorative research and systematic research, art and science.

But what kind of musical creativity research are we talking about here, and how did it come into existence? What conditions are necessary for art and science to go hand in hand? What is the output of musical creativity research? What do we gain with research on musical creativity? Given the huge amounts of money needed to support this type of activity, these are pertinent questions.

We start with a distinction between two concepts of creativity—namely, the romantic concept and the rationalist concept. Both have groundings in different social and economical contexts and their analysis reveals structures and tendencies of the actual situation. Next, the basic conditions that contributed to the emergence of the modern rational concept of creativity are sketched, with reference to social economical, scientific technological, and artistic factors. An analysis of the context of creation is given with particular attention to the role of institutionalization. Finally, an overview of music creation tools for artistic exploration is presented, and a flavor of the concrete environments of creation, their particular results, as well as directions for the future is given. This supports our central theses that (a) postindustrial art calls for the advanced information-processing technologies, and (b) relevant artistic contributions require the support of an institutionalized context of creation.

TWO CONCEPTS OF MUSICAL CREATIVITY

Is musical creation driven by irrational forces such as instinct, feelings, emotions, or is it a rational process completely controlled by our thinking? The classical dichotomy between ratio and affect, or thinking and emotional experience, has led to two rather opposite views, called the romantic view and the rationalist view.

The Romantic View

The romantic view assumes that creation is driven by inspiration independent from the machinery of reason or the compulsions of instinct. Ultimately, musical creativity is believed to come from a muse or divine being, and it is much like a gift or talent to extraordinary people who serve their lives as a medium for a supernatural being's immanent appearance in the world. Others may assume that the muse has its origin in the brain's quantum uncertainty or maybe in affective diseases. But whatever the origin may be, the romantic view entails that creativity cannot be educated, that it is independent from context, and that it must flow out of a divine or natural drive or emotional engagement and inspiration. The outstanding and incomprehensible nature of creativity has been associated with the concept of a genius, whose origin of creation is beyond any reasonable understanding, effective exploitation, or education.

Artistic Versus Scientific Creativity. The romantic view makes a distinction between a scientific genius and an artistic genius. Newton is said to have discovered gravity when he saw an apple falling from a tree. The chemist Kekulé, when falling asleep in a chair, saw in the fireplace before him a snake biting its tail, and discovered the structure of the benzene ring. All these people, like Pasteur, Fleming, and many others, obviously were geniuses who made their discoveries by accident and surprise.

And yet, the genius of an artist is slightly different from the scientific genius, according to the romantic view. Artists are stigmatized, and are characterized by certain tendencies to unadapted social and often psychotic, extravagant, or bizarre behavior. Their creative talents exhibit diabolic powers (like the violinist Paganini), radiate sex appeal (like the pianist and composer Liszt), or stem from tormented minds (like the composers Berlioz and Beethoven). Who knows, but maybe derangements such as depression, mania, substance abuse, or personality disorder are important for having an unusual creativity! Due to the nature of their creativity and these artists' genius, society has to accept such behavior because it is in the very nature of being creative to be either possessed or mad. Case studies, however, have pointed out that there is no compelling evidence that there is pathology in musical creativity (Frosch, 1988; Simonton, 1991).

The distinction between artistic and scientific creativity draws on the idea that the scientific genius seems to be inspired by *divine* forces, whereas the artist's creativity is often associated with *diabolic* forces. In essence, both sources of creativity are sacred and untouchable (at least as long as we deal with geniuses).

Origins of the Romantic View. The romantic view can be traced back to the work of Jean-Jacques Rousseau (1712–1778) who, in his *Emile, ou L'éducation* (1762), defended informal education and the natural origin of creativity. The romantic view did not become popular, however, until the beginning of the 19th century, in the context of the famous Beethoven memorials (Buch, 1999). These international events, organized for the first time in 1845 in Bonn, were supported by celebrated composers such as Berlioz, Schumann, Liszt, and they marked the beginning of a commercial trend going hand in hand with idolatry.

The origins of the romantic view can be related to revolutionary developments in Europe, leading to democracy in France and industrialization in England, that inaugurated the decline of the *ancien régime* and its associated hierarchical and patronized organization of music life. A new type of music life emerged, and led to the installation of a new type of professional framework based on the principles of *free market*. In that framework, composers and musicians were no longer working in service of a court but instead became individual entrepreneurs who worked in free competition conditions with other entrepreneur artists (Sabbe, 1998). The cults of the child prodigy, the virtuoso, and the tormented genius whose work is first misunderstood and later hailed were an emerging effect of a dynamic that was inherent in this new organization of musical life. It was first experienced by the late Mozart, and put into practice by Beethoven.

The free market conditions of the capitalist society of the 19th century provided musical quality consumption goods for the bourgeois class (Hobsbawn, 1987). Although worker classes were first excluded from this free market, it created a dynamics so powerful and all encompassing that its influence remained a dominant factor until the late 20th-century organization of music life. Indeed, even with the decline of the bourgeois society after the World War I (1914–1918) and the advent of mass consumption, mass media, and mass movement in the United States and Europe (Hobsbawn, 1994), the free organization of music life remained the major paradigm in which an industry composed of major recording companies, impresario houses, and state broadcasting companies determines the market (Pichevin, 1997).

The development of this music business was pushed forward thanks to technological innovations that allowed sounds to be stored onto a materialized object. Recording media such as wax cylinders, magnetic wires, vinyl disks, magnetic tapes, up digital disks, and computer hard disks initiated an increasingly facile process of musical reification, in which volatile sounds became a material good, a commodity, a product to be distributed and sold as such. The free market conditions favored a tendency to consider audio music as a commodity whose return sales are in direct proportion to the success of commercial strategies in exploiting the concept of a romantic musical creativity. The romantic view goes hand in hand with the development of industrialization and liberalism.

Romantism in the 20th Century. Although the music industry started with classical music in the 19th century, it continued to generate major business activities up to the postindustrialized world of the second half of the 20th century. Jazz music and, after the World War II, rock 'n' roll in the 1950s and pop music in the 1960s found their way to the masses, and the music industry became one of the most important industries of the postindustrial societies (Laing, 1996). The market conditions, as a natural effect, favored the romantic concept of creativity, and this was easily extended toward all forms of classical and popular music.

The music industry today, in the 21st century, is still perfectly aware of the force of the popular romantic view on musical creativity. The vague ideas of the creative genius, its diabolical origins, are at the center of the mechanisms in which idolization and excess worship are subject to marketing strategies of major commercial companies. As a matter of fact, the very irrationality behind the romantic concept of creativity makes it ideally suited to commercial exploitation. Extravagant behavior, sex appeal, and the use of religious symbols are associated features that contribute to image building. Nigel Kennedy, the classical violist in punk dress, was an example of carefully planned mass consumption strategies that aimed at commercially exploiting idolatry and worship in consumption patterns. In many respects, therefore, the romantic concept of creativity is an effect of musical reification and commodification, a process that started in the 19th century and that continues to generate effects today in popular music.

The Rationalist View

The postindustrial society favors a romantic view on creativity for commercial purposes. Yet, this same postindustrial society has allowed professionals in music research to develop an alternative approach in which creation is seen as the outcome of a rational process and sometimes even as a mechanical process. It led to the erection of institutes for creation—a concept that is radically opposed to the romantic idea.

Origins of the Rationalist View. The origins of this view have to be situated in the rationalist tradition originating with René Descartes (1596–1650). The rationalist view became popular in the 18th century when, during the period of the Enlightenment, the first successes of the methods of deduction, induction, and abduction were taken as models for the development of science and as the foundation of a new worldview. A central idea of the rationalist approach is that if creativity is integral to reason, and reason can be formalized, then aspects of creativity can be formalized and ultimately captured in a formalized and computational system. Composers and scientists of the 17th and 18th centuries explored this view using combinatorial mathematics and dice to create music (Knobloch, 2002). Even today, this idea of the computer as creator remains very popular, and it has been inspired and promoted by the successes of cybernetics and artificial intelligence (Ames, 1987). Yet, it would be rather naïve to believe that all aspects of creation can be and should be put into a mechanical process, just as it is naïve to believe that research on creation is solely aimed a building creative engines that surpass people. Creation is a complex issue, and although machines can be used in creative processes, most experts in the field will deny that machines thus far have ever been able to produce a masterpiece. After all, machines have to be programmed, and the programmer, after all, is a creator! On the other hand, machines have been great tools in the hands of proficient composers (Risset, 1994).

Rationalism in the 20th Century. The difference between the modern conception of creativity and the 17th–18th-century rationalist conception is related to *technology* and the *institutionalized research environment*. It is moreover the achievement of the 20th century musical avant-garde (1950s–1960s) to have paved the way to this new artistic road of musical creativity. The consistent manner in which creativity has been associated with novelty, technology, and institutions indeed forms the foundation of the modern approach to musical creativity. Creation is no longer just the invention of a good idea, nor is it the exploration of a new tool; rather, it is a connected ensemble of invention, novelty, justification, realization, and communication of results, involving rational as well emotional processes.

A core idea of the modern rational approach to creativity is that even without a thorough understanding of all the brain processes underlying creativity, creativity may be guided and tools may be developed that foster its exploration. Also, the old dichotomy between pure rational thinking and the emotions is no longer a problematic issue in creative research (Damasio, 1994). Pure rational thinking is no longer seen as the sole foundation for creativity.

The fact that certain aspects of creativity are badly understood does not imply that creativity is beyond any rational understanding. Instead, most researchers now believe that analysis, observation, and exploration can refine our understanding of the creative process. The modern technological environment implies that creativity—in itself based on thinking, intuition, and emotional experiences—can be controlled and guided through scientific investigation. Yet, the latter doesn't imply that creativity is simply a matter of machine thinking either; machines have become useful as extensions of musical creativity, just like electronic calculators are useful in taking over some parts of mathematical calculation. The tools developed for creative explorations require navigation and intelligent decision making within a space of constrained possibilities.

CONTEXTS OF MUSICAL CREATION

Governments of modern postindustrial states spend considerable amounts of money to set up musical creativity research institutions.[1] Is this a good investment for the future? To understand the nature and consequences of

---

[1]For France, see http://www.culture.fr/culture/mrt/cmr/assises_96/md-anex.htm#Retour

musical creativity research, it is helpful to have a look at the conditions and frameworks through which such a policy might have come into existence. Several factors should be taken into consideration, including social, economical, and political factors; scientific and technological factors; and artistic factors.

Social, Economical, and Political Factors

First, let's consider social, economical, and political factors, along with the central hypothesis that after World War II (1940–1945) the social and economical conditions were present in which a *novel framework* for musical creation could emerge.

The framework was entirely different from the one established in the late 19th century that was, and still continues to be, based on free market conditions. The music industry is dominated by a few big private companies, called *majors*, with globalist or worldwide aspirations, and a few minor private companies, called *minors*, with smaller-scale aspirations in niche markets. Private companies have control over the recording and distribution of almost the entire music scene of the developed and underdeveloped world. They thus provide studios; pay musicians; control production, multiplication, and distribution; organize concerts; and often recruit and establish the successful groups (e.g., boys/girls bands). Besides the recording and distribution sector, there is an additional considerable business in instrument making and concert organization. The main focus is not only on the popular music (jazz, rock 'n' roll, dance music) but also popular classical music (e.g., musicals; Laing, 1996).

In contrast to this, the novel framework for musical creation that emerged after World War II was inaugurated along with the rise of the information society. The information society adds a level of economical activity, on top of or parallel to traditional commodities based on goods and materials (Bell, 1973). The focus, however, is not on fabrication and energy provision, but instead on information processing, communication, and technology (ICT). In the first half of the 20th century, national institutes for mass media (radio) became powerful players in society in general and also in music life. They continued to be important, and in fact their power even increased after World War II up to the 1960s, until the advent of television (Hobsbawn, 1994). National radio and television broadcasting institutions were controlled by the state and characterized by a centralized management. Many of these institutions provided the incentive for the institutionalization of music creation research, often in collaboration with universities. Thus, the questions to be asked are: Why was the institutionalization of music creation research needed? How did it happen? What consequences did it have for musical creativity?

Several explanatory factors could be taken into account, such as the successes of capitalism creating social welfare and sustained democracy. Also, the successes of electro-acoustics should be mentioned, because they opened a new world of possibilities ready to be explored and broadcasted in radiophonic applications.

From a political point of view, too, the support for totally unbound musical creativity within the context of centralized state-owned institutions demonstrated in actuality what it meant to have freedom of thinking and expressing. European governments in particular seem to have willingly supported a European high culture after the calamities of World War II and the ensuing commercialization (in Europe, called "Americanization") of music life.

All these factors define a global context for the development of a novel model for creativity. Already in the 1920s and 1930s, the film industry was calling for experiments in the domain of sound montage (Scaldaferri, 2002). Demands for better techniques for sound manipulation would sooner or later have generated studios for musical creative research. Also, mass media developed fast in the period between the two world wars and they too would sooner or later have led to studios for music research.

Scientific and Technological Factors

From the viewpoint of the history of science, institutionalized creation brought together two traditions in musical research that had existed since ancient times (Barker, 1989). One tradition had a focus on acoustics. Its origins can be traced back to Pythagoras and his disciples, who studied relationships between tones in terms of the length of a monochord. In the 17th and 18th centuries, this tradition was taken up by philosophers and mathematicians such as Descartes, Huygens, Mersenne, Kepler, Euler, and many others (Cohen, 1984), and it culminated in the 19th-century *experimental* physics of sound with major figures as Helmholtz and Lord Rayleigh. The other tradition had a focus on musical practice and composition, and its origins can be traced back to Aristoxenos. This tradition was further developed by music theorists of the medial times. Later on, in the 17th and 18th centuries, it was developed into a genuine composition theory with musicologists such as Zarlino and Rameau.

Attempts at building bridges between acoustics and musical practice were undertaken at the end of the 19th century both by Helmholtz, in his contribution to psychophysics (Helmholtz, 1863/1968), and by Stumpf, in his contribution to music psychology (Stumpf, 1883/1890). The novel contribution to music research in the information society (20th century) has been technology. Powerful electronic analog and digital technology has put the enterprise of musical creativity research in an entirely new light, providing a binding factor for a new synergy between art and science. Through technology, in particular electro-acoustics in the 1950s and digital technology since the last quarter of the 20th century, musical creation became founded on a single framework for acoustics, musical practice, psychoacoustics, and music psychology.

Not only were the social economical conditions available, but the scientific conditions were also set for the development of a rather unique institutionalized network of centers that had musical creativity in the center of their focus. In that respect, music research explored totally new frontiers and paved the way to cross over in science and art. This crossover culminated in studios and research institutes, first associated with broadcasting companies and universities in the 1950s and 1960s at different places in Europe and the United States, and later on with large independent research institutes (e.g., IRCAM) and university research centers (CCRMA)[2] (Veitl, 1997).

Artistic Factors

Along with social, economical, political, scientific, and technological factors, one should also mention the artistic factors that have contributed to the emergence of institutionalized musical creativity research. The main artistic factor of the 1950s and 1960s was called *avant-garde*.

The term *avant-garde* applies to an international group of composers whose creative thinking led to a new type of music, very different from the music of the romantic tradition (Griffiths, 1995). The composition principles of early avant-garde compositions were founded on principles for varying note series—the so-called *serial technique*, first explored by Schoenberg, Berg, and Webern. (The so-called Second Viennese School was coined after the first Viennese School of Haydn and Mozart.) Avant-garde pioneers such as Boulez, Stockhausen, Nono, Xenakis, and Berio developed a new musical style with a particular focus on sound colors (timbre), sound movements with particular beginnings and endings (gestures), and spatial sounds propagated from different directions in a room. These avant-garde composers were inspired by late 19th-century and early 20th-century composers such as Debussy and, later on, Varèse.

However, avant-garde was more than a musical style—it was a mission. Composers pronounced themselves as the mission's leading persons, to be followed and understood by the masses during the course of history. The avant-garde composers understood music history in terms of an inherent logic of musical developments that they had to complete. Their mission was

---

[2]See http://www.iua.upf.es/~xserra/links/universities.html for a list of these institutes.

to continue the musical development according to its inherent logical development. One of these developments related to the decline of tonality and the "liberation" of the 12 chromatic tones using the serial technique of variation and combination. Another development was the interest in structure of sound. The use of electronic technology allowed for the exploration of entirely new frontiers in the world of sound, and it demanded new knowledge about the possible frontiers of human perception and cognition. The electronic technology provided microscopic devices through which sound could be visualized and manipulated.

Dealing directly with both concrete or natural sounds and electronic sounds through magnetic tape recorders and filtering devices was a natural extension of the avant-garde focus on innovation. If creative thinking has to result in a leading role for society, then innovation has to be its major force. One such innovative idea was that the structure at the microlevel of a musical piece can be repeated in the structure at the macrolevel of the musical piece. As such, the structure of sound and the organization of a musical piece can be connected by one and the same principle. Such principles quickly led to the idea that musical structures could be grown from small seeds (sounds, short fragments), or that musical structures could be generated by stochastic procedures. Composers such as Xenakis and Koenig started to experiment with automated procedures for generating and processing music. It was the logical consequence that compositional strategies and thinking procedures themselves should be automated.

Creativity was no longer focusing on this or that particular note to be played—it was no longer driven by a musical model or reference, but instead by processes to be deployed, by designing and constraining spaces from which eventually notes could be chosen at random. This was the spirit of avant-garde. The pioneering work of avant-garde composers has had great consequences for how we think today about musical creation. In fact, it was the first phase of a development in which art and science became connected. It was the first example of a typical postindustrial creation process.

Of particular interest at the time of the avant-garde explosion (1950s, 1960s) were the meetings of the avant-garde movement in Darmstadt and Donaueschingen, the one more didactical, the other one more artistic. The start of the Internationale Ferienkurse für Neue Musik Darmstadt, for example, can be understood as a typical outcome of the democratic reflex to bring Germany back to the edge of modern music after the disaster of Nazional Socialismus. From 1950 on Darmstadt became a main center for new music, and its activities went hand in hand with the emergence of institutions and music production studios. The avant-garde presented itself as the antipode of the musical commodification and commercialization tendencies of the free market framework, and took profit (from about 1950) from state-supported initiatives that lead to the installation of creation institutions.

As such, music creation became institutionalized and associated with a technological environment, often in the context of state-owned mass media institutions. Music creation, from this point on, required the knowledge of particular nonmusical skills in acoustics, psychoacoustics, electronics, and computing in order to be able to record on magnetic tapes; use techniques of cut and paste, stretching, compressing, and filtering; and perform many other sound manipulations.

Science was enough advanced to support the artistic aspirations, and the social economical conditions were favorable for this idea. In short, the advent of new conditions for musical creativity can be explained by a combination of factors involving the state-of-the-art in science and technology, the development of mass media, the politics of state-supported music production institutions, and—last but not least—the artistic developments that imposed an antiromantic modernist (globalist) view on music as a high-culture phenomenon.

CONTEMPORARY CENTERS FOR MUSICAL CREATIVITY RESEARCH

Developments in society have led to a worldwide network of music studios that evolved into genuine research centers for musical creativity research (Geslin, 2002; Veitl, 1997). In the postindustrial society (post-World War II), the institutes or centers formed unique areas in which science and artistic research went hand in hand (Born, 1995). And although the advent of postmodernism and neoliberal politics in the 1980s might have augured the end of the era of such institutions and the restoration of a new era of creational individualism and romantism, it is quite remarkable to observe that there are nowadays more centers than ever before, and moreover these centers are very active. Despite the introduction of the personalized digital music studio on PC, which allowed composers to build private studios at home, music creation institutions haven't lost their appeal. Their attraction is basically due to new possibilities offered by interactive music making. As tendencies toward integrated arts (theater, music, visual art of all kinds) become more important, the domain of creative exploration gradually incorporates the whole audiovisual area. As a matter of fact, this requires very advanced technology and scientific support. Several aspects of this development deserve further analysis, in particular the role of institutionalization, the problem of legitimation, the phenomenon of networked collaboration, and the development of creative tools.

Institutionalization

The institutionalization of music creation can be addressed from three contexts: infrastructure, professional organization, and artistic paradigm.

Infrastructure. The *infrastructure* defines the production environment for music creation. In the early 1950s, it was typically associated with a production or rehearsal studio of a broadcasting company or higher-lever education center that provided equipment and personnel. The founding father of *musique concrète*, Pierre Schaeffer, for example, was a sound technician working at the *Radio-diffusion-Television Française* (RTF) in Paris. Similarly, the early studies at Milan and Cologne were associated with broadcasting. The *Studio di Fonologia Musicale* was founded by Luciano Berio in 1950 at the Milan Radio, and one in Cologne was founded in 1952 at the *Nordwestdeutscher Rundfunk* (later *Westdeutscher Rundfunk*).[3]

The production machinery in the 1960s typically consisted a set of analogue equipment, including magnetophones and sound generators. Nowadays, it is a network of computers with digital audio equipment (Decroupet, 2002). In both cases, however, the infrastructure offers a methodology for the creation process, and very often it also challenges the methodology of the creation process. This methodology involves the planning and realization of ideas with the help of the available technology and personnel. The modern technology provides not only hardware, but also software or tools that allow the manipulation of information. All software tools constrain the creation process in the sense that the creator has to follow the logics of the software developer in order to master its creative possibilities, similar in a way to the machine logics imposed by the old analogue machinery. However, many composers tend to go beyond what is currently available and enjoy the exploration of new frontiers and new possibilities rather than using old tools and defined methodologies.

In this respect, musical creativity has been compared with navigation in a space of possibilities provided by the software tools, or as interaction with a "game of hermeneutic significance" (Hamman, 1999). Computer tools may be designed so as to foster serendipity: the fortunate accident that meets with sagacity (keenness of insight), or, in other words, the faculty of making fortunate and unexpected discoveries by accident (Diaz de Chumaceiro, 1999).

The Professional Context. As with all modern infrastructures, music creation infrastructure also calls for a division of labor. At broadcasting compa-

---

[3]See http://music.dartmouth.edu/~wowem/electronmedia/music/eamhistory.html for a history of electroacoustic music.

nies, producers of radio programs, often themselves composers, could rely on a staff of technical assistants, each devoted to a specific task. Therefore, in creation research, boundaries between artistic creation and technical support are often diffuse, as demonstrated in the case of the pioneers H. Schaeffer, H. Eimert, and many others. It is known, but rarely mentioned, that in the early days of the electronic music studio, technicians and scientists (A. Moles, W. Meyer-Eppler) often contributed to the creation process in finding new solutions to problems posed by the composer. This happens to be the case nowadays as well, with powerful digital real-time applications. Technicians know very well the limits and possibilities of hardware and software, and their contributions in solving creative problems with practical methods is necessary and appreciated.

This professional context forces the creative process to become subdivided into different parts. Especially if music is used with other artistic modalities (dance, visual arts)—which is often the case in modern applications—the situation may not be very different from an opera house where curator, director, composer, librettist, conductor, singers, musicians, and technical personnel comprise the staff members of a huge creative machinery. As a matter of fact, creation then becomes a collective process that emerges from the interactions of smaller contributing creative units.

The Artistic Paradigm. A paradigm may be conceived as an institutionalized set of concepts, but also as a reference frame for creation. As such, it is a powerful conditioner of the creative process (Kuhn, 1962). The avant-garde movement provides an example of this. Although it was strongly involved with the exploration of new possibilities of sound production, transformation, and manipulation using new technology within an institutionalized infrastructure, avant-garde creativity seemed to be rather sensitive to artistic reference points. In the mid 1950s, pieces by Stockhausen (*Gesang der Jünglinge*) and Berio (*Ommagio a Joyce*) became examples for electro-acoustic music creation: If a new piece was created, it would be typically judged with reference to a set of pieces that were considered to be the masterpieces of the avant-garde. If a new piece had to be created, many a composer would take this as the reference point, and its particular features would typically constrain the concept and creation of a new piece.

It is beyond the scope of this chapter to try to characterize the avant-garde paradigm in great detail. Yet, some major distinctions can be easily made. Schaeffer's *Musique Concrète* and Stockhausen's *Elektronische Musik*, for example, provide two paradigms of the early avant-garde period. The one was focused on concrete sound phenomena and perception-based processing, the other (much influenced by Goeyvaerts) on abstract composition and metaphors. In the 1980s, the perception and timbre-based approaches (Wishart, Saariaho, etc.) developed into another influential

Schaefferian paradigm, often called the *spectromorphological paradigm* (Smalley, 1986), whereas the focus on abstract composition and metaphors was further developed in more AI-oriented approaches (Koenig, Ames, Rowe). A paradigm will typically imply a particular methodology that guides creative thinking, and it often will impose a stylistic idiom, a kind of musical worldview, a typical *sound* as well.

Infrastructure, division of labor, and the artistic paradigm depend on and reinforce each other. Together they provide an institutional framework within the larger social context, in which creative actions take place.

Legitimating Musical Creativity

Of particular interest to musical creation is the effect of institutionalization and paradigm formation on artistic legitimation. In the free market framework, the creative context is characterized by *heteronymous* legitimation, which implies that the ultimate justification of musical creativity is in function of the feedback of the consumer market—the number of sales as a measure of success. In the past, creative contexts have always been heteronymous. Musical creativity was directed to God or church in medieval times, to the king or prince in the Renaissance and Baroque periods, or to nature or the will in romantic music.

The fact that postindustrial artistic creation could evolve toward a state of autonomous legitimation can only be explained by its advanced degree of institutionalization, which, in itself, is due to an advanced use of technology. As a consequence, production centers have adopted an organization of artistic research according to the organization of scientific research.

Legitimation is *autonomous* when no forces other than the inherent forces of institutionalization play a role in the justification of the creative process. Nonexperts, such as ordinary audiences, are not allowed to interfere in this process. The previously mentioned meetings at Darmstadt and Donaueschingen indeed provided an international forum for legitimating the creative process in autonomous terms, very similar to the way in which legitimation works in science. Similar to science, findings were evaluated by colleagues, and no single nonspecialist person was allowed to interfere with the process of musical creation. Autonomous legitimation flourished in the high days of avant-garde. In the post-postmodern area, it seems that authorities prefer a kind of feedback from the audience.

Institutionalized creativity was assumed to be free of any constraint, even from the audience that listens to the music. The professional environment was organized in a way similar to the organization of a scientific enterprise. Composers became artists in residence at institutions or teachers at universities. They received a monthly salary for musical research and compositional activities, and their creative output was meticulously analyzed by peer researchers from the same or similar institutes.

Networked Collaboration

Apart from institutionalization, and the problem of legitimating creative output, centers for musical creation are nowadays involved in research and development. They typically develop platforms for creative exploration, often in collaboration with other creative research laboratories worldwide. The network of collaborative institutions is a recent step in institutionalization. It is the natural outcome of the embedded scientific and technological activities of creative research since the 1950s, 1960s, and 1970s. With the advent of worldwide networks of digital communication (the Internet), this process of institutionalization has led to intensive international collaboration and the emergence of a global community of creative research centers, whose critical mass is impressive, in terms of scientific and artistic activities. Creativity research, in this second phase of the postindustrial society, has become mature, and its impact seems to have become even important for the industrial development of the postindustrial society.

The science and technology that underlie the development of creative content-processing tools offer new possibilities in many domains, such as entertainment, therapy, and education. Modern societies have noticed the importance of these developments and support projects in different areas of creativity research. In the United States and Europe, for example, projects are currently being financed that aim at developing and packaging all kinds of audio/multimedia software in order to create a common platform for music/multimedia creation. PlanetCCRMA[4] and Agnula[5] are two projects that aim at developing a Libre Software platform devoted to professional and consumer audio applications, delivering distributions for the Linux platform. Other forms of modern state-supported creation research focus on conferences and meetings. The series of DAFx conferences (supported by the EU COST action), for example, created a huge interest in digital audio effects (Arfib, 2002; Zölzer, 2002). Its current successor, ConGAS, focuses on gestures. Still other forms of support focus on scientific development of creative research (e.g., MEGA-IST).[6]

---

[4]http://ccrma-www.stanford.edu/planetccrma/software/
[5]http://www.agnula.org/project
[6]http://www.megaproject.org

Tools for Creative Music Research

The internationally supported networks often focus on the development of digital tools for creative exploration. Such tools allow the study of musical creation through its exploration and use. Tools for creative exploration allow users to constrain spaces of possibilities and provide frameworks for the navigation, manipulation, and organization of materials.

Given the digital domain in which creation nowadays is situated, low-level interactions between different media such as body movement and music, and music and computer animation, open new frontiers for creative expressiveness. Features of expressiveness in the movement of a dancer, for example, can be extracted and used in computer-generated music in real time. Roughness in sound can be extracted and projected as texture on the scene.

Multimedia in art is no longer just a matter of bringing together different art forms on the scene. Instead, the digital forum offers manipulation and integration at microlevels of information processing. In this context, it is appropriate to briefly mention different areas of contemporary tool making, such as automatic composition, digital audio effects, gestural control, and interactive multimedia.

Automatic Composition

Automated musical creativity is a goal that is sometimes pursued in the contemporary exploration of creative thinking, but it is by no means an entirely modern invention. In the 15th and early 16th centuries, canonic riddles were already embedded within compositions. Dice music—composed by throwing a die iteratively and choosing, on the basis of its outcome, a possible motive from a table of musical figures—was quite popular in the second half of the (rational) 18th century. Mersenne, Kircher, Leibniz, Euler, and Mozart all made use of combinatorial mathematics to create and compose music (Knobloch, 2002).

In modern approaches to automated composition, combinatorics have been incorporated into stochastic or statistic modeling. Pioneers in this area such as Xenakis and Hiller made use of Markov Chains, statistical analysis, and stochastic procedures in algorithmic composition. Apart from stochastic modeling, composers have been using chaos models, as well as rule-based and AI modeling (see, e.g., Tarbor, 1999).

Whether musical creativity can be fully automated remains a philosophical question. As mentioned before, few or no masterpieces have been created by fully automated methods, yet automated techniques and procedures can be developed that may help the creator in organizing and manipulating musical structures. Automated creativity thus becomes a high-level, and often even intelligent, tool for the organization and manipulation of the creator's materials, which, after all, have to be put together to convince an audience.

Digital Audio Effects

Digital audio effects apply to tools for the manipulation of sounds rather than sound structures. Straightforward effects can be obtained using analysis and synthesis methods based on spectral modeling (Zölzer, 2002). Sounds can be split into deterministic (sinusoid) and stochastic (noise) parts. The deterministic part allows a straightforward manipulation of different parameters such as frequency and amplitude as well as higher-level attributes such as noisiness, harmonicity, vibrato, and spectral centroid. Sounds can be given a totally new character by means of spectral domain transformations that affect the original analyzed parameters: Time can be stretched, pitch and timbre can be changed, vibrato can be added, timbres can be combined, all in real time (Risset, 2002). The stochastic parts are more difficult to deal with from a modeling point of view, but they can be filtered and transformed to some extent as well. They can be used in combination with transformed deterministic parts in order to give the sound its original natural flavor. The techniques offer a straightforward platform for digital effects with applications in many domains of musical creation, including more lucrative ones such as karaoke.

Gestural Control

Gestural control is often related to musical performance and in particular also to techniques of synthesis based on physical modeling (although in music analysis people also tend to speak of gestures; Wanderley & Battier, 2000). Research has focused on finding new ways of dealing with gestural control, through the use of all kinds of devices and a wide variety of interactions (Paradiso, 2003). The main reason to develop models of gestural control is to enhance the naturalness of human computer interaction through more cognitive and intuitive interfaces.

An active domain of gesture control research is related to physical modeling (Karjalainen et al., 2001). A physical model emulates computationally the generation and behavior of the sound of natural objects; for example, of natural musical instruments. The control parameters of physical models can be manipulated using gestural controls. This is in fact how music is played on natural musical instruments and it is a source of inspiration for developing musical human–machine interactions.

Gestural control of digital environments will make the digital creative environment more expressive (Camurri et al., 2000). Thus far, creation research has been heavily biased toward the development of tools that require thought and logics, thereby neglecting the importance of emotions, affects, moods, and all kinds of expressiveness. Gestural control will make the difference between a piece played strictly according to the written (stored) score, and a piece played in an expressive way by a human performer. The first one sounds dull, whereas the second one may sound interesting. Gestural control, therefore, is an extremely important aspect of musical creation.

Interactive Multimedia

Last but not least, tools for creative interactive multimedia should be mentioned. They are concerned with software and hardware tools for real-time human–machine interaction in multimodal (including the different senses) environments. This includes the design of new hardware tools, in particular of interfaces and technologies, including wireless devices; tactile, haptic, and pressure sensitive devices; virtual reality interfaces; force-feedback devices; and so on—new types of human computer interfaces as enhancement and supplements to the traditional keyboards, sliders, and potentiometer controllers. The software aspect deals with real-time analysis, synthesis, and networked communication of content through multisensory interfaces, from a multimodal perspective. Platforms as Max or PD,[7] EyesWeb,[8] and others have set a new standard for creative music making. The MEGA-IST[9] project, supported by the European Union, for example, focused on the exploration of expressive and emotional content in nonverbal interaction through multisensory interfaces designed for the artistic context (Camurri, De Poli, Leman, & Volpe, 2001). In the project, music (including vocal) and movement (including dance) are considered channels for conveying expressive and emotional content. The project focuses on music performance and full-body movements as conveyors of expressive and emotional content. Real-time quantitative analysis and processing of expressive content comprise a promising area of research for musical creation.

CONCLUSION

Our conception of musical creativity is grounded in the social and economical context of the postindustrial society. Analysis of the context in which musical creation occurs is important for a better understanding of the na-

---

[7]http://www.pure-data.org/
[8]http://infomus.dist.unige.it/sito_inglese/research/r_current/eyesweb.html
[9]http://www.megaproject.org

ture of creativity and its complex interactions with history, society, technology, infrastructures, and organizations. All these aspects define frameworks that guide and constrain creative processes.

Although creativity in the postindustrial society has been largely influenced by science and technology, romantic and rationalist approaches exist next to each other in different frameworks. The romantic view, in which aspects of divine and diabolic creativity are exploited for commercial purposes, is basically supported by commerce and the music industry. The heritage of the rationalist approach, on the other hand, is supported by modern governments and maintained by the understanding that creative research has an important potential for the development of the postindustrial society. Research and educational institutions form the context in which creativity can be developed and explored. Recent developments reveal the activity of large international networks of musical creation research. Creative research nowadays forms part of a collaborative network of institutes defining the conceptualization and development of creative communication, information, and technology in the postindustrial society.

Developments in automated creation, audio effects, gestural control, and interactive multimedia show an ever-growing use of real-time interactive digital tools, integration of audio within multimedia (combining audio with video and animation), and networked applications. This development has led to the formation of new digital platforms for musical creation. Many composers are already working within these new digital environments for musical creation, often in interaction with performing artists.

REFERENCES

Ames, C. (1987). Automated composition in retrospect: 1956–1986. *Leonardo, 20*(2), 169–185.
Arfib, D. (Ed.). (2002). *Musical implications of digital audio effects* [Special issue of *Journal of New Music Research*]. Lisse: Swets & Zeitlinger.
Barker, A. (1989). *Greek musical writings—volume II: Harmonic and acoustic theory.* New York: Cambridge University Press.
Bell, D. (1973). *The coming of post-industrial society.* New York: Basic Books.
Born, G. (1995). *Rationalizing culture. IRCAM, Boulez, and the institutionalization of the musical avant-garde.* Berkely: University of California Press.
Buch, E. (1999). *La Neuvième de Beethoven—une histore politique.* Paris: Gallimard.
Camurri, A., De Poli, G., Leman, M., & Volpe, G. (2001, November). *A multi-layered conceptual framework for expressive gesture applications.* Paper presented at the Workshop on Current Research Directions in Computer Music, Barcelona.
Camurri, A., Hashimoto, S., Ricchetti, M., Trocca, R., Suzuki, K., & Volpe, G. (2000). EyesWeb—toward gesture and affect recognition in dance/music interactive systems. *Computer Music Journal, 24,* 57–69.
Cohen, H. F. (1984). *Quantifying music: The science of music at the first stage of the scientific revolution, 1580–1650.* Dordrecht: Reidel.
Damasio, A. (1994). *Descartes error: Emotion, reason, and the human brain.* Chatham, UK: Mackays.

Decroupet, P. (2002). Komponieren im analogen Studio—eine historisch—systematische Betrachtung. In E. Ungeheuer (Ed.), *Elektroakustische musik* (pp. 36–66). Laaber, Germany: Laaber-Verlag.
Diaz de Chumaceiro, C. L. (1999). Serendipity. In M. Runco & S. Pritzker (Eds.), *Encyclopedia of creativity* (pp. 543–549). San Diego: Academic Press.
Frosch, W. A. (1988). Moods, madness, and music: Major affective disease and musical creativity. *Comprehensive-Psychiatry, 28*(4), 315–322.
Geslin, Y. (2002). Digital sound and music transformation environments: A twenty-year experiment at the Groupe de Recherches Musicales. *Journal of New Music Research, 31*(2), 99–108.
Griffiths, R. (1995). *Modern music and after.* New York: Oxford University Press.
Hamman, M. (1999). From symbol to semiotic: representation, signification, and the composition of music interaction. *Journal of New Music Research, 28*(2), 90–104.
Helmholtz, H. V. (1863/1968). *Die Lehre von den Tonempfindungen als physiologische Grundlage für die Theorie der Musik.* Hildesheim, Germany: Georg Olms Verlagsbuchhandlung.
Hobsbawn, E. (1987). *The age of empire.* London: Abacus.
Hobsbawn, E. (1994). *Age of extremes—the short twentieth century.* London: Abacus.
Karjalainen, M., Tolonen, T., Välimäki, V., Erkut, C., Laurson, M., & Hiipakka, J. (2001). An overview of new techniques and effects in model-based sound synthesis. *Journal of New Music Research, 30*(4), 203–212.
Knobloch, E. (2002). The sounding algebra: Relations between combinatorics and music from Mersenne to Euler. In G. Assayag, H. Feichtinger, & J. Rodrigues (Eds.), *Mathematics and music—a Diderot mathematical forum* (pp. 7–48). Berlin: Springer-Verlag.
Kuhn, T. (1962). *The structure of scientific revolutions.* Chicago: University of Chicago Press.
Laing, D. (1996). The economic importance of music in the European union. http://www.icce.rug.nl/~soundscapes/DATABASES/MIE/Part1_contents.html.
Paradiso, J. (Ed.). (2003). New Interfaces for Musical Expression [Special issue]. *Journal of New Music Research.*
Pichevin, A. (1997). *Le disque à l'heure d'Internet: L'industrie de la musique et les nouvelles technologies de diffusion.* Paris: L'Harmattan.
Risset, J. C. (1994). Sculpting sounds with computers: Music, science, technology. *Leonardo, 27,* 257–261.
Risset, J. C. (2002). Examples of the musical use of digital audio effects. *Journal of New Music Research, 31*(2), 93–97.
Rousseau, J. J. (1762). Emile, or On education. On-line English translation. http://www.ilt.columbia.edu/Projects/emile/emile.html
Sabbe, H. (1998). *La musique et l'Occident: Démocratie et capitalisme (post-)industriel: incidences sur l'investissement esthétique et économique en musique.* Brussels: Mardaga.
Scaldaferri, N. (2002). Montage und Synchronisation: Ein neues musikalisches Denken in der Musik von Luciano Berio und Bruno Maderna. In E. Ungeheuer (Ed.), *Elektroakustische Musik* (pp. 66–82). Laaber, Germany: Laaber-Verlag.
Simonton, D. K. (1991). Emergence and realization of genius: The lives and works of 120 classical composers. *Journal of Personality and Social Psychology, 61*(5), 829–840.
Smalley, D. (1986). Spectro-morphology and structural processes. In S. Emmerson (Ed.), *The language of electroacoustic music* (pp. 61–93). New York: Harwood Academic.
Stumpf, C. (1883/1890). *Tonpsychologie.* Leipzig, Germany: Hirzel.
Tabor, J. N. (1999). *Otto Laske: Navigating new musical horizons.* Westport, CT: Greenwood.
Veitl, A. (1997). *Politiques de la musique contemporaine—le compositeur, la "recherche musicale" et l' Etat en France de 1958 à 1991.* Paris: L'Harmattan.
Wanderley, M., & Battier, M. (2000). *Trends in gestural control of music* [Edition électronique]. Paris: IRCAM.
Zölzer, U. (Ed.). (2002). *DAFX—digital audio effects.* New York: Wiley.

Chapter 7

Domain-Specific Creativity in the Physical Sciences

Gregory J. Feist
University of California, Davis

Why do magic tricks entertain us so? Human bodies float and/or get sawed in half. Solid objects pass through other solid objects and back again. Birds and rabbits appear from thin air or from hats much smaller than their bodies. None of these things of course can or does happen, and we know this even as we see them apparently occurring right before our eyes. But we love to think they are happening, and they entertain us so because they juxtapose the impossible onto the possible. Magic plays with and appears to violate the most fundamental principles of our intuitive understanding of physics. What is equally amazing is that children, sometimes very young children, especially love these tricks, because they too have the same intuitive understanding of the physical world, of what is possible and what is impossible.

In addition to the intuitive understanding we seem to have for the impossibility of certain physical events, there also is the question of an even more basic psychological process involving objects—namely, how we learn to perceive the "objectness" of objects. Of course, this is precisely what psychologists who study physiology and perception (in this case vision) do, best exemplified by the classic work of Hubel and Wiesel (1962). As it turns out, brains in general and ours in particular have specific receptor cells in the visual cortex that are uniquely sensitive to certain dimensions of objects. Some are sensitive to horizontal lines, some vertical, and others diagonal. Still others are sensitive to black/white contrast and others to color. In short, our brains come ready made, but still must also learn, to perceive objects.

This chapter focuses on the evidence for a specific domain involved in human knowledge of objects and the physical world, which I ultimately argue is the foundation for the physical sciences (physics, astronomy, chemistry, geology). Furthermore, implicit and folk physical knowledge has been critical for much of human evolution, and I propose that there are multiple sources of evidence that converge on the conclusion that our brains, as well as the brains of many other species, have made use of ever-more complex physical knowledge guided by first principles of object knowledge.

WHAT IS PHYSICAL KNOWLEDGE?

At first glance, the ubiquity of physical knowledge may not be self-evident, but when it is defined and its components are made clear, then its pervasiveness becomes obvious. Physical knowledge concerns the inanimate world of physical objects (including tools); their movement, positioning, and causal relations in space; and their inner workings (machines). Because the tool-use element is a large component of physical knowledge, some archeologists refer to this domain as *technical intelligence* (cf. Byrne, 2001; Mithen, 1996). An "implicit physics" is also seen in children's automatic sense that physical objects obey different rules than living things (inanimate vs. animate rules). Inanimate objects fall to the ground and do not get up. Moreover, spatial knowledge and skills are involved in the physical objects domain. To jump to one of my conclusions, the physical sciences (physics, astronomy, chemistry, geology)—as well as applied science, technology, and engineering—stem from this domain of implicit knowledge.

DOMAIN SPECIFICITY AND THEIR CRITERIA

First, I define a domain of mind by borrowing from Gelman and Brenneman (1994), who defined a domain as a "given set of principles, the rules of their application, and the entities to which they apply" (p. 371). The principles are interrelated and are specific to a class of entities (cf. Karmiloff-Smith, 1992). Domains are not to be confused with modules, however, because the latter are encapsulated information-processing units that are concerned with inputs of perceptions (cf. Fodor, 1983; Karmiloff-Smith, 1992; Sperber, 1994). Domains, on the other hand, are internally consistent cognitive and learning principles that apply to specific classes of entities. In short, modules are perceptual and domains are conceptual.

I argue for two major categories of criteria for an evolved domain of mind, namely evolutionary and developmental. The evolutionary criteria are five in number: fossil, comparative psychology, neuroscience, universality, and genetic. The developmental criteria are two in number: automatic and spontaneous expression in early childhood, and precocity and giftedness. By these criteria, I maintain that there are seven implicit (folk) domains of mind: psychology, physics, biology, math, linguistics, art-aesthetics, and music (Feist, in press). Using some subset of these criteria, other theorists argue for three (Gopnik, Meltzoff, & Kuhl, 1999), four (Carey & Spelke, 1994; Mithen, 1996; Parker & McKinney, 1999), five (Karmiloff-Smith, 1992; Pinker, 1997), or eight (Gardner, 1983, 1999) domains of intelligence. This chapter focuses only on the evidence for an evolved domain for physical knowledge.

EVOLUTIONARY EVIDENCE

Fossil Evidence

One method for establishing a domain of mind is the study of stones and bones (fossils). Such a capacity is evidence of an implicit physics domain because it not only demonstrates implicit knowledge of physical material, it also requires an understanding of both their causal relationship (i.e., "If I do this, that will happen") and their representation in three-dimensional space.

The first stone tools were relatively simple objects known as Omo tools, dating from between 2 and 3 million years ago (myr), are difficult to distinguish from naturally occurring rocks, and are attributed to pre-homo Australopithecus (Binford, 1989; Mithen, 1996; Nobel & Davidson, 1996). However, a revolutionary advance began with the first species of *Homo*, and in fact their name is "handy human," (aka *H. habilis*). Their technology industry is referred to as *Oldowan* and it represents the greatest behavioral difference between early *Homo* and *Australopithecus*. The major advance with this technology is that we see the first examples of flakes being removed from rocks. But even Oldowan tools were used for little more than chopping. Another advance occurred at about 1.4 myr, with the first bifacial hand-axes (developed Oldowan). However, not until roughly a quarter of a million years ago was there a real advancement, namely precise "arrowhead" flakes (the Levallois industry). One really remarkable point to make (no pun intended) is the relative slowness at which advances occurred in stone tool technology (Binford, 1989; Mithen, 1996). For over 2 million years, there was almost no significant advance in stone tool technology. Not until perhaps 750 thousand years ago (kyr) was there a new source material, namely bone, and not until less than 100 kyr were there complex, multicomponent tools (Mithen, 1996). Domain-specific knowledge of the physical world has been a crucial part of the human mind almost as long as there has been a human mind.

As essential and informative as fossils are, they are inherently random, spotty, somewhat ambiguous, and destined to be changed with each major find. They are most informative when combined with the other evolutionary disciplines, such as comparative psychology, neuroscience, cross-cultural psychology and anthropology, and genetics.

Comparative Evidence

The comparative approach is one of the oldest in psychology (with Robert Yerkes, Wolfgang Köhler, and Harry Harlow being early well-known figures). The fundamental idea started with the Darwinian notion of commonality between species and examined the similarities in cognitive abilities of different species, with emphasis placed on primate comparisons (this field is also known as "animal cognition"). The science of cladistics is closely aligned with comparative analysis of different species. Comparative psychologists and archeologists can make inferences about the origins of behavior by seeing which species posses that behavior and where the common branch in the clade is (a field known as *cladistics*). The logic of cladistics is simple: If many species do something, then that behavior must be much older than a behavior performed by only a few species. Wood tool use, for instance, is demonstrated in modern chimps as well as humans and must be older than use of stone tools, which is unique to the human lineage.

Technical-spatial-physical intelligence is best represented in comparative research on tool use and object permanence. Parker and McKinney (1999) argued that physical cognition is the most widely researched cognitive domain in comparative psychology. They also asserted that physical knowledge has three main subsets: object knowledge, space relations, and causal relations. Most comparative intelligence research has been conducted with Piagetian or neo-Piagetian models as the common orientation; therefore, the conclusions are in terms of Piagetian stages and their substages. In object permanence, for instance, the 4th substage is when an individual will look for an object only under the original cloth (A) after it was initially hidden under that cloth but now is hidden in plain view under a second cloth (B). The 5th substage is characterized by searching for an object under the last cloth under which it was seen, even if the object is hidden under a second cloth directly in front of the infant. The 6th substage consists of not only looking for the object under the last place seen, but, if not finding it, systematically looking for it in reverse order.

Nonhuman primates tend to peak at the first 2 stages, and therefore most research has used sensorimotor and preoperational tasks. Indeed, the 6 substages of the sensorimotor stage are markers for monkey and ape cognitive development. For instance, macaque monkeys peak at the 5th substage of sensorimotor development with object permanence, and they reach that stage at 8 to 12 months of age (Parker & McKinney, 1999). Gorillas reach all 6 substages of the sensorimotor stage, and do so by 9 to 10 months of age. By comparison, humans reach the 6th substage of the sensorimotor stage between 11 and 21 months of age, and ultimately reach formal operations by adolescence (see Table 7.1). In general, apes perform about as well as 24-month-old humans on object permanence tasks (Call, 2001). On tasks such as assembling blocks, drawing, tying knots, and reading maps, great apes tend to peak at levels reached by 3- or 4-year-old humans.

Although Köhler and Yerkes demonstrated tool use in captive great apes in the 1920s, it was only after Jane Goodall's observations on chimps in the wild that it become generally recognized that humans were not the only users and makers of tools (Goodall, 1986). The question then became not whether they used tools, but how and with what level of complexity. As with all other domains, there are systematic differences in complexity of tool use and tool manufacturing as we ascend the phylogenetic scale, from monkeys to apes to humans. Monkeys in the wild have seldom been observed using any tools, and in captivity seldom go beyond the simplest tool use, such as using a stick to get food that is visible (Byrne, 2001). Chimps, on the other hand, have been observed in the wild using complex tools and even meta-tools (tools on tools); for instance, wild chimps have used wedges to stabilize their anvils (Matsuzawa, 1996). Chimps also have been observed using compound tools or a complex sequence of tools, such as sequentially using a chisel, awl, and dipstick to extract honey (McGrew, 1992). Experiments that manipulate the complexity of problems using captive primates have confirmed this phylogenetic increase in complexity of tool use and tool

TABLE 7.1
Table of Phylogenetic Comparison of Maximum Development of Physical Knowledge (Object Knowledge and Object Permanence)

Taxon	Piagetian Stage						
Monkeys	ESM	LSM					
Great apes	ESM	LSM	EPO	LPO			
Australopithecus	*ESM*	*LSM*	*EPO*	*LPO?*			
Early Homo (habilis, etc.)	*ESM*	*LSM*	*EPO*	*LPO*			
Homo erectus	ESM	LSM	EPO	LPO	ECO		
Archaic Homo sapiens	ESM	LSM	EPO	LPO	ECO	LCO	
Homo neanderthalensis	ESM	LSM	EPO	LPO	ECO	LCO	
Modern Homo sapiens	ESM	LSM	EPO	LPO	ECO	LCO	FO

Note. E = early, L = late, SM = sensorimotor, PO = preoperational, CO = concrete operational, FO = formal operational. Taxa in italics are based on inferences from the archeological record and are hypotheses and conjecture as much as description of fact (cf. Donald, 1991; Mithen, 1996; Parker & McKinney, 1999).

production (Parker & McKinney, 1999; Visalberghi, Fragaszy, & Savage-Rumbaugh, 1995).

The overall conclusions from comparative research on the distinct spatial, physical, and technical tasks are that different species actually acquire the same capacities in the same order, but at different ages and with different end points (Parker & McKinney, 1999; see Table 7.1). Monkeys tend to end their physical cognitive development in Piagetian Substages 4 or 5 of the sensorimotor stage, which in humans is achieved around 18 months of age. Great apes tend to peak at the late (intuitive) preoperational stage, which in humans is achieved around age 4 or 5 years. Humans go on to peak at the formal operational stage of development.

Cross-Cultural Universality Evidence

Universality evidence is ubiquitous for the tool-making and tool-use part of the physical domain. That tool making in humans is universal is almost tautological. Every human culture has used and produced tools; indeed, it was a defining behavioral characteristic that separated early *Homo* from *Australopithecus* (see, e.g., Mithen, 1996, for a review). Every *H. sapien* culture is defined by its tool use and tool production. Just like other domains of mind, that humans use tools is a universal; *how* they do so is culturally determined.

However, other aspects of physical knowledge—spatial ability and object permanence—are so ingrained in human behavior that few studies have explicitly been undertaken to study them cross-culturally. One exception is a geologist, Jim Blaut, and his colleagues, who have conducted research on the universality of untaught mapping abilities in preschool children from the United Kingdom, United States, Mexico, South Africa, and Iran. Children in each of these cultures used very similar cognitive processes in reading a map and orienting with a map (Snowden, Stea, Spencer, Blades, & Blaut, 1996; Stea, Blaut, Elguea, & Stephens, 1996). Furthermore, the authors argued, maplike models have been used in all cultures going back to prehistory. Similarly, research on the universality of spatial ability per se is almost nonexistent, although there is a fairly robust literature on the universality of gender differences in spatial ability (Gaulin, 1992; Silverman & Eals, 1992; Voyer, Voyer, & Bryden, 1995). Although men are in fact better than women at mental rotation, women are better at contextualized object location and recall (Silverman & Eals, 1992), suggesting different abilities in the genders rather than overall superiority of one gender over the other. Research on object permanence and object knowledge has been conducted on hundreds if not thousands of samples of humans from many different cultures, but little explicit cross-cultural comparison has been conducted to determine the commonalities and differences among different cultures.

Neuroscience

If our brains have evolved specific mechanisms for solving specific problems, there should be some degree of anatomical specificity in brain function and these areas should correspond at least globally with the domains of mind. Historically, there have been two categories of method for examining brain specificity, namely disease and injury with humans or lesions on rats as well as the more recent brain imaging techniques. With the advent of brain imaging techniques over the last 30 years, in particular positron emission tomography (PET) in the 1970s and functional magnetic resonance imaging (fMRI) in the 1990s, we now know much more about the distinct regions of brain that are involved in different tasks in normal-functioning adults.

The importance of the hippocampus and the parahippocampus in spatial orientation and navigational knowledge has been known for some time (O'Keefe & Nadel, 1978; cf. Aguirre, Detre, Alsop, & D'Esposito, 1996). More recently, researchers have reported that one particular area of the brain—parahippocampal cortex or parahippocampal place area (PPA)—is involved in perceiving photos of indoor or outdoor scenes but not of faces or objects in general (Epstein, DeYoe, Press, Rosen, & Kanwisher, 2001; Epstein & Kanwisher, 1998). The PPA was activated by a photo only if it depicted a place that one could navigate—faces or objects were not sufficient. Finally, there appears to be some hemispheric laterality with chess, with the right hemisphere being dominant (Cranberg & Albert, 1988), but the evidence as a whole concerning laterality of spatial knowledge is equivocal (Cooper & Wojan, 2000; Sergent, Ohta, & MacDonald, 1992).

Genetic Evidence

DNA evidence is also evolutionary evidence because, as inherited material, it provides a record of evolutionary change. It tells us where we have been and when genes evolved. Genetic evidence, however, is of at least four distinct kinds, each with a different methodology. Two of these methods rely on analysis of DNA from the nucleus (chromosome), and two of them on DNA from mitochondria. First, there is behavioral genetic evidence of living people that comes from nuclear DNA. The best-known behavioral genetic research is twin-adoption studies that disentangle genetic and environmental effects by examining the similarities and differences in identical and fraternal twins reared apart and together. Another, more recent form of behavioral genetics research is known as "quantitative trait loci" (QTL), and it looks more directly at the locations on the chromosome that are involved in certain personality or behavioral differences. Second, there is comparison of the genome (nuclear DNA) of different species and the degree to which there is similarity or difference in the genome between species, which provides a clue as to when two species may have shared a common ancestor.

The second two forms of genetic evidence come from mitochondrial rather than nuclear DNA (mtDNA). Mitochondrial DNA is not subject to recombination and is therefore passed on unchanged from one generation to the next (from mothers only). Also, mitochondrial DNA is much simpler and easier to extract than is nuclear DNA, because the entire human mitochondrial genome consists of only 16,000 base pairs (compared to 3 billion in the nuclear genome; Foley, 2000). Indeed, the entire human mtDNA genome was sequenced years before the nuclear human genome was. Additionally, there is mtDNA analysis of living groups of people throughout the world for clues of population changes and when branching off from other species might have occurred (such as Neanderthal). Finally, there is mtDNA analysis of the ancient (< 50 kyr) fossil record, which provides clues of whether specific species such as Neanderthal are our direct ancestors. MtDNA analysis consistently points to distinct lineages for Neanderthal and modern humans, suggesting that the former is not our ancestor (Adcock et al., 2001; Krings et al., 1997).

The current problem with genetic evidence for domain specificity is that the brain structures involved in specific tasks are not usually localized to one specific region only (even if there is a primary site involved). Additionally, these brain regions and behaviors are results of "quantitative genetic traits"; that is, they are expressed on a continuum rather than discrete categories and are the result of hundreds if not thousands of genes (Clark & Grunstein, 2000). Therefore, isolating even a handful of the genes involved is tedious, complicated, and a long way off. At the current time we have little research devoted to the genetics of specific cognitive capacities, such as object perception, partly because there is no such thing as an "object perception" gene. Genes code for protein synthesis—that is how they are defined. But the path from gene to amino acid to protein to neurotransmitter and neuron to brain structure to behavior is a long and complicated one. To complicate matters even more, the brain structures themselves are complex and diverse, even if we are getting a handle on their specificity. The Human Genome Project promises to uncover some of the missing pieces of the genetics puzzle, but that is probably years away.

DEVELOPMENTAL EVIDENCE

There are two developmental criteria: early and automatic expression, and precocity/giftedness. For other overviews of developmental evidence for object knowledge, spatial intelligence, tool use, and mechanical knowledge, see Gopnik et al. (1999) and Karmiloff-Smith (1992).

Early and Automatic Expression (Theory Construction)

One of the best-known developmental psychologists in the area of physical knowledge is Elizabeth Spelke, who has argued that principles of cohesion, contact, and continuity guide and constrain perception and understanding of physical objects in early infancy (Carey & Spelke, 1994; Spelke, 1990). Four-and-a-half-month-old infants already understand how objects are distinct from one another and how they move about in space based on principles of cohesion, contact, and continuity. Single objects are recognized if their parts are connected, if their surfaces are in contact, and if the object moves continuously over one path and one path only in space and time. Spelke, also one of the pioneers in the now-ubiquitous preferential eye-gaze technique, showed that infants look much longer at "impossible events" such as two objects apparently taking up the same space. Furthermore, she and her colleagues demonstrated that these principles override and develop prior to the Gestalt principles of perception such as similarity, closure, and simplicity (Carey & Spelke, 1994).

Our understanding of "things" and the physical world only begins with perception of objects. The real trick comes from understanding their permanence, how they move, predicting where they will be, where they are located in space, and how they affect one another. Regarding the permanence of objects, Piaget again was the first to systematically investigate the development of children's understanding of the physical world. He took a constructivist position and argued that the first stage of learning (in infancy) was guided not by any perceptual or attentional biases or constraints, but rather by pure sensory experience. He argued that the first year is when the infant understands the world only through operating (manipulating) objects and experiencing them through the senses. Knowledge is strictly and directly sensory. If an object is not being sensed, it does not exist. There is no cognitive representation independent of sensation. This was the basis for Piaget's well-known concept of "object permanence." Because infants are tied to the sensory, they will not grab for an object that has just disappeared from their view. They act as if it no longer exists once it is out of sight. It is not until around the age of 9 to 11 months that internal representations of the external world start to develop—that is, object permanence (Piaget & Inhelder, 1967).

Piaget's criterion was motoric—whether the child continued to reach for an object just hidden from sight. However, psychologists and neuroscientists had known for years about the principles of "center-out" and "head-to-toe" development of motor skills (Gesell & Thompson, 1938; McGraw, 1943). That is, motoric command at the center of the body matures before the extremities and the head before the arms, which in turn mature before the legs and feet. Developmental psychologists in the 1960s and 1970s started to take advantage of such knowledge and developed assessment techniques that involved movement of the eyes and mouth rather than the arms and hands. As mentioned previously, Spelke was a pioneer in using the "eye-gaze preference" technique, wherein interest was measured by which of two simultaneously presented stimuli the infant looked at the longest. With regard to object permanence, Rene Baillargéon challenged Piaget's claim of its onset occurring around 9 to 12 months of age and argued instead for around 4 months (Baillargéon, 1987; Baillargéon, Spelke, & Wasserman, 1985). She did this by first habituating 4- and 5-month-old infants to a screen that moved in a 180° fashion, from flat pointing toward the child to flat pointing away from the child. Then, in clear view of the infants, a box was placed in the path of the screen (at the point where the screen reaches 112° of its arc; it should also be pointed out that the infants were positioned in such a way that once the screen reached 90° the box was completely occluded from view by the screen). Next, half of the infants saw a perfectly normal event: The screen stopped when it got to the now-unseen box. But the other half (who had not seen that an adult had surreptitiously removed the box) saw something that was "impossible"—namely, the screen continued to move all the way past the box at the 112° mark and was flat and pointing away. If Piaget were correct, and 4-month-olds possess no object permanence, they should not have been at all surprised by this "impossible" event. After all, the box was out of sight and therefore out of mind. However, they were surprised (by the eye-gaze attentional method), which suggests they do have some degree of understanding that objects still exist after no longer being perceived directly. That is, infants have some kind of mental representation of the object. Critics of this research point out that these are perceptual rather than conceptual phenomena and therefore do not constitute object permanence (Bogartz, Shinskey, & Schilling, 2000).

Precocious Talent-Giftedness

Giftedness in the physical-technical domain is seen most readily in the area of physics, mechanics, chess, and computer science, which tap into the spatial and mechanical elements of physical knowledge, respectively (Cranberg & Albert, 1988; Rimland & Fein, 1988). Chess is one example of a visual-spatial ability that manifests its extreme talent often very early in life, with future masters sometimes becoming national champions at the age of 12 or 14 years (Cranberg & Albert, 1988). Indeed, "only in chess, music, and mathematics have profound, original insights been contributed by preadolescents" (Cranberg & Albert, 1988, p. 167).

Extreme creative talent in theoretical physics—like chess, pure math, and lyric poetry—is also likely to peak earlier than in some fields of study, such as biology, geology, history, and philosophy (Lehman, 1953; Moulin, 1955; Simonton, 1988a). It is not uncommon for major theoretical contributions in physics to be made in the decade of one's 20s (Einstein being the most obvious but not only case), and the general peak of productivity occurring during the late 20s or early 30s (Simonton, 1988a). In contrast to chess, pure math, and music, however, there are few instances of creative contributions in physics prior to age 20 (Charness, 1988; Lehman, 1953).

An intriguing connection with such physical giftedness is the fact that special talents in the physical domain are often manifested in children who are blatantly lacking in the social domain, namely autistic children (Baron-Cohen et al., 1998; Baron-Cohen, Wheelwright, Stott, Bolton, & Goodyer, 1997; Rimland & Fein, 1988). For instance, some autistic children are experts at mechanics, able to take clocks, radios, and so on apart and put them back together without error. In at least one recorded instance, an autistic boy could determine with a high degree of accuracy an object's dimensions, such as a room, fence, or driveway. With objects smaller than 20 feet, he was accurate within a quarter inch (Rimland & Fein, 1988).

PERSONALITY UNDERPINNINGS OF PHYSICAL CREATIVITY

Various lines of evidence, sometimes direct and sometimes indirect, converge on the conclusion that physical scientists from very early in life have temperaments and personalities that are thing oriented rather than people oriented. For instance, indirect evidence comes from Baron-Cohen and colleagues, who have demonstrated a thing orientation versus people orientation as early as 36 hours after birth, with male neonates showing a slight preference for things over people and females showing no real preference one way or the other (Connellan, Baron-Cohen, Wheelwright, Batki, & Ahluwalia, 2000). Whether this effect, assuming it can be replicated, has an influence on interest in science has yet to be demonstrated, but it is an intriguing hypothesis because males are still disproportionately represented in the physical sciences and math (National Science Foundation, 1999). In addition, Baron-Cohen and his colleagues have shown that engineers, mathematicians, and physical scientists score much higher on measures of high-functioning autism and Asperger's syndrome than do nonscientists, and that physical scientists, mathematicians, and engineers are higher on a nonclinical measure of autism than are social scientists (Baron-Cohen, Wheelwright, Skinner, Martin, & Clubley, 2001; Baron-Cohen, Wheelwright, Stone, & Rutherford, 1999). Lastly, autistic children are more than twice as likely as nonautistic children are to have a father or grandfather who was an engineer (Baron-Cohen et al., 1997, 1998).

Second, the research that has been conducted explicitly on the personality traits of scientists has confirmed a personality constellation that is relatively introverted, asocial, and thing oriented (Feist, 1998). For instance, in summarizing the results from 26 studies (and 41 samples), Feist (1998) reported the median effect size (Cohen's d) for introversion comparing scientists to nonscientists was .26 or about a quarter of a standard deviation higher in scientists—a small but non-zero effect size. More specifically the cluster of social traits (i.e., introversion, independence, arrogance, dominance, hostility, and self-confidence) suggests a relatively low threshold for social stimulation in physical scientists. The problem with the research on personality and science is that it is not specific to physical scientists, but rather covers scientists in general. Very little if any research has compared the personality dispositions of natural, biological, and social scientists to examine whether the more social the scientist is the more sociable his or her personality is. Of most interest would be developmental research that examined whether a preference for things is evident early in life for future physical scientists, and likewise whether a preference for people is evident early in life for future social scientists. The next line of research for the personality psychology of science is to explore differences in personality among physical, biological, and social scientists. My hunch is that the physical scientists as a group will be more introverted and thing oriented (i.e., have more developed implicit physical domain knowledge) than will the social scientists.

In sum, my argument is that talent and creativity shown in the physical sciences does not develop randomly in some people and not others. The disposition to be interested in and have a talent for understanding the physical and inanimate world has been shaped by evolutionary pressures, and humans in general have a specific domain of mind devoted to solving just such problems. In that sense, we all have some implicit capacity for physical knowledge. Only some of us, however, take these implicit capacities and develop a real talent for formal and explicit skill in understanding the physical world. Like interest and talent in the other folk domains (psychology, biology, math, linguistics, art, and music), physical science talent stems from and is built on the implicit, evolved constraints, capacities, and first principles (Carruthers, 2002; Mithen, 1996). These constraints and implicit first principles sometimes facilitate the development of explicit formal physical knowledge and sometimes hinder such knowledge. Indeed, scientific interest and talent in general is a function of many psychological processes (development, cognition, personality, and social influences, to name just the most obvious), and the explication and analysis of these processes is the task for the psychology of science (Feist, in press; Feist & Gorman, 1998; Houts, 1989; Simonton, 1988b). Physical knowledge and physical science is a perfect place for the psychology of science to focus its attention. But then again, so are biological science and social science, as well as engineering and math. Understanding the physical and inanimate world is indeed part of what we do intuitively and implicitly and sometimes explicitly, and understanding those who understand the physical world is part of what psychologists of science do.

REFERENCES

Adcock, G. J., Dennis, E. S., Easteal, S., Huttley, G. A., Jermilin, L. S., Peacock, W. J., & Thorne, A. (2001). Mitochondrial DNA sequences in ancient Australians: Implications for modern human origins. *Proceedings of the National Academy of Sciences, 98*, 537–542.

Aguirre, G. K., Detre, J. A., Alsop, D. C., & D'Esposito, M. (1996). The parahippocampus subserves topographical learning in man. *Cerebral Cortex, 6*, 823–829.

Baillargéon, R. (1987). Object permanence in 3.5- and 4.5-month-old infants. *Developmental Psychology, 23*, 655–664.

Baillargéon, R., Spelke, E., & Wasserman, S. (1985). Object permanence in five month old infants. *Cognition, 20*, 191–208.

Baron-Cohen, S., Bolton, P., Wheelwright, S., Short, L., Mead, G., Smith, A., & Scahill, V. (1998). Autism occurs more often in families of physicists, engineers, and mathematicians. *Autism, 2*, 296–301.

Baron-Cohen, S., Wheelwright, S., Stott, C., Bolton, P., & Goodyer, I. (1997). Is there a link between engineering and autism? *Autism, 1*, 101–109.

Baron-Cohen, S., Wheelwright, S., Stone, V., & Rutherford, M. (1999). A mathematician, a physicist, and a computer scientist with Asperger syndrome: Performance on folk psychology and folk physics tests. *Neurocase, 5*, 475–483.

Binford, L. R. (1989). Isolating the transition to cultural adaptations: An organizational approach. In E. Trinkaus (Ed.), *The emergence of modern humans: Biocultural adaptations in the later Pleistocene* (pp. 18–41). Cambridge, UK: Cambridge University Press.

Bogartz, R. S., Shinskey, J. L., & Schilling, T. H. (2000). Object permanence in five-and-a-half-month-old infants. *Infancy, 1*, 403–428.

Byrne, R. W. (2001). Social and technical forms of primate intelligence. In F. B. M. de Waal (Ed.), *Tree of origin: What primate behavior can tell us about human social evolution* (pp. 147–172). Cambridge, MA: Harvard University Press.

Call, J. (2001). Object permanence in orangutans (*Pongo pygmaeus*), chimpanzees (*Pan troglodytes*), and children (*Homo sapiens*). *Journal of Comparative Psychology, 115*, 159–171.

Carey, S., & Spelke, E. (1994). Domain specific knowledge and conceptual change. In L. A. Hirschfeld & S. A. Gelman (Eds.), *Mapping the mind: Domain specificity in cognition and culture* (pp. 169–200). Cambridge, UK: Cambridge University Press.

Carruthers, P. (2002). The roots of scientific reasoning. In P. Carruthers, S. Stich, & M. Siegal (Eds.), *The cognitive basis of science* (pp. 73–95). Cambridge, UK: Cambridge University Press.

Charness, N. (1988). Expertise in chess, music, and physics: A cognitive perspective. In L. K. Obler & D. Fein (Eds.), *The exceptional brain: Neuropsychology of talent and special abilities* (pp. 399–426). New York: Guilford.

Clark, W. R., & Grunstein, M. (2000). *Are we hardwired? The role of genes in human behavior.* Oxford, UK: Oxford University Press.

Connellan, J., Baron-Cohen, S., Wheelwright, S., Batki, A., & Ahluwalia, J. (2000). Sex differences in human neonatal social perception. *Infant Behavior and Development, 23*, 113–118.

Cooper, E. E., & Wojan, T. J. (2000). Differences in the coding of spatial relations in face identification and basic-level object recognition. *Journal of Experimental Psychology: Learning, Memory, and Cognition, 26,* 470–488.

Cranberg, L. D., & Albert, M. L. (1988). The chess mind. In L. K. Obler & D. Fein (Eds.), *The exceptional brain: Neuropsychology of talent and special abilities* (pp. 156–190). New York: Guilford.

Donald, M. (1991). *Origins of the modern mind: Three stages in the evolution of culture and cognition.* Cambridge, MA: Harvard University Press.

Epstein, R., DeYoe, E. A., Press, D. Z., Rosen, A. C., & Kanwisher, N. (2001). Neuropsychological evidence for a topographical learning mechanism in parahippocampal cortex. *Cognitive Neuropsychology, 18,* 481–508.

Epstein, R., & Kanwisher, N. (1998). A cortical representation of the local visual environment. *Nature, 392,* 598–601.

Feist, G. J. (1998). A meta-analysis of the impact of personality on scientific and artistic creativity. *Personality and Social Psychological Review, 2,* 290–309.

Feist, G. J. (in press). *The scientific mind: An introduction to the psychology of science.* New Haven, CT: Yale University Press.

Feist, G. J., & Gorman, M. E. (1998). Psychology of science: Review and integration of a nascent discipline. *Review of General Psychology, 2,* 3–47.

Fodor, J. A. (1983). *The modularity of mind: An essay on faculty psychology.* Cambridge, MA: MIT Press.

Foley, J. (2000). *Fossil hominids: Mitochondrial DNA.* Retrieved September 4, 2002, from http:www.talkorigins.org/faqs/homs/mtDNA.html

Gardner, H. (1983). *Frames of mind: The theory of multiple intelligences.* New York: Basic Books.

Gardner, H. (1999). *Intelligence reframed: Multiple intelligences for the 21st century.* New York: Basic Books.

Gaulin, S. J. C. (1992). Evolution of sex differences in spatial ability. *Yearbook of Physical Anthropology, 35,* 125–151.

Gelman, R., & Brenneman, L. (1994). First principles can support both universal and culture-specific learning about number and music. In L. A. Hirschfeld & S. A. Gelman (Eds.), *Mapping the mind: Domain specificity in cognition and culture* (pp. 369–390). New York: Cambridge University Press.

Gesell, A., & Thompson, H. (1938). *The psychology of early growth including norms of infant behavior and a method of genetic analysis.* New York: Macmillan.

Goodall, J. (1986). *Chimpanzees of the Gombie.* Cambridge, MA: Harvard University Press.

Gopnik, A., Meltzoff, A. N., & Kuhl, P. K. (1999). *The scientist in the crib: Minds, brains, and how children learn.* New York: Morrow.

Houts, A. (1989). Contributions of the psychology of science to metascience: A call for explorers. In B. Gholson, W. R. Shadish, R. A. Neimeyer, & A. C. Houts (Eds.), *Psychology of science: Contributions to metascience* (pp. 47–88). Cambridge, UK: University of Cambridge Press.

Hubel, D. H., & Wiesel, T. N. (1962). Receptive fields, binocular interaction, and functional architecture in the cat's visual cortex. *Journal of Physiology (London), 160,* 106–154.

Karmiloff-Smith, A. (1992). *Beyond modularity: A developmental perspective on cognitive science.* Cambridge, MA: MIT Press.

Krings, M., Stone, A., Schmitz, R. W., Krainitzki, H., Stoneking, M., & Pääbo, S. (1997). Neanderthal DNA sequences and the origin of modern humans. *Cell, 90,* 19–30.

Lehman, H. C. (1953). *Age and achievement.* Princeton, NJ: Princeton University Press.

Matsuzawa, T. (1996). Chimpanzee intelligence in nature and in captivity: Isomorphism of symbol use and tool use. In W. McGrew, L. Marchant, & T. Nishida (Eds.), *Great ape societies* (pp. 196–209). Cambridge, UK: Cambridge University Press.

McGraw, M. (1943). *The neuromuscular maturation of the human infant.* New York: Columbia University Press.

McGrew, W. (1992). *Chimpanzee material culture.* New York: Cambridge University Press.
Mithen, S. (1996). *The prehistory of the mind: The cognitive origins of art and science.* London: Thames & Hudson.
Moulin, L. (1955). The Nobel prizes for the sciences from 1901–1950: An essay in sociological analysis. *British Journal of Sociology, 6,* 246–263.
National Science Foundation. (1999). *Women, minorities, and persons with disabilities in science and engineering: 1998* (NSF 99-87.) Arlington, VA: Author.
Nobel, W., & Davidson, I. (1996). *Human evolution, language, and mind: A psychological and archeological inquiry.* Cambridge, UK: Cambridge University Press.
O'Keefe, J., & Nadel, L. (1978). *The hippocampus as a cognitive map.* Oxford, UK: Oxford University Press.
Parker, S. T., & McKinney, M. L. (1999). *Origins of intelligence.* Baltimore, MD: Johns Hopkins University Press.
Piaget, J., & Inhelder, B. (1967). *The child's conception of space.* New York: Norton.
Pinker, S. (1997). *How the mind works.* New York: Norton.
Rimland, B., & Fein, D. (1988). Special talents of autistic savants. In L. K. Obler & D. Fein (Eds.), *The exceptional brain: Neuropsychology of talent and special abilities* (pp. 474–492). New York: Guilford.
Sergent, J., Ohta, S., & MacDonald, B. (1992). Functional neuroanatomy of face and object processing. *Brain, 115,* 15–36.
Silverman, I., & Eals, M. (1992). Sex differences in spatial abilities: Evolutionary theory and data. In J. H. Barkow, L. Cosmides, & J. Tooby (Eds.), *The adapted mind: Evolutionary psychology and the generation of culture* (pp. 533–549). Oxford, UK: Oxford University Press.
Simonton, D. K. (1988a). Age and outstanding achievement: What do we know after a century of research? *Psychological Bulletin, 104,* 251–267.
Simonton, D. K. (1988b). *Scientific genius: A psychology of science.* Cambridge, UK: Cambridge University Press.
Snowden, S., Stea, D., Spencer, C., Blades, M., & Blaut, J. (1996). Mapping abilities of four-year-old children in York, England. *Journal of Geography, 95,* 107–111.
Spelke, E. (1990). Principles of object perception. *Cognitive Science, 14,* 29–56.
Sperber, D. (1994). The modularity of thought and epidemiology of representations. In L. A. Hirschfeld & S. A. Gelman (Eds.), *Mapping the mind: Domain specificity in cognition and culture* (pp. 39–67). Cambridge, UK: Cambridge University Press.
Stea, D., Blaut, J., Elguea, S., & Stephens, J. (1996). Mapping as a cultural universal. In J. Portugali (Ed.), *The construction of cognitive maps* (pp.). New York: Kluwer.
Uzgiris, I., & Hunt, M. (1975). *Assessment in infancy: Ordinal scales of psychological development.* Urbana: University of Illinois Press.
Visalberghi, E., Fragaszy, D., & Savage-Rumbaugh, S. E. (1995). Performance in a tool-using task by common chimpanzees (*Pan troglodytes*), bonobos (*Pan paniscus*), orangutan (*Pongo pygmeaus*), and capuchin monkeys (*Cebus apella*). *Journal of Comparative Psychology, 109,* 52–60.
Voyer, D., Voyer, S., & Bryden, M. P. (1995). Magnitude of sex differences in spatial abilities: A meta-analysis and consideration of critical variables. *Psychological Bulletin, 117,* 250–270.

Chapter 8

Creativity in Psychology: On Becoming and Being a Great Psychologist

Dean Keith Simonton
University of California, Davis

Of all the chapters in this volume, this could be the most difficult to write. Why? Because it is the only one in which the author examines creativity in his or her own domain of creativity. Psychologists may examine creativity in the arts, the other sciences, or in various practical domains, such as business, with relative impunity. After all, as outsiders looking in, the investigator can adopt an objective stance most concordant with a bona fide scientific analysis. However, when a psychologist looks at psychologists, it is easier for personal biases to interfere. The analysis might be tainted by alliances to particular subdisciplines or to specific theoretical or methodological orientations (Cronbach, 1957; Kimble, 1984; Simonton, 2000c). In addition, because psychology tends to be a more personal enterprise than the other sciences, there is perhaps more latitude for the intrusion of individual idiosyncrasies of a more subtle kind. Many have noted, for example, how much a psychologist's ideas tend to reflect his or her distinctive background and personality makeup (Johnson, Germer, Efran, & Overton, 1988). It was no freak accident that Sigmund Freud, the inventor of the Oedipal Complex, had an attractive, young mother. Neither was it mere coincidence that Alfred Adler, a middle-born child, spoke somewhat derisively of the firstborn as the "dethroned king." Neither, finally, was it just happenstance that Carl Jung, an advocate of the significance of archetypes in the collective unconscious, had a sometimes psychotic fascination with the mysterious and the occult that extended back to childhood. Given these intimate connections between psychologist as person and psychologist as creator, how are we to trust anything that psychologists have to say about creativity in psychology?

The only possible response is to focus on the scientific facts as much as possible. Although not entirely free from bias, the scientific method ensures a reasonable degree of objectivity. Moreover, scientific research has generated a vast amount of literature that addresses the topic of this chapter. These investigations provide information about what distinguishes highly creative psychologists from their less creative, even noncreative, colleagues. Moreover, these findings permit us to examine highly creative psychologists from four perspectives (cf. Simonton, 2002).

First, creative psychologists can be considered as just one specific manifestation of eminent achievers in general. A Jean Piaget or an Ivan Pavlov can be said to belong to the same category of luminaries as a Napoleon or a Lenin. The former two may not be quite so famous as the latter two, but all share the quality of having "made a name" for themselves by leaving some "mark on history" (Simonton, 1994).

Second, creative psychologists can be examined as a specific case of outstanding creators of various kinds, whether artistic or scientific (Gardner, 1993; Simonton, 1999b). In this comparison, Wilhelm Wundt might be placed in the same group as fellow Leipziger Johann Sebastian Bach, just as Francis Galton might be associated with fellow Londoner William Shakespeare.

Third, creative psychologists can be viewed as a subclass of the broad group of distinguished scientists, including notable creators in the physical, biological, and social sciences (Simonton, 1988). Here, John B. Watson, Clark Hull, and B. F. Skinner would rub shoulders with Laplace, Lavoisier, and Pasteur.

Fourth and last, illustrious psychologists may constitute a distinctive group possessing characteristics that set them apart from other scientists, creators, or achievers (Simonton, 2002). A Pavlov, Galton, or Piaget can be distinguished from a Lenin, Shakespeare, or Pasteur because there is something about the very discipline of psychology that requires creative psychologists to have a different psychological makeup than anyone else.

Next I consider each of these possible perspectives.

EMINENT ACHIEVERS

Before I write anything more, let me first make clear that creativity is not a categorical variable (Simonton, 2000b). People cannot be divided into two discrete classes of creative and noncreative. Instead, creative behavior should be defined as a continuum ranging from the zero point of no creativity to creativity of the level of Galileo, Descartes, Dante, Beethoven, and

Michelangelo. Arrayed somewhere along the middle of the implicit scale will be found more everyday forms of creativity. Only at the high end of this underlying dimension does exceptional creativity become equivalent to achieved eminence (Galton, 1869). Hence, when I class creative psychologists with eminent achievers, I am deliberately focusing on the upper end of the underlying continuum. However, as shortly becomes apparent, the factors that distinguish highly eminent psychologists from less eminent psychologists are largely the same factors that separate the less eminent psychologists from the noneminent psychologists. And these factors all have to do with how creative the psychologist tends to be (Simonton, 2002). That nicety in mind, I can now draw the following three conclusions from the research.

First, *intelligence* is positively associated with being both an exceptional achiever (Cox, 1926; Simonton, 1986b, 1991c; Walberg, Rasher, & Hase, 1978) and a creative psychologist (Roe, 1953a). This assertion is based both on investigations using standard intelligence tests as well as more indirect content analytical or biographical measures (Suedfeld, 1985). However, this statement does not mean that all great psychologists have genius-level IQs. On the contrary, eminent psychologists, like eminent achievers in general, tend to be noticeably more intelligent than the average person of their time and place (Simonton, 1994). Indeed, under special circumstances it sometimes possible for individuals to be too smart to attain distinction in their fields (Simonton, 1985a), yet there is no record of anyone attaining distinction as a creator without a markedly above-average intellectual capacity (Barron & Harrington, 1981; Cox, 1926). At the minimum, creators are intellectually gifted even if not intellectual geniuses.

Second, eminent achievement in all domains is strongly correlated with *motivation* (Cox, 1926; Simonton, 1991c), and psychology is by no means an exception (Helmreich, Spence, Beane, Lucker, & Matthews, 1980; Helmreich, Spence, & Pred, 1988; Matthews, Helmreich, Beane, & Lucker, 1980; Taylor, Locke, Lee, & Gist, 1984; Wispé, 1963). In fact, drive, persistence, and determination are more crucial to success than is intelligence. The main reason why many individuals can attain distinction without a genius-grade intellect is that they are willing to put in the necessary hard work to compensate. This factor is especially important in light of the final attribute.

Third, it is rare to achieve fame without first acquiring a sufficient amount of domain-specific *expertise* (Ericsson, 1996b). This requirement is often expressed as the "10-year rule" because ambitious youth must typically spend many hours every day for a full decade before they can attain world-class competence in a given achievement domain, whether it be in sports, chess, musical performance, or creative achievement (Ericsson, 1996a). Nevertheless, it is necessary to add the stipulation that the individual only must acquire *sufficient* competence, not *total* mastery. In fact, training can often have a curvilinear relationship with achievement, creative or otherwise (Simonton, 1976, 2000a). This inverted-U curve appears because excessive expertise can often undermine creativity, an absolute necessity for any domain of creative achievement (Simonton, 2000a).

Insofar as psychologists display intelligence, motivation, and expertise, they can be can be considered in the same class as other kinds of high achievers, whether great leaders, athletes, or performers.

OUTSTANDING CREATORS

Something is missing in the foregoing conclusion. Intelligence, motivation, and expertise are clearly not sufficient to attain a high degree of distinction. A person can satisfy all three requirements and still not attain eminence. Fame and fortune only follow when these three assets are translated into concrete contributions. The specific nature of these accomplishments is what distinguishes various kinds of achievement domains. Legislators must write legislation, decision makers must make decisions, athletes must win competitions, musicians must perform in concert halls and recording studios, and so on. In the case of accomplished creators, these achievements take the form of creative products; that is, creators must exhibit *creative productivity* (Albert, 1975; Simonton, 1997). Indeed, it is characteristic of highly creative individuals that they begin productivity at an exceptionally precocious age, end such productivity at an unusually advanced age, and maintain a high rate of output throughout their career (Blackburn, Behymer, & Hall, 1978; Clemente, 1973; Raskin, 1936; Simonton, 1991a, 1991b, 1997). Highly creative psychologists are no exception to this general pattern (Albert, 1975; Simonton, 1992a, 2002). To be sure, occasionally there appear late bloomers who got a delayed start in their fields, and sometimes creative output is tragically terminated by an early death. However, these cases are too rare to overthrow the generalization.

Several features of creative productivity deserve emphasis. First, the distribution of output is so highly skewed that a small percentage of creators account for most of the total contributions to a given discipline (Lotka, 1926; Walberg, Strykowski, Rovai, & Hung, 1984). On average, the top 10% in lifetime output account for about 50% of the products, a productive elitism that holds for all of the arts and sciences (Dennis, 1954a, 1955), including psychology (Dennis, 1954b). Second, total quantity of output is strongly correlated with total quality of output for both psychologists (Crandall, 1978; Platz & Blakelock, 1960; Rodgers & Maranto, 1989; Rushton, 1984; Simonton, 1985b) and other varieties of creators (Busse & Mansfield, 1984; Feist, 1993, 1997; Stewart, 1983). Those who produce the most high-impact works also produce the most low-impact works. Third, creative productivity is strongly associated with ultimate eminence (Albert, 1975; Feist, 1993; Simonton, 1977, 1991a). The most eminent psychologists, on average, tend to be the most prolific psychologists (Myers, 1970; Simonton, 2002). In fact, it is this finding that provides a behavioral basis for the continuous scale mentioned earlier. Psychologists, like other creators, can be arrayed along a scale that is anchored by the zero point of no contribution whatsoever to the field. At the top of the scale are psychologists who can be considered the creative geniuses of the discipline (Albert, 1975; Simonton, 2002).

Now some questions naturally arise: What determines a creator's placement along this productivity dimension? Why are some psychologists much more prolific than are their colleagues? The three factors underlying exceptional achievement provide only a partial answer. Highly prolific creators are not necessarily more intelligent or more expert than their less prolific contemporaries, albeit they will most likely be more strongly motivated. More is still required in the case of creative achievement. In particular, creativity is associated with the following additional personal characteristics.

First, the individual should have what can be termed a *creative cognitive style* (Martindale, 1989; Simonton, 1999a; Sternberg & Lubart, 1995). More specifically, he or she should exhibit flexible thinking that takes alternative points of view into consideration and that remains open to the implications of unexpected experiences (James, 1880). Many highly intelligent people fail to display creativity because they tend to be constrained by rigid, preconceived ideas.

Second, the person should be relatively *introverted* (Cattell, 1963; Cattell & Drevdahl, 1955; Simonton, 1999a). Creative problem solving requires a considerable amount of pure mental effort that is disrupted by social situations or communication (Simonton, 1999b). This is not to say that creative people do not collaborate, because they do (Over, 1982; Smart & Bayer, 1986). It is merely a matter that an excessive extrovert is someone who enjoys social interaction for its own sake, whereas an introvert more often confines such interaction to the creative tasks at hand.

Third, the person should display a high degree of *independence* and *autonomy* (Feist, 1998; Simonton, 1999a). After all, an essential attribute of creativity is originality, and originality tends to be incompatible with conformity. Thus, the highly creative individual must be willing to "defy the crowd" whenever necessary (Sternberg & Lubart, 1995). This independence, when coupled with a high degree of motivation, enables creators to overcome the many obstacles that are often thrown in their paths. For example, it makes the creator less vulnerable to the devastating attacks of critics and competitors.

To some extent, the just-listed personal attributes could be the gifts of genetic inheritance (Simonton, 1999c, 2002). Thus, in part, creative genius is born rather than made. Nevertheless, environmental or experiential factors also play a major role a well. Creativity is a matter of both nurture and nature. A case in point is the critical impact of role models and mentors in creative development (Walberg, Rasher, & Parkerson, 1980), an influence important in both the arts (Simonton, 1975, 1977, 1984) and sciences (Crane, 1965; Simonton, 1992b). In the specific case of psychology, highly creative psychologists are more likely to have studied under highly creative psychologists (Boring & Boring, 1948; Simonton, 1992a; Wispé, 1965).

DISTINGUISHED SCIENTISTS

I must tighten the comparisons yet another notch. Psychology purports not merely to represent a domain of creative achievement but rather a specific subset of such domains—those that pass by the name of *science*. Thus, psychologists are more properly compared to physicists, chemists, and biologists than to painters, composers, and poets. This distinction is central insofar as scientific creators differ from artistic creators in two major ways.

First, creative scientists differ from creative artists with respect to certain *personality traits* (Feist, 1998). Probably the most significant of these contrasts concerns mental health (Simonton, 1999b). Artistic creators are much more likely to suffer from emotional or mental instability relative to scientific creators (Ludwig, 1995; Post, 1994; Raskin, 1936). This instability may take the form of deep depression, suicide, or complete psychotic breakdown. Although creative scientists are not completely immune from such unfortunate conditions, they tend to be much closer to the "normal" end of the spectrum. The only qualification that must be placed on this generalization is that there is a modest tendency for the more eminent contributors to a domain, whether scientific or artistic, to exhibit somewhat higher rates of psychopathology in comparison to their less illustrious colleagues (Ludwig, 1995; Simonton, 1999b).

Second, creative scientists differ from creative artists with respect to certain *biographical experiences* (Simonton, 1999b). For instance, scientists are more likely to be the firstborn children in their families (Clark & Rice, 1982; Galton, 1874; West, 1960), whereas artists are more likely to be laterborns (Bliss, 1970; Eisenman, 1964). The two main qualifications on this generalization are (a) revolutionary scientists may be more prone to be laterborns (Sulloway, 1996) and (b) classical composers are more disposed to be firstborns (Schubert, Wagner, & Schubert, 1977). Because firstborns tend to be more conventional than are laterborns, this result fits in with a more general finding: Creative scientists tend to come from more conventional backgrounds than do creative artists (Raskin, 1936; Schaefer & Anastasi, 1968). For example, scientists are more likely to have grown up in stable, intact families with well-educated parents engaged in professional occupations (Berry, 1981; Eiduson, 1962; Galton, 1874; Moulin, 1955; Roe, 1953a; Zuckerman, 1977). The odds are also greater that scientists did very well in school and progressed rapidly to an advanced degree in their chosen field (Cattell, 1906; Chambers, 1964; Poffenberger, 1930; Taylor & Ellison, 1967; Van Zelst & Kerr, 1951). The artists, in contrast, are more likely to have had traumatic experiences, such as parental loss, in childhood or adolescence (Berry, 1981; Post, 1994; Raskin, 1936; Simonton, 1986a), and they are more likely to have not done as well in the educational system (Goertzel, Goertzel, & Goertzel, 1978; Simonton, 1986a). Needless to say, there may exist some yet-to-be-determined connection between this contrast and the contrast in emotional stability.

When we turn our attention to the research on creative psychologists, we find that they fall closer to the creative scientists than to the creative artists. With respect to personality traits, eminent psychologists tend to be more emotionally stable than are eminent artists (Ludwig, 1995; Simonton, 2002), albeit there is some evidence that some degree of pathological symptoms is positively correlated with creativity in the field (Rushton, 1990; cf. Wispé & Parloff, 1965). Highly creative psychologists are also more likely to be firstborns (Roe, 1953b; Terry, 1989), a family status that even predicts a psychologist's citation rate in the literature (Helmreich et al., 1980). Successful psychologists also have a greater likelihood of growing up in the same kind of home environment as other eminent scientists (Wispé, 1965), and to have done almost as well academically in school, college, and university (Rodgers & Maranto, 1989; Wispé, 1965). Hence, the overall picture is that the personality traits and biographical experiences of psychologists are more similar to those of scientists than artists. Not surprisingly, therefore, the values of eminent psychologists are strongly inclined toward the sciences (Campbell, 1965).

ILLUSTRIOUS PSYCHOLOGISTS

So what separates the creative psychologist from the creative scientists in the other sciences? Judging from the empirical evidence, the answer is: Not much. Because psychologists tend to be more extroverted than are other scientists (Cattell, 1963) they lead somewhat more active social lives with respect to extracurricular activities and love relationships (Roe, 1953a). They also tend to be more unconventional in their beliefs and to lead somewhat less conventional lives, as illustrated by their higher divorce rates (Roe, 1953a). Psychologists are also prone to exhibit less scholastic prowess than do other scientists, especially physicists and chemists, and to have been less intellectually precocious (Roe, 1953a; Terman, 1954). There are also some noticeable contrasts in career trajectories—psychologists get a later start and peak somewhat later than do scientists in the natural sciences (Lehman, 1953, 1966; Simonton, 1992a, 2002). Other than that, the main difference is that psychologists study psychological phenomena, whereas physicists investigate physical phenomena, biologists examine biological phenomena, and so forth.

Therefore, it seems safe to draw the following three conclusions. First, creative psychologists are like eminent achievers in that they display intelligence, motivation, and expertise. Second, they are similar to outstanding creators in that they exhibit creative productivity, a creative cognitive style, and an introverted and independent personality, and their creative development is influenced by notable role models and mentors. Third, creative psychologists are like distinguished scientists in that they are inclined to be emotionally stable, to be firstborn children from stable, professional families, and to have performed well in school and higher education. Taken together, these attributes and experiences provide the typical profile of a creative psychologist. Furthermore, to the degree that a given psychologist fits this profile, he or she can be considered an illustrious psychologist. Especially crucial are certain key components of this profile, such as creative productivity, expertise, motivation, and independence.

But, unfortunately, there's a catch—a big one. Eminent achievers do not represent a homogeneous group, but rather consists of creators, leaders, athletes, performers, and luminaries in a host of other domains. Neither do outstanding creators constitute a coherent class, for at the very least the scientists must be distinguished from the artists. And it is clear that there exists more than one kind of distinguished scientist. Thus, what makes us so sure that the distinctions can stop once we get to the category of illustrious psychologists? Why can't there be more than one type of psychologist, each type having its own form of creativity with corresponding correlates and antecedents?

In point of fact, creative psychologists do not form a homogeneous group. For instance, scientific psychology can be divided into two subdisciplines, one experimental and the other correlational (Cronbach, 1957). So disparate are their orientations that experimental and correlational psychologists ignore each other's work even when they address the same substantive topic, such as scientific discovery (Simonton, 2003). The within-discipline diversity extends well beyond this division, however, because at least these two subdisciplines view psychology as a natural science. Not all psychologists do so; rather, they subscribe to a human science, or even humanistic model (Coan, 1979; Kimble, 1984). For instance, where experimental psychologists favor determinism, objectivism, laboratory investigation, nomothetic analysis, concrete mechanisms, elementism, cognition, and reactivity, psychotherapists favor indeterminism, intuitionism, field study, idiographic analysis, abstract concepts, holism, and creativity (Kimble, 1984). Moreover, this division between natural and human science psychologists separates not just the rank and file psychologists, but also distinguishes highly creative psychologists (Simonton, 2000c). At one extreme are the illustrious psychologists like Sigmund Freud, Carl Jung, Alfred Adler, William James, Gordon Allport, and Carl Rogers, who favor the subjectivistic, qualitative, holistic, personal, dynamic, and endogenist side of psychology, and at the other extreme are the distinguished psychologists B. F. Skinner, Harry Harlow, E. R. Thurstone, and William Estes, who favor the objectivistic, quantitative, elementaristic, impersonal, static, and exogenist side of psychology.

Why does this matter? Why can't we just view these differences as comparable to the contrast between, say, theoretical and experimental physicists or between zoologists and botanists? The reason why this distinction cannot be dismissed so easily is that the facts show that the scientific psychologists differ from the humanistic psychologists on a host of behavioral, personality, and developmental variables (Brems, Johnson, & Gallucci, 1996; Coan, 1979; Conway, 1988; Zachar & Leong, 1992). In general, psychologists who lean toward the human sciences tend to have profiles more comparable to those of artistic creators. Moreover, these differences do not necessarily represent extreme positions on an overall normal distribution (Simonton, 2002). Instead, to some degree, psychology as a discipline is polarized along this dimension, so that the underlying distribution may be bimodal. This polarization then has consequences for the degree of eminence a creative psychologist can display. For example, those psychologists who stand closer to the middle of the distribution on the natural versus human science dimension may be less influential than are those at the extremes. Hence, J. R. Angell, G. E. Müller, and J. M. Cattell had much less impact than either Freud, Jung, Adler, James, Allport, and Rogers or Skinner, Harlow, Thurstone, and Estes (Simonton, 2000c). Moreover, although creative psychologists at the natural science end of the spectrum are more likely to receive such honors as election to the National Academy of Sciences (Over, 1981), those at the other end are more likely to have higher citation rates in the discipline (Simonton, 2000c).

Perhaps the best conclusion to draw from these complications—and here I am going beyond the hard data—is that psychology is among the most creative of the sciences. I base this conclusion on the fact that there is more than one way to become a creative psychologist.

REFERENCES

Albert, R. S. (1975). Toward a behavioral definition of genius. *American Psychologist, 30,* 140–151.
Barron, F. X., & Harrington, D. M. (1981). Creativity, intelligence, and personality. *Annual Review of Psychology, 32,* 439–476.

Berry, C. (1981). The Nobel scientists and the origins of scientific achievement. *British Journal of Sociology, 32,* 381–391.

Blackburn, R. T., Behymer, C. E., & Hall, D. E. (1978). Correlates of faculty publications. *Sociology of Education, 51,* 132–141.

Bliss, W. D. (1970). Birth order of creative writers. *Journal of Individual Psychology, 26,* 200–202.

Boring, M. D., & Boring, E. G. (1948). Masters and pupils among the American psychologists. *American Journal of Psychology, 61,* 527–534.

Brems, C., Johnson, M. E., & Gallucci, P. (1996). Publication productivity of clinical and counseling psychologists. *Journal of Clinical Psychology, 52,* 723–725.

Busse, T. V., & Mansfield, R. S. (1984). Selected personality traits and achievement in male scientists. *Journal of Psychology, 116,* 117–131.

Campbell, D. P. (1965). The vocational interests of American Psychological Association presidents. *American Psychologist, 20,* 636–644.

Cattell, J. M. (1906). *American men of science: A biographical directory.* New York: Science Press.

Cattell, R. B. (1963). The personality and motivation of the researcher from measurements of contemporaries and from biography. In C. W. Taylor & F. Barron (Eds.), *Scientific creativity: Its recognition and development* (pp. 119–131). New York: Wiley.

Cattell, R. B., & Drevdahl, J. E. (1955). A comparison of the personality profile (16 P. F.) of eminent researchers with that of eminent teachers and administrators, and of the general population. *British Journal of Psychology, 46,* 248–261.

Chambers, J. A. (1964). Relating personality and biographical factors to scientific creativity. *Psychological Monographs: General and Applied, 78* (7, Whole No. 584).

Clark, R. D., & Rice, G. A. (1982). Family constellations and eminence: The birth orders of Nobel Prize winners. *Journal of Psychology, 110,* 281–287.

Clemente, F. (1973). Early career determinants of research productivity. *American Journal of Sociology, 79,* 409–419.

Coan, R. W. (1979). *Psychologists: Personal and theoretical pathways.* New York: Irvington.

Conway, J. B. (1988). Differences among clinical psychologists: Scientists, practitioners, and scientist-practitioners. *Professional Psychology: Research and Practice, 19,* 642–655.

Cox, C. (1926). *The early mental traits of three hundred geniuses.* Stanford, CA: Stanford University Press.

Crandall, R. (1978). The relationship between quantity and quality of publications. *Personality and Social Psychology Bulletin, 4,* 379–380.

Crane, D. (1965). Scientists at major and minor universities: A study of productivity and recognition. *American Sociological Review, 30,* 699–714.

Cronbach, L. J. (1957). The two disciplines of scientific psychology. *American Psychologist, 12,* 671–684.

Dennis, W. (1954a, September). Bibliographies of eminent scientists. *Scientific Monthly, 79,* 180–183.

Dennis, W. (1954b). Productivity among American psychologists. *American Psychologist, 9,* 191–194.

Dennis, W. (1955, April). Variations in productivity among creative workers. *Scientific Monthly, 80,* 277–278.

Eiduson, B. T. (1962). *Scientists: Their psychological world.* New York: Basic Books.

Eisenman, R. (1964). Birth order and artistic creativity. *Journal of Individual Psychology, 20,* 183–185.

Ericsson, K. A. (1996a). The acquisition of expert performance: An introduction to some of the issues. In K. A. Ericsson (Ed.), *The road to expert performance: Empirical evidence from the arts and sciences, sports, and games* (pp. 1–50). Mahwah, NJ: Lawrence Erlbaum Associates.

Ericsson, K. A. (Ed.). (1996b). *The road to expert performance: Empirical evidence from the arts and sciences, sports, and games.* Mahwah, NJ: Lawrence Erlbaum Associates.

Feist, G. J. (1993). A structural model of scientific eminence. *Psychological Science, 4,* 366–371.

Feist, G. J. (1997). Quantity, quality, and depth of research as influences on scientific eminence: Is quantity most important? *Creativity Research Journal, 10,* 325–335.
Feist, G. J. (1998). A meta-analysis of personality in scientific and artistic creativity. *Personality and Social Psychology Review, 2,* 290–309.
Galton, F. (1869). *Hereditary genius: An inquiry into its laws and consequences.* London: Macmillan.
Galton, F. (1874). *English men of science: Their nature and nurture.* London: Macmillan.
Gardner, H. (1993). *Creating minds: An anatomy of creativity seen through the lives of Freud, Einstein, Picasso, Stravinsky, Eliot, Graham, and Gandhi.* New York: Basic Books.
Goertzel, M. G., Goertzel, V., & Goertzel, T. G. (1978). *300 eminent personalities: A psychosocial analysis of the famous.* San Francisco: Jossey-Bass.
Helmreich, R. L., Spence, J. T., Beane, W. E., Lucker, G. W., & Matthews, K. A. (1980). Making it in academic psychology: Demographic and personality correlates of attainment. *Journal of Personality and Social Psychology, 39,* 896–908.
Helmreich, R. L., Spence, J. T., & Pred, R. S. (1988). Making it without losing it: Type A, achievement motivation, and scientific attainment revisited. *Personality and Social Psychology Bulletin, 14,* 495–504.
James, W. (1880, October). Great men, great thoughts, and the environment. *Atlantic Monthly, 46,* 441–459.
Johnson, J. A., Germer, C. K., Efran, J. S., & Overton, W. F. (1988). Personality as the basis for theoretical predilections. *Journal of Personality and Social Psychology, 55,* 824–835.
Kimble, G. A. (1984). Psychology's two cultures. *American Psychologist, 39,* 833–839.
Lehman, H. C. (1953). *Age and achievement.* Princeton, NJ: Princeton University Press.
Lehman, H. C. (1966). The psychologist's most creative years. *American Psychologist, 21,* 363–369.
Lotka, A. J. (1926). The frequency distribution of scientific productivity. *Journal of the Washington Academy of Sciences, 16,* 317–323.
Ludwig, A. M. (1995). *The price of greatness: Resolving the creativity and madness controversy.* New York: Guilford.
Martindale, C. (1989). Personality, situation, and creativity. In J. A. Glover, R. R. Ronning, & C. R. Reynolds (Eds.), *Handbook of creativity* (pp. 211–232). New York: Plenum.
Matthews, K. A., Helmreich, R. L., Beane, W. E., & Lucker, G. W. (1980). Pattern A, achievement striving, and scientific merit: Does Pattern A help or hinder? *Journal of Personality and Social Psychology, 39,* 962–967.
Moulin, L. (1955). The Nobel prizes for the sciences from 1901–1950: An essay in sociological analysis. *British Journal of Sociology, 6,* 246–263.
Myers, C. R. (1970). Journal citations and scientific eminence in contemporary psychology. *American Psychologist, 25,* 1041–1048.
Over, R. (1981). Affiliations of psychologists elected to the National Academy of Sciences. *American Psychologist, 36,* 744–752.
Over, R. (1982). Collaborative research and publication in psychology. *American Psychologist, 37,* 996–1001.
Platz, A., & Blakelock, E. (1960). Productivity of American psychologists: Quantity versus quality. *American Psychologist, 15,* 310–312.
Poffenberger, A. T. (1930). The development of men of science. *Journal of Social Psychology, 1,* 31–47.
Post, F. (1994). Creativity and psychopathology: A study of 291 world-famous men. *British Journal of Psychiatry, 165,* 22–34.
Raskin, E. A. (1936). Comparison of scientific and literary ability: A biographical study of eminent scientists and men of letters of the nineteenth century. *Journal of Abnormal and Social Psychology, 31,* 20–35.
Rodgers, R. C., & Maranto, C. L. (1989). Causal models of publishing productivity in psychology. *Journal of Applied Psychology, 74,* 636–649.

Roe, A. (1953a). *The making of a scientist.* New York: Dodd, Mead.
Roe, A. (1953b). A psychological study of eminent psychologists and anthropologists, and a comparison with biological and physical scientists. *Psychological Monographs, 67* (2, Whole No. 352).
Rushton, J. P. (1984). Evaluating research eminence in psychology: The construct validity of citation counts. *Bulletin of the British Psychological Society, 37,* 33–36.
Rushton, J. P. (1990). Creativity, intelligence, and psychoticism. *Personality and Individual Differences, 11,* 1291–1298.
Schaefer, C. E., & Anastasi, A. (1968). A biographical inventory for identifying creativity in adolescent boys. *Journal of Applied Psychology, 58,* 42–48.
Schubert, D. S. P., Wagner, M. E., & Schubert, H. J. P. (1977). Family constellation and creativity: Firstborn predominance among classical music composers. *Journal of Psychology, 95,* 147–149.
Simonton, D. K. (1975). Sociocultural context of individual creativity: A transhistorical time-series analysis. *Journal of Personality and Social Psychology, 32,* 1119–1133.
Simonton, D. K. (1976). Biographical determinants of achieved eminence: A multivariate approach to the Cox data. *Journal of Personality and Social Psychology, 33,* 218–226.
Simonton, D. K. (1977). Eminence, creativity, and geographic marginality: A recursive structural equation model. *Journal of Personality and Social Psychology, 35,* 805–816.
Simonton, D. K. (1984). Artistic creativity and interpersonal relationships across and within generations. *Journal of Personality and Social Psychology, 46,* 1273–1286.
Simonton, D. K. (1985a). Intelligence and personal influence in groups: Four nonlinear models. *Psychological Review, 92,* 532–547.
Simonton, D. K. (1985b). Quality, quantity, and age: The careers of 10 distinguished psychologists. *International Journal of Aging and Human Development, 21,* 241–254.
Simonton, D. K. (1986a). Biographical typicality, eminence, and achievement style. *Journal of Creative Behavior, 20,* 14–22.
Simonton, D. K. (1986b). Presidential personality: Biographical use of the Gough Adjective Check List. *Journal of Personality and Social Psychology, 51,* 149–160.
Simonton, D. K. (1988). *Scientific genius: A psychology of science.* Cambridge, UK: Cambridge University Press.
Simonton, D. K. (1991a). Career landmarks in science: Individual differences and interdisciplinary contrasts. *Developmental Psychology, 27,* 119–130.
Simonton, D. K. (1991b). Emergence and realization of genius: The lives and works of 120 classical composers. *Journal of Personality and Social Psychology, 61,* 829–840.
Simonton, D. K. (1991c). Personality correlates of exceptional personal influence: A note on Thorndike's (1950) creators and leaders. *Creativity Research Journal, 4,* 67–78.
Simonton, D. K. (1992a). Leaders of American psychology, 1879–1967: Career development, creative output, and professional achievement. *Journal of Personality and Social Psychology, 62,* 5–17.
Simonton, D. K. (1992b). The social context of career success and course for 2,026 scientists and inventors. *Personality and Social Psychology Bulletin, 18,* 452–463.
Simonton, D. K. (1994). *Greatness: Who makes history and why.* New York: Guilford.
Simonton, D. K. (1997). Creative productivity: A predictive and explanatory model of career trajectories and landmarks. *Psychological Review, 104,* 66–89.
Simonton, D. K. (1999a). Creativity and genius. In L. A. Pervin & O. John (Eds.), *Handbook of personality theory and research* (2nd ed., pp. 629–652). New York: Guilford.
Simonton, D. K. (1999b). *Origins of genius: Darwinian perspectives on creativity.* New York: Oxford University Press.
Simonton, D. K. (1999c). Talent and its development: An emergenic and epigenetic model. *Psychological Review, 106,* 435–457.

Simonton, D. K. (2000a). Creative development as acquired expertise: Theoretical issues and an empirical test. *Developmental Review, 20,* 283–318.
Simonton, D. K. (2000b). Creativity: Cognitive, developmental, personal, and social aspects. *American Psychologist, 55,* 151–158.
Simonton, D. K. (2000c). Methodological and theoretical orientation and the long-term disciplinary impact of 54 eminent psychologists. *Review of General Psychology, 4,* 1–13.
Simonton, D. K. (2002). *Great psychologists and their times: Scientific insights into psychology's history.* Washington, DC: APA Books.
Simonton, D. K. (2003). Scientific creativity as constrained stochastic behavior: The integration of product, process, and person perspectives. *Psychological Bulletin, 129,* 475–494.
Smart, J. C., & Bayer, A. E. (1986). Author collaboration and impact: A note on citation rates of single and multiple authored articles. *Scientometrics, 10,* 297–305.
Sternberg, R. J., & Lubart, T. I. (1995). *Defying the crowd: Cultivating creativity in a culture of conformity.* New York: Free Press.
Stewart, J. A. (1983). Achievement and ascriptive processes in the recognition of scientific articles. *Social Forces, 62,* 166–189.
Suedfeld, P. (1985). APA presidential addresses: The relation of integrative complexity to historical, professional, and personal factors. *Journal of Personality and Social Psychology, 47,* 848–852.
Sulloway, F. J. (1996). *Born to rebel: Birth order, family dynamics, and creative lives.* New York: Pantheon.
Taylor, C. W., & Ellison, R. L. (1967, March 3). Biographical predictors of scientific performance. *Science, 155,* 1075–1080.
Taylor, M. S., Locke, E. A., Lee, C., & Gist, M. E. (1984). Type A behavior and faculty research productivity: What are the mechanisms? *Organizational Behavior and Human Performance, 34,* 402–418.
Terman, L. M. (1954). Scientists and nonscientists in a group of 800 gifted men. *Psychological Monographs: General and Applied, 68* (7, Whole No. 378), 1–44.
Terry, W. S. (1989). Birth order and prominence in the history of psychology. *Psychological Record, 39,* 333–337.
Van Zelst, R. H., & Kerr, W. A. (1951). Some correlates of technical and scientific productivity. *Journal of Abnormal and Social Psychology, 46,* 470–475.
Walberg, H. J., Rasher, S. P., & Hase, K. (1978). IQ correlates with high eminence. *Gifted Child Quarterly, 22,* 196–200.
Walberg, H. J., Rasher, S. P., & Parkerson, J. (1980). Childhood and eminence. *Journal of Creative Behavior, 13,* 225–231.
Walberg, H. J., Strykowski, B. F., Rovai, E., & Hung, S. S. (1984). Exceptional performance. *Review of Educational Research, 54,* 87–112.
West, S. S. (1960). Sibling configurations of scientists. *American Journal of Sociology, 66,* 268–274.
Wispé, L. G. (1963, September 27). Traits of eminent American psychologists. *Science, 141,* 1256–1261.
Wispé, L. G. (1965). Some social and psychological correlates of eminence in psychology. *Journal of the History of the Behavioral Sciences, 7,* 88–98.
Wispé, L. G., & Parloff, M. B. (1965). Impact of psychotherapy on the productivity of psychologists. *Journal of Abnormal Psychology, 70,* 188–193.
Zachar, P., & Leong, F. T. L. (1992). A problem of personality: Scientist and practitioner differences in psychology. *Journal of Personality, 60,* 665–677.
Zuckerman, H. (1977). *Scientific elite.* New York: Free Press.

Chapter 9

Creativity in Computer Science[1]

Daniel Saunders
Paul Thagard
University of Waterloo

INTRODUCTION

Computer science only became established as a field in the 1950s, growing out of theoretical and practical research begun in the previous two decades. The field has exhibited immense creativity, ranging from innovative hardware such as the early mainframes to software breakthroughs such as programming languages and the Internet. Martin Gardner worried that "it would be a sad day if human beings, adjusting to the Computer Revolution, became so intellectually lazy that they lost their power of creative thinking" (Gardner, 1978, pp. vi–viii). On the contrary, computers and the theory of computation have provided great opportunities for creative work.

This chapter examines several key aspects of creativity in computer science, beginning with the question of how problems arise in computer science. We then discuss the use of analogies in solving key problems in the history of computer science. Our discussion in these sections is based on historical examples, but the sections that follow discuss the nature of creativity using information from a contemporary source—a set of interviews with practicing computer scientists collected by the Association of Computing Machinery's online student magazine, *Crossroads*. We then provide

---

[1]For helpful suggestions, we are grateful to Peter Buhr, Gordon Cormack, Amyrose Gill, Patrick Gill, Ming Li, and C. I. Stolarski. Financial support was provided by the Natural Sciences and Engineering Research Council of Canada.

a general comparison of creativity in computer science and in the natural sciences.

NATURE AND ORIGINS OF PROBLEMS IN COMPUTER SCIENCE

Computer science is closely related to both mathematics and engineering. It resembles engineering in that it is often concerned with building machines and making design decisions about complex interactive systems. Brian K. Reid wrote, "Computer science is the first engineering discipline ever in which the complexity of the objects created is limited by the skill of the creator and not limited by the strength of the raw materials" (Frenkel, 1987, p. 823). Like engineers, computer scientists draw on a collection of techniques to construct a solution to a particular problem, with the creativity consisting in development of new techniques. For example, during the creation of the first large-scale electronic computer, Eckert and Mauchly solved numerous engineering problems, resulting in solutions that became important contributions to computer science (Goldstine, 1972).

Computer science also has a strong mathematical component. An early example came in 1935, with Alan Turing's invention of an abstract, theoretical computing machine to solve David Hilbert's decidability problem in the foundations of mathematics (Hodges, 1983). The Turing machine has proven to be a very powerful tool for studying the theoretical limitations of computers. The theory of the class of NP-Complete problems, which appear to be computationally intractable, is another result in both mathematics and computer science (Cook, 1971; Garey & Johnson, 1979).

Computer science is like engineering in that it is often concerned with questions of how to accomplish some technological task rather than with scientific questions of why some natural phenomenon occurs. Like mathematics, computer science is largely preoccupied with manipulating abstract symbols. In contrast to natural science, stories of serendipitous discovery are uncommon: Computers often do unexpected things, but rarely in a way that leads to new discoveries. In a company, problems can come from commercial motivations such as the desire to enter into a new market, to improve on an existing product, or to overcome some difficulties that are preventing a project from being delivered. In the academic world, questions often arise from reading already-published papers that mention extant problems.

There is in addition a source of problems that is especially important in computer science. Computers are unusual machines in being not only tools but also tools for making tools. What computer scientists study is also a machine that can help with its own investigation, as if microbiologists studied

9. CREATIVITY IN COMPUTER SCIENCE   155

their electron microscopes rather than bacteria. In a typical scenario, a computer scientist becomes frustrated with a repetitive, boring, and difficult task that might be relieved by new technology. When someone with the right background and ideas experiences such frustration, creative contributions to computer science can be made.

A major example occurred during the final months of work on the ENIAC, the first general-purpose electronic computer, started at the Moore School of Electrical Engineering in 1943 (Goldstine, 1972). The ENIAC had been built with the assumption that only one problem would be run on it for a long period of time, so it was difficult and time consuming to reprogram; in essence, the ENIAC had to be rewired by physically plugging in wires to make a new circuit. This led to great frustration, especially when the team's machine was pitted against the much slower and more primitive Harvard-IBM Mark I machine, which did not use vacuum tubes: "To evaluate seven terms of a power series took 15 minutes on the Harvard device of which 3 minutes was set-up time, whereas it will take at least 15 minutes to set up ENIAC and about 1 second to do the computing" (Goldstine, 1972, pp. 198–199).

The solution to this problem, primarily due to John von Neuman, was the concept of a stored program, which enabled the instructions for the computer to perform in the same memory as the data on which the instructions were to operate. With stored programs, a computer could be set to work on a new problem simply by feeding it a new set of instructions. The key insight was that instructions could be treated just the same as data in an early memory device in which numbers were stored as sound waves echoing back and forth in tubes of mercury.

Another example of frustration-based creativity is the invention of the first high-level language, FORTRAN, by John Backus in 1953. FORTRAN allowed computer programs to be written in comprehensible, algebralike commands instead of assembly code (Shasha, 1995). Assembly code consists of lists of thousands of inscrutable three-letter commands, designed to communicate with the machine at its lowest level. Backus was a programmer at IBM, who said later: "Assembly language was time-consuming; it was an arduous task to write commands that were specific to a particular machine and then to have to debug the multitude of errors that resulted" (Shasha, 1995, p. 10). The layer of abstraction that FORTRAN placed between the underlying electronics and the human was very important to the subsequent development of computer science. Programs could be written faster and with fewer errors, making possible larger and more complex uses of the computer, including building yet more powerful tools and programming languages.

There are many other examples of creativity inspired by frustration in computer science, such as the Unix operating system, Larry Wall's programming language Perl, and Donald Knuth's typesetting system T_EX. Larry Wall declared that the three virtues of the computer programmer are "laziness, impatience, and hubris" (Wall, 1996, p. xiii). It is thus clear that frustration with the limitations of a machine or the repetitive nature of a task is an important motivating force in producing creative answers in computer science. For a survey of important innovations in computer software, see Wheeler (2001).

Although technological frustration may be the origin of many problems in computer science, we should not neglect the intrinsic pleasure for many people of building computers and writing computer programs. According to Brooks (1982): "The programmer, like the poet, works only slightly removed from pure thought-stuff. He builds castles in the air, from air, creating by exertion of the imagination. Few media of creation are so flexible, so easy to polish and rework, so readily capable of realizing grand conceptual structures" (p. 7). The term *hacker* referred originally not to people who use programs for destructive purposes such as breaking into the computers of others, but instead referred to creative young programmers who reveled in producing clever and useful programs (Levy, 1984; Raymond, 1991). Presumably, there are also computer scientists whose creativity is fueled by financial interests: Excitement can derive from the prospect that novel software and hardware can make the inventor rich.

Not all computer scientists are concerned with practical problems. The theory of NP-completeness originated because of Stephen Cook's interest in mathematical logic, although he was also interested in computational implications. As Cook reflected, "My advisor at Harvard, Hao Wang, was doing research on the decision problem for predicate calculus. Validity in the predicate calculus is r.e. complete, and this was what gave me the idea that satisfiability in the propositional calculus might be complete in some sense" (Cook, personal communication, July 4, 2002). Thus, Cook formulated a new problem in theoretical computer science by analogy to a familiar problem in mathematical logic. Analogies can also be a fertile source of solutions to problems.

CREATIVE ANALOGIES IN COMPUTER SCIENCE

Once computer scientists have posed a problem, how do they solve it? Creative problem solving about computers requires all the cognitive processes that go into scientific research, including means-ends reasoning with rules, hypothesis formation, and generation of new concepts. This section focuses on one important source of creative problem solving—the use of analogies. Analogy is far from being the only source of creative solutions in computer science, but its importance is illustrated by many historical examples.

Following Dunbar (2001) and Weisberg (1993), we distinguish between *local* analogies, which relate problems from the same domain or from very similar domains, and *distant* analogies, which relate problems from different domains. Distant leaps from one domain to another have contributed to important scientific discoveries, such as Benjamin Franklin's realization that lightning is a form of electricity (Holyoak & Thagard, 1995). Distant analogies have also played an important role in the history of computer science, but local analogies have also been important for creativity in computer science.

An early distant analogy in computer science was made by Charles Babbage, when he realized that the punch cards that controlled the intricate weaving on the automatic Jacquard looms of the day might be used with his hypothetical computing machine, the Analytical Engine (Goldstine, 1972). Lady Ada Lovelace, his friend and collaborator, wrote, "We may say most aptly that the Analytical Engine weaves algebraic patterns just as the Jacquard-loom weaves flowers and leaves" (Goldstine, 1972, p. 22).

Biological analogies have been particularly important in computer science: In 1945, Von Neumann was influenced by McCulloch and Pitts' theories of how the human nervous system could be described mathematically, and used their notation in his "First Draft of a Report on the EDVAC" (Goldstine, 1972). Another example is the invention by Bob Baran of the packet-switching network, the technology underlying the Internet (Hafner & Lyon, 1996). In the context of the nuclear fears of the time, Baran wanted to build a network that could survive with numerous nodes knocked out. He took for his inspiration the structure of the human brain with its redundancy and decentralization. The massively parallel Connection Machine of Danny Hillis was built to emulate the parallelism in the brain (Shasha, 1995). More recently, genetic algorithms and neural networks have proved to be powerful biologically based ideas that are gradually being incorporated into the mainstream of computer science.

The Wright brothers, in building the first manned, powered flying machine, also used a biological analogy, modeling the turning system of their aircraft after that used by birds (Weisberg, 1993). However, the Wright brothers also drew on decades of work on flight, carefully studying analogs close to their goal such as sophisticated gliders and attempts at powered flights that had preceded their own. The same phenomenon is also found in computer science, in which original ideas are often variations and improvements on existing technologies that furnish local analogies.

Eckert and Mauchly had a local inspiration, in the form of John Atanasoff's ABC computer (Slater, 1987). The ABC was a special-purpose machine, designed only to solve differential equations, and there is some argument about whether it was fully operational; however, it was the first of its kind, using vacuum tubes to perform its operations. Mauchly was keenly interested in the machine, and came to visit Atanasoff for 4 days, talking computers with him the whole time. Only after the mountain of publicity on the ENIAC's unveiling in 1946 did Atanasoff realize how many ideas they had borrowed from his machine. In 1975, at the end of a drawn-out lawsuit sparked by the pair's attempts to defend patents on their invention, Atanasoff was declared the legal inventor of the automatic electronic digital computer.

Whether or not this was a case of intellectual plagiarism, it is typical of how inventors absorb technological ideas and build on them. FORTRAN was preceded by Speedcoding and A-0, and Babbage was familiar with the machines of Leibniz and Pascal. Creative inventors do not work in a vacuum, but instead are usually very aware of other creative work going on in their field. Atanasoff said later, "What each man accomplishes depends on his brains and energy, but also on the surroundings in which he works.... In a larger sense, no man invents anything; he builds and extends a little with his friends and on the shoulders of others" (Huisman, 1999).

Similarly, in 1979 Steven Jobs and engineers from Apple Computers took a tour of the Xerox Palo Alto Research Center, where they saw menus, windows, and user-friendly word processors years before they would be available to the public. At least one member of the team has regretted the effect of the story on the perception of the creativity of the Macintosh group, saying, "Those one and a half hours tainted everything we did, and so much of what we did was original research" (Hiltzik, 1999, p. 343n). Later, Microsoft borrowed many of the same ideas for its Windows operating system, another case of problem solving with local analogies.

What, then, is the role of distant analogies if most important inventions have local antecedents? Consider the case of the invention of object-oriented programming by Alan Kay in the early 1970s. As a graduate student, Kay was exposed to a pioneering computer graphics program called Sketchpad, which had the concept of "master" drawings and "instance" drawings, and the computer language Simula. He was struck with the ideas in Simula, and it stimulated his thinking along analogical lines: "When I saw Simula, it immediately made me think of tissues ... [it] transformed me from thinking of computers as mechanisms to thinking of them as things that you could make biological-like organisms in" (Kay, 1996b, p. 575). Kay gave this description of how the cumulative effect of the various examples to which he was exposed led to the ideas that culminated in Smalltalk: "The sequence moves from 'barely seeing' a pattern several times, then noting it but not perceiving the 'cosmic' significance, then using it operationally in several areas; then comes a 'grand rotation' in which the pattern becomes the center of a new way of thinking" (Kay, 1996a, p. 514). Many of the parts of Smalltalk can be traced back to local analogies with Simula and Sketchpad, but the general principles of object-oriented programming that were crucial to the final design of Smalltalk did not occur to Kay until he had seen the distant biological analogy. He noted, "The big flash was to see this as biological cells. I'm not sure where that flash came from but it didn't happen when I looked at Sketchpad. Simula didn't send messages either" (Shasha, 1995, p. 43). Similarly, when James Gosling invented the programming language Java, he was inspired by local analogies, particularly to the programming language C++, and also by a distant analogy to networks of sound and light he experienced at a rock concert (Thagard & Croft, 1999).

Distant analogies in computer science are useful not only for generating new ideas, but also in communicating ideas and suggesting deeper principles underlying the accumulation of technological ideas. Notice the reliance on metaphorical names for the new entities, such as *files* and *folders*, *words* and *pages* of memory, and even stranger appropriations, such as *firewall* and *zombie*. Some terms, such as *software engineering* and *virus*, began as metaphors but later expanded and conceptually deepened the source words, so that there are now more kinds of engineering and more kinds of viruses than there used to be.

EVERYDAY CREATIVITY

The previous sections have described some of the most important historical cases of creativity in computer science, but have ignored the day-to-day creative processes of working computer scientists in both academia and industry. For insight into this more prosaic topic, we have examined surveys compiled by *Crossroads*, the online student magazine of the Association for Computing Machinery (2002). This magazine includes a feature called "A Day in the Life of . . ." that highlights interviews with practicing computer scientists. We have looked at their answers to two questions: "What do you do to get yourself thinking creatively?" and "What is your problem-solving strategy?" The answers were often brief, and sometimes seemed to reflect different interpretations of the questions, but they displayed some interesting patterns. Out of the people profiled in the "A Day in the Life of . . ." feature, we chose 50 with either an academic position in computer science or a job title of "computer scientist" in industry. All quotations without references are taken from this source.

We have not found evidence that the creativity behind famous inventions is fundamentally different from the everyday creativity of ordinary computer scientists. Not all the respondents to the *Crossroads* questions are ordinary—they include Herbert Simon and Internet pioneer Leonard Kleinrock. One famous name in computer science, Leslie Lamport, said: "When I look back on my work, most of it seems like dumb luck—I happened to be looking at the right problem, at the right time, having the right background" (Shasha, 1995, p. 138). This quote underemphasizes the important roles of motivation and intelligence in achievement, but plausibly suggests that creativity is not a rare or supernatural gift.

Only 2 of the 50 examined respondents to the creativity survey mentioned analogies, and those went no further than simply "think of analogies." The others either did not use analogies in their creative work or were not aware of using them.

In the answers to the survey's creativity questions, two modes of creative work were evident, usually one or the other being emphasized in a particular person's answer. We may call them the *intense* mode and the *casual* mode, and they are illustrated by two images of the artist or scientist at work. In the intense mode, the creative individual is hunched over a desk, scribbling madly on pads of paper. In the casual mode, the researcher is lying in the bath relaxing when a solution to a laid-aside problem suddenly hits.

THE INTENSE MODE OF CREATIVITY

The intense mode is the one that most looks like work, and it is characterized by either writing on many sheets of paper or else conducting animated conversation. This writing is very different from the work involved in communicating one's ideas. The result is not a draft of a paper but instead pages covered in scrawls and doodles, showing the evidence of prolonged attacks on an idea from many directions at once: experimentation, examples, pictures, lists, restatements of the problem—anything that could help crack it open. It is most often seen as problem solving, and work in this mode feels relatively rational and systematic. Many of the respondents used systematic language like "first lay out all the options," "ask myself questions," and "create a list of the various issues," and two respondents even provided a numbered list of the steps they take in solving a problem, such as "2. Determine the components and parameters of the problem."

For thinkers in intense mode, the pencil and paper provide a kind of feedback loop, an extension of normal human capabilities that helps to capture thoughts and preserve them beyond the span of short-term memory. Other people can also serve to record and amplify ideas. The phrases "bouncing ideas off" and "brainstorming with" were often used in the computer scientists' responses about their creative method. Social mechanisms to encourage such creative communication are found in both academic and corporate workplaces.

FORTRAN inventor John Backus once said, "It's wonderful to be creative in science because you can do it without clashing with people and suffering the pain of relationships" (Shasha, 1995, p. 20). However, computer scientists depend on social relationships to foster their creativity as much as other researchers do. Twelve of the respondents to the survey explicitly mentioned the importance of talking to people in their creative process, and in the last 5 years of the *Journal of the Association for Computing Machinery* (January 1997–April 2002) 132 out of 164 articles (80.5%) had more than one author.

It is surprising that, for this group of experienced computer scientists, the tool of choice for focused assault on a problem was usually ordinary writing materials such as pencil and paper. Comments included "I probably do best by writing stuff down, often free-flow," "Lots of writing on paper," "Open my notebook to a blank sheet of paper," and "[Problem solving] usually takes A LOT of paper to scribble on, some is just doodling while you stare at the pieces, others is actual notes that help with solutions." Others mentioned dry-erase whiteboards, ubiquitous in every high-tech company and research institute, as critical to their creative process, sometimes even using them as a verb, as in "Whiteboard it!" Typical is a description of Xerox PARC whiteboards covered "with boxes filled with other boxes and arrows pointing to yet more boxes with pointers across to new boxes and so on" (Hiltzik, 1999, p. 225).

Why are computers considered inadequate for the most critical part of the development of creative ideas? One reason may be the distracting clutter of computer displays. Another reason may be the comparable robustness and portability of a notepad and pen. However, Robert Smith's answer to this question suggested there may be deeper problems: "It is very difficult to use a computer when you are trying to birth new ideas. The computer limits your ideas to the shape of documents you know how to create (immediately turns everything into a text document or briefing slide). Blank paper lets you develop an idea in any form you can scribble." Perhaps someday there will be computer software that incorporates such superior characteristics of plain paper as the lack of distracting features; the ease of movement among text, formulas, and drawings; and the freedom to lay out the page flexibly.

THE CASUAL MODE OF CREATIVITY

In contrast to the intense mode, the casual mode of creative thinking usually involves inspiration striking during a break from work. Many of the *Crossroads* respondents reported that their best insights occurred not when they were diligently working at their desks, but rather in nonwork situations. A number of the respondents mentioned their time spent running or hiking as prime creative time, and nine believed that physical exercise was important for creative thinking. One respondent reported this strategy for creative thinking: "Go to the beach and run and run and run! Then think and jot things down quickly, saving the refinements for later." The father of computer science, Alan Turing, was an avid long-distance runner, often running the 50 km between Cambridge and Ely. According to his biographer, Andrew Hodges, he came to his idea of the Turing Machine when lying in the middle of a field after a long run (Hodges, 1983). Other respondents mentioned hiking, bike riding, or martial arts as important to helping them in thinking creatively.

Driving was emphasized by one respondent: "I drive an hour each way to work which gives me a lot of time to contemplate and just let my mind range from topic to topic. Most of the time I spend the drive looking at the scenery and then seeing where that topic takes me." Other researchers also reported that their daily drive or subway ride often constituted their most important creative period of the day.

The shower also seems to be an excellent place for generating creative ideas. One respondent reported, "Once I have a problem, it becomes part of me, and ideas come up mostly in non-work situations. I came up with a major idea for my thesis while in the shower." Alan Kay, the inventor of object-oriented programming and the graphical user interface, believed he got his best ideas in the shower. He even had a shower stall to himself in the basement of the Xerox PARC research facility, where he made some of his most startling inventions. He used the shower in the morning, his most productive time of the day (Hiltzik, 1999).

Finally, several computer scientists reported getting great ideas in bed, in the middle of the night or on waking. One reported that her response to getting badly stuck on a problem was to go to bed and "wake up at 2 AM with the solution suddenly obvious." The original inventor of public key cryptography, J. H. Ellis, reportedly made his discovery in the middle of the night, after spending some days mulling over the problem of how to allow secure communication by two parties who had never met (Ellis, 1987).

These occasions of casual mode creativity share the following characteristics: immersion in a problem domain, absence of immediate pressure to focus on the problem, absence of distractions, mental relaxation, unstructured time, and solitude. Physical activities are an important way of reaching a relaxed state of mind in which ideas that had been studied intensely before are free to combine in various ways without immediate pressure to solve a problem. This increased freedom helps to overcome problems that have become obstacles.

An important illustration of the casual mode in computer science history is the story of John Atanasoff (Slater, 1987). Atanasoff was a professor at Iowa State College and had become very concerned with the problems his graduate students were having in doing calculations with the primitive analogue machines available at the time. He had thought intensely about the problems of computing, but felt stuck. He went for a very fast drive in his car until he crossed the border into Illinois, where he stopped at a roadhouse and ordered a drink. Atanasoff recounted, "Now, I don't know why my mind worked then when it had not worked previously, but things seemed to be good and cool and quiet. . . . I would suspect that I drank two drinks perhaps, and then I realized that thoughts were coming good and I had some positive results" (Mackintosh, 1988, p. 74). In the few hours he spent at the roadhouse, he formed several important ideas for his computer, including the use of binary numbers and the use of vacuum tubes instead of relays to increase the speed of calculations. Atanasoff described the feeling of having heightened creativity, of being inspired: "I remember it perfectly, as if it were yesterday. Everything came together in that one night. All of a sudden I realized that I had a power that I hadn't had before. How I felt that so strongly in my soul, I don't know. I had a power—I mean I could do things, I could move, and move with assurance" (Slater, 1987, p. 55).

The casual mode contributes to the phenomenon of sudden insight, described by Hadamard (1945) as "those sudden enlightenments which can be called inspirations" (p. 21). He quoted Helmholtz: "Creative ideas . . . come mostly of a sudden, frequently after great mental exertion, in a state of mental fatigue combined with physical relaxation" (p. 34). Hadamard proposed that creative insights happen in four stages, which he called preparation, incubation, illumination, and "precising." But the incubation stage, in which little directed thought is given to the problem, could only lead to illumination when preceded by hard work on the problem. As Louis Pasteur said, chance favors the prepared mind. Thus, insight in the casual mode requires previous work in the intense mode.

According to Jack Goldman, who was head of research at Xerox and responsible for the famously creative computer science lab at the Palo Alto Research Center, "Invention can result from a flash of genius or painstaking pursuit of a technical response to an identified or perceived need—sometimes perceived only by the inventor himself" (Alexander & Smith, 1988, p. 34). Although the intense mode feels less special and creative than when ideas come out of the blue in the casual mode, it is a critical part of creative work, and responsible for many important discoveries. Creative researchers typically construct their days to give some time to both modes.

In the *Crossroads* survey, some computer scientists reported getting stimulated creatively by any kind of creative work, not just work in computer science and its related disciplines: "A good film or art exhibit or any creative work done with excellence can inspire me as much as computing," "Reading someone else's creative material starts the juices flowing again," "Reading articles in *Science* magazine about biology or something else completely outside of what I usually do is also stimulating." This seems to be more than just a case of noticing distant analogies between whatever one is reading and one's own work. Why should creative work in one domain inspire creativity in a researcher in a totally different domain? Perhaps inspiration derives from stimulation of excitement that facilitates work in general; Isen (1993) reviewed research showing that induction of positive mood enhances creative decision making.

COMPARISON WITH NATURAL SCIENCE

We now compare what we have learned about creativity in computer science with aspects of creativity in the natural sciences. Problems in physics, chemistry, and biology can take the form of several different kinds of questions. Some questions are empirical, inquiring about the relations between two or more variables with observable values. On the more theoretical side, there are "why" questions that ask for an explanation of observed empirical relations. Sciences such as biology often also ask "how" questions that can be answered by specifying a mechanism that shows how observed functions are performed. Finally, applied science, such as biomedicine, asks "how" questions concerning how what is known about mechanisms might be used to solve some practical problem, such as treating disease. Computer science is not concerned with empirical questions involving naturally observed phenomena, nor with theoretical "why" questions aimed at providing explanations of such phenomena. Neither does it study naturally occurring mechanisms. Rather, computer science usually aims at producing new mechanisms, both hardware and software, that can provide solutions to practical problems. This is computer science as engineering. The problems in theoretical computer science are more like problems in pure and applied mathematics than like problems in the natural sciences. They usually involve very abstract notions of computation and can often be only tangentially relevant to practical concerns of computing.

In the natural sciences, the origins of problems are often empirical, when surprising observations lead to experimentation and theorizing aimed at replacing surprise by understanding. Some problems arise for conceptual reasons; for example, when two plausible theories are incompatible with each other. The motivation for theoretical computer science is largely conceptual, but much work in computer science originates from practical frustrations with available technology. Thus, the origins of problems in most computer science are like the origins of problems in applied sciences, such as biomedicine. Many emotions—including frustration, need, surprise, interest, and ambition—can motivate novel work in both science and engineering (Thagard, 2002). We said earlier that there seems to be less serendipity in computer science than in natural science, so perhaps frustration is a more important emotion than surprise for technological innovation.

9. CREATIVITY IN COMPUTER SCIENCE

How does finding solutions to problems in computer science compare with finding solutions to the empirical and theoretical problems in the natural sciences? Thagard and Croft (1999) compared scientific discovery with technological innovation, and concluded:

> Scientists and inventors ask different kinds of questions. Because scientists are largely concerned with identifying and explaining phenomena, they generate questions such as: Why did X happen? What is Y? How could W cause Z?
>
> In contrast, inventors have more practical goals that lead them to ask questions of the form: How can X be accomplished? What can Y be used to do? How can W be used to do Z?
>
> Despite the differences in the form of the questions asked by scientists from the form of the questions asked by inventors, there is no reason to believe that the cognitive processes underlying questioning in the two contexts are fundamentally different. Scientists encounter a puzzling X and try to explain it; inventors identify a desirable X and try to produce it. (p. 134)

In computer science, the desirable X is a better way of computing. Like all problem solvers, computer scientists use means-ends reasoning and analogies to generate solutions to problems. Hence, creativity in computer science seems very similar cognitively to creativity in thinking in the natural sciences. For further discussion of the cognitive processes involved in scientific creativity, see Thagard (1988, 1992, 1999).

We are not aware of any systematic studies of the roles of intense and casual modes of thinking the natural sciences. Cognitive psychologists have primarily investigated the intense mode, but there is anecdotal evidence that the casual mode contributes to creativity in the natural sciences. For example, Kekulé reported apprehending the structure of benzene during a dream. It would be interesting to conduct a survey, analogous to the *Crossroads* interviews with computer scientists, to determine whether other kinds of thinkers are also sometimes inspired in casual contexts. It would not be surprising if natural scientists also can benefit from physical exercise, showers, concerts, and lying in bed. (Thagard got one of his best ideas, the computational theory of explanatory coherence, while watching a boring movie, *Beverly Hills Cop 2*.)

In sum, the cognitive and social processes that foster creativity in computer science do not seem to be different in kind from the processes that underlie success in the natural sciences, especially applied sciences such as medicine. Computer science is certainly different in that it studies an artifact—computers and computation—rather than naturally occurring phenomena. However, natural science, technology, and mathematics all involve asking novel questions to pose hard problems and then answering them by using analogies and other kinds of reasoning to form new hypotheses and concepts.

CONCLUSION

We conclude by summarizing the major findings of our investigation of creativity in computer science. Problems in computer science originate in both engineering and mathematical contexts. Many engineering problems in computer science arise from frustration with available computational tools, but creativity can also be fueled by financial interests and the pleasure of building computers and writing software. Both local and distant analogies can be useful in solving problems. Everyday creativity in computer science operates in both an intense mode of focused concentration and a casual mode in which inspiration strikes during nonwork activities. Answering computational questions seems to involve the same kinds of cognitive processes that generate answers to empirical questions in the natural sciences. Creativity requires caring about a problem sufficiently to work on it intensely, using analogies and other means of generating novel solutions.

REFERENCES

Alexander, R. C., & Smith, D. K. (1988). *Fumbling the future: How Xerox invented, then ignored, the first personal computer.* New York: Morrow.

Association for Computing Machinery. (2002). *A day in the life of.* . . . Retrieved April 15, 2002, from http://www.acm.org/crossroads/dayinlife/index.html

Brooks, F. P. (1982). *The mythical man-month: Essays on software engineering.* Reading, MA: Addison-Wesley.

Cook, S. A. (1971). The complexity of theorem proving procedures. In ACM Special Interest Group on Algorithms and Computation Theory, *Proceedings of the third annual ACM symposium on Theory of computing* (pp. 151–158). New York: ACM Press.

Dunbar, K. (2001). The analogical paradox: Why analogy is so easy in naturalistic settings, yet so difficult in the laboratory. In D. Gentner, K. J. Holyoak, & B. K. Kokinov (Eds.), *The analogical mind* (pp. 313–334). Cambridge, MA: MIT Press.

Ellis, J. H. (1987). *The history of non-secret encryption.* Retrieved March 20, 2002, from http://www.cesg.gov.uk/publications/media/nsecret/ellis.pdf

Frenkel, K. A. (1987). Profiles in computing: Brian K. Reid: A graphics tale of a hacker tracker. *Communications of the ACM, 30,* 820–823.

Gardner, M. (1978). *Aha! Insight.* New York: Scientific American/Freeman.

Garey, M., & Johnson, D. (1979). *Computers and intractability.* New York: Freeman.

Goldstine, H. (1972). *The computer from Pascal to Von Neumann.* Princeton, NJ: Princeton University Press.

Hadamard, J. (1945). *The psychology of invention in the mathematical field.* New York: Dover.

Hafner, K., & Lyon, M. (1996). *Where wizards stay up late: The origins of the Internet.* New York: Simon & Schuster.

Hiltzik, M. A. (1999). *Dealers of lightning: Xerox PARC and the dawn of the computer age.* New York: HarperCollins.

Hodges, A. (1983). *Alan Turing: The enigma.* London: Burnett.

Holyoak, K. J., & Thagard, P. (1995). *Mental leaps: Analogy in creative thought.* Cambridge, MA: MIT Press/Bradford.

Huisman, D. (1999, Oct./Nov). Stories behind John Vincent Atanasoff's computer. *The Academic Information Technologies Newsletter, 33*(65). Retrieved April 15, 2002, from http://www.ait.iastate.edu/newsletter/199910/article4.html

Isen, A. M. (1993). Positive affect and decision making. In M. Lewis & J. M. Haviland (Eds.), *Handbook of emotions* (pp. 261–277). New York: Guilford.

Kay, A. C. (1996a). The early history of SmallTalk. In T. J. Bergin & R. G. Gibson (Eds.), *History of programming languages II* (pp. 511–579). New York: Addison-Wesley.

Kay, A. C. (1996b). Transcript of SmallTalk presentation. In T. J. Bergin & R. G. Gibson (Eds.), *History of programming languages II* (pp. 579–589). New York: Addison-Wesley.

Levy, S. (1984). *Hackers: Heroes of the computer revolution.* Garden City, NY: Anchor/Doubleday.

Mackintosh, A. R. (1988). *Dr. Atanasoff's computer.* Retrieved April 15, 2002, from http://www.geocities.com/computerresearchassociated/Atanasoff.htm

Raymond, E. S. (1991). *The new hacker's dictionary.* Cambridge, MA: MIT Press.

Shasha, D. (1995). *Out of their minds: The lives and discoveries of 15 great computer scientists.* New York: Copernicus.

Slater, R. (1987). *Portraits in silicon.* Cambridge, MA: MIT Press.

Thagard, P. (1988). *Computational philosophy of science.* Cambridge, MA: MIT Press/Bradford.

Thagard, P. (1992). *Conceptual revolutions.* Princeton, NJ: Princeton University Press.

Thagard, P. (1999). *How scientists explain disease.* Princeton, NJ: Princeton University Press.

Thagard, P. (2002). The passionate scientist: Emotion in scientific cognition. In P. Carruthers, S. Stich, & M. Siegal (Eds.), *The cognitive basis of science* (pp. 235–250). Cambridge, UK: Cambridge University Press.

Thagard, P., & Croft, D. (1999). Scientific discovery and technological innovation: Ulcers, dinosaur extinction, and the programming language Java. In L. Magnani, N. Nersessian, & P. Thagard (Eds.), *Model-based reasoning in scientific discovery* (pp. 125–137). New York: Plenum.

Wall, L. (1996). *Programming Perl* (2nd ed.). Sebastopol, CA: O'Reilly.

Weisberg, R. W. (1993). *Creativity: Beyond the myth of genius.* New York: Freeman.

Wheeler, D. A. (2001). *The most important software innovations.* Retrieved April 15, 2002, from http://www.dwheeler.com/innovation/innovation.html

Chapter 10

Engineering Creativity: A Systems Concept of Functional Creativity

David Cropley
University of South Australia

Arthur Cropley
University of Hamburg

CREATIVITY AND THE "FAILURE" OF ENGINEERS

Creativity has been a topic of interest to writers in different areas for many years, stretching back to antiquity. However, earlier discussions focused mainly on art, literature, music, dance, and similar areas, what we refer to later in this chapter as "aesthetic" or "artistic" creativity. This situation changed drastically about 50 years ago. The turning point was the successful launching in 1957 by the then-Soviet Union of the first artificial earth satellite, Sputnik I. In the United States of America and most North American-Western European societies, this event led to a wave of self-criticism that centered mainly on the argument that the Western world's *engineers* had failed.

At first it was not clear where the cause of their failure rested. However, the 1949 address of the incoming president of the American Psychological Association (Guilford, 1950) had already laid the groundwork for an answer that was quickly seized on when the crisis occurred. Guilford argued that psychologists (and, as a result, teachers, educational theorists, parents, even politicians) had in their definitions of human intellectual functioning placed too much emphasis on acquiring factual knowledge, recalling it rapidly and accurately, reapplying it in a logical manner in order to find the single best answer to a problem, applying existing skills in a well-practiced, economical, and tidy way to new situations, having clearly defined and concretely specified goals, working quickly, resisting distractions, following instructions, and similar processes. According to Guilford, these define "convergent" thinking. They are undoubtedly of great value. Indeed, as Sternberg (1997) pointed out, abilities of this kind have dominated the definition of intelligence from the beginning of its widespread use in about 1920.

However, Guilford argued that people are capable of applying their intellect in a different way by using what he called "divergent" thinking. This involves branching out from the given to envisage previously unknown possibilities and arrive at unexpected or even surprising answers, and thus generate novelty. By the time of the Sputnik shock, the idea that convergent thinking leads to conventional products (even if they are useful in a limited way), whereas divergent thinking leads to novelty, was well established among theorists, and divergent thinking had come to be associated with *creativity*—indeed, Guilford's paper introducing the idea of divergent thinking was entitled "Creativity." An intense discussion was already under way, and the failure of American engineers to make the breakthrough that the Soviets had achieved was quickly attributed to defects in their creativity. Thus, from the very beginning of the modern era, creativity was seen as a practical problem centering on engineers.

The general argument is easy to summarize: In the face of rapid change that is biotechnological (e.g., communications, health), environmental (e.g., global warming, gene-modified crops), industrial (e.g., offshore manufacturing, globalization), demographic (e.g., breakdown of the family, aging of the population), social (e.g., adaptation of immigrants, integration of minorities), and political (e.g., terrorism, achieving fairness in international relations), societies will stagnate, even perish, unless their leaders in all fields become more creative. Thus, creativity is no longer seen as purely the domain of aesthetes and intellectuals concerned with questions of truth and beauty (as important as these issues may be), but also as a pathway to national prosperity and as a means for making the nation strong and safe.

CREATIVITY AS AN ASPECT OF ENGINEERING

The shift away from aesthetics in discussions of creativity has continued and has opened up new perspectives on the topic. Adopting a human capital approach (e.g., Walberg & Stariha, 1992), writers have given considerable attention to creativity in applied and theoretical sciences ("scientific/intellectual" creativity) as well as in management and manufacturing on the one hand, and administration and even the military on the other ("survival/prosperity" creativity). According to economic theory, returns on investments in rich countries should have been lower during the second half of the 20th century than during the first, because the stock of capital was rising faster than was the workforce. However, the fact is that returns were considerably higher. The decisive factor that defeated the law of diminishing returns is now seen to be the *addition to the system of new knowledge and technology* ("Thanksgiving for Innovation," 2002). Higgins (1994) described 10 challenges faced by business in the first decade of the 21st century. These challenges—which include the accelerating rate of change of all facets of business, increasing competition, globalization, and the transformation of First World economies from industrial to knowledge-based economies—act as sources of problems and opportunities. Higgins proposed that the mechanism that will enable businesses to survive and prosper in this new environment (to solve the problems and utilize the opportunities) is innovation—the process of applying creativity to generate new and valuable ideas, products, and processes.

Creativity has thus come to be seen as a vital factor in "good" engineering, which is now viewed as "a career full of discovery, *creativity* and excitement" (our italics; Horenstein, 2002, p. 1). Burghardt (1995, p. 2) defined it as "a professional life devoted to the *creative* solution of problems" (our italics). At the level of the individual engineer, this means that creativity is seen as essential for a successful career (Dekker, 1995). One result is that creativity training is becoming widespread (Clapham, 1997; Thackray, 1995). According to the 1995 U.S. Industry Report, corporations are now budgeting billions of U.S. dollars for creativity training programs, and demand for such training is even outstripping the supply of trainers (Hequet, 1995). Among other things, this indicates the importance of creativity in the early education of engineers (see later discussion in this chapter). We turn now to the question of what engineering creativity is.

THE CREATIVITY OF PRODUCTS

Although Cropley (2001), among others, has emphasized that there are common elements to creativity in all domains, creativity in engineering clearly differs from creativity in, for instance, fine arts. Horenstein (2002, p. 2) defined these differences succinctly by pointing out that engineers "produce devices or systems that *perform tasks or solve problems*" (our italics). Burghardt (1995, p. 4) made this contrast explicit: According to him, fine art is "a manifestation of creativity with no *functional* purpose [our italics], only aesthetic purpose." By contrast, engineering creativity "results from creativity *with a purpose*" (our italics). This purpose is to create *products* (in the broadest sense of the word—including physical objects, complex systems, and processes) that, to repeat Horenstein's definition, "perform tasks or solve problems." We refer to this as "functional" creativity. Its most important aspect is the devices or systems that perform tasks or solve problems—that is, its practically useful *products*.

Although earlier discussions of creativity gave considerable emphasis to tangible products (e.g., Clifford, 1958; Gordon, 1961; Roe, 1952; Rossman, 1931), this aspect of creativity has not received as much attention as might be expected in recent years, perhaps because modern research has been dominated by psychologists and educators. Writers such as Albert (1990) have even concluded that it is too difficult to define creative products in a practical, objective way because the concept is so subjective, and have recommended focusing instead on creative *processes* and characteristics of the creative *person*. Amabile (1983) and Csikszentmihalyi (1996) gave support to this view by suggesting that "creativity" as a property of products is no more than a positive category of judgment in the minds of observers, a term that they used to praise products that they found exceptionally good. This view can be seen as a warning against reifying "creativity," thus repeating the mistake made by treating "intelligence" as though it were a real and tangible entity rather than simply an explanatory construct used to make sense of observable behavior. Despite this, we show later in this chapter that the creativity of products is not as diffuse a concept as might at first appear to be the case. We believe that in a certain sense there really is creativity. The purpose of this chapter is to work out a definition that can be applied in engineering.

There is widespread agreement among contemporary writers on engineering (e.g., Burghardt, 1995; Dekker, 1995; Horenstein, 2002; Steiner, 1998) that engineers must produce products, and that creativity is a vital component of engineering practice and, therefore, of the products they produce. Of course paintings, musical compositions, poems, or novels—or even systems of ideas as in, let us say, philosophy or mathematics—are products. Some writers would also argue that such products "perform tasks or solve problems" of their own kind, such as capturing the essence of beauty or communicating a feeling to another person. However, as Burghardt (1995, p. 4) put it, "*technology* is the manifestation of engineering creativity" (our italics). Functional creativity leads to one or two products or outcomes: either an effective complex system of some kind, such as a submarine or a business information system, or a process in the sense of a service, technique, or method (a manufacturing process, a control process, a logistics service). Each of these examples is drawn directly from a particular subspecialization of engineering ranging from mechanical engineering to systems engineering. The idea of product thus has a particular quality in engineering that is different from its meaning in the context of aesthetic creativity. We turn now to the issue of defining the creativity of functional products.

In principle, creativity can be regarded as either a cause (i.e., some power or capacity in people that causes them to produce creative products), or as an effect (i.e., a property of certain products that makes them creative and sets them off from other, noncreative ones). It makes intuitive sense to examine creativity by looking at its effects (i.e., to focus on products) in order to work out a model of functional creativity, although we subsequently apply the results in order to make suggestions for how to encourage engineers to be more creative (i.e., creativity as cause). In essence, we work from specific products to develop general rules (inductive thinking) and then reapply these rules to make specific suggestions (deductive thinking). As Cropley (2002) argued, this way of working seems to be common in physical and applied science, but is less common in social sciences, where the hypothetico-deductive paradigm is more common (i.e., the general rule already exists at the beginning of research).

It seems more or less self-evident that the first characteristic of a creative product is *novelty*—creativity always leads to something new. As the psychologist Bruner (e.g., 1962) put it, creativity must create "surprise." However, novelty (surprisingness) is not sufficient on its own. If it were, every crazy idea or absurd suggestion would be creative. Thus, creative products must be not only novel, but also *relevant* and *effective* (Bruner, 1962). This is especially true of engineering: Bridges or buildings are not supposed to collapse, no matter how unusual they are (although, of course, some do). Thus, the first two criteria of functional creativity are (a) relevance and effectiveness and (b) novelty. The order of these criteria is not irrelevant: Although novelty seems intuitively to take precedence over effectiveness, our view is that in the case of *functional* creativity there can be no discussion of creativity without first dealing with the issue of effectiveness. To take a simple example, a bridge must first solve the problem of getting traffic across a river. If it does not accomplish what the engineers were hired to build it for, it is a bad product, no matter how beautiful or how surprising it is. Higgins (1994, p. 6) reiterated this is a more general, business sense when he stated that "to be a true creative product it must have value and not just be original. To be innovative, it must have *significant* value" (our italics).

In this sense, functional creativity differs from other forms, such as aesthetic creativity, where novelty may have precedence. There may even be a conflict between the two ways of looking at creativity. A famous example in our homeland is the Sydney Opera House. After several decades it is still hailed as a piece of extraordinary architectural creativity because of its high level of novelty. Its only fault is that it is a less than optimal venue for the large-scale staging of operas, the purpose for which it was originally commissioned! Critics who emphasize the criteria of functional creativity and insist that it should be capable of solving the problem for which it was built (i.e., who place relevance and effectiveness before novelty) are dismissed as soulless curmudgeons by those who give preference to the criteria of aesthetic creativity.

In the case of aesthetic creativity, the relationship in products between relevance and effectiveness on the one hand, and novelty on the other, may be more or less open, or even optional. To take a simple example: A book might be acclaimed by critics for opening new perspectives in literature and also sell well (i.e., be both novel and functionally effective). However, it might sell well without critical acclaim (i.e., effectiveness without novelty), or be critically acclaimed without good sales (novelty without effectiveness). All three combinations might be regarded as involving creativity, with only the combination of poor sales accompanied by lack of acclaim being "uncreative." By contrast, in the case of functional creativity, the sequence is not optional. This can be demonstrated by a second Australian example.

In 1999, the Australian Minister for Defence requested a report to investigate problems associated with the performance of a new class of diesel-electric submarine (the Collins class) under construction for the Royal Australian Navy (RAN). By 1999, three of the planned six submarines had been delivered to the RAN, yet there were serious and widely publicized problems with the submarines. Aside from substantial delays in their completion (the third boat was 28 months late in delivery) the report found that the submarines "cannot perform at the levels required for military operations." MacIntosh and Prescott (1999) further determined that 6 years after the launch of the first boat there were still many outstanding deficiencies. Among the most serious problems were several that related specifically to the functional performance of the submarines (as military systems, rather than simply as underwater vehicles). These included problems with the diesel engines, with the submarines' noise signature, with the propellers, the periscopes, and the masts, and with the combat systems. At the same time the report determined that "there has been much high quality work carried out and the internal layout and the housekeeping of the boats are of a high order" (MacIntosh & Prescott, 1999, p. 5).

This represents a clear case in which relevance and effectiveness, in terms of the fundamental purpose of the submarines, were lacking. The designers' task was to provide a system for seeking out and destroying enemy ships and submarines, something the Collins class boats could not do effectively with defects such as an easily detectable noise signature and defective combat systems. The aspects that received praise—for example, the internal layout—may well represent innovative approaches to comfort and conditions in a submarine, and thus involve production of substantial novelty. However, the boats seem to offer an example of novelty without effectiveness. According to the earlier discussion, this might be acceptable in aesthetic creativity, but in a military context novelty without effectiveness would have literally fatal results. Thus, novelty is of necessity secondary to the functional purpose of the system. Because of a lack of clarity on this, informed opinion in Australia is sharply divided on whether the submarines are a success or not: The two sets of criteria (aesthetic vs. functional) lead to different assessments of the boats, although because of lack of clarity on the issues there is poor understanding in public discussions of how it is possible for disagreement to exist.[1]

THE CRITERIA OF FUNCTIONAL CREATIVITY

In defining creativity of products, Besemer and O'Quin (1987) emphasized "novelty" (the product is original, surprising, and germinal), "resolution" (the product is valuable, logical, useful, and understandable), and "elaboration and synthesis" (the product is organic, elegant, complex, and well crafted). *Resolution* refers to what we call relevance and effectiveness, whereas *elaboration* and *synthesis* involve not the presence or absence of novelty but instead the nature of the novelty. Taylor (1975) also emphasized relevance and originality. However, he went beyond these dimensions to include "generation," "reformulation," "complexity," "condensation," and "hedonics." Generation and reformulation are related to novelty, but—like elaboration and synthesis—complexity and condensation involve the nature of the creativity. The criterion of hedonics is reminiscent of Jackson and Messick's (1965) distinction between *external* criteria of the effectiveness of a novel product (i.e., Does it work?) and *internal* criteria such as logic, harmony among the elements of the product, and pleasingness (i.e., Is it beautiful?). Paradoxically, Taylor thus added what are to some extent *aesthetic* criteria to the definition of *functional* creativity.

It is interesting to note that even untrained judges can agree on whether such criteria are present in a product, and can do it in a consistent (reliable) way (e.g., Besemer & O'Quin, 1987), whereas there is substantial agreement among raters, especially those who are knowledgeable in a domain (Amabile, 1983). In other words people have a common understanding of novelty, complexity, elegance, and the like, and can recognize them when they see them. This is the phenomenon of consensus described by Amabile (1983). We argue later that consensus is particularly evident in the case of engineers.

Cropley and Cropley (2000) rated products designed and built by engineering students (wheeled vehicles propelled by the energy stored in a mousetrap) on four dimensions: *effectiveness* (ability to propel itself), *novelty* (originality and surprisingness), *elegance* (understandability and workman-like finish), and *germinality* (usefulness, ability to open up new perspectives). They found that these dimensions could be assessed by an engineer

---

[1] The situation is made more difficult by the fact that both politicians and senior officers in the RAN have a vested interest in obfuscation, because they do not wish to be seen as having made costly mistakes.

TABLE 10.1
The Hierarchical Organization of Problem Solutions

	Kind of Solution				
Criterion	Routine	Original	Elegant	Innovative	Aesthetic
Effectiveness	+	+	+	+	?
Novelty	−	+	+	+	+
Elegance	−	−	+	+	?
Generalizability	−	−	−	+	?

acting as rater with a substantial degree of reliability and with satisfactory validity (ratings of the four dimensions had low correlations with each other and correlated with scores on a creativity test in a logical way). In this chapter, we propose a similar four-dimensional model for defining the creativity of engineering products (i.e., of functional creativity). The four dimensions are:

1. *Relevance and effectiveness*: The product solves the problem it was intended to solve.
2. *Novelty*: The product is original and "surprising."
3. *Elegance*: The product is "beautiful" or pleasing, and goes beyond a simple mechanical solution; for instance, by introducing a "bonus" such as being cost effective.
4. *Generalizability*: The product is broadly applicable—it can be transferred to situations other than the present one and opens up perspectives for solving other problems.[2]

It is helpful to conceptualize the products of *functional* creativity as solutions to problems. Indeed, the idea of solving a problem was emphasized by both Horenstein and Burghardt. The systematic relationships among the four criteria just stated become apparent when they are related to a hierarchical model of problem solutions ranging from the "routine" solution (characterized by relevance and effectiveness alone) at one pole to the "innovative" solution (characterized by effectiveness, novelty, elegance, and generalizability) at the other, with "original" and "elegant" solutions between these poles. This relationship is shown in Table 10.1. The schematic in Table 10.1 can also be used to demonstrate the position of what we call "aesthetic" creativity. The table shows that each solution higher in the hierarchy incor-

---

[2]Finally, most writers nowadays accept that a product must be ethical if it is to be acclaimed as creative (e.g., Grudin, 1990). Ethical issues are readily recognizable in areas such as biotechnology.

porates all the properties of solutions at lower levels, but also adds something to them. According to our criteria (see previous discussion) routine solutions are not creative, because the second necessary criterion (novelty) is missing. This does not mean, however, that such solutions are useless.

FUNCTIONAL CREATIVITY AS A SYSTEM

For our purposes, the most important aspect of the four-dimensional model of functional creativity is that the dimensions form a *hierarchy*. Relevance and effectiveness on the one hand, and novelty on the other, are fundamental and necessary conditions for a creative product, but neither is sufficient on its own. Only when both are present is it possible to talk about creativity. Furthermore, the first criterion (effectiveness) must be met before the second (novelty) becomes relevant. Elegance and generalizability come lower in the hierarchy: It is possible to talk about creativity without them, and they are only interesting when the first two criteria have been met. The relationship among the criteria is also *dynamic*. To put this slightly differently, addition of the criteria lower in the hierarchy *adds value* to those above them. To take the most obvious example, novelty increases effectiveness. Elegance adds to both novelty and effectiveness and generalizability adds to novelty as well as increasing relevance and effectiveness. Thus, although elegance and generalizability are not absolutely indispensable for creativity, they add value to the creativity of a product. For an example of how generalizability adds value to a solution, see the refueling example later in the chapter.

There is an interesting nexus of aesthetic values (e.g., elegance) and effectiveness that manifests itself in engineering. A documented heuristic in the field of systems engineering reinforces the idea that elegant products tend to be more effective than are inelegant ones. In our terminology, elegance adds value. Rechtin and Maier (1997) quoted Wernher von Braun's aphorism: "The eye is a fine architect. Believe it!" (p. 237). This principle captures what is intuitively understood by many engineers, namely that good engineering solutions usually *look like good solutions*. In the language of functional creativity, they are elegant and understandable. A similar point was made by Einstein. He argued that it is not difficult to find solutions to problems—the difficult part is finding solutions that are *elegant* (see Miller, 1992). Grudin (1990) reinforced this idea when he gave his book the title *The Grace of Great Things* (our emphasis). Such solutions not infrequently cause a more or less instantaneous "shock of recognition" (Cropley, 1967, p. 21) when they occur, and provoke a "Why didn't I think of that?" reaction. To return to an earlier point, there is "consensus" among observers. Indeed, an elegant solution may look so simple and obvious—after the fact—that viewers may underrate its creativity or denigrate it as "obvious."

A further important point is that products do not occur in a vacuum. As both Miller (2000) and Sternberg (1999) emphasized, creativity most commonly involves what Sternberg called "propelling a field," usually by adding to what already exists, seeing it in a new light, transferring it to a new context, and so on. Bolts from the blue are the exception. A simple example occurred when practices well known in the refueling of commercial aircraft were transferred to Formula One motor racing. Although commonplace at the previous place of work, the practices were unknown at the new (i.e., in that context they were novel). Thus, the generalizability of the practices added value to them and made them capable of being applied in a new setting, where they were regarded as novel. Importantly, a change in the context or particular purpose can also have the opposite effect, destroying the relevance and effectiveness of a product, as can be seen in the Falklands War case study later in this chapter. Thus, *the context determines creativity* by defining not only a product's relevance and effectiveness, but also its degree of novelty. In a sense, creativity is not an aspect of the product at all, but instead one of the context. This is one of the "paradoxes" of creativity referred to by Cropley (1997).

A CASE STUDY

The dynamic nature of functional creativity can be illustrated by the following example from the Anglo-Argentinean Falklands War of 1982. It is characteristic of wartime that it produces many examples of engineering creativity. These examples are particularly valuable for the present discussion, because the criterion of effectiveness is often starkly obvious. As a result, examples from war are very instructive, although we do not want to create the impression that we are admirers of armed conflict. As the fighting in the Falklands developed, both sides used high-performance fighter jets. For the British, this was the "Harrier" V/STOL (vertical/short take-off and landing) aircraft operating from aircraft carriers, whereas for the Argentineans it was "Mirage" and "Dagger" jets. Considered in isolation, each country's aircraft met a particular need defined for that country's anticipated military operations. In the British case, the need was for jet aircraft capable of operating from aircraft carriers within a given framework of cost and performance. In the Argentinean case, the need was for supersonic land-based fighters to counter similar aircraft from potential adversaries. There is little doubt that both countries considered the aircraft they possessed to be relevant and effective for their particular needs. Of course, if these aircraft had been intended for some quite different task, such as transporting passengers, they would have been irrelevant and ineffective, immediately changing the nature of their claims to engineering creativity. This notion is discussed more fully later.

The importance of the particular context in defining functional creativity is illustrated by what happened when the British and Argentinean aircraft met in combat. The British aircraft quickly achieved superiority over the Argentineans, to the point that no British Harriers were lost in air-to-air combat in the conflict, whereas they accounted for the loss of 11 Argentinean fighters and a number of other, lesser aircraft. The particular capabilities of the Harriers, on paper inferior to the Mirages and Daggers, became assets, because the context of aircraft operations in the Falklands War forced the Argentinean aircraft to operate at low altitudes, where their superior speed could not be capitalized on. Although they would have been relevant and effective in meeting a threat from other, similar, land-based fighter jets, they were ineffective under the particular conditions of the fighting in the Falklands. The context for which the Argentinean aircraft had been designed was not the one in which they had to fight. This immediately rendered them far less relevant and effective than had been thought to be the case. At the same time, the context enhanced the Harriers' relevance and effectiveness, because they were ideally suited to the actual combat conditions encountered. In other words, the ability of the Harriers to function well in a setting that had not been foreseen (i.e., their generalizability) added value to their novelty. Possibly more interesting, the Harriers' generalizability *subtracted* value from the Mirages and Daggers. Subtraction of value is a special issue that becomes relevant when there are *competing solutions*, a situation that is discussed in more detail later.

The case study also illustrates the dynamic nature of the other dimensions that define functional creativity. The Harrier is regarded, in a general sense, as a novel aircraft. For example, it has the ability to fly backwards and to take off and land vertically. This is a quality that is certainly original and surprising in fixed-wing aircraft. The Harrier possesses other characteristics that were also hailed as highly innovative when the craft was first introduced into the market. These qualities distinguish it from other aircraft. It is unique, unusual, and—at the time it was introduced—its capabilities would not have been anticipated by competing manufacturers. The Mirages and Daggers, on the other hand, are routine high-performance jet aircraft. They have no particular features that set them apart from competing products. They certainly do not evoke surprise. In fact, it is likely that when introduced they represented a combination of design factors that was entirely predictable and commonplace. This takes nothing away from their ability to solve a particular problem (their relevance and effectiveness in a given context), but it means that they exhibit very little, if any, novelty, and as we now know, a fatal lack of generalizability. We see, then, that relevance and effectiveness alone are insufficient to define engineering creativity, although they are vitally necessary. The generalizable creative product is capable of solving a given problem in a novel manner, *even if this is not what it was originally designed for.*

The greater novelty of the Harrier had important consequences in the context of the particular problem defined by operations in the Falklands War. Specifically, the unusual and surprising ability of the Harrier to use a maneuver known as VIFFing (vectoring in forward flight) made a significant improvement to its relevance and effectiveness. In air-to-air combat, the Harrier was able turn disadvantage into decisive advantage when being pursued by an Argentinean jet by suddenly VIFFing, or using the controllable exhaust nozzles of the engine to alter speed and direction radically. This maneuver enabled the Harrier to jump out of the path of a pursuing aircraft and rapidly reposition itself behind the attacker, which was almost impossible for the conventional, routine Argentinean jets to counter. It thus transferred the Harriers from a position of danger into one in which they could destroy the attacking aircraft. There can be little doubt of the surprise that this tactic must have caused Argentinean pilots who succumbed to it. The addition of generalizable novelty in the design of the Harrier added value to its relevance and effectiveness. Furthermore, this novelty in the Harrier had the effect of reducing the relevance and effectiveness of the Mirage and Dagger jets (i.e., it subtracted value from the competing product).

LATENT FUNCTIONAL CREATIVITY

In Table 10.1, we touched on the possibility that "aesthetic" solutions to problems, although displaying novelty, may or may not involve other criteria such as effectiveness. This raises the possibility that, despite our earlier insistence on the necessity of effectiveness, even in the case of functional creativity there may be two kinds of novelty that are worth taking seriously: one kind that is actually observed to add value to the product (in terms of solving a particular given problem) and another kind that has not yet been seen to do this, but may eventually do so if and when appropriate problem conditions are encountered—a kind of *abstract* novelty that yields *potential* creativity. We cannot dismiss large numbers of products as lacking creativity simply because they fail to solve a particular problem in a given context. If we did this, we would have had to rate the Harrier as lacking creativity if, for instance, it had chanced to be applied to the problem of transporting passengers, because of its low level of effectiveness in this particular context, despite the fact that we have shown that the aircraft has a great deal of novelty that gives it creative merit in an engineering sense, regardless of the problem context, and which proved to be extremely effective when the right circumstances occurred.

For this reason, it is necessary to view engineering creativity as consisting of two fundamental categories: (a) functional creativity and (b) "latent" functional creativity. If neither of these applies, then any creative merit must, by definition, be (c) aesthetic creativity. These three categories can be defined as follows:

1. *Functional creativity* is driven by a specific functional purpose (relevance and effectiveness in a particular context).
2. *Latent functional creativity* characterizes products that possess novelty without a particular functional purpose, although this novelty has the potential to become relevant and effective when the right circumstances occur.
3. *Aesthetic creativity* involves novel products with no functional purpose, present or potential. "Functional" purpose is used here with the particular meaning worked out previously.

This distinction means that despite its lack of effectiveness as, let us say, a passenger transport aircraft, the Harrier was not relegated to the status of "art" but instead had *latent* functional creativity that was realized when the product was placed in the appropriate context (i.e., used as a low-level fighter aircraft). It does not lose its novel abilities in the "wrong" context (e.g., as a means of mass passenger transport), but simply realizes no benefit from them because of an absence of relevance and effectiveness to the particular situation, which nullifies the usefulness of its novelty in the setting in question, but not in absolute terms.

This issue becomes particularly important in a situation in which a product is forced to compete with a *rival solution*. In a sense, this was the problem faced by the pilots of the Argentinean Mirages and Daggers. It is also a common situation in commercial settings. Indeed, this may be one of the main practical ways in which functional creativity differs from aesthetic creativity. Although there are many examples of highly "commercial" aesthetic creators, such as some of the Italian painting masters or 5-cents-a-word authors, the artist does not usually compete directly for market shares and the like, and many are reluctant to sell their work at all. However, in the case of functional creativity, a novel product may have its effectiveness and thus its functional creativity destroyed by its rival, in the way that, to take a single example, the vacuum tube's relevance was destroyed by the silicon chip. Nonetheless, the vacuum tube continues to have been creative in its day, although it is no longer in general use because of the existence of a more effective rival. The need to make a product's value robust in the face of a rival product or even capable of subtracting value from the rival supports the importance of "loading" new products with novelty, and suggests several reasons for doing this:

1. Novelty may add so much value to a product that it is immune to value subtractions resulting from a rival's novelty.
2. The product's novelty may also give it the capacity to subtract value from a rival product (i.e., to nullify the rival's effectiveness).
3. "Extra" novelty may add to a product's generalizability.

However, because the nature of the rival may be unknown at the time a product is being developed (i.e., the exact problem the product must solve may be unknown), added value resulting from novelty may initially be only *latent*.

IMPLICATIONS FOR PRACTICE—FOSTERING CREATIVITY IN ENGINEERS

Despite the importance of creativity, a recent survey in Australia (Government of Australia, 1999) showed that three quarters of new graduates there are "unsuitable" for employment because of "skill deficiencies" in creativity, problem solving, and independent and critical thinking. A U.K. study (Cooper, Altman, & Garner, 2002) concluded that the education system militates against innovation. In the United States, university-level teaching of engineering is widely regarded as indifferent or even hostile to creativity, and empirical studies support this view. Snyder (1967), for instance, showed that students at an American university who preferred trying new solutions dropped out of engineering courses three times more frequently than did those who preferred conventional solutions. Gluskinos (1971) found no correlation between creativity as measured by a creativity test and GPAs in engineering courses. Despite this, the literature over the years demonstrates the existence of a continuing interest in fostering the creativity of engineering students (e.g., Gawain, 1974; Masi, 1989; Olken, 1964).

Attempts in the past to train engineering students to be more creative have produced mixed results. Rubinstein (1980) and Woods (1983) reported some success in training these students in problem solving. More recently, in a pretest-posttest study, Basadur, Graen, and Scandura (1986) showed that a program emphasizing divergent thinking increased the preference of manufacturing engineering students for generating new solutions, although the study did not report any changes in actual performance. Clapham and Schuster (1992) administered creativity tests to engineering students from a variety of majors. About half of them then received creativity training that emphasized brainstorming, incubation, idea-getting techniques, and deferment of judgment, whereas the remainder acted as controls. The statistical analysis showed that the test scores of the trained students had increased significantly more than had those of the controls.

Clapham (1997) reviewed possible mechanisms through which beneficial effects of training might occur, and concluded that they can be attributed to programs' ability to foster development of appropriate thinking skills, acquisition of positive attitudes to creativity and creative performance, motivation to be creative, perception of oneself as capable of being creative, reduction of anxiety about creativity, and experience of positive mood in problem-solving situations. It is apparent that this list goes beyond simply thinking skills, and encompasses attitudes, motivation, self-image, and similar factors.

Cropley and Cropley (2000) pursued Clapham's analysis further in a study in which engineering students received three lectures from a psychology specialist (the second author of this chapter) on the following topics: What is creativity? What has creativity got to do with engineering students? Why do engineers have problems with creativity? What are the psychological elements of creativity? What are the characteristics of a creative product? How can you solve problems creatively? What blocks creativity? Lectures also emphasized the issues touched on previously in this chapter (importance of creativity in modern engineering practice and as a factor in developing a career in the field; nature of engineering creativity). Finally, it was emphasized that creative products must not only be novel and germinal but must also reflect a high level of engineering knowledge (i.e., be effective and relevant).

Subsequently, the students were required to build "a wheeled vehicle powered by a mousetrap." It was emphasized that the novelty of their vehicle would be an important source of points, although they were also reminded that the vehicle would have to be capable of propelling itself (i.e., effective). The students were also reminded of the four dimensions on which their products would be evaluated (effectiveness, novelty, elegance, and germinality). Finally, the students were given individual "creativity counseling" based on the connection between psychological aspects of creativity such as nonconformity, originality, openness, or risk taking and their own behavior on a creativity test, for instance drawing their attention to unfavorable aspects of their own personality such as fear of taking a risk or excessive conformity.

Both longitudinal comparisons of test scores (before and after training) as well as comparisons with the work of a control group indicated that the program had had beneficial effects on participants' originality of thinking and willingness to depart from the conventional, as well as on the novelty of the machines they built. However, it is scarcely conceivable that the brief training provided in this project would bring about profound and long-lasting changes in participants' fundamental psychological potential to be creative, although it was possible to show the students a different way of solving an engineering problem that they found enjoyable, as well as to give them a convincing demonstration of their own ability to come up with ideas. In this sense, the study offers hints about how to influence the development of knowledge concerning creativity and divergent cognitive strategies, as well as a positive attitude to novelty. However, there seems little likelihood that such attributes will persist unless they are further developed by appropriate follow-up activities.

REFERENCES

Albert, R. S. (1990). Identity, experiences, and career choice among the exceptionally gifted and talented. In M. A. Runco (Ed.), *Theories of creativity* (pp. 13–34). Newbury Park, CA: Sage.

Amabile, T. M. (1983). *The social psychology of creativity*. New York: Springer.

Basadur, M., Graen, G. B., & Scandura, T. (1986). Training effects of attitudes toward divergent thinking among manufacturing engineers. *Journal of Applied Psychology, 71*, 612–617.

Besemer, S. P., & O'Quin, K. (1987). Creative product analysis: Testing a model by developing a judging instrument. In S. G. Isaksen (Ed.), *Frontiers of creativity research: Beyond the basics* (pp. 367–389). Buffalo, NY: Bearly.

Bruner, J. S. (1962). The conditions of creativity. In H. Gruber, G. Terrell, & M. Wertheimer (Eds.), *Contemporary approaches to cognition* (pp. 1–30). New York: Athaneum.

Burghardt, M. D. (1995). *Introduction to the engineering profession* (2nd ed.). New York: Addison-Wesley.

Clapham, M. M. (1997). Ideational skills training: A key element in creativity training programs. *Creativity Research Journal, 10*, 33–44.

Clapham, M. M., & Schuster, D. H. (1992). Can engineering students be trained to think more creatively? *Journal of Creative Behavior, 26*, 156–162.

Clifford. P. I. (1958). Emotional contacts with the external world manifested by selected groups of highly creative chemists and mathematicians. *Perceptual and Motor Skills, 8*, 3–26.

Cooper, C., Altman, W., & Garner, A. (2002). *Inventing for business success*. New York: Texere.

Cropley, A. J. (1967). *Creativity*. London: Longmans.

Cropley, A. J. (1997). Creativity: A bundle of paradoxes. *Gifted and Talented International, 12*, 8–14.

Cropley, A. J. (2001). *Creativity in education and learning*. London: Kogan Page.

Cropley, A. J. (2002). *Qualitative research methods: An introduction for students of psychology and education*. Riga, Latvia: Zinātne.

Cropley, D. H., & Cropley, A. J. (2000). Fostering creativity in engineering undergraduates. *High Ability Studies, 11*, 207–219.

Csikszentmihalyi, M. (1996). *Creativity: Flow and the psychology of discovery and invention*. New York: HarperCollins.

Dekker, D. L. (1995). Engineering design processes, problem solving and creativity. In *Proceedings of the 1995 International Association for Engineering Education Frontiers in Education Conference* (pp. 16–19). Atlanta, GA: American Society for Engineering Education.

Gawain, T. H. (1974). Reflection on education for creativity in engineering. *International Association for Engineering Education Transactions in Education, 17*, 189–192.

Gluskinos, U. M. (1971). Criteria for student engineering creativity and their relationship to college grades. *Journal of Educational Measurement, 8*, 189–195.

Gordon, W. J. (1961). *Synectics*. New York: Harper.

Government of Australia. (1999). *Higher education funding report, 1999*. Canberra: Government Printer.

Grudin, R. (1990). *The grace of great things: Creativity and innovation.* New York: Ticknor and Fields.
Guilford, J. P. (1950). Creativity. *American Psychologist, 5,* 444–454.
Hequet, M. (1995, October). Doing more with less. *Training,* pp. 76–82.
Higgins, J. M. (1994). *101 creative problem solving techniques—the handbook of new ideas for business.* Winter Park, FL: New Management.
Horenstein, M. N. (2002). *Design concepts for engineers* (2nd ed.). Upper Saddle River, NJ: Prentice-Hall.
Jackson, P. W., & Messick, S. (1965). The person, the product, and the response: Conceptual problems in the assessment of creativity. *Journal of Personality, 33,* 309–329.
MacIntosh, M. K., & Prescott, J. B. (1999). *Report to the Minister for Defence on the Collins Class Submarine and related matters.* Canberra: Commonwealth of Australia.
Masi, J. V. (1989). Teaching the process of creativity in the engineering classroom. In *Proceedings of the 1989 International Association for Engineering Education Frontiers in Education Conference* (pp. 288–292). San Juan, Puerto Rico: American Society for Engineering Education.
Miller, A. I. (1992). Scientific creativity: A comparative study of Henri Poincaré and Albert Einstein. *Creativity Research Journal, 5,* 385–418.
Miller, A. I. (2000). *Insights of genius.* Cambridge, MA: MIT Press.
Olken, H. (1964, December). Creativity training for engineers—its past, present and future. *International Association for Engineering Education Transactions in Education,* pp. 149–161.
Rechtin, E., & Maier, M. (1997). *The art of systems architecting.* Boca Raton, FL: CRC.
Roe, A. (1952). *The making of a scientist.* New York: Dodd Mead.
Rossman, J. (1931). *The psychology of the inventor: A study of the patentee.* Washington, DC: Inventors' Publishing Co.
Rubinstein, M. F. (1980). A decade of experience in teaching an interdisciplinary problem solving course. In D. T. Turna & F. Reif (Eds.), *Problem solving and education* (pp. 35–48). Hillsdale, NJ: Lawrence Erlbaum Associates.
Snyder, B. (1967). Creative students in science and engineering. *Universities Quarterly, 21,* 205–218.
Steiner, C. J. (1998). Educating for innovation and management: The engineering educator's dilemma. *International Association for Engineering Education Transactions in Education, 41,* 1–7.
Sternberg, R. J. (1997). Intelligence and lifelong learning. What's new and how can we use it? *American Psychologist, 52,* 1134–1139.
Sternberg, R. J. (1999). A propulsion model of types of creative contributions. *Journal of General Psychology, 3*(2), 83–100.
Taylor, A. (1975). An emerging view of creative actions. In I. A. Taylor & J. W. Getzels (Eds.), *Perspectives in creativity* (pp. 297–325). Chicago: Aldine.
Thackray, J. (1995, July). That vital spark (creativity enhancement in business). *Management Today,* pp. 56–58.
Thanksgiving for innovation. (2002, September 21). *Economist Technology Quarterly,* pp. 13–14.
Walberg, H. J., & Stariha, W. E. (1992). Productive human capital: Learning, creativity and eminence. *Creativity Research Journal, 5,* 323–340.
Woods, D. R. (1983). Introducing explicit training in problem solving into our courses. *Higher Education Research and Development, 2,* 79–102.

Chapter 11

Creativity as a General and a Domain-Specific Ability: The Domain of Mathematics as an Exemplar[1]

Roberta M. Milgram
School of Education, Tel Aviv University, and College of Judea and Samaria

Nava L. Livne
School of Education, Tel Aviv University

Guilford's 1950 address to the American Psychological Association led to a new era in the study of creativity. His distinction between convergent and divergent cognitive processes in problem solving (1956, 1967) dominated conceptions of creativity and provided the impetus for studies that focused, almost exclusively, on establishing the discriminant validity of measures of creative thinking from intelligence. Wallach (1970, 1971) summarized the literature that had accumulated on creativity over a period of 20 years, and concluded that when divergent thinking was operationally defined as scores on measures of ideational fluency, intelligence and creativity (i.e., convergent and divergent thinking) were indeed cognitive processes that were empirically distinguishable from each other.

The emphasis on the intelligence–creativity distinction led to neglect of the important ways in which intelligence and creativity are similar. For example, both intelligence and creativity are best viewed as "raw abilities"

---

[1]This chapter was written by Roberta M. Milgram, Professor Emerita, School of Education, Tel Aviv University, and Coordinator, Department of Education, College of Judea and Samaria, and Nava L. Livne, School of Education, Tel Aviv University. Nava Livne is now at the Department of Education, University of California, Irvine. This chapter was based on data collected for the dissertation submitted by the second author in partial fulfillment of the requirements for the Ph.D. degree at Tel Aviv University, School of Education. The first author directed the research.

Correspondence concerning this article should be addressed to Roberta M. Milgram, POB 157, Kochav Yair, Israel, 44864. E-mail: milgram@post.tau.ac.il

(Barron & Harrington, 1981). Just as convergent intellectual abilities as measured in IQ tests are productive only if they are applied to a specific domain, so too, in order to be productive, divergent thinking abilities must be realized in real-world creative products. Another similarity between convergent and divergent thinking is that both were viewed by Guilford (1956, 1967) as being normally distributed. This postulation was very different from widely held views (Feldman, 1986; Gruber & Davis, 1988) that creativity is the gift of a rare few, a belief that led to emphasis on understanding high creative abilities and ignoring the fact that creative thinking, like intelligence, occurs at lower levels as well. People who use original thinking solve everyday problems at work or in their personal lives more successfully.

Despite the findings that demonstrated the reliability, convergent validity, and discriminant validity from intelligence of ideational fluency-based measures of creativity cited previously, several investigators criticized this psychometric approach to the measurement of creative thinking as having many methodological flaws (Plucker & Renzulli, 1999). The most serious criticisms were that fluency measures lacked predictive validity (Baer, 1993; Gardner, 1993; Kogan & Pankove, 1974; Plucker & Renzulli, 1999; Wallach, 1985; Weisberg, 1993). It was suggested that improvement of scoring of divergent thinking measures would lead to greater predictive validity (Hocevar & Bachelor, 1989). Efforts were made to improve the scoring of ideational fluency and/or to control for the effect of fluency on divergent thinking scores (Hocevar, 1979; Hocevar & Michael, 1979). Plucker and Runco (1998) summarized the research on creativity measurement. They concluded that the issue of methodological improvement of ideational fluency measures of creativity retained its importance, but they also cited as a positive development the fact that the field of creativity measurement has broadened to include many aspects in addition to ideational fluency. None of the previously cited studies stressed the critical contribution of general ideational fluency to creative problem solving in a specific domain.

Creativity is often conceptualized as a component of giftedness. Authoritative summaries and discussion of the different theories of giftedness and talent that were developed in the 1980s and 1990s appeared in the literature (Cohen & Ambrose, 1993; Horowitz & O'Brien, 1985; Runco & Albert, 1990; Sternberg & Davidson, 1986). Among the better-known conceptualizations that emerged were those of Sternberg (1988), Gardner (1983, 1993), and Tannenbaum (1983, 1986). Many of the current theories include creativity; however, even those that are broad in scope and recognize the role of environment and experience in realization of creative abilities do not specifically distinguish between general and specific creative abilities and do not distinguish among levels.

In the 1980s, the general–domain-specific creativity controversy appeared. A number of well-respected authorities in the field of creativity offered the opinion that creativity was not a general but instead a domain-specific ability (Amabile, 1983a, 1983b; Feldman, 1986; Gardner, 1983; Wallach, 1985). Some investigators argued that not only was creativity domain specific, but that it was necessary to specify abilities even within domains. There is no serious doubt about domain differences in creativity. A major statement of both positions that appeared in two articles designated as "point–counterpoint" that appeared in the *Creativity Research Journal* (Baer, 1998; Plucker, 1998) concluded that divergent thinking has been a wrong direction taken for many years in the study of creativity, in that it has not led to theoretical clarity about the process of creative thinking, nor to its assessment.

The modern trend that places emphasis on understanding domain-specific creativity was reflected, for example, in the first three articles presented in a 2002 issue of the *Creativity Research Journal* (vol. 14, no. 1). Of the first four studies that appeared in the issue, three were of domain-specific creativity: one of the performing arts (Kogan, 2002), one of creative writers (Kaufman, 2002), and one of creativity in art and design (Christiaans, 2002). Not one of these articles postulated creative thinking as contributing to creative attainment in any one of the areas, nor did they include an empirical ideational fluency assessment of it. On the other hand, Plucker (1998) insisted that the general versus domain-specific nature of creativity is still an open question, and pointed out serious methodological weaknesses that make the empirical evidence supporting the domain-specific position far from compelling.

More and more discussion has focused on the domain-specific nature of creative thinking and creative performance (Baer, 1998; Plucker, 1998; Plucker & Runco, 1998). However, empirical investigations of the domain-general versus the domain-specific nature are uncommon. Milgram dealt with the efficacy of ideational fluency measures of creativity by raising the question, "Creativity: An Idea Whose Time Has Come and Gone?" (Milgram, 1990). She concluded her paper with the following statement:

> Creativity is *not* an idea whose time has come and gone. Numerous researchers have objected to the heavy emphasis placed upon ideational fluency measures of creativity. *I do not agree with these criticisms.* Ideational fluency is not in and of itself creativity. It is, however, probably a critical component of talent. The trend in research on creativity is clearly to focus more on real-world performance, on products, rather than on process. I am an enthusiastic supporter of this development. (p. 229)

The volume in which this current chapter appears is an effort to systematize the knowledge that has accumulated on the question of creativity as a general versus a domain-specific ability. In this chapter, we report a study, conducted with a very large representative sample, that used an advanced statistical technique to empirically examine the relationship of general creativity to domain-specific creative performance in mathematics. This study is based upon the Milgram 4 × 4 model of the structure of giftedness as applied to mathematics.

Milgram's (1989, 1991) multidimensional 4 × 4 model of the structure of giftedness (see Fig. 11.1) explains giftedness as the result of the complex interaction of cognitive, personal-social, and sociocultural influences. Giftedness is depicted in terms of four dimensions. The first dimension includes four distinct types of ability, two having to do with aspects of intelligence (general intellectual ability and domain-specific intellectual ability) and two with aspects of original thinking (general original/creative thinking and domain-specific creative talent). The second dimension of the struc-

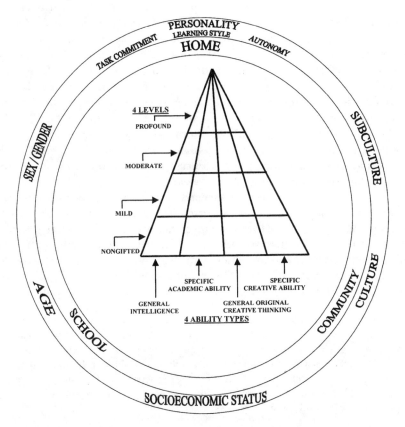

FIG. 11.1. Milgram: 4 × 4 structure of giftedness model. *Source:* "Teaching Gifted and Talented Children in Regular Classrooms: An Impossible Dream or a Full-Time Solution for a Full-Time Problem?" by R. M. Milgram (Ed.), *Teaching gifted and talented children learners in regular classrooms, 1,* p. 10. Copyright 1989 by Springfield, IL: Charles C. Thomas.

ture of giftedness refers to four distinct levels of ability: one level of nongifted ability, and three levels of gifted (mild, moderate, and profound) abilities. The four ability levels represent different combinations of cognitive processes that are qualitatively differentiated by the complexity of the cognitive processes at each level. These distinct ability levels are hierarchically ordered by their degree of difficulty, so that the higher the level, the more infrequently it occurs. Each of the four types of ability may obtain at each of the four levels. The model postulates relationships between general intellectual ability and domain-specific intellectual ability and between general original/creative thinking and domain-specific creative talent.

The third dimension of the 4×4 model refers to the influence of three interrelated learning environments (home, school, and community) on the degree of realization of abilities. The fourth dimension postulates the effect of individual difference characteristics such as age, sex/gender, socioeconomic status, culture, subculture, and especially personality characteristics such as task commitment, learning style, autonomy, motivation, persistence, and many others on the actualization of potential abilities. To the best of our knowledge, this is the only theory that distinguishes between the general and domain-specific creative thinking abilities, at four levels, and postulates a relationship between the two.

The construct validity of the 4×4 structure of giftedness model (Milgram, 1989, 1991) as applied to literature was examined by Hong and Milgram (1996). The research participants were boys and girls in Grades 7 to 9 ($n = 392$) and Grades 10 to 12 ($n = 381$) who represented the wide range of abilities and talents postulated by current multidimensional conceptualizations of giftedness. Using confirmatory factor analyses, the 4×4 model and five alternative models were evaluated and compared with respect to a number of goodness-of-fit indexes to determine which model fits the data best from among the alternative models. Among the alternative models in this study, the best fit was the hypothesized 4×4 model, validating that giftedness in the domain of literature may be conceptualized in terms of general intellectual ability, domain-specific intellectual ability, general creative thinking, and domain-specific creative talent.

In discussing the results of their study, Hong and Milgram (1996) made two observations that influenced the current research. First, they suggested that domain-specific creativity could be represented by indicators other than the self-report scales used in their study. They recommended ratings by experts of portfolios supplied by research participants. Second, they concluded that results that demonstrated domain-specific ability in literature, to be independent from the other three types of abilities postulated by the 4×4 model, did not necessarily apply to all domains. The question of whether specific abilities in other domains, such as mathematics, are equally distinct remained to be investigated. Hong and Milgram suggested that future investigations were needed in order to establish the interrelationships of the underlying cognitive processes of each type of gifted abilities.

In this current chapter, we are focusing on the cognitive components of giftedness in mathematics as postulated in the 4 × 4 model. The challenge was to develop operational definitions of domain-specific creative ability in mathematics, to assess them reliably, and to investigate their relationship to general creative thinking ability. In addition, we investigated the interrelationships between general and specific creative ability in mathematics and general and specific academic ability in mathematics. This required the development of two new instruments to assess domain-specific creativity in mathematics, the *Multiscale Academic and Creative Abilities in Mathematics* (Livne & Livne, 1999a) and the *Tel Aviv Activities and Accomplishments Inventory: Mathematics* (Livne & Milgram, 1999). We followed the example provided by Guttman (Guttman, 1968, 1971, 1991) and developed two mapping sentences to provide an exact and detailed conceptual description of the postulated academic and creative abilities in mathematics at four levels of understanding (Livne, 2002; Livne, Livne, & Milgram, 1999; Livne & Milgram, 2000). We used the two mapping sentences, as presented in Figs. 11.2 and 11.3, to guide the process of building the items to assess specific academic and specific creative thinking abilities in mathematics, respectively.

In addition, a precise scoring guide was developed to operationally define differences in academic and creative abilities in mathematics *between* and *within* four ability levels (Livne & Livne, 1999b). The *between-level* measurement refers to four qualitatively distinct levels of cognitive process ordered by level of difficulty based on an ordinal scale. The *within-level* measurement refers to eight qualitatively distinct levels of cognitive processes, ordered by degree of complexity.

ASSESSMENT OF GENERAL AND DOMAIN-SPECIFIC ABILITIES

In this chapter, we report on a large-scale study in which two basic questions were investigated: Is there a distinction between specific academic and specific creative ability in mathematics, and what is the relationship of each of these specific abilities to the general intellectual and general creative abilities? The research participants were 1,090 students (565 males and 525 females) in the 10th and 11th grades (mean age = 16.50, SD = .59). The subjects represented a wide range of intellectual abilities, and were drawn from 22 public schools that constituted a nationally stratified and representative sample of students in urban and rural schools. The instruments were group

Domain: academic and creative mathematical abilities at four levels

An item presents a mathematical problem
A Type of problem
- a1 *numerically*
- a2 *verbally*

relates to:

B Mathematical fields
- b1 combinatorics
- b2 geometry
- b3 linear algebra
- b4 probability
- b5 others

An item measures mathematical abilities
C Type of abilities
- c1 *academic* *
- c2 creative

An item is defined globally as:
D Type of framework
- d1 *highly specific well defined*
- d2 a set of dynamic, nonspecific, not well defined formulations

its elements are:
E Item elements
- e1 *very specific*
- e2 not specific to the problem

An item measures a theoretic level in mathematical abilities:
F Levels of mathematical understanding: Theoretical definition
- f1 ordinary - initial impression from examination of the data on the surface
- f2 mild - attention to details
- f3 moderate - integration
- f4 profound - transfer/application

The level of each item's data is defined as:
G Number of Relevant data units
- g1 a given number of data units
- g2 the given number of data units +1
- g3 the given number of data units +2
- g4 the given number of data units +3

which are:
H Data generality
- h1 specific (usually numerical)
- h2 general (usually verbal)

The level of each item's distractors is defined as:
I Number of Distractors units
- i1 1
- i2 2
- i3 3
- i4 4

which are:
J Distractors generality
- j1 specific (usually numerical)
- j2 general (usually verbal)

An item combines a certain number of units and generality of data and distractors to operationally define a level of mathematical understanding as:
K Levels of mathematical understanding: Empirical definition
- k1 a given number of (mainly) specific data units and a specific distractor
- k2 the given number of (mainly) specific data units + 1 and two (usually) general distractors
- k3 the given number of (mainly) general data units + 2 and three (mainly) specific distractors
- k4 the given number of (mainly) general data units + 3 and four (mainly) general distractors

The solution process is based on:
L Cognitive preconditions
- l1 *mainly learned knowledge*
- l2 basic knowledge and creative thinking
- l3 creative thinking alone

leads to:

M Number of solution paths
- m1 *one formal solution path (not intuitive)*
- m2 *variations on one formal path*
- m3 several disjoint solution paths

The quality of solution is:
N Quality of solution paths
- n1 *standard*
- n2 creative: original, surprising, high quality aesthetic

reach a solution type which is:
O Type of Solution
- o1 *one dichotomic - correct/incorrect*
- o2 varied: correct/partially correct/incorrect

FIG. 11.2. Mapping sentence of academic and creative abilities in mathematics at four levels of understanding: A schematic representation. *Note:* Italics represent academic abilities.

Domain: creative talent in mathematics at four levels

A Type of activity

An item represents an out-of-school mathematical activity that is:
- a1 unchallenging
- a2 partly unchallenging
- a3 partly challenging
- a4 challenging

B Type of cognitive process

The activity uses:
- b1 mainly convergent thinking
- b2 more convergent than divergent thinking
- b3 more divergent than convergent thinking
- b4 mainly divergent thinking

C Quality of activity process

The quality of the activity process is defined as:
- c1 popular and low quality
- c2 popular and high quality
- c3 unusual and low quality
- c4 unusual and high quality

D Quality of product

The activity results in a product that is:
- d1 popular and low quality
- d2 popular and high quality
- d3 unusual and low quality
- d4 unusual and high quality

E Level of motivation

The activity is:
- e1 extrinsically motivated
- e2 more extrinsically than intrinsically motivated
- e3 more intrinsically than extrinsically motivated
- e4 intrinsically motivated

F Level of task-commitment

The activity reflects:
- f1 low task commitment
- f2 mild task commitment
- f3 moderate task commitment
- f4 high task commitment

G Level of personal initiative

The activity expresses:
- g1 low initiative
- g2 mild initiative
- g3 moderate initiative
- g4 high initiative

H Level of Intensity

The degree of intensity with which the activity is done is:
- h1 low
- h2 mild initiative
- h3 moderate initiative
- h4 high initiative

I Theoretical definition: Levels of creative talent in mathematics in terms of out-of-school activities

An item measures a theoretical level of creative talented mathematical activity that is:

i1 ordinary – an unchallenging activity in mathematics. It uses mainly popular and low quality convergent thinking and results in a popular and low quality product. The activity is extrinsically motivated, reflects low task commitment, low initiative and the degree of intensity with which it is performed is low

h2 mild – a partly unchallenging activity in mathematics. It uses more popular and high quality convergent thinking than divergent thinking and results in a popular and high quality product. It is more extrinsically than intrinsically motivated, reflects mild task commitment, mild initiative and it is performed with a and it is performed with a mild degree of intensity

h3 moderate – a partly challenging activity in mathematics. It uses more unusual and low quality divergent thinking than convergent thinking and results in an unusual and low quality product. It is more intrinsically than extrinsically motivated, reflects moderate task commitment, moderate initiative and the degree of intensity with which it is performed is moderate

h4 profound – a challenging activity in mathematics. It uses mainly unusual and high quality divergent and results in an unusual and high quality product It is intrinsically motivated, reflects high task commitment, high initiative and the degree of intensity with which it is performed is very high

FIG. 11.3. *(Continued)*

J Frequency of activity performance

The activity is done:
- j1 very frequently
- j2 frequently
- j3 infrequently
- j4 very infrequently

K Time duration of activity

The activity may be described as:
- k1 brief – a given time range
- k2 somewhat longer – at least twice as long as the given time range
- k3 long – at least three times as long as the given time range
- k4 very long – at least four times as long as the given time range

L Degree of focus of activity

The degree of focus of activity in mathematics is:
- l1 not focused on one specific field
- l2 more unfocused than focused on one specific field
- l3 more focused on one specific field than unfocused
- l4 focused on one specific field

M Degree of activity comprehensiveness

The degree of comprehensiveness of the activity is dictated by:
- m1 fixed, specific limits
- m2 fixed, general limits
- m3 flexible, specific limits
- m4 flexible, general limits

N Percentage of activity performers

The activity is performed by:
- m1 50% - 70% of adolescents
- m2 25% - 35% of adolescents
- m3 10% - 20% of adolescents
- m4 1% - 2% of adolescents

O Empirical definition: Levels of creative talent in mathematics in terms of out-of-school activities

An item combines a frequency and time duration of activity with degree of focus of activity and percentage of adolescents who perform the activity to operationally define the level of an out-of-school activity as:

- o1 ordinary – the activity is done very frequently, is of brief time duration. The activity is general and not focused on one specific field and is dictated by fixed, specific limits. It is performed by 50% - 70% of adolescents
- o2 mild – the activity is done frequently, is of somewhat longer time duration. The activity is more unfocused than focused on one specific field in mathematics and is dictated by fixed, general limits. It is performed by 25% - 35% of adolescents
- o3 moderate – the activity is done infrequently, is of long time duration. The activity is more focused on one specific field in mathematics than unfocused and is dictated by flexible, specific limits. It is performed by 10% - 20% of adolescents
- o4 profound – the activity is done very infrequently, is of very long time duration. The activity is focused on one specific field in mathematics and is dictated by flexible, general limits. It is performed by 1% – 2% of adolescents

FIG. 11.3. Mapping sentence of creative talent in mathematics at four levels in terms of out-of-school activities.

administered in a complex cross-balanced procedure that was described in detail elsewhere (Livne, 2002).

The instrument, used to measure both domain-specific academic and domain-specific creative abilities in mathematics, was the *Multiscale Academic and Creative Abilities in Mathematics* (Livne, 2002; Livne & Livne, 1999a) cited earlier. It consisted of 16 open-ended items. Eight items required standard-logical thinking for solution and provided an index of specific academic ability in mathematics at four levels. The other eight items required nonstandard creative thinking for solution and provided an index of specific creative ability in mathematics at four levels. The internal consistencies of the eight-item measures of each of the domain-specific abilities, academic and creative in mathematics, were .67 and .68, respectively. The corresponding Spearman–Brown (Brown, 1910; Spearman, 1910) internal consistencies for scales with five times the number of items would be .90 and .91, respectively.

A second index of domain-specific academic ability in mathematics was the final grade point average for achievement in mathematics for the first semester of the academic year in which the study was conducted. This grade ranged from 0 to 100 and was provided by school authorities.

A second index of domain-specific creative ability in mathematics was the *Tel Aviv Activities and Accomplishments Inventory: Mathematics* (Livne & Milgram, 1999). This instrument consisted of 36 self-report biographical items designed to assess creative ability in mathematics at four levels. Each item required the research participant to indicate by answering yes or no to whether he or she had or had not participated in the particular extracurricular, challenging activity or had attained the accomplishment in mathematics. This measure provided an index of specific creative ability in mathematics at four levels. The process by which this instrument was developed and evidence of its construct validity was reported by Livne and Milgram (2000). The Kuder–Richardson internal consistency of the 36-item measure of domain-specific creative ability in mathematics as used in the study reported here was .95 (Kuder & Richardson, 1937).

General creative and general intellectual ability were assessed by measures of confirmed validity. General creative ability was measured by two verbal items selected from the Tel Aviv Creativity Test (Milgram & Milgram, 1976a), an instrument designed to assess ideational fluency. The number of distinct ideas generated in response to the stimulus item represented the degree of general creative thinking. The Tel Aviv Creativity Test yields scores that are highly reliable, distinct from intelligence (Milgram & Milgram, 1976a), and characterized by both construct and concurrent validity (Milgram & Arad, 1981). The quantity of ideational fluency was considered a valid index of general original thinking based on the findings of Milgram and Rabkin (1980) and Milgram, Milgram, Rosenbloom, and

Rabkin (1978). The internal consistency of the two-item measure of general creative thinking was .77. The corresponding Spearman–Brown (Brown, 1910; Spearman, 1910) internal consistency for a scale with three times the number of items would be .91.

General intellectual ability was measured by both verbal and nonverbal measures. The *Abstract Verbal Thinking Test* (Glanz, 1996)—a group intelligence test widely used in Israel—was the measure of general verbal intelligence. Prior evidence for the reliability and validity of the instrument was reported by Glanz (1996). The Kuder–Richardson internal consistency of the 180-item measure of general intelligence was .98. The *Advanced Progressive Matrices* (Raven, 1962) was a 36-item nonverbal measure of general intelligence. Evidence for the reliability and validity of the measure was reported by Raven, Raven, and Court (1998). The Kuder–Richardson internal consistency of the nonverbal measure of general intelligence as used in the current study was .90.

Structural equation modeling was used as a unified analysis (Bollen & Long, 1993) for testing the construct validity of the proposed interrelationships among the conceptual components of the two dimensions of the 4 × 4 model (Milgram, 1989, 1991) as applied to mathematics, ability type, and ability level. It has been recommended as the best advanced technique for this purpose, because it takes into account the validity, reliabilities, and error measurement of each of the scales (Byrne, 1994; Hair, Anderson, Tatham, & Black, 1995). The findings of construct validity of the 4 × 4 model reported in the next section were reported in detail by Livne (2002) and by Livne and Milgram (2002b).

EVIDENCE OF CONSTRUCT VALIDITY OF THE 4 × 4 MODEL AS APPLIED TO MATHEMATICS

Using the EQS 5.7 program (Bentler, 1997; EQS, 1997), a confirmatory factor analysis was conducted on the entire sample of 1,090 students. The findings provided evidence of a good fit for the postulated 4 × 4 model as applied to mathematics, and constituted good evidence of overall construct validity.

DISCRIMINANT VALIDITY OF THE TWO DIMENSIONS: ABILITY TYPES AND ABILITY LEVELS

The findings provided evidence of the discriminant validity of the two postulated dimensions of mathematical giftedness. No significant causal relationships were found among the four component concepts of the ability type dimension (i.e., general intelligence, specific academic ability in mathematics, general original creative thinking, and specific creative ability in mathematics) and the four component concepts of the hierarchical ability level dimension (i.e., nongifted, mild, moderate, and profound). The correlation coefficients ranged between .001 and .19. These findings provided strong evidence of the construct validity of the two postulated dimensions (ability type × ability level) of the 4 × 4 model as applied to mathematics.

CONVERGENT AND DISCRIMINANT VALIDITY OF THE FOUR ABILITY TYPES

A positive unidirectional causal relationship was found between general intellectual ability and specific academic ability in mathematics. The relationship between general creative thinking and specific creative ability in mathematics as measured by both creative solutions of mathematical problems and creative out-of-school activities and accomplishments in mathematics was also positive and unidirectional. Of the two measures, the causal relationship between general creative thinking and creative solutions was significantly higher compared with out-of-school activities in mathematics (rs = .57 and .22, $p < .001$, respectively). No significant causal relationships were found between general intelligence and either general creative thinking ability or specific creative thinking ability in mathematics. Similarly, no significant causal relationships were found between specific academic ability in mathematics and either of the two creative ability types. These findings constituted good evidence of the convergent and discriminant validity of the postulated general and domain-specific intellectual and creative abilities in mathematics.

Among the alternative models compared in the study, the best fit was the hypothesized four-factor model, validating that giftedness in the domain of mathematics might be conceptualized in terms of general intellectual ability, specific academic ability in mathematics, general creative thinking, and specific creative ability in mathematics.

DISCRIMINANT VALIDITY OF THE FOUR ABILITY LEVELS

The causal relationship coefficients supported all the postulated causal relationships among the ability levels in mathematics as well. The causal relationships were all statistically significant, positive, and moderate to high in magnitude. As predicted, the intercausal relationships between each two levels diminished significantly with increasing ordinal distance between them, representing the hierarchical order between them. These findings constituted good evidence of the discriminant validity of the four hierarchical ability levels in mathematics.

To determine whether the four hierarchical ability levels (nongifted, mild, moderate, and profound) in mathematics represented distinct levels that could be empirically supported, seven alternative models were compared with the current four level estimated (null) model (Bollen 1989; Bollen & Long, 1993; Hair et al., 1995; Hoyle & Panter, 1995). The findings indicated that the null model provided evidence of a significantly better fit to the data compared with the alternative models. These findings provided solid evidence of validity for the four distinct and hierarchical ability levels that were postulated by the 4×4 model.

DISCUSSION

The major finding reported in this chapter is that creativity in mathematics is *both* a general and a domain-specific ability. On the one hand, the findings constitute impressive evidence for the domain-specific view of creativity in mathematics. On the other hand, the findings support the conceptualization of creative thinking as a general ability evident in mathematics and probably in a wide variety of other domains.

The data reported here were based on a study conducted on a very large, representative sample of research participants, using advanced structural equation modeling (SEM; Bollen & Long, 1993) technique (Livne, 2002). The instruments were carefully constructed, highly reliable, and characterized by excellent construct validity. Accordingly, the data that resulted from the SEM analyses, indicating that general creative thinking ability and specific creative problem-solving ability in mathematics were empirically distinguishable, provide strong support for the domain-specific position. On the other hand, general creative thinking—an ability frequently operationally defined as ideational fluency—was found to be strongly related to the ability to generate creative solutions to problems in mathematics. When the criterion for specific creative thinking ability in mathematics was solving problems that offered the possibility of generating more than one correct answer at varying levels of quality of solution, the relationship between general creative thinking ability and creative thinking ability in mathematics was strong. On the basis of these data one can conclude that the ability to generate a large number of ideas, some of which are unusual and of high quality, in the process of general problem solving contributes to the production of creative (i.e., unusual and high-quality) solutions to problems in mathematics. These findings support the conceptualization of creativity in mathematics as an example of a general ability.

In effect, the findings support the conceptualization of creativity in mathematics as *both* a general and a domain-specific ability. The percentages of explained variance between divergent thinking as the predictor and the two indexes of creativity in mathematics used in the current study were 33% and 5% for the creative solutions index and the creative activities index, respectively. The difference between the percentages of explained variance for the two indexes can be explained in terms of the degree to which each index represents real-world behavior. The more the index of creative ability in mathematics—in this instance, the creative solutions index—resembles real-world problem-solving behavior in mathematics, the better it is predicted by general creative thinking.

These data document the important contribution of general ideational fluency ability to creativity in mathematics. However, they also clearly indicate that creative thinking ability alone is *not enough*. Many other general cognitive abilities certainly contribute to the creative process. For example, curiosity, fantasy, imagery, problem finding, metaphoric production, and selective attention deployment have been cited as components of general creative thinking. Undoubtedly, there are many others as well. Accordingly, one reasonable interpretation of the data presented here is that it provides support for Milgram's (1990) view that general creative thinking ability is *necessary*, but *not sufficient*, to explain domain-specific creativity in a wide variety of domains, including mathematics.

Three practical applications emerge from this research. One application is for mathematics education. Measures of both general creative thinking and specific creative ability in mathematics could be profitably added, in addition to IQ scores and school grades, to selection batteries of instruments used to identify mathematical talent. Using measures of all the four ability types and all four levels would lead to more effective identification of pupils with a wide range of abilities, and would help these students to realize their abilities in mathematics. Moreover, in order to best identify potential completely mathematical abilities, it is desirable to assess both academic and creative abilities.

The Multiscale Academic and Creative Abilities in Mathematics and the Tel Aviv Activities and Accomplishments Inventory: Mathematics are useful psychometric instruments for identifying the four different types of mathematical abilities at each of the four levels. The scores on these instruments could be used to guide teachers in tailoring curricula and teaching strategies to match each pupil's individual needs. For example, a curriculum could take the form of computerized units for individual instruction matched to type and level of ability.

The second practical application of the findings is psychometric. The two-stage technique for instrument development reported here could serve as a prototype for developing measures of the cognitive processes of domain-specific creative thinking in a wide variety of domains in addition to mathematics. The first stage refers to the development of a mapping sentence that provided a detailed key for the development of test items, and the second stage to development of theoretical scoring guidelines and an operational scoring guide based on these guidelines. Both stages would be useful in many other domains, such as science, technology, or the arts.

Finally, there is a methodological application that follows from the results reported in this chapter. Many theories of creativity appear in the professional literature (Cohen & Ambrose, 1993; Gardner, 1993; Horowitz & O'Brien, 1985; Runco & Albert, 1990; Sternberg & Davidson, 1986). However, the empirical research conducted to investigate the validity of these theories is sparse indeed. The structural equation modeling used in the current study can be used to assess the construct validity of other multidimensional theoretical models of creativity and the instruments designed to operationally define their component concepts.

To sum up, our findings indicate that creativity in mathematics is both a general and a domain-specific ability. The evidence reported here supports the position held by Amabile (1996), Anderson, Reder, and Simon (1996), and Conti, Coon, and Amabile (1996), who argue for both domain-general and domain-specific creative thinking skills as important in creative performance in particular domains. It seems reasonable to assume that general creative thinking ability plays a similar important role in creativity in many and probably all other specific domains. This assumption, however, must be investigated separately for each domain.

REFERENCES

Amabile, T. M. (1983a). The social psychology of creativity: A componential conceptualization. *Journal of Personality and Social Psychology, 45*, 357–376.
Amabile, T. M. (1983b). *The social psychology of creativity.* New York: Springer-Verlag.
Amabile, T. M. (1996). *Creativity in context: Update to the social psychology of creativity.* Boulder, CO: Westview.
Anderson, J. R., Reder, L. M., & Simon, H. A. (1996). Situated learning and education. *Educational Researcher, 25*(4), 5–11.
Baer, J. (1993, December/January). Why you shouldn't trust creativity tests. *Educational Leadership,* 80–83.
Baer, J. (1998). The case for domain specificity in creativity. *Creativity Research Journal, 11*, 173–177.
Barron, F., & Harrington, D. M. (1981). Creativity, intelligence and personality. *Annual Review of Psychology, 32*, 439–476.
Bentler, P. M. (1997). *EQS structural equations program manual.* Encino, CA: Multivariate Software, Inc.
Bollen, K. A. (1989). *Structural equations with latent variables.* New York: Wiley.
Bollen, K. A., & Long, J. S. (1993). *Testing structural equation models.* Newbury Park, CA: Sage.

Brown, W. (1910). Some experimental results in the correlation of mental abilities. *British Journal of Psychology, 3*, 296–322.
Byrne, B. M. (1994). *Structural equation modeling with EQS and EQS/Windows: Basic concepts, applications, and programming.* Newbury Park, CA: Sage.
Christiaans, H. H. C. M. (2002). Creativity as a design criterion. *Creativity Research Journal, 14*(1), 41–54.
Cohen, L. A., & Ambrose, D. C. (1993). Theories and practices of differentiated education for the gifted and talented. In K. A. Heller, F. J. Mönks, & A. H. Passon (Eds.), *International handbook of research and development of giftedness and talent* (pp. 336–364). Oxford, UK: Pergamon.
Conti, R., Coon, H., & Amabile, T. M. (1996). Evidence to support the componential model of creativity: Secondary analyses of three studies. *Creativity Research Journal, 9*, 385–389.
EQS for Windows 5.7 [Computer software]. (1997). User interface Copyright © 1992–1997.
Feldman, D. H. (1986). *Nature's gambit: Child prodigies and the development of human potential.* New York: Basic Books.
Gardner, H. (1983). *Frames of mind: The theory of multiple intelligence.* New York: Basic Books.
Gardner, H. (1988). Creative lives and creative works: A synthetic scientific approach. In R. J. Sternberg (Ed.), *The nature of creativity* (pp. 298–321). New York: Cambridge University Press.
Gardner, H. (1993). *Multiple intelligences: The theory in practice.* New York: Basic Books.
Glanz, I. (1996). *CHEMED: A comprehensive testing battery.* Barak: Information Processing, Tel Aviv.
Gruber, H. E., & Davis, S. N. (1988). Inching our way up Mount Olympus: The evolving-systems approach to creative thinking. In R. J. Sternberg (Ed.), *The nature of creativity* (pp. 243–270). New York: Cambridge University Press.
Guilford, J. P. (1950). Creativity. *American Psychologist, 5*, 444–454.
Guilford, J. P. (1956). The structure of intellect. *Psychological Bulletin, 53*, 267–293.
Guilford, J. P. (1967). *The nature of human intelligence.* New York: McGraw-Hill.
Guttman, L. (1968). A general nonmetric technique for finding the smallest coordinate space for a configuration of points. *Psychometrika, 33*, 469–506.
Guttman, L. (1971). Measurement as structural theory. *Psychometrika, 36*, 329–347.
Guttman, L. (1991). *Louis Guttman on facet theory: Excerpts from unfinished writings.* Jerusalem: The Israel Academy of Science and Humanities and the Hebrew University of Jerusalem.
Hair, J. F., Jr., Anderson, R. E., Tatham, R. L., & Black, W. C. (1995). *Multivariate data analysis with readings* (4th ed.). Englewood Cliffs, NJ: Prentice-Hall.
Hocevar, D. (1979). Ideational fluency as a confounding factor in the measurement of originality. *Journal of Educational Psychology, 71*, 191–196.
Hocevar, D., & Bachelor, P. (1989). A taxonomy and critique of measurements used in the study of creativity. In J. A. Glover, R. R. Ronning, & C. R. Reynolds (Eds.), *Handbook of creativity* (pp. 53–75). New York: Plenum.
Hocevar, D., & Michael, W. B. (1979). The effects of scoring formulas on the discriminant validity of tests of divergent thinking. *Educational and Psychological Measurement, 39*, 917–921.
Hong, E., & Milgram, R. M. (1996). The structure of giftedness: The domain of literature as an exemplar. *Gifted Child Quarterly, 40*, 31–40.
Horowitz, F. D., & O'Brien, M. (Eds.). (1985). *The gifted and talented: Developmental perspectives.* Washington, DC: American Psychological Association.
Hoyle, R. H. (Ed.). (1995). *Structural equation modeling: Concepts, issues, and application.* Newbury Park, CA: Sage.
Hoyle, R. H., & Panter, A. T. (1995). Writing about structural equation models. In R. H. Hoyle (Ed.), *Structural equation modeling: Concepts, issues, and applications* (pp. 1–16). Newbury Park, CA: Sage.

Kaufman, J. C. (2002). Dissecting the golden goose: Components of studying creative writers. *Creativity Research Journal, 14*(1), 27–40.

Kogan, N. (2002). Careers in the performing arts: A psychological perspective. *Creativity Research Journal, 14*(1), 1–16.

Kogan, N., & Pankove, E. (1974). Long-term predictive validity of divergent-thinking tests: Some negative evidence. *Journal of Educational Psychology, 66,* 802–810.

Kuder, G. F., & Richardson, M. W. (1937). The theory of estimation of test reliability. *Psychometrica, 2,* 151–160.

Livne, N. L. (2002). *Giftedness as a bi-dimensional phenomenon: Theoretical definition and psychometric assessment of levels of academic and levels of creative abilities in mathematics.* Unpublished doctoral dissertation, Tel Aviv University, School of Education, Ramat Aviv, Israel.

Livne, N. L., & Livne, O. E. (1999a). *Multiscale academic and creative abilities in mathematics (MACAM).* Ramat Aviv, Israel: Tel Aviv University, School of Education.

Livne, N. L., & Livne, O. E. (1999b). *A scoring guide for the multiscale academic and creative abilities in mathematics (MACAM).* Ramat Aviv, Israel: Tel Aviv University, School of Education.

Livne, N. L., Livne, O. E., & Milgram, R. M. (1999). Assessing academic and creative abilities in mathematics at four levels of understanding. *Journal of Mathematical Education in Science and Technology, 30*(2), 227–242.

Livne, N. L., & Milgram, R. M. (1999). *Tel Aviv activities and accomplishments inventory: Mathematics.* Ramat Aviv, Israel: Tel Aviv University, School of Education.

Livne, N. L., & Milgram, R. M. (2000). Assessing four levels of creative mathematical ability in Israeli adolescents utilizing out-of-school activities: A circular three-stage technique. *Roeper Review: A Journal on Gifted Education, 22*(2), 111–116.

Messick, S. (1995). Validity of psychological assessment: Validation of inferences from person's responses and performances as scientific inquiry into score meaning. *American Psychologist, 50*(9), 741–749.

Milgram, R. M. (Ed.). (1989). *Teaching gifted and talented children learners in regular classrooms.* Springfield, IL: Charles C. Thomas.

Milgram, R. M. (1990). Creativity: An idea whose time has come and gone? In M. A. Runco & R. S. Albert (Eds.), *Theories of creativity* (pp. 215–233). Newbury Park, CA: Sage.

Milgram, R. M. (1991). *Counseling gifted and talented children: A guide for teachers, counselors, and parents.* Norwood, NJ: Ablex.

Milgram, R. M., & Arad, R. (1981). Ideational fluency as a predictor of original problem-solving. *Journal of Educational Psychology, 73,* 568–572.

Milgram, R. M., & Feldman, N. O. (1979). Creativity as a predictor of teacher effectiveness. *Psychological Reports, 45,* 899–903.

Milgram, R. M., & Milgram, N. A. (1976a). *Tel Aviv creativity test (TACT).* Ramat Aviv, Israel: Tel Aviv University, School of Education.

Milgram, R. M., & Milgram, N. A. (1976b). Creative thinking and creative performance in Israeli children. *Journal of Educational Psychology, 68,* 255–259.

Milgram, R. M., Milgram, R. M., Rosenbloom, G., & Rabkin, L. (1978). Quantity and quality of creative thinking in children and adolescents. *Child Development, 49,* 385–388.

Milgram, R. M., & Rabkin, L. (1980). A developmental test of Mednick's associative hierarchies of original thinking. *Developmental Psychology, 16,* 157–158.

Plucker, J. A. (1998). Beware of simple conclusions: The case for the content generality of creativity. *Creativity Research Journal, 11,* 179–182.

Plucker, J. A., & Renzulli, J. S. (1999). Psychometric approaches to the study of human creativity. In R. J. Sternberg (Ed.), *Handbook of creativity* (pp. 35–61). New York: Cambridge University Press.

Plucker, J. A., & Runco, M. A. (1998). The death of creativity measurement has been greatly exaggerated: Current issues, recent advances, and future directions in creativity assessment. *Roeper Review: A Journal on Gifted Education, 21*(1), 36–40.

Raven, J., Raven, J. C., & Court, J. H. (1998). *Manual for Raven's Advanced Progressive Matrices and Vocabulary Scales: Section 4.* Oxford Psychologist Press.
Raven, J. C. M.Sc. (1962). *Advanced progressive matrices—APM SET II.* London: H. K. Lewis.
Runco, M. A., & Albert, R. S. (Eds.). (1990). *Theories of creativity.* Newbury Park, CA: Sage.
Satorra, A., & Bentler, P. M. (1988). Scaling corrections for chi-square statistics in covariance structure analysis. *Proceeding of American Statistical Association,* 308–313.
Satorra, A., & Bentler, P. M. (1994). Corrections to test statistics and standard errors in covariance structure analysis. In A. von Eye & C. C. Clogg (Eds.), *Latent variables analysis: Application for developmental research* (pp. 399–419). Thousand Oaks, CA: Sage.
Spearman, C. (1910). Correlation calculated from faculty data. *British Journal of Psychology, 3,* 271–295.
Sprites, P., Glymour, L., & Scheines, R. (1993). *Causation, prediction and search.* New York: Springer-Verlag.
Sternberg, R. J. (1988). *The nature of creativity: Contemporary psychological perspectives.* New York: Cambridge University Press.
Sternberg, R. J., & Davidson, J. E. (Eds.). (1986). *Conceptions of giftedness.* New York: Cambridge University Press.
Tannenbaum, A. J. (1983). *Gifted children: Psychological and educational perspectives.* New York: Macmillan.
Tannenbaum, A. J. (1986). Giftedness: A psychosocial approach. In R. J. Sternberg & J. E. Davidson (Eds.), *Conceptions of giftedness* (pp. 21–52). New York: Cambridge University Press.
Wallach, M. A. (1970). Creativity. In P. H. Mussen (Ed.), *Carmichael's manual of child psychology, vol. 1* (3rd ed., pp. 1211–1272).
Wallach, M. A. (1971). *The intelligence/creativity distinction.* Morristown, NJ: General Learning Press.
Wallach, M. A. (1985). Creativity testing and giftedness. In F. D. Horowitz & M. O'Brien (Eds.), *The gifted and talented: Developmental perspectives* (pp. 99–123). Washington, DC: American Psychological Association.
Wallach, M. A., & Kogan, N. (1965). *Modes of thinking in young children: A study of the creativity-intelligence distinction.* New York: Holt, Rinehart & Winston.
Wallach, M. A., & Wing, C. W., Jr. (1969). *The talented student: A validation of the creativity-intelligence distinction.* New York: Holt, Rinehart, & Winston.
Weisberg, R. W. (1993). *Creativity: Beyond the myth of genius.* New York: W. H. Freeman.

Chapter 12

Creative Problem-Solving Skills in Leadership: Direction, Actions, and Reactions[1]

Michael D. Mumford
Jill M. Strange
Gina Marie Scott
Blaine P. Gaddis
The University of Oklahoma

Few people would dispute the statement that Winston Churchill was a leader. Through his actions before and during World War II, Churchill exercised a powerful influence over the course of 20th-century history. Lost in the pages of history texts, however, is "another" Churchill—one whose behavior was aptly summarized in a quote drawn from Jenkins' (2001) biography: "Once a week or oftener, Mr. Churchill came into the office bringing with him some adventurous or impossible projects; but after half an hour's discussion something evolved which was still adventurous but not impossible" (p. 129). Apparently, Churchill was not just a leader but an unusually creative person as well. Biographies of Benjamin Franklin (Brands, 2000), George Washington (Ellis, 2001), Theodore Roosevelt (Morris, 1979), and J. P. Morgan (Strouse, 1999) all make a similar point. Historically, notable leaders have tended to be highly creative people.

If the historic record so clearly impresses us with the creativity of notable leaders, one must ask why has the role of creative thinking skills in leadership received what is, at best, scant attention (Mumford & Connelly, 1999)? One answer to this question may be found in our stereotypic conception of

---

[1]We would like to thank Shane Connelly, Fran Yammarino, and Steve Zaccaro for various discussions contributing to the ideas presented here. Parts of this effort were supported by a series of grants from the United States Department of Defense, Michael D. Mumford, Principal Investigator. Correspondence should be addressed to Dr. Michael D. Mumford, Department of Psychology, The University of Oklahoma, Norman, OK 73019.

the creative act. Following the romantic tradition (Abra, 1995; Eisenberger & Shanock, 2003), scholars have, more often than not, seen creativity as an autonomous act in which individual genius must struggle against the forces of social order. Given this image, it is easy to conclude that leaders, as people who must direct and structure the work of others, are not only unlikely to exhibit creativity but they may, in fact, be the ultimate enemy of the creative person. In this chapter, however, we apply a functional perspective to argue that leaders are not the enemies of creativity but, instead, rely on creative problem-solving skills as a basis for effective performance.

Another answer to the question posed earlier—Why do we discount the role of creative thinking skills in leader performance?—may be found in the ways in which leaders express creativity. Traditionally, students of creativity have sought to define, and frame, studies of creativity with respect to uniquely identifiable products (e.g., Mumford & Gustafson, 1988), often products whose "authorship" can be attributed to a single individual (e.g., Gruber & Wallace, 1999). Of course, leaders' creative efforts involve others interacting on complex projects unfolding over substantial periods of time. As a result, it becomes difficult to isolate the leaders' unique contribution (Mumford, 2002). Because, moreover, leaders work with and through others in producing new ideas, new procedures, new products, and new systems (Damanpour, 1991), the skills leaders rely on may be different than those found in other domains of creative work, both in the emphasis placed on certain skills and the type of creative problem-solving skills needed (Lubart, 2001; Mumford, 2002; Mumford & Connelly, 1991). Accordingly, in this chapter we examine in some detail the nature of these skills with respect to three key leadership functions: direction, actions, and reactions.

DIRECTION

Problem Solving

Although a number of different models have been used to understand leader emergence and performance (Bass, 1990; Dansereau & Yammarino, 1998; Yukl, 2001), most models converge on one key point: Ultimately, leaders must direct and structure the activities of group members so as to ensure the maintenance of the group and the attainment of organizational goals (Hackman & Walton, 1986; Katz & Kahn, 1978). This traditional and rather straightforward definition of the leader's job has an important, albeit commonly overlooked, implication: A leader's direction is required when group members must address complex, ill-defined problems (Mumford, Zaccaro, Connelly, & Marks, 2000; Mumford, Zaccaro, Harding, Jacobs, & Fleishman, 2000). Thus, leaders must coach people in solving problems, they must identify the goals to be pursued by the group, and they must determine the "best" ways to achieve these goals. Moreover, because organizational environments are turbulent—involving changes in people, technology, and markets—the complex, ill-defined problems confronting the group are often novel problems for which leaders must formulate an adaptive response to change (Jaques, 1976; Tushman & O'Reilly, 1997).

These observations, of course, imply that in directing people leaders must address the kind of complex, novel, ill-defined problems that call for creative thought (Lubart, 2001). As a result, one would expect that creative problem-solving skills would play an important role in shaping leader performance by enabling requisite directive activities. Indeed, evidence pointing to the importance of creative problem-solving skills in this regard has been provided by studies of divergent thinking, or idea generation, skills (Mumford, Peterson, & Childs, 1999). For example, Scratchley and Hakstain (2001) obtained measures of change initiation by some 200 managers and found that divergent thinking was an effective predictor of change initiation. Along similar lines, Bray, Campbell, and Grant (1974), Chusmir and Koberg (1986), and Mumford, Marks, Connelly, Zaccaro, and Johnson (1998) have shown that measures of divergent thinking skills are effective predictors of leader performance, producing correlations in the .20 to .40 range across multiple alternative indexes of performance even when other potential influences on leader performance (e.g., intelligence, motivation, and social skills) are taken into account.

Perhaps the most comprehensive investigation of the role of creative thinking skills in leaders' organizational problem solving, the basis for their directive activities, may be found in a series of studies conducted by Mumford and his colleagues (Connelly et al., 2000; Marshall-Mies et al., 2000; Mumford, Marks, Connelly, Zaccaro, & Reiter-Palmon, 2000; Mumford, Zaccaro, Johnson, et al., 2000; Zaccaro, Mumford, Connelly, Marks, & Gilbert, 2000). In this series of studies, the creative problem-solving skills of 1,818 Army officers, ranging in grade from Second Lieutenant (roughly 30 subordinates) to Full Colonel (roughly 2,000 subordinates) were assessed using a complex military combat scenario involving an invasion of a hostile country. These officers were to assume the role of the Army commander and answer a series of probe questions indicating how they would approach this situation. These probe questions were devised to assess the creative problem-solving skills identified by Mumford, Mobley, Uhlman, Reiter-Palmon, and Doares (1991): problem construction, information encoding, category search, category selection, conceptual combination and idea generation, idea evaluation, implementation planning, and monitoring.

In addition to this measure of creative problem-solving skills, four measures of leader performance were obtained. These performance measures examined organizational problem solving, critical incident performance, and objective achievement (e.g., medals won) as well as attained rank. In a series of correlational and regression analyses, it was found that these skill indexes would predict performance on all of the criterion measures, including objective achievement, as well as organizational problem solving and critical incident performance, typically yielding correlations in the .40s. However, certain skills were found to be more important for more senior, as opposed to more junior, leaders—a result attributable to the greater complexity and novelty of the problems confronting people in more senior leadership positions (Yukl, 2001).

In this regard, the findings obtained in the Mumford, Marks, et al. (2000) study are particularly noteworthy. In this study, changes in creative problem-solving skills were assessed as people moved from junior to mid-level and from mid-level to more senior positions. The results obtained in a series of discriminant analyses indicated that, as leaders moved into more senior positions, two skills—problem construction and idea evaluation—showed particularly large increases. This finding suggested that problem construction and idea evaluation may be particularly important skills for leaders. Some support for this proposition was provided by Farris (1972) in a study examining the conditions under which research and development personnel were likely to communicate with their managers. In accordance with observations concerning the importance of problem construction and idea evaluation skills, he found that contact was highest during initial definition of the problem and after an idea, or potential problem solution, had been formulated.

Problem construction activities represent an attempt to define the problem and frame problem-solving activities, with this frame exerting a profound influence on the nature of subsequent solutions (Getzels & Csikszentmihalyi, 1976; Okuda, Runco, & Berger, 1991; Redmond, Mumford, & Teach, 1993; Rostan, 1994). In problem construction, a search and screening of available representations is used to identify goals, procedures for use in problem solving, restrictions, and key information to be considered (Mumford, Baughman, Threlfall, Supinski, & Costanza, 1996; Reiter-Palmon, Mumford, Boes, & Runco, 1997). Accordingly, as more time is spent analyzing alternative representations, performance improves. Moreover, with experience (especially diverse experience), performance improves by providing a range of relevant representations. The goals, procedures, and restrictions abstracted from these representations, in turn, allow leaders to structure people's work without placing undue limitations on their autonomy. Moreover, the goals specified and restrictions identified provide leaders with a basis for integrating followers' problem-solving efforts with both other group activities and broader organizational concerns.

Idea evaluation has received less attention in studies of creativity than has problem construction (Runco & Chand, 1994). It is clear, however, that creative problem solutions, by virtue of their novelty, will prove difficult to evaluate (Sharma, 1999). Accordingly, effective evaluation will require the creative problem-solving skills needed to recognize viable new ideas (Basadur, Runco, & Vega, 2000). From the perspective of leaders, however, evaluative activities provide a basis not only for deciding whether an idea is worth pursuing, but also for extending and revising initial ideas to enhance their value within the setting at hand (Barlow, 2000; Lubart, 2001). In fact, leaders' idea evaluation efforts appear to enhance performance particularly when the leader points out flaws or alternative hypotheses, encourages elaboration of an initial idea, seeks to integrate alternative perspectives bearing on the idea, and examines the implications of the idea from a broader organizational standpoint (Lubart, 1994; Maier & McRay, 1972; Schwenk & Crozier, 1980).

Vision

Although it appears that problem construction and idea evaluation represent critical skills needed by leaders to direct people's work, leaders must also structure the interactions occurring within the group. Group interactions, of course, might be structured using a variety of different strategies. For example, to generate new ideas, it may be useful to increase the diversity of the group and the projects being pursued (Murmann & Tushman, 1997; Pelz & Andrews, 1976). Alternatively, establishing a flat, organic structure with clear output expectations appears to contribute to creativity and innovation (Cardinal, 2001). In discussions of leadership, however, the structure underlying group members' interactions is commonly held to be tied to the leader's vision (Bass, 1985; Dunham & Freeman, 2000).

Vision refers to an image of the future that specifies an idealized end state for the group or organization. This image of an idealized future not only serves to motivate followers by providing meaning, placing followers' activities in a larger context (Conger & Kanungo, 1998; Shamir, House, & Arthur, 1993), it also provides an overarching structure guiding project selection, decision making, the definition of group norms, and acceptable patterns of interpersonal relationships (Jacobsen & House, 2001). In fact, studies by Howell and Avolio (1993), Kirkpatrick and Locke (1996), Lowe, Koreck, and Sivasubamaniam (1996), and Sosik, Kahai, and Avolio (1998, 1999) indicated that a leader's articulation of an evocative vision is a powerful influence on group performance and perceived leader effectiveness.

Although a number of studies have looked at the impact of vision on leader performance, studies examining the origins of vision have been few and far between. A notable exception to this general trend may be found in Strange and Mumford (2002) and Mumford and Strange (2002). These authors argued that visions are based on a mental model of how an organizational system operates. Reflection on this mental model, in relation to personal values and perceived social needs, allows leaders to abstract the key goals that should be pursued by an organization and the key causes influencing goal attainment. These key goals and key causes are used to construct a prescriptive mental model describing an idealized organization that, with feedback, provides the basis for emergence of a vision.

Mumford and Strange (2002) and Strange and Mumford (2002) provided some support for this model by showing that it can be used to account for behavioral differences observed among ideological and charismatic leaders—leadership styles that both, in one form or another, rely on vision. Other studies by Ellis (2001) and Thomas and McDaniel (1990) supplied evidence for certain key tenets of this model. For example, in a study of hospital chief executive officers, Thomas and McDaniel (1990) found that CEOs based their decisions on a limited number of key goals and key causes. Ellis (2001), moreover, showed that the vision articulated in George Washington's "Farewell Address" emerged from reflection on the events that led to American success in the Revolutionary War.

These observations about the origins of a leader's vision are noteworthy because vision formation may be the most powerful manifestation of creative thought on the part of leaders. However, these observations are also significant because they point to certain creative thinking skills needed by leaders. To begin, this model of vision formation hinges on the notion that leaders must be able to abstract key causes and key goals from a complex dynamic system. This observation in turn suggests that leaders need two key skills: penetration and systems thinking. *Penetration* refers to the leader's ability to abstract key causes and goals. In fact, prior research by Kettner, Guilford, and Christensen (1959) demonstrated the importance of this skill in some creative efforts. *Systems thinking* refers to the leader's ability to identify and articulate complex causal relationships emerging over time (Maccoby, 2001). Within this framework, systems thinking provides a basis for generating requisite descriptive and prescriptive mental models. In fact, Drazin, Glynn, and Kazanjian (1999) and Kazanjian, Drazin, and Glynn (2000), in a study of leaders' contributions to large complex technical development projects (e.g., building a new airplane), found that leaders' sensemaking activities, an activity contingent on penetration and systems thinking, represents a crucial influence on group performance.

In addition to penetration and systems thinking, these observations about vision formation suggest that leaders may need another set of skills. More specifically, the need for self-reflection, and the need to frame goals in terms of broader organizational and social concerns, suggest that wisdom may be a necessary component of leadership. Indeed, in their study of the skills linked to leader performance among Army officers, Connelly et al. (2000) and Mumford, Marks, et al. (2000) found that wisdom-related skills, as assessed using a social judgment task, were related to indexes of leader performance. Three facets of wisdom—reflection, judgment, and appraisal of solution fit—proved to be particularly important in more senior leadership positions.

ACTIONS

Planning

Unlike creativity in other domains, for leaders it is not enough to "simply" generate new ideas. Instead, leadership requires the introduction of new ideas within the social system under consideration (Mumford, Scott, Gaddis, & Strange, 2002). In fact, one might argue that the "value added" that leaders bring to creative efforts is their ability to organize action to ensure the development of innovative products. We often assume, following the romantic tradition, that the actions that guide innovation (product production) require little or no creative thought, involving only substantial expertise and the ability to get things done in an organization (Vincent, Decker, & Mumford, 2002). However, one must remember that innovation occurs in a complex, dynamic organizational environment in which successful introduction of a new idea is by no means ensured (Quinn, 1989). As a result, implementation will present a number of novel problems—problems that the leader must solve and problems that may call for substantial creative thinking skills.

In complex organizational systems, the successful introduction of a new idea depends on the coordination of people, resources, and technology (Dougherty & Hardy, 1996; Drazin & Schoonhoven, 1996). The coordination of people, resources, and technology in idea implementation, of course, implies that planning will be required (Castrogiovani, 1996; Dean & Sharfman, 1996). Planning, the historic prerogative of leaders (Yukl, 2001), has unfortunately often been seen as little more than a simple lock-step implementation of a set of predefined action scripts (e.g., Miller, Galanter, & Pribram, 1960; Schank & Abelson, 1977). More recent work, however, indicates that planning is inherently an active, conscious, constructive activity guiding action on complex, ill-defined tasks (Mumford, Schultz, & Osburn, 2002; Patalano & Seifert, 1997; Xiao, Milgram, & Doyle, 1997).

Although multiple models of planning have been proposed over the years (Mumford, Schultz, & VanDoorn, 2001), planning appears best described as a process of envisioning action. It begins with an analysis of the environment and the idea, to identify past cases that might be used to provide a template for understanding performance requirements in the situation at hand (Hammond, 1990). This initial template is then used to identify the key causes, restrictions, resources, and contingencies that might influence performance (Xiao et al., 1997). With formation of the initial plan, it becomes possible for people to forecast, or project, the consequences of plan implementation within the particular setting (Doerner & Schaub, 1994). These projected outcomes are then used as a basis for plan revision and the formation of backup plans needed to handle various contingencies (Kuipers, Moskowitz, & Kassinger, 1988; Xiao et al., 1997). This revised plan, or one or more of the backup plans, are then implemented in an opportunistic fashion (Hayes-Roth & Hayes-Roth, 1979).

This thumbnail sketch of planning processes is noteworthy because it suggests that certain creative thinking skills will play a role in leaders' planning efforts. Perhaps the most clear-cut implication of this model pertains to the need for divergent thinking. Leaders, in planning, must identify *multiple* resources, restrictions, contingencies, and potential influences on performance—often constructing plans in such a way as to offset unworkable contingencies, resource deficiencies, or inappropriate restrictions. Of course, the identification of multiple influences of this sort will require divergent thinking. Indeed, one might argue that one of the reasons divergent thinking measures are consistently related to leader performance (e.g., Bray et al., 1974; Chusmir & Koberg, 1986; Scratchley & Hakstain, 2001) is that divergent thinking provides a basis for identifying a wider range of potential influences on plan implementation.

By the same token, however, the role of divergent thinking in planning suggests that leaders' expression of divergent thinking skills may differ from those of people in general. Some evidence supporting this point was provided by Mumford, Marks, et al. (1998). They scored a consequences test (a standard measure of divergent thinking) for attributes of consequences—such as time frame, realism, and complexity—expressly relevant to leaders' planning activities, and found that this domain-specific scoring resulted in better prediction of leader performance. Along similar lines, one might expect, given the nature of leaders' planning activities, that scoring divergent thinking tests for planning attributes, such as the restrictions and contingencies implied, might also prove to be of value.

In addition to divergent thinking, there is also reason to suspect that leaders' creative efforts will call for substantial forecasting skills. In a series of exploratory factor analytic investigations, Berger, Guilford, and Christensen (1957) and Merrifield, Guilford, Christensen, and Frick (1962) obtained evidence for the existence of forecasting as a distinct aspect of creative thought. This factor was defined by tests in which people were asked to suggest improvements in social institutions, identify the questions to be asked in reaching a decision, and list the conditions calling for use of an object. What should be recognized here, however, is that leaders' forecasting activities may be rather complex, because leaders need to apply a relatively long time frame in making forecasts (Jaques, 1976); incorporate multiple, nonlinear relationships (Doerner & Schaub, 1994); find an appropriate balance of positive and negative outcomes (Mumford, Schultz, & Osburn, 2002); and take a range of different outcomes into account (Quinn, 1989).

The complex nature of leaders' forecasting activities reflect the nature of the environment in which plans are implemented. Given the complexity and ambiguity of organizational environments, it can be expected that both cognitive complexity and flexibility will be needed in planning. In fact, the need for and capability to move to backup plans also underscores the need for these skills. In complex organizational environments, however, there are many risks and ambiguities associated with plan implementation, whereas plans may well threaten others when they are to be implemented in a competitive social context. This apparently straightforward observation has two noteworthy implications for the creative problem-solving skills needed by leaders. First, leaders, in planning, must avoid negative organizational outcomes suggesting that a skeptical, critical evaluation of plans may be required, with leaders asking what is the worst that could happen. Second, because leaders must envision and manage other reactions to their plans, leaders' creative thinking will necessarily involve an element of social gaming. Although there is reason to suspect that social gaming and critical evaluation, often based on worst-case scenarios, are necessary skills for leaders (Kuhn & Kuhn, 1991), these topics have not traditionally received the attention they warrant.

Plan Implementation

Plans, of course, however valuable, are useful only if they can be successfully implemented. In turbulent multifaceted organizational environments, plans are not implemented in a lock-step fashion but instead appear to be implemented opportunistically (Finkelstein, 2002; Hayes-Roth & Hayes-Roth, 1979). The term *opportunistic*, although an apt description of leaders' plan implementation (Bluedorn, 2002), may not fully convey the dynamics that surround a leader's attempt to put plans into action. Mintzberg (1975), in a quantitative study of managers' day-to-day planning activities, found that plans tend to be implemented in a piecemeal fashion over time, as managers go about dealing with a host of different demands. Moreover, plans and plan implementation activities appear to be updated and revised "on line"[2] to take into account emerging opportunities and handle the unforeseen problems likely to occur in any complex system (Drazin et al., 1999).

---

[2] In this discussion, "on line" means during implementation; it has nothing to do with the Internet in this context.

Although this description of plan implementation rings true, it has a number of noteworthy implications, not only for planning activities but also the kind of creative thinking skills evidenced by leaders. Perhaps the most unambiguous conclusion emerging from Mintzberg's (1975) observations is that, during plan implementation, leaders will not typically have the attentional and cognitive resources needed for in-depth analysis of the implications of various decisions. As Isenberg (1986, 1991) and Kaufmann (1991) pointed out, this temporal pressure not only requires leaders to be able to manage stress, it also places a premium on prior planning as a vehicle to permit rapid "on-line" decisions. In fact, Noice (1991), like Berger et al. (1957), argued that the significance of elaboration, or imaging the implications of plan implementation, is that it provides a way of constructing a pool of available action scripts for "on-line" plan implementation.

Elaboration, no matter how extensive, cannot cover every contingency likely to be encountered in plan implementation. The need to rapidly adjust plans, under conditions in which time and attentional resources are lacking, suggests that intuition (the use of low demand associational reasoning, as opposed to active, conscious processing) may play a critical role in leaders' problem-solving efforts (Mumford & Gustafson, in press; Policastro, 1995). Some support for this proposition has been provided by studies of executives conducted by Agor (1991) and Isenberg (1991). In interviews with executives, and observations of their actions, these authors found that decisions with respect to plan implementation were often based on intuition. Leaders' effective use of intuition, moreover, appeared to depend on an open, nonpredetermined approach to available information; attention to unexpected, surprising information; the rapid construction of associational linkages; awareness, and active monitoring, of effective markers; and sufficient experience with people, the work, and the organization to provide the tacit knowledge needed for viable associational networks (Mintzberg, 1991; Mumford, 1998; Mumford & Gustafson, in press; Reber, 1989).

Although intuition appears necessary for leaders when implementing, and potentially formulating, plans in complex dynamic systems, it is unlikely to prove of value in responding to problems in plan implementation unless two conditions are met. First, the leader must be actively seeking information bearing on the status of the plan implementation. Second, the leader must be sensitive to or aware of the implications of this information, especially negative information, for plan implementation. In fact, evidence is available indicating that both information monitoring and problem sensitivity represent noteworthy skills involved in leader performance. For example, Komaki, Deselles, and Bowman (1989), in a study of team leaders, found that more-effective leaders engaged in an active monitoring of critical performance markers, often identifying these monitoring benchmarks as part of their initial plan. Along somewhat different lines, Fleishman and Quantance (1984), as well as Mumford (2001), provided evidence that problem sensitivity is needed by leaders. Mumford (2001), however, noted that leaders are most likely to attend to and identify emergent problems when the signaling events are salient, multiple parties call the leaders' attention to the problem, and the parties calling the leader's attention to the problem are credible, high-status people. Thus, leaders' planning and plan implementation may be strongly influenced by social information—a point underscoring the distinctly social nature of leaders' problem-solving efforts (Zaccaro, Gilbert, Thor, & Mumford, 1991).

REACTIONS

Support

Our foregoing observations about social information alluded to a broader point: Leaders' problem solutions and plans are constructed and implemented in a distinctly social context. Resources and support must be accrued for the effort, and members of the group must be committed to the effort. The requirements for accruing support and commitment have traditionally been framed in terms of social skills and persuasion (Simonton, 1984; Zaccaro et al., 1991). However, there is reason to suspect that certain cognitive skills may also play a role in both the acquisition of support and the engagement of followers.

Hitt, Hoskisson, Johnson, and Moesel (1996) and Rodgers and Adhikurya (1979) examined the conditions that lead people to support new ideas. Broadly speaking, the findings obtained in these studies suggested that support increases when the idea is framed in terms of broader strategy, there are short-term as well as long-term benefits, the idea is consistent with existing technologies and organizational capabilities, and the idea is consistent with broader cultural values. From the perspective of a leader trying to acquire support for an idea, however, these observations suggest that the leader must have the capacity to appraise social needs.

Some support for the importance of this needs assessment skill has been provided by Mumford and VanDoorn (2001) in their examination of Benjamin Franklin's leadership style. In an analysis of 10 cases of outstanding leadership exhibited by Franklin, they found that his ability to identify and appeal to the common social good was a key determinant of the success of his efforts in establishing public libraries, a police force, fire departments, and a public hospital. Moreover, in building support for these projects, Franklin would expressly seek low-cost solutions, compatible with existing systems, illustrating their value through low-cost demonstration projects.

The Mumford and VanDoorn (2001) study, as well as studies of social innovation by Mumford (2002) and Mumford and Moertl (2003), are also of interest because they suggest another social problem-solving skill that might be involved in leaders' creative efforts. Again, this skill, one that might be referred to as *motive appraisal*, was evident in Franklin's leadership style. For example, in framing arguments for the introduction of paper currency, Franklin provided a detailed analysis of the reasons that some social groups would, and would not, find paper currency attractive. He then used this appraisal to suggest a strategy for introducing paper currency, by tying it to a land standard that would appeal to the majority of the relevant constituencies. There is reason to suspect that a motive appraisal skill may, in fact, exert a persuasive influence over leaders' creative efforts, allowing them to build requisite coalitions, acquire product champions, navigate political disputes, and establish elite support (Mumford, Scott, Gaddis, & Strange, 2002; Mumford & VanDoorn, 2001). Indeed, it is possible that one of the more significant forms of leader creativity is manifest in the use of needs assessment and motive appraisal skills to build requisite coalitions.

These observations about needs assessment and motive appraisal point to a third, and final, social-cognitive skill likely to be needed by leaders in acquiring support. Here, of course, we refer to political/negotiation skills. As Kacmar and Baron (1999) pointed out, politics and negotiation are a pervasive activity in most organizations, particularly when the organization is confronting complex, novel problems. Leaders, moreover, by virtue of expectations for representation and boundary spanning, will play a central role in political negotiations. What is of note here, however, is that the leader must, in order to manage conflict through politics and negotiation, have acquired an understanding of different groups and be able to manage disagreements in such a way to create win-win situations. Thus, politics and negotiation may call for a unique form of creative thought—one that may be as necessary in the leaders' direction of followers, especially diverse autonomous followers, as it is in acquiring support.

Engagement

Political, needs assessment, and motive appraisal skills are needed as leaders interact and manage relations with other groups, people, and institutions. Leaders, however, must also manage relations in the group they are responsible for in such a way as to maximize involvement, motivation, and performance. However, the various, often contradictory, social pressures characterizing groups place leaders in a demanding role that requires not only creative problem solving on the part of the leader but also social perceptiveness. This point was nicely illustrated in a study by Keller (2001), who found that although the use of diverse, multifunctional teams contributes to innovation in research and development groups, it also results in increased stress. Under these conditions, group performance will be maximized only if leaders attend to others' reactions and intervene at appropriate times to reduce stress.

As important as it is for leaders to manage people and their relationships through social perceptiveness and social intelligence (Dansereau & Yammarino, 1998; Zaccaro et al., 1991), leaders face another, perhaps more important, task—they must engage people in the efforts the leaders are advocating. Of course, engagement can be brought about through a variety of mechanisms, including articulation of a vision (Sosik et al., 1999), rewards (Eisenberger & Shanock, 2003), and participation (Mossholder & Dewhurst, 1980). In addition to these structural engagement techniques, however, it appears that leaders must also be able to inspire. This inspirational activity in turn appears to require a final noteworthy skill—leaders must be able to act.

Some support for this proposition may be found in a study by Feldhusen and Pleiss (1994). In this study, students participating in a youth leadership program were rated by teachers in terms of both leadership and dramatic skills. The resulting correlation between dramatic skills, acting, and leadership lay in the low .30s. Acting, of course, is a complex domain in its own right. Nonetheless, the relevance of acting skills to leadership suggests that role elaboration, anticipation of others' reactions, and effective timing of affective expression may be required of truly outstanding leaders (Noice, 1991). Indeed, when one thinks of leaders like Churchill and Roosevelt, it seems that their dramatic skills, by providing inspiration and calling attention to their vision, were a crucial influence on performance.

CONCLUSIONS

Before turning to the broader conclusions flowing from the present effort, it would seem germane to consider certain limitations inherent in the approach we took in preparing this chapter. To begin, in this chapter we have treated leadership as a general phenomenon. However, it should be recognized that a number of different styles of leadership have been identified over the years (Bass, 1990; Mumford & VanDoorn, 2001). As a result, it is likely that some of the conclusions drawn herein may vary somewhat by style. For example, it seems likely that dramatic skills are more important for visionary leaders (e.g., Winston, Churchill) than for more pragmatic leaders (e.g., George C. Marshall). Along similar lines, we have examined leadership as a general phenomenon. Thus, differences among leaders across organizational settings or hierarchical levels have not received much attention. It is possible, however, that institution type and organizational level might represent significant moderators of the relationships discussed herein (Mumford, Zaccaro, Harding, et al., 2000).

Even bearing these caveats in mind, we believe that the evidence reviewed in the present chapter has some noteworthy implications for understanding leadership. Perhaps the most clear-cut conclusion that can be drawn from this discussion is that leaders are, apparently, also creators. Not only are the key characteristics of creative problems evident in the problem-solving tasks presented to leaders (e.g., novelty, complexity, ill-definition), it is clear that measures of creative problem-solving skills are effective predictors of leader performance (e.g., Connelly et al., 2000). One implication of these findings, of course, is that they indicate that leadership may indeed represent a noteworthy domain of creative work.

What should be recognized in this regard, however, is that it may not be desirable to reflexively apply models of creativity—particularly models developed in other domains such as the arts and sciences (Fiest, 1999)—to understanding leadership and leaders' creative problem-solving skills. Although it appears that many of the problem-solving skills that play a role in other creative ventures are also relevant to understanding leader performance, the unique demands made by leadership roles and the ways leaders go about doing their work apparently result in a greater weight being placed on certain skills. More specifically, due to the directive demands placed on leaders, a premium is placed on problem construction and idea evaluation skills (Mumford, Marks, et al., 2000).

In addition to placing a greater emphasis on certain skills, it appears that creative problem-solving skills are applied in different ways by leaders, vis-à-vis people working in other domains. This point is illustrated in our observations with regard to idea generation or divergent thinking. As is the case in other domains of creative activity, divergent thinking skills were found to be related to leader performance. However, the role of divergent thinking was not simply to produce ideas. Rather, its key contribution to leader performance was apparently derivative of the need for planning.

Not only do leaders apply traditional creative problem-solving skills in unique ways, it appears that creative efforts in the leadership domain may also call for at least some creative problem-solving skills that are not frequently seen in other forms of creative work. For example, penetration and foresight are apparently skills critical for leaders who must construct visions and action plans in a complex, dynamic social setting. It is open to question, however, whether these skills are needed by a bench scientist or a painter. Certainly, the gaming skills—as well as political, needs assessment, and motive appraisal skills—needed by leaders are not thinking skills likely to be found in every other domain of creative work.

These observations about social-cognitive skills bring us to a final comment about creativity in the domain of leadership. Leaders' creative efforts are not isolated, independent, technical productions. Instead, leaders' creative efforts occur in response to, and through, others—others working in a complex, ever-changing social system. As a result, leaders' creative efforts represent a distinctly social phenomenon in which adaptation to social demands is at a premium. One implication of this statement is that many of the skills identified herein can be expected to operate in a synergistic fashion. Thus, motive appraisals may shape plans just as intuition plays a role in the analysis of motives. Another, perhaps more important, implication, however, is that by virtue of its complexity and multifaceted expression in direction, actions, and reactions, leaders' creative problem-solving efforts may provide an unusually rich domain in which to study creativity and creative problem-solving skills—a domain suggesting both new skills and new ways of applying these skills.

REFERENCES

Abra, J. (1995). Do the muses dwell in Esyleum: Thoughts on death as a motive for creativity. *Creativity Research Journal, 8*, 132–149.

Agor, W. H. (1991). The logic of intuition: How top executives make important decisions. In J. Henry (Ed.), *Creative management* (pp. 165–174). London: Sage.

Barlow, C. M. (2000). Deliberate insight in team creativity. *Journal of Creative Behavior, 34*, 101–112.

Basadur, M., Runco, M. A., & Vega, L. A. (2000). Understanding how creative thinking skills, attitudes, and behaviors work together: A causal process model. *Journal of Creative Behavior, 34*, 77–100.

Bass, B. M. (1985). *Leadership and performance beyond expectation.* New York: Harper.

Bass, B. M. (1990). *Bass and Stogdill's handbook of leadership.* New York: Free Press.

Berger, R. M., Guilford, J. P., & Christensen, P. R. (1957). A factor analytic study of planning abilities. *Psychological Monographs, 71*, 1–29.

Bluedorn, A. C. (2002). Commentary on "Planning in organizations: Performance as a multilevel phenomenon." *Annual Review of Research in Multi-Level Issues, 1*, 64–71.

Brands, H. W. (2000). *The first American: The life and times of Benjamin Franklin.* New York: Doubleday.

Bray, D. W., Campbell, R. S., & Grant, D. C. (1974). *Formative years in business.* New York: Wiley.

Cardinal, L. B. (2001). Technological innovation in the pharmaceutical industry: The use of organizational control in managing research and development. *Organizational Science, 12*, 19–36.

Castrogiovani, G. T. (1996). Pre-start-up planning and the survival of new small businesses: Theoretical linkages. *Journal of Management, 22*, 801–822.

Chusmir, K., & Koberg, E. (1986). Creativity differences among managers. *Journal of Vocational Behavior, 29*, 240–253.

Conger, J. A., & Kanungo, R. S. (1998). *Charismatic leadership in organizations.* Thousand Oaks, CA: Sage.

Connelly, M. S., Gilbert, J. A., Zaccaro, S. J., Threlfall, K. V., Marks, M. A., & Reiter-Palmon, R. (2000). Exploring the relationship of leadership skills and knowledge to leader performance. *Leadership Quarterly, 11*, 65–86.

Damanpour, F. (1991). Organizational innovation: A meta-analysis of effects of determinants and moderators. *Academy of Management Journal, 34,* 555–590.

Dansereau, F., & Yammarino, F. J. (1998). *Leadership: The multiple-level approaches.* Stamford, CT: JAI.

Dean, J. S., & Sharfman, M. P. (1996). Does decision process matter? A study of strategic decision making effectiveness. *Academy of Management Journal, 39,* 368–396.

Doerner, D., & Schaub, H. (1994). Errors in planning and decision making and the nature of human information processing. *Applied Psychology: An International Review, 43,* 433–453.

Dougherty, D., & Hardy, B. F. (1996). Sustained innovation production in large mature organizations: Overcoming organization problems. *Academy of Management Journal, 39,* 826–851.

Drazin, R., Glynn, M. A., & Kazanjian, R. K. (1999). Multilevel theorizing about creativity in organizations: A sense making prospective. *Academy of Management Review, 24,* 286–329.

Drazin, R., & Schoonhoven, C. B. (1996). Community population, and organizational effects on innovation: A multilevel perspective. *Academy of Management Journal, 39,* 1065–1083.

Dunham, L., & Freeman, R. E. (2000). There is business like show business: Leadership lessons from the theater. *Organizational Dynamics, 29,* 108–122.

Eisenberger, R., & Shanock, L. (2003). Rewards, intrinsic motivation, and creativity: A case study in conceptual and methodological isolation. *Creativity Research Journal, 15,* 221–230.

Ellis, J. (2001). *Founding brothers.* New York: Knopf.

Farris, G. F. (1972). The effect of individual role on performance in innovative groups. *R & D Management, 3,* 23–28.

Feldhusen, J. F., & Pleiss, M. K. (1994). Leadership: A synthesis of social skills, creativity, and histrionic ability. *Roeper Review, 16,* 293–296.

Fiest, G. J. (1999). The influence of personality on artistic and scientific creativity. In R. J. Sternberg (Ed.), *Handbook of creativity* (pp. 273–298). Cambridge, UK: Cambridge University Press.

Finkelstein, S. (2002). Commentary: Planning in organizations: One vote for complexity. *Annual Review of Research in Multi-Level Issues, 1,* 72–80.

Fleishman, E. A., & Quantance, M. K. (1984). *Taxonomies of human performance: The description of human tasks.* Orlando: Academic Press.

Getzels, J. S., & Csikszentmihalyi, M. (1976). *The creative vision: A longitudinal study of problem finding in art.* New York: Wiley.

Gruber, H. E., & Wallace, D. B. (1999). The case study method and evolving systems approach for understanding unique creative people at work. In R. J. Sternberg (Ed.), *Handbook of creativity* (pp. 93–115). Cambridge, UK: Cambridge University Press.

Hackman, J. R., & Walton, R. E. (1986). Leading groups in organizations. In P. S. Goodman (Ed.), *Designing effective work groups.* San Francisco: Jossey-Bass.

Hammond, K. J. (1990). Case-based planning: A framework for planning from experience. *Cognitive Science, 14,* 385–443.

Hayes-Roth, B., & Hayes-Roth, F. (1979). A cognitive model of planning. *Cognitive Science, 3,* 275–310.

Hitt, M. A., Hoskisson, R. E., Johnson, R. A., & Moesel, D. D. (1996). The market for corporate control and firm innovation. *Academy of Management Journal, 39,* 1084–1096.

Howell, J. M., & Avolio, B. J. (1993). Transformational leadership, transactional leadership, loss of control, and support for innovation. *Journal of Applied Psychology, 78,* 891–902.

Isenberg, D. J. (1986). Thinking and managing: A verbal protocol analysis of managerial problem-solving. *Academy of Management Journal, 29,* 775–788.

Isenberg, D. J. (1991). How senior managers think. In J. Henry (Ed.), *Creative management* (pp. 43–57). London: Sage.

Jacobsen, C., & House, R. J. (2001). Dynamics of charismatic leadership: A process theory, simulation model, and tests. *Leadership Quarterly, 12,* 75–112.

Jaques, E. (1976). *A general theory of bureaucracy.* London: Heinemann.

Jenkins, R. (2001). *Churchill: A biography.* New York: Farrar, Straus & Giroux.
Kacmar, K. M., & Baron, R. R. (1999). Organizational politics: The state of the field, links to related processes, and an agenda for future research. *Research in Personnel and Human Resources Management, 17,* 1–39.
Katz, D., & Kahn, R. L. (1978). *The social psychology of organizations.* New York: Wiley.
Kaufmann, G. (1991). Problem-solving and creativity. In J. Henry (Ed.), *Creative management* (pp. 103–133). London: Sage.
Kazanjian, R. K., Drazin, R., & Glynn, M. A. (2000). Creativity and technological learning: The roles of organization, architecture, and crisis in large-scale projects. *Journal of Engineering Technology Management, 17,* 273–298.
Keller, R. T. (2001). Cross-functional project groups in research and new product development: Diversity, communications, job stress, and outcomes. *Academy of Management Journal, 44,* 546–555.
Kettner, N. W., Guilford, J. P., & Christensen, P. R. (1959). A factor analysis study across the domains of reasoning, creativity, and evaluation. *Psychological Monographs, 9,* 1–31.
Kirkpatrick, S., & Locke, E. A. (1996). Direct and indirect effects of three core charismatic leadership components on performance and attitudes. *Journal of Applied Psychology, 81,* 36–51.
Komaki, J. C., Deselles, M. C., & Bowman, E. D. (1989). Definitely not a breeze: Extending an operant model to the effective supervision of teams. *Journal of Applied Psychology, 74,* 522–529.
Kuhn, R. L., & Kuhn, L. (1991). Decision making and deal making: How creativity helps. In J. Henry (Ed.), *Creative management* (pp. 72–80). London: Sage.
Kuipers, B., Moskowitz, A. J., & Kassinger, J. P. (1988). Critical decisions under uncertainty: Representation and structure. *Cognitive Science, 12,* 177–210.
Lowe, K. B., Koreck, K. G., & Sivasubamaniam, N. (1996). Effectiveness correlates of transformational and transactional leadership: A meta-analytic review of the MLQ literature. *Leadership Quarterly, 7,* 385–425.
Lubart, T. I. (1994). *Product-centered self-evaluation and the creative process.* Unpublished doctoral dissertation, Yale University, New Haven, CT.
Lubart, T. I. (2001). Models of the creative process: Past, present, and future. *Creativity Research Journal, 13,* 295–308.
Maccoby, M. (2001). Successful leaders employ strategic intelligence. *Research Technology Management, 44,* 58–66.
Maier, N. R. F., & McRay, E. P. (1972). Increasing innovation in change situations through leadership skills. *Psychological Reports, 31,* 343–354.
Marshall-Mies, J. C., Fleishman, E. A., Martin, J. A., Zaccaro, S. J., Baughman, W. A., & McGee, M. C. (2000). Development and evaluation of cognitive and meta-cognitive measures for predicting leadership potential. *Leadership Quarterly, 11,* 135–154.
Merrifield, P. R., Guilford, J. P., Christensen, P. R., & Frick, J. W. (1962). The role of intellectual factors in problem-solving. *Psychological Monographs, 76,* 1–21.
Miller, G. A., Galanter, E., & Pribram, K. H. (1960). *Plans and the structure of behavior.* New York: Holt, Rinehart & Winston.
Mintzberg, H. (1975, July/August). The manager's job: Folklore and fact. *Harvard Business Review,* 66–75.
Mintzberg, H. (1991). Planning on the left side and managing on the right. In R. J. Henry (Ed.), *Creative management* (pp. 58–71). London: Sage.
Morris, E. (1979). *The rise of Theodore Roosevelt.* New York: Coward, McCann, & Geohegan.
Mossholder, K. W., & Dewhurst, H. D. (1980). The appropriateness of management by objectives for development and research personnel. *Journal of Management, 6,* 145–156.
Mumford, M. D. (1998). Creative thought: Structure, components, and educational implications. *Roeper Review, 21,* 14–20.

Mumford, M. D. (2001). Something old, something new: Revising Guilford's conception of creative problem-solving. *Creativity Research Journal, 13*, 267–276.

Mumford, M. D. (2002). Social innovation: Ten cases from Benjamin Franklin. *Creativity Research Journal, 14*, 253–266.

Mumford, M. D., Baughman, W. A., Threlfall, K. V., Supinski, E. P., & Costanza, D. P. (1996). Process-based measures of creative problem-solving skills: I. Problem construction. *Creativity Research Journal, 9*, 63–76.

Mumford, M. D., & Connelly, M. S. (1991). Leaders as creators: Leader performance and problem-solving in ill-defined domains. *Leadership Quarterly, 2*, 289–315.

Mumford, M. D., & Connelly, M. S. (1999). Leadership. In M. A. Runco & S. Pritzker (Eds.), *Encyclopedia of creativity: Volume II* (pp. 139–146). San Diego: Academic Press.

Mumford, M. D., & Gustafson, S. B. (1988). Creativity syndrome: Integration, application, and innovation. *Psychological Bulletin, 103*, 27–43.

Mumford, M. D., & Gustafson, S. B. (in press). Creative thought: Cognition and problem solving in a dynamic system. In M. A. Runco (Ed.), *Creativity research handbook: Volume II* (pp.). Cresskill, NJ: Hampton.

Mumford, M. D., Marks, M. A., Connelly, M. S., Zaccaro, S. J., & Johnson, T. F. (1998). Domain based scoring of divergent thinking tests: Validation evidence in an occupational sample. *Creativity Research Journal, 11*, 151–164.

Mumford, M. D., Marks, M. A., Connelly, M. S., Zaccaro, S. J., & Reiter-Palmon, R. (2000). Development of leadership skills: Experience, timing, and growth. *Leadership Quarterly, 11*, 87–114.

Mumford, M. D., Mobley, M. I., Uhlman, C. E., Reiter-Palmon, R., & Doares, L. (1991). Process analytic models of creative capacities. *Creativity Research Journal, 4*, 91–122.

Mumford, M. D., & Moertl, P. (in press). Social innovation: Lessons from two innovations in the 20th century. *Creativity Research Journal, 15*, 261–266.

Mumford, M. D., Peterson, N. G., & Childs, R. A. (1999). Basic and cross-functional skills: Taxonomies, measures, and findings in assessing job skill requirements. In N. G. Peterson, M. D. Mumford, W. C. Borman, P. R. Jeanneret, & E. A. Fleishman (Eds.), *An occupational information system for the 21st century: The development of the O*NET* (pp. 49–70). Washington, DC: American Psychological Association.

Mumford, M. D., Schultz, R. A., & Osburn, H. K. (2002). Planning in organizations: Performance as a multi-level phenomenon. *Annual Review of Research in Multi-Level Issues, 1*, 3–63.

Mumford, M. D., Scott, G. M., & Gaddis, B. P. (in press). Leadership in scientific organizations. In J. Hurley (Ed.), *The organizational dimension of scientific effectiveness* (pp.). New York: Wiley.

Mumford, M. D., Scott, G. M., Gaddis, B., & Strange, J. M. (2002). Leading creative people: Orchestrating expertise and relationships. *Leadership Quarterly, 13*, 705–750.

Mumford, M. D., & Strange, J. M. (2002). Vision and mental models: The case of charismatic and ideological leadership. In B. J. Avolio & F. J. Yammarino (Eds.), *Charismatic and transformational leadership: The road ahead* (pp. 109–142). Oxford, UK: Elsevier.

Mumford, M. D., & VanDoorn, J. (2001). The leadership of pragmatism: Reconsidering Franklin in the age of charisma. *Leadership Quarterly, 12*, 279–312.

Mumford, M. D., Zaccaro, S. J., Connelly, M. S., & Marks, M. A. (2000). Leadership skills: Conclusions and future directions. *Leadership Quarterly, 11*, 155–170.

Mumford, M. D., Zaccaro, S. J., Harding, F. D., Jacobs, T. D., & Fleishman, E. A. (2000). Leadership skills for a changing world: Solving complex social problems. *Leadership Quarterly, 11*, 11–36.

Mumford, M. D., Zaccaro, S. J., Johnson, J. F., Diana, M., Gilbert, J. A., & Threlfall, K. V. (2000). Patterns of leader characteristics: Implications for performance and development. *Leadership Quarterly, 11*, 115–134.

Murmann, J. P., & Tushman, M. L. (1997). Organizational responsiveness to environmental shock as an indicator of foresight and oversight: The role of executive team characteristics and organizational content. In R. Garud & P. R. Nayyar (Eds.), *Technological innovations: Oversights and foresights* (pp. 260–278). New York: Cambridge University Press.

Noice, H. (1991). The role of explanations and plan recognition in the learning of theatrical scripts. *Cognitive Science, 15*, 425–460.

Okuda, S. M., Runco, M. A., & Berger, D. E. (1991). Creativity and the finding and solving of real-world problems. *Journal of Psychoeducational Assessment, 9*, 145–153.

Patalano, A. L., & Seifert, C. M. (1997). Opportunistic planning: Being reminded of pending goals. *Cognitive Psychology, 34*, 1–36.

Pelz, D. C., & Andrews, F. M. (1976). *Scientists in organizations: Productive climates for research and development*. New York: Wiley.

Policastro, E. (1995). Creative intuition: An integrative review. *Creativity Research Journal, 8*, 99–113.

Quinn, J. B. (1989). Technological innovation, entrepreneurship, and strategy. In M. L. Tushman, C. O'Reilly, & D. A. Adler (Eds.), *The management of organizations* (pp. 549–581). New York: Harper & Row.

Reber, D. S. (1989). Implicit learning and tacit knowledge. *Journal of Experimental Psychology: General, 118*, 219–235.

Redmond, M. R., Mumford, M. D., & Teach, R. J. (1993). Putting creativity to work: Leader influences on subordinate creativity. *Organizational Behavior and Human Decision Processes, 55*, 120–151.

Reiter-Palmon, R., Mumford, M. D., Boes, J. O., & Runco, M. A. (1997). Problem construction and creativity: The role of ability, cue consistency, and active processing. *Creativity Research Journal, 10*, 25–32.

Rodgers, E. M., & Adhikurya, R. (1979). Diffusion of innovations: Up to date review and commentary. In D. Nimmo (Ed.), *Communication yearbook 3* (pp. 67–81). New Brunswick, NJ: Transaction.

Rostan, S. M. (1994). Problem finding, problem-solving, and cognitive controls: An empirical investigation of critically acclaimed productivity. *Creativity Research Journal, 7*, 97–110.

Runco, M. A., & Chand, I. (1994). Problem finding, evaluative thinking, and creativity. In M. A. Runco (Ed.), *Problem finding, problem-solving, and creativity* (pp. 40–76). Norwood, NJ: Ablex.

Schank, R. C., & Abelson, R. P. (1977). *Scripts, plans, goals, and understanding: An inquiry into human knowledge structure*. Hillsdale, NJ: Lawrence Erlbaum Associates.

Schwenk, C. R., & Crozier, R. A. (1980). Effects of the expert, devil's advocate, and dialectical inquiry methods on performance prediction. *Organizational Behavior and Human Decision Processes, 26*, 409–424.

Scratchley, L. S., & Hakstain, A. R. (2001). The measurement and prediction of managerial creativity. *Creativity Research Journal, 13*, 367–384.

Shamir, B., House, R. J., & Arthur, M. B. (1993). The motivational effects of charisma: A self-concept based theory. *Organizational Science, 4*, 577–594.

Sharma, A. (1999). Central dilemmas of managing innovation in large firms. *California Management Review, 41*, 146–164.

Simonton, D. K. (1984). *Genius, creativity, and leadership: Historiometric inquiries*. Cambridge, MA: Harvard University Press.

Sosik, J. M., Kahai, S. S., & Avolio, B. J. (1998). Transformational leadership and dimensions of creativity: Motivating idea generation in computer mediated groups. *Creativity Research Journal, 11*, 111–122.

Sosik, J. M., Kahai, S. S., & Avolio, B. J. (1999). Leadership style, anonymity, and creativity in group decision support systems. *Journal of Creative Behavior, 33*, 227–257.

Strange, J. M., & Mumford, M. D. (2002). The origins of vision: Charismatic versus ideological leadership. *Leadership Quarterly, 13,* 343–377.

Strouse, J. (1999). *Morgan: American financier.* New York: HarperCollins.

Thomas, J. B., & McDaniel, R. R. (1990). Interpreting strategic issues: Effects of strategy and information processing structure of top management teams. *Academy of Management Journal, 32,* 286–306.

Tushman, M. L., & O'Reilly, C. A. (1997). *Winning through innovation: A practical guide to leading organizational change and renewal.* Cambridge, MA: Harvard Business School Press.

Vincent, A. H., Decker, B. D., & Mumford, M. D. (2002). Divergent thinking, intelligence, and expertise: A test of alternative models. *Creativity Research Journal, 14,* 163–178.

Xiao, Y., Milgram, P., & Doyle, D. J. (1997). Planning behavior and its functional role in interactions with complex systems. *IEEE Transactions on Systems, Man, and Cybernetics, 27,* 313–325.

Yukl, G. L. (2001). *Leadership in organizations.* Englewood Cliffs, NJ: Prentice-Hall.

Zaccaro, S. J., Gilbert, J., Thor, K. K., & Mumford, M. D. (1991). Leadership and social intelligence: Linking social perceptiveness and behavioral flexibility to leader effectiveness. *Leadership Quarterly, 2,* 317–331.

Zaccaro, S. J., Mumford, M. D., Connelly, M. S., Marks, M. A., & Gilbert, J. A. (2000). Leader skill assessment: Measure and methods. *Leadership Quarterly, 11,* 37–64.

Chapter **13**

Emotions as Mediators and as Products of Creative Activity

James R. Averill
University of Massachusetts, Amherst

Emotions are related to creativity in many ways—as facilitators, inhibitors, and simply as adventitious by-products. In this chapter, I consider two of the more positive ways—namely, emotions as mediators and as products of creative activity. These two ways involve different meanings of *emotion*. In the first (mediational) sense, *emotion* refers to the broad matrix of experience in which all behavior is embedded. Various names have been given to emotions in this sense; for example, *feeling tones* (Getz & Lubart, 2000), *affective tones* (Isen, 2000), and *background feelings* (Damasio, 1994). A common theme that runs through these formulations is that *emotional feelings* (the term I use here) can act as catalysts to creativity without, however, entering into the final product. Until emotional feelings are given symbolic form and made manifest in behavior, there is little reason to speak of them as either creative or noncreative in and of themselves.

Emotion in the second sense refers to specific patterns of response that *are* manifested in behavior and that *are* symbolized in ordinary language by such names as *anger, fear,* and *love.* I call emotions in this sense *emotional syndromes* to distinguish them from emotional feelings as defined previously. Emotional syndromes can be creative products in their own right. How such creativity is possible, the criteria for its assessment, and its relation to other kinds of creativity are the major concerns of this chapter.

I begin with a brief discussion of how emotional feelings can help mediate creativity. This is an important topic in its own right, but I also want to short-circuit at the outset a potential source of confusion. Emotional feelings are only part or one component of emotional syndromes. What is true of the part need not be true of the whole, and vice versa.[1]

EMOTIONAL FEELINGS AS MEDIATORS OF CREATIVITY

Building associations among seemingly disparate ideas, as in the formation of metaphors, is critical to creativity in a variety of domains—art, business, science, and literature (Martindale, 1993; Mednick, 1962; Simonton, 1988). Therefore, in discussing emotional feelings as catalysts for creativity, I focus on the formation of metaphors and, in particular, on the emotional resonance model of Getz and Lubart (2000; Lubart & Getz, 1997).

In traditional accounts of metaphor (e.g., Gluksberg & Keysar, 1993; Ortony, 1993; Tourangeau & Sternberg, 1982), two seemingly disparate concepts become linked when their lexical representations overlap (and hence the activation of one directly activates the other), or because both concepts are instances of a more generic concept that mediates the link between them. These two cognitive mechanisms are depicted graphically in Panels A and B of Fig. 13.1.

According to Getz and Lubart (2000), neither of these two mechanisms is sufficient to account for the formation of truly novel metaphors (i.e., metaphors with no prior conceptual links), whether direct (Panel A) or mediated (Panel B). Getz and Lubart therefore proposed an emotional resonance model (ERM), which is illustrated in Panel C of Fig. 13.1. This model assumes that some associations between concepts are mediated by emotional profiles or feeling tones. When a concept is activated, a corresponding feeling tone presumably spreads as a global "wave" throughout the memory system, where it may resonate with another concept that has a similar emotional profile.

Feeling tones become attached to events through direct experience, particularly events that are self-involving. But people, as opposed to infrahuman animals, not only experience events directly, they also give meaning to experience within a conceptual system. When direct experience is conceptualized, a feeling tone becomes linked to the relevant concept. For example, the feeling tone associated with separation from a friend or loved one may be conceptualized as grief in Western cultures, but as illness or fatigue by the Tahitians (Levy, 1984), with corresponding differences in be-

---

[1] *Feeling* is one of the vaguest terms in the English language; to adapt Wittgenstein's familiar metaphor, it covers a large, extended family, one united more by name than by resemblance (Averill, 1994). Thus, the use of *feeling* in this chapter should not be generalized uncritically to other contexts.

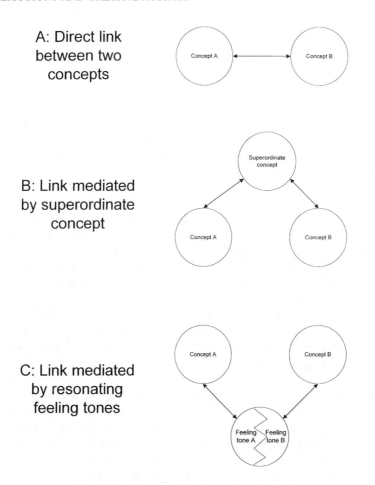

FIG. 13.1. Three models of metaphor formation.

havior and social interactions. The conceptualization of feelings is most evident with respect to concepts such as "fear," "anger," and "love" that have an explicitly emotional connotation. However, nearly all concepts have affective qualities attached to them. Some of those qualities, such as overall feelings of pleasantness or unpleasantness, are general across persons and even cultures (cf. Snider & Osgood, 1969); other qualities are multifaceted (combinations of feeling tones) and idiosyncratic to the individual. The latter are the focus of Getz and Lubart's (2000) emotional resonance model; it is what sets their model apart from related models that focus almost exclusively on the positive–negative dimension of feeling.

Concepts necessarily have shared meaning. For example, my concept of a "lawyer" must overlap with your concept of a "lawyer," otherwise we would not be able to communicate about lawyers. However, how I feel about lawyers, based on my experience, need not correspond with how you feel about lawyers, based on your experience. On the other hand, the way I feel about lawyers may "resonate" with the way I feel about broccoli. Creative metaphors are generated, according to Getz and Lubart (2000), when individuals with a rich store of idiosyncratic feelings access in working memory two resonating tones, thus leading to the formation of an original link between the otherwise remote concepts to which these feeling tones were experientially attached. For example, "Lawyers are the broccoli of the judicial system."

How are such links made? We can address this question from both a psychological and a neurophysiological perspective. Psychologically, Getz and Lubart (2000) postulate a threshold value for the detection of resonating feeling tones. When this threshold value is reached, the associated concepts can be brought into working memory and a metaphor can be established. A person's threshold value for detection can presumably be raised or lowered by a variety of personal (e.g., motivation) and situational (e.g., priming) variables.

From a neurophysiological perspective, memory for emotional events—and hence corresponding feeling tones—depends on a network of neural and chemical signals distributed widely in the brain; the same is true of the networks that mediate conceptual (e.g., declarative) knowledge. Because of their widespread distribution, emotional and conceptual networks interconnect in many ways, thus making possible the kind of linkages postulated by Getz and Lubart. Indeed, it is only in the abstract that we can speak of separate emotional and conceptual systems, as opposed to a single, integrated emotional-conceptual system. As the title of one of Damasio's books (*Descartes' Error*, 1994) suggests, Descartes made a fundamental error in making a sharp distinction between cognitive (mental) and emotional (physiological) processes.

I have used the emotional resonance model of Getz and Lubart (2000) to illustrate one way that emotions might mediate creativity in general. This is currently an active area of research about which I say more later. The major focus in this chapter, however, is not on emotional feelings as mediators of creativity, but instead on emotional syndromes as potentially creative products in their own right.

FROM EMOTIONAL FEELINGS TO EMOTIONAL SYNDROMES

As defined earlier, emotional syndromes are organized patterns of response that are symbolized in ordinary language by such terms as *anger, love, grief,* and the like. (Art and music are also important symbolic forms for expressing emotion; for simplicity, however, I focus on language.) Emotional feelings and emotional syndromes are often conflated, both in psychological theory and everyday discourse, as when such phrases as "I feel angry" and "I am angry" are used interchangeably. However, emotional feelings are neither necessary nor sufficient conditions for the attribution of emotion, whether the attribution is to another person or to oneself (Averill, 1994). Feelings are simply one component—albeit a very central component—of most emotional episodes.

New concepts are continually being introduced into language, for example, on the forefront of scientific discovery. Arieti (1976) used the term *endocept* to refer to refer to such concepts in the making. Arieti's concern was with creativity in the intellectual and artistic domains, but similar considerations apply to the emotions. As new emotional concepts come into common use, or old concepts pass out of use, corresponding changes occur in the emotional feelings—no less than in the thoughts and actions—symbolized by those concepts. The change, however, does not occur suddenly. Typically, there is a stage in which the emerging emotional syndrome is represented in ordinary language only by circumlocution or metaphor. Adapting Arieti's terminology, I refer to such embryonic syndromes as *endoceptual.*

Endoceptual emotional syndromes typically do not last. As humans, we have a strong need to impose order on, or make sense of, events—especially when those events include our own behavior. Hence, there is a tendency to short-circuit endoceptual experiences by assimilating events into some readily available conceptual category. Assimilation can sometimes be a creative solution; in terms of criteria to be discussed shortly, it may lead to behavior that is authentic but not particularly novel. More creative, and more difficult, is to change the category to better accommodate the new behavior.

Emotional Syndromes as Products of Creative Activity

A fully formed emotional syndrome is an organized pattern of responses (feelings, thoughts, and actions). The operative term here is *organized*—an emotional syndrome presumes principles of organization. Biological principles (information encoded in the genes) may predispose the individual to respond in some ways more than in others. This is particularly evident in the case of simple emotions, such as fright. For most emotions, however, the proximal organizing principles are more social than biological. That is, culturally specific beliefs (implicit folk theories) provide the blueprint according to which otherwise disparate components are integrated into a coherent whole.

Two types of beliefs can be distinguished: existential beliefs and social rules. These are illustrated in Fig. 13.2. Existential beliefs concern what *is*,

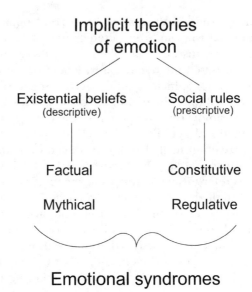

FIG. 13.2. Emotional syndromes as constituted by implicit (folk) theories of emotion.

what exists. Some existential beliefs about emotions may be true in the sense that they are accurate reflections of how people respond when emotional. For example, it is true that when people are in love they generally want to be together. Other existential beliefs are mythical; for example, that love is made in heaven, that there is only one "true" love, and so forth. Needless to say, myths can lend meaning and significance to experience, sometimes even more than true beliefs. The important point is that emotional syndromes are organized, in part, by the existential beliefs we hold about them.

Emotional syndromes are also constituted, in part, by social rules. Succinctly put, our folk theories of emotion not only describe what *is*, whether in fact or myth, they also prescribe what *should be*. It is widely recognized that emotions are regulated by rules; for example, that you should not laugh at a funeral. But many rules also have an enabling functions. To illustrate with a nonemotional example, consider grammatical rules: They not only regulate how a person speaks a language, they help constitute the language that is spoken. Thus, without an English grammar, there would be no English language. The same is true with respect to the rules of emotion. Without the rules of anger, say, there would be no anger, only inarticulate expressions of rage or frustration.

Existential beliefs and social rules provide the prototypes according to which the emotions commonly recognized within a culture are socially constructed. However, beliefs change and rules can be broken. As an emotional syndrome diverges from its prototype, its conceptual representation becomes increasingly fuzzy and difficult to articulate. If the resulting behavior is detrimental, it may simply be labeled "neurotic." However, not all innovations are detrimental. On occasion, the behavior may prove effective for the individual or group, in which case it can be regarded as creative.

THE CRITERIA FOR CREATIVITY, WITH SPECIAL REFERENCE TO AUTHENTICITY

Implicit in the previous analysis are two of the most frequently mentioned criteria for assessing creativity: namely, novelty and effectiveness. A creative response is (typically) different from what is standard for the individual or group, and it is of some value (e.g., aesthetically as in art, theoretically as in science, or practically as in business). Most discussions of creativity stop with these two criteria. But a third needs to be added: authenticity. I examine this criterion in some detail, both because it is important in its own right and because it illustrates some conditions (e.g., the necessity of external standards) that also apply to the criteria of novelty and effectiveness.

To illustrate the importance of authenticity, imagine a very talented artist who copies a masterwork in every detail, so that there are now two paintings—one original and one copy—that are indistinguishable from each other. Because they are identical, both paintings are equally novel and equally effective (beautiful). Yet we prize the original for the creativity it manifests and only marvel at the copy for its technical competence. What makes the difference?

Arnheim (1966, p. 298) wrote of the "pregnant sight of reality" as a hallmark of the creative artist. In the previous hypothetical example, the original painting reflects the artist's own vision—his or her beliefs and values—about the world. The copy, no matter how well done, remains an imitation; its inspiration comes from another, not from the self.

Because the origin of an authentic response lies within the self, the response may also be novel; that is, idiosyncratic to the individual. In individualistic (e.g., Western) societies, therefore, the criteria of novelty and authenticity tend to converge. By contrast, in collectivist (e.g., East Asian) societies in which the self is more identified with the group and its traditions, authenticity and novelty are more easily distinguishable as criteria for creativity (Averill, Chon, & Hahn, 2001).

At first, the criterion of authenticity might seem more relevant to creativity in the arts than in the sciences. Scientific discoveries are objective; that is, divorced of idiosyncracies of the individual scientist. However, disputes over priority are as common in the sciences as in the arts. Moreover, Arnheim's (1966) phrase, the "pregnant sight of reality," would seem to apply to science scientific discoveries (and their heuristic value) even more than to innovations in art. (This is not to deny an important difference between authenticity in art and science: If Darwin had never lived, someone else would discovered the principle of natural selection; but if Picasso never lived, no one would have painted *Guernica*. This difference, however, is not critical to our present discussion.)

The criterion of authenticity raises particularly interesting questions when applied to the emotional creativity. The experience of emotion is often taken as prima facie evidence for authenticity, especially if the emotion is intensely felt and sincerely expressed. For example, the vivid emotions experienced by some persons as they recount being "abducted" by space aliens can be so convincing as to mislead even sophisticated observers (Kenny, 1998). But, of course, not all emotions are authentic, no matter how keenly felt or sincerely expressed. One need not adhere to psychoanalytic principles to realize how misleading emotional experiences can be, even to the person doing the experiencing.

Authenticity is not an inherent feature of emotion, but instead a judgment we make about emotions; and, like other kinds of judgment, a standard of comparison is implied. To take a nonemotional example, a painting attributed to Titian is judged authentic only if it matches other paintings by that artist, and a statue attributed to classical Greece is judged authentic only if it matches other statues bearing similar cultural characteristics. I am oversimplifying, of course. One might argue that the painting must not only match others by Titian, but that it must have been painted *by* Titian, and that the statue must have been sculpted *by* a person living in classical Greece. But these added stipulations raise complications of their own (Startwell, 1988), and they do not alter the basic argument I wish to make, namely, that judgments of authenticity involve some standard of comparison or frame of reference. By what standards do we judge the authenticity of an emotional response?

Sincerity is one standard but, for reasons mentioned earlier, sincerity is at best a necessary, not a sufficient, condition for authenticity. Sincerity, it might be said, is simply believing in the authenticity of one's own experience. The belief must still be justified.

In search of a firm foundation for judging authenticity, many theorists fall back on the hoary notion that "real" emotions are grounded in our biological heritage. The sociologist Arlie Hochschild (1983) illustrated this position. She analyzed the "emotional labor" expected by some organizations of their employees. She described, for example, how flight attendants are trained to smile and be polite even when confronted with rude and obnoxious passengers, and how bill collectors may feign anger to collect a debt, even while sympathizing with the plight of the debtor. No doubt, many employees, following company policies, are inauthentic in their expression of emotion; moreover, the stress of feigning emotion can exert a heavy toll on the employee (for a review, see Steinberg & Figart, 1999). The toll may be especially insidious when the emotions dictated by an organization—or society as a whole (Mestrovic, 1997)—are adopted and experienced as one's own; that is, when they acquire a faux authenticity.

But what is nature of the presumably authentic emotions from which a person becomes estranged in the furtherance of corporate or societal interests? The position adopted by Hochschild (1983) was that authentic emotions are akin to simple sensory experiences, such as "hearing, touch, and smell" (p. 219). This appeal to elementary biological processes hardly does justice to the complexity of the issue. Nevertheless, I believe an answer may be found in Hochschild's implicit assumption that inauthentic emotions are, in the long term, detrimental to an individual's welfare. Stated in positive terms, an emotion is judged authentic when it is consistent with a person's own best interests. This is admittedly a difficult standard to apply, because a person's best interests may not be recognized until long after the fact. The authenticity of an emotion can thus always be reevaluated as circumstances change.

The ancient Greeks had a saying: Count no man happy until he is dead. Most emotions are not as global in their implication as is happiness and hence are subject to more frequent reevaluation. For example, as a person matures, what was once considered the epitome of true love may with hindsight be dismissed as mere sexual infatuation. On an even shorter time scale, the events of tomorrow may make today's anger (fear, hope, etc.) seem less than genuine.

To summarize, authenticity is one of three criteria by which a response is judged creative; the other two are novelty and effectiveness. I have focused on authenticity not because I believe it to be more important than the other two criteria, but because it is the most neglected in contemporary theoretical discussions. All three criteria are important and, to an extent, compensatory: A response that is particularly novel and authentic may be judged creative even while its effectiveness (value) remains uncertain. Likewise, a response that is particularly effective and authentic may be considered creative even though it is not especially novel, and similarly for a response that is novel and effective, although it falls short on authenticity.

One final point before leaving this topic. I have emphasized how judgments of authenticity presume some standard of comparison. The same is, of course, true of novelty and effectiveness. A response can be novel only in comparison to the commonplace, and a response is effective only within a context. In other words, judgments of creativity are implicitly relative. I emphasize this fact for reasons that become evident later in this chapter, when I discuss the domain generality and specificity of creativity. But first, I need to review briefly the empirical evidence for emotional creativity.

EMPIRICAL EVIDENCE

The evidence for emotional creativity can be divided into three main categories: cultural variations in emotional syndromes, individual differences in the ability to be emotionally creative, and improvisations during the course (microgenesis) of emotional episodes. These categories form a rough progression from the macro (cultural) to the micro (episodic) levels of analysis, and each helps to explain the others in a top-down or bottom-up fashion.

Cultural Variations

Some of the best, albeit indirect, evidence for emotional creativity comes from cultural differences in emotional syndromes. Much of the cross-cultural research on emotion has involved facial expressions, and has tended to favor the universality of at least as few "basic" emotions (e.g., Matsumoto, 2001); or it has involved linguistic expressions, and has tended to favor cultural specificity (e.g., Russell, 1991). However, expressive reactions and verbal behavior are only two of the many components that, taken together, help constitute an emotional syndrome. As evidence for emotional creativity, the most relevant research involves "thick" descriptions in which emotional syndromes are treated as integrated wholes and interpreted within the culture of which they are a part. The research of Lutz (1988) on the emotional life of the Ifaluk, a people of Micronesia, provides a good example.

Although cultural variations in emotional syndromes are well documented, their theoretical significance has not always been appreciated. As alluded to earlier, the tendency has been to interpret cultural variations as a result of regulatory or "display" rules, ignoring the enabling or constitutive function of social norms. Stated differently, cultural variations have too often been dismissed as mere patina or overlay on more "basic" (biologically primitive) emotions. Needless to say, cultural variations do not negate the importance of biology. However, the conception of emotions as biologically primitive ("animallike"), and hence relatively impervious to change, is based more on custom than on empirical evidence (Averill, 1996).

Given that cultural variations exist in emotional syndromes, the question becomes: How did they arise? The answer, I argue, is to be found in the emotional creativity of individuals within the society. That is, differences that exist today between cultures would not have occurred except for the ability of individuals within a culture to introduce variations on "received" emotional syndromes.

Individual Differences

William James (1902/1961) observed that "when a person has an inborn genius for certain emotions his life differs strangely from that of ordinary people" (p. 215). I don't know whether emotional geniuses are different in this regard than geniuses in other domains. James did not mention names. But my concern is not with creative genius, in whatever domain; rather, it is with the emotional equivalent of "everyday creativity" (Richards, 1990).

To assess individual differences in everyday emotional creativity, a 30-item emotional creativity inventory (ECI) was constructed (Averill, 1999). The ECI consists of three facets. The first facet, comprising 7 items, assesses *preparedness*, that is, a person's background knowledge about, and the importance placed on his or her emotional life; the second facet (14 items) relates to the criterion of *novelty*; and the third facet (9 items) represents a combination of the other two criteria for creativity, namely, *effectiveness* and *authenticity*. (Using self-report measures, it has proved difficult to distinguish the perceived effectiveness of a response from its authenticity; people tend to judge their own emotions effective to the extent they are authentic, and vice versa.)

The ECI was developed as a research instrument, not for use in applied settings. Its purpose is to explore the correlates of emotional creativity on the individual level. People who score high on the ECI are rated by their peers as being emotionally more creative than are low scorers, presumably on the basis of everyday behavior, and high scorers are better able to express unusual emotions symbolically in stories and pictures (Averill, 1999; Averill & Thomas-Knowles, 1991; Gutbezahl & Averill, 1996). In terms of the "Big Five" personality dimensions (McCrae, 1992), the ECI is most closely related to openness to experience, but is independent of extraversion and neuroticism, two traits closely related to positive and negative emotionality, respectively (Averill, 1999). Scores on the ECI are negatively related to alexithymia, and positively to self-reported spiritual or mysticlike experiences (Averill, 2002). Both alexithymia and mysticlike experiences are marked by an inability to name the emotions one is experiencing. The reasons for the difficulty are, however, very different: Alexithymia reflects an external orientation and lack of discernment of one's own emotional state; mysticlike experiences involve an internal orientation and emotions that are inherently difficult to describe in ordinary language. People who score high on the ECI are also better able than are low scorers to benefit from solitude, a condition that traditionally has been associated with creative pursuits (Long, Seburn, Averill, & More, 2003).

Differences can be as informative as similarities. Therefore, let me contrast emotional creativity with a closely related construct, namely, emotional intelligence. As formulated by Salovey, Mayer, and their colleagues (e.g., Salovey, Bedell, Detweiler, & Mayer, 2000), emotional intelligence comprises four related "branches": namely, the ability (a) to identify accurately emotions in oneself and others; (b) to use emotions to facilitate thought and action; (c) to understand the meaning or significance of emotions; (d) to manage emotions in oneself and others. These branches form a rough hierarchy, from the most elementary to the most complex.

Research on emotional intelligence has been extensively reviewed elsewhere (Bar-On & Parker, 2000; Mathews, Zeidner, & Roberts, 2002). My concern here is limited to a single question. The abilities attributed to emotional intelligence would also be conducive to emotional creativity: Wherein, then, lies the difference?

In their numerous publications, Salovey, Mayer, and colleagues have been commendably clear on the criteria for assessing an "intelligence" (e.g., that there be explicit standards for success or failure), and they have constructed performance tests to assess each branch of their model: the multifactor emotional intelligence scale (MEIS) and its successor, the MSCEIT (Mayer, Salovey, & Caruso, 2000). They have been less clear on what counts as an emotion. "A reasonably canonical definition," Mayer et al. (2001) asserted, "might be that an emotion is an organized mental response to an event that includes physiological, experiential, and cognitive aspects, among others" (pp. 233–234). To narrow this very inclusive definition, Mayer et al. added two stipulations, namely, that emotions "typically occur in the context of relationships" and that they "show some universality across human beings and even closely related mammalian species" (p. 234).

In the Salovey et al. four-branch model, emotional intelligence may be related to creativity in two ways. First, at Branch 2 (using emotions), "emotional information" may facilitate thinking and creativity. This is consistent with our earlier discussion of emotional feelings as mediators of creativity. Second, at Branches 3 (understanding emotions) and 4 (managing emotions), different emotions may be combined and expressed in unusual ways. This might seem to correspond to changes in emotional syndromes. However, the concept of an emotional syndrome presented earlier is fundamentally different than the concept of emotion in Salovey et al.'s model of emotional intelligence. This difference is made explicit in the following observation by Mayer et al. (2001): "Discovering a new way of expressing an emotion doesn't necessarily involve inventing new emotional rules or having idiosyncratic emotional reactions" (p. 238). In contrast, emotional creativity as here conceived involves precisely that—a change in the beliefs and rules that help constitute emotional syndromes.

To complicate matters further, emotional intelligence as assessed by the MEIS emphasizes conformity to group standards rather than the novelty and authenticity of a response. That is, a correct response to an item on the MEIS is determined by its agreement with the pooled responses of a large group of test takers, or with the responses of a smaller group of presumed experts on emotion. Such consensus scoring may be a valid indicator of effectiveness, but it downplays the importance of novelty and authenticity, two of the criteria for creativity discussed earlier. In response to this objection, originally raised by Roberts et al. (2001), Mayer et al. (2001) noted that the MEIS is, like most intelligence tests, a measure of convergent rather than divergent thinking/feeling. That may be true, but it doesn't settle the issue. It is well known that a certain degree of abstract intelligence is necessary for creativity in a given domain—no one with an IQ of 60 will be a creative astrophysicist. However, beyond a threshold necessary for success in a field, there is only a modest relation between intelligence as measured by IQ tests and creativity. The same is true, I assume, of the relation between emotional intelligence and creativity.

To summarize, individuals differ in their ability to be emotionally creative, and those differences presume some of the same abilities encompassed under the broader rubric of emotional intelligence. However, intelligence is no guarantee of creativity in the emotional domain any more than it is in the intellectual domain. Moreover, individual differences in abilities do not explain the *processes* by which new emotional syndromes actually develop or come into being. For that, we must examine how an emotion unfolds within an episode—its microgenesis.

The Microgenesis of Emotional Episodes

The beliefs and rules that help organize an emotional syndrome (see Fig. 13.2) allow for a great deal of improvisation as an episode develops. In this respect, an emotional episode can be compared to a rhetorical argument—both involve the "art of persuasion" (Averill, 2001). To change metaphors, emotional episodes are constructed "on line" (Parkinson, 1995). In forming the sequence of responses that constitute an emotional episode, a person has recourse to a large database of previous experiences stored in memory, as well as beliefs about what the emotion is and should be like.

For obvious methodological reasons, it is difficult to study emotions as they develop on line. However, a study by Morgan and Averill (1992) illustrated some of the issues involved, especially as related to emotional creativity. Participants in this study were asked to recount incidents in which they experienced "true feelings," a common colloquialism for authentic emotional experiences. The feature that most distinguished true-feeling episodes from other emotional episodes of approximately equal intensity was that the former implicated deeply held beliefs and values. This might occur, for example, when a participant was facing a moral dilemma or during the breakup of a romantic relationship.

Although the study by Morgan and Averill (1992) was retrospective, care was taken to assess participants' reactions toward the beginning, middle, and end of an episode. A typical episode began with confusion and was followed by a kaleidoscope of nebulous and ever-shifting emotions. This was basically a reversion to the endoceptual stage discussed earlier. As the episode progressed, one of two processes might have become dominant, corresponding to Piagetian assimilation and accommodation. One process (assimilation) led to a "normalization" of the experience, for example, by giving it meaning within a standard emotional category, such as anger or love, in which case the beliefs and rules that helped constitute that emotion were reinforced. The other process (accommodation) led to a change in the relevant beliefs and rules, resulting in an emotional variant, one difficult to describe in conventional terms.

Generalizing from an individual to a social level of analysis, it is easy to imagine how beneficial variants, if effectively communicated, might accumulate and diffuse through society. The ultimate result would be a new or transformed emotional syndrome. We thus come full circle, accounting for the historical and cultural differences in emotions discussed earlier.

GENERALITY VERSUS SPECIFICITY

One of the central issues addressed by the chapters in this volume is the degree to which creativity is general across domains or specific to a domain. This issue has been the object of considerable research and speculation for decades—and the answer seems to be an unequivocal *both*—creativity is general *and* specific. The question then becomes: Under what conditions do we find generality, and under what conditions do we find specificity?

Behavior is hierarchically organized. Whether or not one finds generality or specificity depends, in part, on the level at which the creative response is identified. Emotional creativity is a "midlevel" construct. Looking upward in the behavioral hierarchy, we can expect to find increasing generality, for example, between emotional creativity and creativity in the arts and sciences. The evidence for overlap between emotional and artistic creativity is largely anecdotal, but too ubiquitous to be dismissed. Poetry, in particular, has often been viewed as a means for giving form to emotions that are inadequately expressed in ordinary language; and, metaphorically speaking, dance is poetry in motion. Acting, too, particularly deep or method acting, involves learning to be emotional in often unusual ways.

At an even broader level of generality, I would expect some overlap between emotional and intellectual creativity. Among university students, emotional creativity as measured by the ECI, is largely independent of intellectual ability as measured by SAT scores (Averill, 1999). This may be due, in part, to a restriction in the range of intellectual abilities among university students. (As noted earlier, even intellectual creativity is poorly related to general intelligence, beyond a threshold level of ability required for success in a field.) Be that as it may, emotional appraisals depend on the capacity to make fine discriminations in situations that are often complex, ambiguous, and stressful; a good deal of information processing also goes on between the appraisal of the situation and the experience of emotion; and, finally, the effective expression of emotion requires a certain finesse, both verbal and behavioral, often in coordination with the behavior of another (e.g., the target or instigator of the emotion). For these reasons alone, I believe it would be a mistake to draw too sharp a distinction between emotional and intellectual creativity.

Looking downward in the behavioral hierarchy, increasing specificity can be expected between emotional creativity in general and creativity in different domains of emotion. Some people are more aggressive than others, some are more nurturing, and some are more timorous. Corresponding to such temperamental differences, we should expect to find differences in the ability to be creatively angry, loving, and fearful.

However, the issue of generality (versus specificity) does not depend solely on the behavioral level at which the construct is defined, or even on attributes of the creative person. As discussed earlier, creativity is a judgment we make about behavior, not an inherent property of behavior. It follows that questions about generality or specificity must also take into account the characteristics of those doing the judging. For example, a literary critic is unlikely to have the expertise to judge a musical composition, and hence may fail to recognize commonalities in creativity across the two domains. In general, the more narrow the expertise of the judges, the greater the specificity of judgments of creativity is likely to be. This presents particular problems in domains that traditionally have not been considered open to creativity—the emotions being a prime example. In such instances, creativity may go unacknowledged.

Still a third factor must be considered. The criteria for judging creativity—novelty, effectiveness, and authenticity—are all relative to the situation; hence, consideration must be given to the "state of the art" in a domain at a given time. A person might potentially be creative in several domains, but if one of those domains is not ripe for exploitation, creativity will be correspondingly restricted or may go unrecognized. This is one implication of Kuhn's (1970) familiar distinction between normal and revolutionary science. In terms of potential, scientists are no less creative during periods of normal science, although the problems they address allow for mostly minor advances on accepted theories, and hence are not generally recognized as being particularly creative (at least as far as the criterion of novelty is concerned). Only as anomalies accumulate do radically new approaches, or paradigm shifts, become feasible. Something similar occurs in the domain of art (Martindale, 1990), and, I would suggest, in the domain of emotion, as periods of traditionalism oscillate with periods of romanticism (as in the sexual revolution of the 1960s).

Three-way interactions are always difficult to visualize, particularly when each part (persons, judges, situations) can be analyzed in a hierarchically fashion (as described earlier for creative persons and their behavior). That is one reason why the issue of generality versus specificity seems so intractable. The tendency is to focus on only one member of the triad, typically creative persons, whereas holding constant (or ignoring) the other two. But the others never remain constant; hence, there always will be exceptions to any conclusion.

Locating creativity in the interaction among creative persons, judges, and situations is consistent with Csikszentmihalyi's (1999) systems approach to creativity. His analysis goes far beyond what I have said here, but to conclude this chapter I want to approach the problem of generality from a different perspective.

CONCLUDING OBSERVATIONS

The three-way interaction of persons, judges, and situations helps to set the boundaries of a domain as more or less inclusive. We can also ask about the interaction *among* domains, regardless of how the boundaries are set. From this perspective, generality takes on a different meaning. It no longer refers to the inclusiveness of a domain, but, rather, to the general "climate" in which creativity in a variety of domains may flourish together, each enhancing the others.

Historically, many societies have "golden ages" in which the arts, sciences, philosophy, politics, and commerce have all flourished. Classical Greece and Renaissance Italy are two familiar examples. However, let me take a recent and more mundane example. In an analysis of metropolitan regions within the United States, Richard Florida (2002) found that those with thriving economies, such as the San Francisco Bay Area and Austin, Texas, have a high proportion of creative people in a variety of domains. The presence of this "creative class" is indexed by such variables as the percentage of college-educated workers in the labor force, the number of patents per capita, the number of artistically talented people, and even the concentration of homosexual couples (a proxy for a tolerance of alternative lifestyles). "On many fronts," Florida (2002) asserted, "the Creative Class lifestyle comes down to a passionate quest for experience. The ideal, as a number of my subjects succinctly put it, is to 'live the life'—a creative life packed full of intense, high-quality, multidimensional experiences" (p. 166).

Florida did not distinguish between emotions as mediators and as products of creativity, but both senses seem implicit in his description of the creative lifestyle. Assuming his analysis proves valid (for a critique, see Malanga, 2004), his findings suggest the potential importance of the emotions for creativity "in general."

REFERENCES

Arieti, S. (1976). *Creativity: The magic synthesis.* New York: Basic Books.
Arnheim, R. (1966). *Toward a psychology of art.* Berkeley: University of California Press.
Averill, J. R. (1994). What influences the subjective experience of emotion? I feel, therefore I am—I think. In P. Ekman & R. J. Davidson (Eds.), *The nature of emotion: Fundamental questions* (pp. 379–385). New York: Oxford University Press.
Averill, J. R. (1996). An analysis of psychophysiological symbolism and its influence on theories of emotion. In R. Harré & W. G. Parrott (Eds.), *The emotions: Social, cultural and biological dimensions* (pp. 204–228). London: Sage.
Averill, J. R. (1999). Individual differences in emotional creativity: Structure and correlates. *Journal of Personality, 67,* 331–371.
Averill, J. R. (2001). The rhetoric of emotion, with a note on what makes great literature great. *Empirical Studies of the Arts, 19,* 5–26.
Averill, J. R. (2002). Emotional creativity: Toward "spiritualizing the passions." In C. R. Snyder & S. J. Lopez (Eds.), *Handbook of positive psychology* (pp. 172–185). New York: Oxford University Press.
Averill, J. R., Chon, K. K., & Hahn, D. W. (2001). Emotions and creativity, East and West. *Asian Journal of Social Psychology, 4,* 165–183.
Averill, J. R., & Thomas-Knowles, C. (1991). Emotional creativity. In K. T. Strongman (Ed.), *International review of studies on emotion* (Vol. 1, pp. 269–299). London: Wiley.
Bar-On, R., & Parker, J. D. A. (Eds.). (2000). *Handbook of emotional intelligence.* San Francisco: Jossey-Bass.
Csikszentmihalyi, M. (1999). Implications of a systems perspective for the study of creativity. In R. Sternberg (Ed.), *Handbook of creativity* (pp. 313–335). Cambridge, UK: Cambridge University Press.
Damasio, A. R. (1994). *Descartes' error: Emotion, reason, and the human brain.* New York: Putnam.
Florida, R. (2002). *The rise of the creative class.* New York: Basic Books.
Getz, I., & Lubart, T. I. (2000). An emotional-experiential perspective on creative symbolic-metaphorical processes. *Consciousness & Emotion, 1,* 283–312.
Gluksberg, S., & Keysar, B. (1993). How metaphors work. In A. Ortony (Ed.), *Metaphor and thought* (2nd ed., pp. 401–424). Cambridge, UK: Cambridge University Press.
Gutbezahl, J., & Averill, J. R. (1996). Individual differences in emotional creativity as manifested in words and pictures. *Creativity Research Journal, 9,* 327–337.

Hochschild, A. R. (1983). *The managed heart.* Berkeley: University of California Press.
Isen, A. M. (2000). Positive affect and decision making. In M. Lewis & J. M. Haviland (Eds.), *Handbook of emotions* (2nd ed., pp. 417–435). New York: Guilford.
James, W. (1961). *Varieties of religious experience.* New York: Collier. (Original work published 1902)
Kenny, M. (1998). The proof is in the passion: Emotion as an index of veridical memory. In J. de Rivera & T. R. Sarbin (Eds.), *Believed-in imaginings: The narrative construction of reality* (pp. 269–293). Washington, DC: American Psychological Association.
Kuhn, T. S. (1970). *The structure of scientific revolutions* (2nd ed.). Chicago: University of Chicago Press.
Levy, R. I. (1984). The emotions in comparative perspective. In K. R. Scherer & P. Ekman (Eds.), *Approaches to emotion* (pp. 397–412). Hillsdale, NJ: Lawrence Erlbaum Associates.
Long, C. R., Seburn, M., Averill, J. R., & More, T. A. (2003). Solitude: Experiences, settings, varieties, and individual differences. *Personality and Social Psychology Bulletin, 29,* 578–583.
Lubart, T. I., & Getz, I. (1997). Emotion, metaphor, and the creative process. *Creativity Research Journal, 10,* 285–301.
Lutz, C. (1988). *Unnatural emotions.* Chicago: University of Chicago Press.
Malanga, S. (2004). The curse of the creative class. *City Journal, 14,* 36–45.
Martindale, C. (1990). *The clockwork muse: The predictability of artistic change.* New York: Basic Books.
Martindale, C. (1993). *Cognitive psychology: A neural network approach.* Belmont, CA: Wadsworth.
Mathews, G., Zeidner, M., & Roberts, R. D. (2002). *Emotional intelligence: Science and myth.* Cambridge, MA: MIT Press.
Matsumoto, D. (2001). Culture and emotion. In D. Matsumoto (Ed.), *Handbook of culture and psychology* (pp. 171–194). New York: Oxford University Press.
Mayer, J. D., Caruso, D., & Salovey, P. (2000). Emotional intelligence meets traditional standards for an intelligence. *Intelligence, 27,* 267–298.
Mayer, J. D., Salovey, P., Caruso, D. R., & Sitarenios, G. (2001). Emotional intelligence as a standard intelligence. *Emotion, 1,* 232–242.
McCrae, R. R. (Ed.). (1992). The five factor model: Issues and application [Special issue]. *Journal of Personality, 60*(2).
Mednick, S. A. (1962). The associative basis of the creative process. *Psychological Review, 69,* 220–232.
Mestrovic, S. G. (1997). *Postemotional society.* Thousand Oaks, CA: Sage.
Morgan, C., & Averill, J. R. (1992). True feelings, the self, and authenticity: A psychosocial perspective. In D. D. Franks & V. Gecas (Eds.), *Social perspectives on emotion* (Vol. 1, pp. 95–124). Greenwich, CT: JAI.
Ortony, A. (1993). The role of similarity in similes and metaphors. In A. Ortony (Ed.), *Metaphor and thought* (2nd ed., pp. 342–356). Cambridge, UK: Cambridge University Press.
Parkinson, B. (1995). *Ideas and realities of emotion.* London: Routledge.
Richards, R. (1990). Everyday creativity, eminent creativity, and health. *Creativity Research Journal, 3,* 300–326.
Russell, J. A. (1991). Culture and the categorization of emotions. *Psychological Bulletin, 110,* 426–450.
Salovey, P., Bedell, B. T., Detweiler, J. B., & Mayer, J. D. (2000). Current directions in emotional intelligence research. In M. Lewis & J. M. Haviland (Eds.), *Handbook of emotions* (2nd ed., pp. 504–520). New York: Guilford.
Simonton, D. K. (1988). Creativity, leadership and chance. In R. J. Sternberg (Ed.), *The nature of creativity* (pp. 386–426). New York: Cambridge University Press.

Snider, J. G., & Osgood, C. E. (Eds.). (1969). *Semantic differential technique: A sourcebook*. Chicago: Aldine.
Startwell, C. (1988). Aesthetics of the spurious. *British Journal of Aesthetics, 28*, 360–367.
Steinberg, R. J., & Figart, D. M. (Eds.). (1999). *The Annals of The American Academy of Political and Social Science: Emotional labor in the service economy* (Vol. 561, special ed.). Thousand Oaks, CA: Sage.
Tourangeau, R., & Sternberg, R. J. (1982). Understanding and appreciating metaphors. *Cognition, 11*, 203–244.

Chapter 14

Selective Retention Processes That Create Tensions Between Novelty and Value in Business Domains

Cameron M. Ford
Diane M. Sullivan
University of Central Florida

Creative action in organizations often requires individuals to risk huge investments of time and credibility in the face of highly uncertain and distant returns. Given the magnitude of the personal and organizational stakes involved even in relatively modest creative endeavors, it would seem unwise to proceed with novel proposals without carefully considering how they produce value for affected stakeholders. In organizational settings, value tends to have a "bottom line" quality to it—at some point, the magnitude, duration, and scope of a novel idea's economic contribution must be articulated. This is not a trivial task. Several different streams of research in the administrative sciences raise important questions regarding the value of novel proposals in organizational environments. Novel proposals often create value and serve as the impetus to important organizational and industrial changes, but more often they do not. A variety of explanations have been offered to explain circumstances when novel proposals are likely to create value, and when they are likely to fail. The purpose of this chapter is to describe a few of these theories in an effort to depict environmental constraints and challenges that affect creativity in organizational settings. In particular, we are taking the rather unconventional approach of describing attributes of business environments outside the boundaries of specific organizations that *are largely beyond the control of specific organizations and organizational actors.* The environmental influences we describe herein place important constraints on creative discretion within organizations, and must be considered by those charged with implementing creative proposals that affect an organization's external constituencies. Consequently, we propose important boundary conditions that should be taken into account by investigators who aim to better contextualize organizational creativity research (Heath & Sitkin, 2001).

We begin by arguing that creativity can be best understood through the lens of evolution theory. A Darwinian variation and selective retention view offers a generic process description that can be applied to creative achievements and social change in varied task domains (Simonton, 1999). Given the generic nature of its descriptions, evolutionary theory offers a unique platform on which insights from different academic disciplines can be generalized to form a robust and useful description of creativity in social settings. Campbell (1960) initially described an evolutionary perspective of creativity by identifying blind variation and selective retention processes that govern the generation and diffusion of novel ideas. Other eminent psychologists such as Csikszentmihalyi (1990) and Simonton (1999) have advocated this description of creativity and social change. Ford (1996) and Ford and Gioia (2000) generalized this approach to creativity in organizational and business domains by describing associations between complementary psychological and sociological perspectives on variation and selective retention processes. Ford's theory emphasizes how variations and environments reciprocally affect each other over time. This emphasis on mutual adaptation reflects the tenets of structuration (cf. Giddens, 1984) and coevolution theory (Lewin, Long, & Carroll, 1999) whereby social structures constrain current patterns of behavior and these patterns either reinforce or invalidate current conventions. Thus, an evolutionary view of creativity provides a means of linking administrative science research that emphasizes selective retention processes enforcing conformity in organizational environments with psychological theories of creativity that emphasize how variations are developed (Ford, 1996).

One of the most significant implications of applying an evolutionary view of creativity to organizations is that it focuses on variation and selective retention processes that are inherently at cross-purposes with one another (Weick, 1979). Specifically, as individuals, teams, organizations, or industries become increasingly adapted to previously retained variations, the motivation and ability to generate and select new variations (creative alternatives) declines. Variation processes (e.g., brainstorming, experimenting, etc.) are more likely to generate a wide range of novel ideas when selective retention processes (e.g., memory, routines, norms, standards, etc.) place few constraints on individuals' thought processes. Alternatively, selective retention processes are more likely to align collective thought and behavior into efficiently organized and synchronized patterns when novel disruptions are few. Campbell's generic description of the tension between variation and selective retention processes is as follows:

For an evolutionary process to take place there need to be variations [as by mutation, trial, etc.], stable aspects of the environment differentially selecting among such variations and a retention-propagation system rigidly holding on to the selected variations. The variation and the retention aspects are inherently at odds. Every new mutation represents a failure of reproduction of a prior selected form. Too high a mutation rate jeopardizes the preservation of already achieved adaptations. There arise in evolutionary systems, therefore, mechanisms for curbing the variation rate. The more elaborate the achieved adaptation, the more likely are mutations to be deleterious, and therefore the stronger the inhibitions on mutation. For this reason we may expect to find great strength in the preservation and propagation systems, which lead to the perpetuation of once-adaptive traits long after environmental shifts have removed their adaptedness. (Campbell, 1965, pp. 306–307)

Administrative science theories have provided extensive descriptions of stable aspects of organizational environments differentially selecting among variations that function to curb the variation rate. These theories describe several different attributes of organizations' operating environments, including their competitive, institutional, and technological environments that curb variations through their impact on individual and collective creativity. Consequently, it is important to understand how environments and individuals interact during the evolutionary processes that characterize creativity.

Campbell's description dramatically illustrates the inevitable tension between variation and selective retention processes in task environments. Weick (1979) was the first administrative scientist to describe this tension from the standpoint of organizations and their environments. He followed Campbell's description of the antagonistic relationship between variation and selective retention processes in organizations by emphasizing that the effectiveness of one process implies the failure of the other in his evolutionary model of organizing processes. Ford (1996) subsequently applied Campbell and Weick's logic more narrowly to describe individual and collective creativity in organizational domains. Ford portrayed the tension between variation and selective retention processes by framing creativity as a choice between novel behaviors whose value is uncertain and previously retained routines whose value has been established. This theory describes factors that lead individuals to choose novel behavior opportunities over habitual or routine behavioral options (variation), and features of groups, organizations, industries, and institutions that affect the fate of novel and common actions (selective retention).

Thus, despite all the breathless hype that surrounds the pursuit of creativity and innovation in the business press, most organizations, employees, and consumers—when given a choice—overwhelmingly favor established routine solutions over unproven novel solutions (Staw, 1995). We argue that this preference is based on two unassailable human tendencies: Individuals tend to prefer known to unknown solutions, and individuals tend to avoid negative information and seek positive information regarding the self. Retention processes in organizational environments typically allow individuals to know with great certainty what will happen if they enact a routine pattern of behavior. Alternatively, consequences associated with novel proposals are usually highly uncertain, distant in time (March, 1991), and portend substantial, often unanticipated changes. The relative ease of recall, justification, and implementation associated with routine solutions makes them preferable for the typical satisficing, heuristic-using decision maker (cf. March & Simon, 1958) in comparison to novel alternatives. Building a case for selecting and retaining novel solutions also requires deviating from the opinions and pointing out the failures of others. This may work in favor of a novel proposal if those indicted by a failure work outside the organization (e.g., a competitor). However, most novel proposals require deviating from ideas held by close associates in a manner that implies blame for current shortcomings. This is likely to evoke defensive responses from those whose self-theories are challenged by the proposed new order. Negative reactions imposed on those holding minority views enforce conformity if positive appraisals from the majority are important to a dissenter's self-image.

Both of these basic human characteristics are called into question when aspects of an organization's environment are taken into consideration by purveyors of novel ideas. Organizational environments provide multiple, redundant normative cues that signal "appropriate" and "inappropriate" or "profitable" and "unprofitable" patterns of individual and organizational action (cf. Ford, 1996). In sum, the preponderance of evidence accumulated by administrative scientists suggests that when individuals in organizations are free to choose they tend to conform to the conventions suggested by others who have successfully navigated the same environment.

This may seem like a strange introduction to a discussion of creativity in business. However, the tensions between novelty and ascribed value present challenges that are unique, or at least substantially more salient, in business domains. In this chapter, we frame these challenges within Campbell's description of variation and selective retention processes in hopes that this discussion is familiar to many readers of this volume. The remainder of this chapter focuses on two principle issues. First, we describe selective retention processes characteristic of organizations' macro environments that place boundaries on creating processes in organizational settings. Second, we explain some of the complexities involved in creating value with novel proposals given the boundaries or constraints that we describe. This discussion suggests that "creativity" is a particularly troublesome construct in organizations because the underlying attributes of novelty and value are often weakly or even negatively associated due to forces in organizations' environments. Our concluding remarks offer suggestions for contextualizing creativity research by considering distinct selective retention processes that affect the fate of novel proposals in organizational environments.

ADMINISTRATIVE SCIENCE THEORIES DESCRIBING SELECTIVE RETENTION PROCESSES

In organizational settings, there exist multiple overlapping influences on individual and collective behavior that collectively represent an organization's operating environment. These influences act as selective retention processes that regulate individual and collective behavior along several different dimensions. Many administrative scientists have contributed theories that support the notion that conforming to behavioral expectations, norms, and routines is fundamental to the process of organizing. Without conformity, organizations or any other social collective would spiral into anarchy. By conforming to standards and routines that facilitate organizing and economic value creation, organizational actors reaffirm previously retained forms of activity that have proven their worth over time. Of course, being "organized" has its problems. Collective behavior that is organized for one purpose can be maladaptive when circumstances change. Also, basing actions on the status quo implies that one will always be a follower of trends rather than a vanguard capable of shaping the environment to one's advantage. The tension between being organized yet flexible, efficient yet creative, reliable yet dynamic, and timeless yet timely has vexed administrative scholars and practitioners for decades. Our view is that this tension is a ubiquitous and inevitable result of the variation and selective retention processes that are characteristic of organizational domains.

Several administrative science theories describing organizations' environments have used evolutionary theory as the basis for their proposals. To simplify our presentation, we have elected to present illustrative examples of theories whose dominant logic is closely aligned with our own. Specifically, we provide brief sketches of representative proposals from population ecology theory, institutional theory, and technological innovation theory that describe selective retention factors that define the character of organizations' operating environments. We also describe how these environmental characteristics affect individual and collective creativity. The selective retention processes addressed by these theories are important for creativity researchers to understand as dynamic contextual features that are distinctive influences on creative action within business contexts. As such, they could be considered as influences to be included in future studies, or as boundary conditions that better contextualize the contributions offered by empirical research (Rousseau & Fried, 2001). Readers interested in reviewing prior research and theory that describes contextual influences *within* organizations may benefit by seeking out complementary reviews offered by Amabile (1988), Ford (1996), and Woodman, Sawyer, and Griffin (1993). It is important to recall, however, that the individual, team, and organizational factors affecting creativity identified in these reviews are subject to the influences of selective retention processes in organizational environments that we describe here.

Population Ecology Theory

Population ecology theory (also referred to as *structural inertia theory*), as its name suggests, seeks to explain the types of organizational forms that exist in specific environmental niches, and how the distribution of forms changes over time (Freeman & Hannan, 1983; Hannan & Freeman, 1977; McKelvey, 1982). This theory is a direct extension of Darwinian logic—an organization's fit with its niche is the primary determinant of its viability. This theory poses problems that affect both novel and established (retained) organizational forms. Novel organizational forms that represent variations from previous selected forms are faced with the "liability of newness" (Stinchcomb, 1965) as a result of limited resources that can buffer them from environmental threats. Organizations face the highest likelihood of failure during this initial founding period. Furthermore, the "liability of adolescence" (Fichman & Levinthal, 1991) occurs when initial investments run dry and firms begin to function with normal operating revenues. Again, youth portends resource constraints that make firms especially vulnerable to unfavorable conditions in their environments. Environmental conditions, largely representing the accumulated affect of previously selected organizational forms, tend to select against novelty. On average, novel forms fair poorly.

However, novel forms do possess one advantage: They tend to have a greater capacity for adapting to environmental changes than do longstanding, previously successful forms. When important aspects of the environment change, possibly as a consequence of the introduction of a new form, selective retention processes will favor those forms that are best able to capture resources in the changed environment. Hannan and Freeman (1984) discussed how inertia increases as firms age, thus making them less able to change strategies or structures in the face of environmental threats. Inertia is particularly problematic when organization members have diverse objectives, as is the case in a firm with many specialists, and when means-ends relationships (i.e., appropriate technology) are unclear. Put more simply, inertia is especially difficult to overcome when personal implications and potential solutions are hard to discern (Hannan & Freeman, 1984). Although one may argue that firms should be able to innovate their way out of this competitive cul-de-sac, empirical evidence suggests that introducing multiple innovations simultaneously increases firm mortality rates by as much as 40% (Barnett & Freeman, 2001). These results suggest that rapid, innovation-based turnarounds are substantially less likely than are rapid, innovation-based fatalities.

Population ecology theory does not explain how new forms arise, or how adaptive responses come to light. Variations are exogenous factors that affect, and are affected by, the environment. So, what can a creativity researcher learn from population ecology theory? First, organizations are limited in their ability to adapt to significant environmental changes. For instance, typewriter companies failed to adopt, or lead in the development of, word-processing technology. Firms that succeeded with word processors failed to adopt personal computing technology. Consequently, virtually all of the typewriter and word-processor manufacturers who once dominated their industry failed shortly after new technology disrupted their markets (Christensen, 1997). Thus, novel proposals are more likely to be selected against in mature, differentiated firms in which individual contributions to firm performance are difficult to articulate. Smaller, organically structured firms are likely to be more favorably positioned with respect to novel proposals. Many large firms now recognize the problems associated with inertia. They often launch novel initiatives as small, independent ventures (spinouts) to free themselves from the tyranny of previously retained organizational routines and values (Christensen, 1997).

However, environmental forces are likely to select against new, vulnerable forms that fit poorly with established industry practices and characteristics. Ultimately, population ecology theory makes the point that organizations within specific environmental niches exhibit relatively little variation. It is difficult for established firms to change, and difficult for novel firms to survive. Creative discretion is, therefore, quite limited. Unless a firm's environment changes significantly, novel proposals are most likely to create value by facilitating incremental improvements on the existing business formula. Because environmental conditions are likely to affect the relative value created by incremental or radical innovations, organizational creativity researchers may want to consider the stability of environmental conditions within an industry when they test their proposals or as a boundary condition on their arguments. For example, the priority, focus, and scope of creative initiatives are likely to be quite different in the information technology and canned food industries.

Institutional Theory

Institutional theory was developed as an attempt to explain the remarkable similarity of organizations in industrialized societies (Mizruchi & Fein, 1999). Early contributors to this perspective argued that similarity was driven not only by competitive forces or technical requirements for efficiency, but also by organizations' need for social legitimacy within their operating environments. Homogeneity across firms is seen as a consequence of historical evolutionary forces. When an organizational field—typically described as a group of organizations affiliated with a particular industry, consumer markets, regulatory agencies, and so on—is relatively undefined, the population of organizations within it may be rather diverse. However, as a consequence of competitive and institutional isomorphism, firm behavior and characteristics become more closely aligned over time. Competitive isomorphism is similar to the forces described by population ecology theory previously and is not the primary focus of institutional theory's arguments (Mizruchi & Fein, 1999). Institutional isomorphism, the main contribution of institutional theory, aims to satisfy an organization's need for political and institutional legitimacy. DiMaggio and Powell (1983) proposed three forces through which institutional isomorphism occur. These forces may be considered as selective retention processes as we have described previously. *Coercive isomorphism* occurs when one organization is dependent on another organization for resources. In this case, one organization's actions will be constrained by the desires and requirements of those who provide resources. *Mimetic isomorphism* occurs when one organization mimics another, more successful organization, as is the case when firms copy "best practices" from industry leaders. Finally, *normative isomorphism* occurs as a consequence of professional socialization whereby organizational actors' beliefs and worldviews lead them to identify with norms, values, and practices previously selected and retained in their professional domain (e.g., accountants, professors, physicians, etc.).

Thus, in addition to selective retention processes within competitive environments emphasized by population ecology theory, this theory identifies multiple, overlapping selective retention processes characteristic of institutional environments. Individuals working in highly institutionalized settings (e.g., banking, insurance, automobile manufacturing) will find their creative discretion limited by the "rationalized myths" (Meyer & Rowan, 1977) representing previously retained (although not necessarily optimal) knowledge that defines "the way things are done" in an industry. Rationalized myths are impersonal prescriptions that often impose specific technical routines that are beyond the discretion of any individual or organization. As such, these routines become taken for granted as legitimate regardless of their actual effectiveness (Meyer & Rowan, 1977).

How can institutional theory enhance our understanding of creativity and organizational settings? In addition to the constraints imposed by competitive forces within an environmental niche, organizational actors must consider how their novel proposals are related to the preferences of potential resource providers, the state of accepted best practices, and the prevailing norms and wisdom held within their industry and profession. For example, in an interesting study of the textbook publishing industry, Levitt and Nass (1989) found textbook content and topic sequencing varied far more in organizational behavior texts than in basic physics texts because institutional forces (especially normative isomorphism) are stronger in more established disciplines like physics. Creators may be very discouraged by the heavy-handed imposition of institutional constraints. Yet, navigating these constraints may provide administrators with opportunities to exercise their unique creative talents. Drazin, Glynn, and Kazanjian (1999) illustrated the utility of this notion by describing dynamic processes whereby creative challenges shift between technical and managerial roles during the evolution of creative projects. Creators may also be able to take advantage of others' unquestioning adherence to an industry's dominant logic. For example, industry outsiders who are typically unaware or have little stake in an industry's routines or norms start novel ventures (Aldrich & Kenworthy, 1998) and introduce disruptive technology (Christensen, 1997) far more often than do incumbent firms.

Overall, organizational creativity researchers should remain cognizant of multiple competitive and institutional constraints that limit discretion in many settings (e.g., nurses may attempt novel approaches to some tasks, but legal requirements and professional norms forbid novel approaches to others). Articulating institutional constraints may be particularly challenging because these constraints often function as tacit, taken-for-granted ideas, rather than as explicitly understood barriers to creativity. These constraints should either be included in theories and research designs, or acknowledged as boundary conditions to research proposals.

Technological Innovation Theory

Technological innovation is one of the primary elements most people think of when they consider how creativity impacts businesses. Clearly, technological innovation is an important source of strategic differentiation that allows firms to capture and maintain competitive advantage. However, selective retention processes afoot in this context suggest that not all novel technologies will be valued. Anderson and Tushman (1990) provided one of the most comprehensive descriptions of an evolutionary model of technological change. The thrust of their arguments is as follows:

> Technological discontinuities [innovations that dramatically advance an industry's price vs. performance frontier] trigger a period of ferment that is closed by the emergence of a dominant design. A period of incremental technical change then follows, which is, in turn, broken by the next technological discontinuity. . . . This cyclical model of technological change focuses on the

social and organizational selection processes that affect the closing on a dominant design and contrast social and technological dynamics during eras of ferment with those in eras of incremental change. (p. 604)

Anderson and Tushman (1990) reviewed prior technology and innovation research and argued that technological change is best characterized, following Campbell, as a "sociocultural evolutionary process of variation, selection and retention" (p. 605).

This line of research has been comprehensively reviewed by Utterback (1994) and cleverly extended by Christensen (1997). This research tradition shows that novel technologies are introduced frequently when no particular design dominates consumer markets. During this phase of technological evolution, many small firms vie for the hearts of consumers by offering novel approaches that address a particular need (Utterback, 1994). At some point, competition among novel forms culminates in the selection of a single "dominant design" (Anderson & Tushman, 1990). For example, Microsoft's Windows became the dominant design for PC operating systems during the 1980s. Subsequently, other operating systems and the companies that offered them disappeared. Rapid industry consolidation and the emergence of a standardized product architecture occur during the second phase of a technology's evolution. After this transition, major innovations are mostly unwelcome because they cause disruptions that exceed any value created. Large firms with large investments in the dominant design, suppliers who benefit by supporting the design, and consumers who develop comfortable routines employing a technology conspire to create an environment that is unfavorable for highly novel technologies. Consequently, the focus of creative efforts shifts to pursuing incremental elaborations and improvements on the dominant design (Utterback, 1994). For instance, laundry detergents have not changed fundamentally for decades but continue to add novel properties that consumers value (contrast this to the current success of no-detergent laundry disks—a novel technology that requires significant changes in consumer beliefs and routines).

In some cases, developing a major technology can be so cost prohibitive that no single firm can justify investing in its development. Institutions, especially the government, may step in to create more favorable selective retention processes. This occurred when the FCC created technical standards for high-definition television, rather than waiting for unpredictable market forces to sort things out (Day, Schoemaker, & Gunther, 2000). What is the lesson in all this for those interested in creativity? It is critically important to understand the stage of technology evolution in an industry one wishes to affect. Immature, fragmented technologies may be receptive to novel entries and new ventures. Mature sectors characterized by a dominant design and few competitors (typically five to seven firms; Utterback, 1994) find little value in highly novel proposals that could ruin the viability of current designs. Once a dominant design is established, initiatives can return the most value at relatively modest or extremely high levels of novelty. Highly novel products that command a decisive cost, performance, or quality advantage over prior product forms may throw an industry back into an era of ferment (Anderson & Tushman, 1990). However, incremental innovations that entail relatively modest degrees of novelty are the primary source of value creation with mature technologies.

CREATIVITY AS A LOOSELY COUPLED CONSTRUCT WITHIN ORGANIZATIONAL CONTEXTS

Creativity researchers and laypersons seem to agree that creativity requires that a proposal be both novel and, in some sense, valuable. In many research domains in which novelty is often intrinsically valued (e.g., art, mathematics, architecture, etc.), value and novelty may be, on average, closely associated. General evolutionary theory would propose that this would be true in any domain in which novelty is favored by relevant selective retention processes. However, the applications of evolutionary theory to organizations and their environments we have described show that novelty is not *intrinsically* valuable in organizational domains. Population ecology theory, institutional theory, and technology innovation theory each show that novel proposals are often rejected by selective retention processes characteristic of all organizations' operating environments. Novel products that violate technological standards and consumer expectations usually fail (Aldrich & Fiol, 1994). New business ventures usually fail (Aldrich & Kenworthy, 1998). Firms that break with tradition often lose support from vital stakeholders, thus making them more likely to fail (DiMaggio & Powell, 1983; Meyer & Rowan, 1977).

Our point is not that novelty is bad, but rather that it is not always good. This is true in all task domains, but we believe it is especially true in organizational settings. For instance, Ford and Gioia (2000) found that two distinct constellation of influences contributed to the novelty and value of managerial choices. Novelty and value had statistically independent antecedents, and were weakly associated with each other as attributes of creativity. Ford and Gioia concluded that managerial decision making involves a complex balancing of solution requirements (selective retention processes), some that favor novelty and some that do not. Deephouse (1999) suggested that the solution to this conundrum is a question of balance; individuals and organizations need to be different enough to offer value that cannot be easily acquired from another source, but not so different as to violate existing standards, norms, and routines. At this point we hope that it is obvious that we believe managing novelty and value are loosely coupled challenges that should be addressed with an appreciation of the different challenges associated with each. Researchers should also consider using multidimensional assessment techniques that allow the relationship between novelty and value to be assessed empirically. Articulating how and when novelty creates value is important for both influencing and investigating creativity in organizations.

Timing also affects the relationship between assessments of novelty and value. One can immediately discern whether a particular proposal is novel to a particular context. This is an empirical question that can be resolved using a cross-sectional research design. The current proposal simply needs to be compared to solutions retained in the past. However, ascertaining the value created by or associated with a novel proposal is an empirical question requiring a longitudinal, and perhaps multilevel, research design. When one begins consideration of a creative episode by describing the genesis of a variation, evolutionary logic would suggest that value would be determined by how the variation fares when subjected to selective retention processes. In social contexts, the time required to assess the outcome of a selective retention process is likely to increase in proportion with the complexity and uncertainty associated with a novel proposal, and the scope or level of the selective retention context one wishes to assess. For example, a group might endorse a novel proposal relatively quickly, perhaps in a matter of days or weeks. Alternatively, it is not uncommon for radical innovations to flounder for years, waiting to be fully endorsed by a sponsoring organization. Achieving success in the marketplace may take even longer (cf. Christensen, 1997). When people are asked to assess the creativity of a particular proposal, they can immediately assess its novelty (of course, the meaningfulness of this assessment is constrained by a judge's familiarity with previously retained solutions in a particular domain), but in most cases they must conduct a thought experiment to imagine value created by the proposal.

In practice, the conceptual and temporal separation of assessments of novelty and value manifest themselves in the "pitching" process (cf. Elsbach & Kramer, 2003). Creators, who have already imagined positive consequences that will be realized if their novel proposals are enacted, typically must convince others to support their endeavors. Appreciating the novelty of a proposal might lead a listener to say "That's cool!" but uncertainty regarding the ultimate value created by the proposal might also lead to asking "So what?" Presenting novel proposals for rigorous value assessments is common in business; stage-gate review processes are often applied to assess the value of innovative projects, and business plan presentations are usually required from those wishing to launch a new venture. Over time, the valuation process may cascade up levels of analysis—from team to organization to market, for example—with assessments at one level influencing assessments at the next level. Creativity researchers should attempt to be as specific as possible regarding the context and magnitude of novelty and value assessments (i.e., Novel to whom? How novel? Valuable to whom? How valuable?). These issues matter. Incremental and radical innovations arise through dramatically different processes, for example (Christensen, 1997).

CONCLUDING REMARKS

Our focus on selection and retention processes is an attempt to better contextualize future organizational creativity research (Heath & Sitkin, 2001; Rousseau & Fried, 2001). It is not sufficient for administrative scientists to study creativity because it may be relevant to organizations or occasionally occurs in organizational contexts. In order for administrative scientists to provide unique insights into organizational creativity, we need to emphasize how the process of creating (variation) is related to the process of organizing (selective retention). This approach has the advantage of articulating the importance of creating to organizing, emphasizing dynamic processes that unfold over time, and encouraging cross-level research (Heath & Sitkin, 2001). Approaching organizational creativity research framed in this manner allows administrative scientists to offer unique insights not likely to be shared by researchers in related disciplines. We suggest that interpretation of organizational creativity research findings can be clarified by attending to the contextual boundaries we have discussed. Specifically, researchers should consider if and how selective retention processes in organizations' environments limit the generalizability of empirical findings.

We have emphasized selective retention processes described by administrative science theories that place boundaries on the value-creating potential of novel proposals. The selective retention processes we presented suggest that competitive context (population ecology), resource networks and regulatory agencies (coercive isomorphism), fads and "best practices" (mimetic isomorphism), industry norms (normative isomorphism), and stage of technology development each limit creative discretion in organizational settings. Christensen (1997), in his description of disruptive innovation, employed the metaphor of learning to fly to describe how managers should consider forces like these. He likened selective retention processes to the laws of physics, which clearly limit the viability of certain novel approaches to flying. However, knowledge of these "laws" can also focus and inspire creative efforts to produce genuinely valuable innovations. Powell (1991) made a similar argument from the perspective of institutional theory. He suggested that knowledge of gaps and tensions between institutional domains can create opportunities for creative approaches and novel business initiatives. For example, new government requirements for medical reporting that conflict with the current routines of hospitals and physicians may create a market for firms that can help medical agencies comply with new requirements. Our point is that the selective retention processes in organizational environments can be viewed as both constraints and facilitators of creative action. Perhaps the ability to view these forces in terms of opportunities is one of the characteristics that distinguish successful creators.

REFERENCES

Aldrich, H. E., & Fiol, C. M. (1994). Fools rush in? The institutional context of industry creation. *Academy of Management Review, 19*, 645–670.

Aldrich, H. E., & Kenworthy, A. (1998). The accidental entrepreneur: Campbellian antinomies and organizational foundings. In J. A. C. Baum & B. McKelvey (Eds.), *Variations in organization science: In honor of Donald T. Campbell* (pp. 19–33). Newbury Park, CA: Sage.

Amabile, T. M. (1988). A model of creativity and innovation in organizations. *Research in Organizational Behavior, 10*, 123–169.

Anderson, P., & Tushman, M. L. (1990). Technological discontinuities and dominant designs: A cyclical model of technological change. *Administrative Science Quarterly, 35*, 604–633.

Barnett, W. P., & Freeman, J. (2001). Too much of a good thing? Product proliferation and organizational failure. *Organization Science, 12*, 539–558.

Campbell, D. T. (1960). Blind variation and selective retention in creative thought as in other knowledge processes. *Psychological Review, 95*, 380–400.

Campbell, D. T. (1965). Variation and selective retention in socio-cultural evolution. In H. R. Barringer, G. I. Blanksten, & R. W. Mack (Eds.), *Social change in developing areas: A reinterpretation of evolutionary theory* (pp. 19–48). Cambridge, MA: Schenkman.

Christensen, C. M. (1997). *The innovator's dilemma: When new technologies cause great firms to fail.* Cambridge, MA: Harvard Business School Press.

Csikszentmihalyi, M. (1990). The domain of creativity. In M. A. Runco & R. S. Albert (Eds.), *Theories of creativity* (pp. 190–212). Newbury Park, CA: Sage.

Day, G. S., Schoemaker, P. J. H., & Gunther, R. E. (Eds.). (2000). *Wharton on managing emerging technologies.* New York: Wiley.

Deephouse, D. L. (1999). To be different, or to be the same? It's a question (and theory) of strategic balance. *Strategic Management Journal, 20*, 147–166.

DiMaggio, P. J., & Powell, W. W. (1983). The iron cage revisited: Institutional isomorphism and collective rationality in organizational fields. *American Sociological Review, 48*, 147–160.

Drazin, R., Glynn, M. A., & Kazanjian, R. K. (1999). Multilevel theorizing about creativity in organizations: A sensemaking perspective. *Academy of Management Review, 24*, 286–307.

Elsbach, K. D., & Kramer, R. M. (2003). Assessing creativity in Hollywood pitch meetings: Evidence for a dual-process model of creativity judgments. *Academy of Management Journal, 46*, 283–302.

Fichman, M., & Levinthal, D. A. (1991). Honeymoons and the liability of adolescence: A new perspective on duration dependence in social and organizational relationships. *Academy of Management Review, 16*, 442–468.

Ford, C. M. (1996). A theory of individual creative action in multiple social domains. *Academy of Management Review, 21*(4), 1112–1142.

Ford, C. M., & Gioia, D. A. (2000). Factors influencing creativity in the domain of managerial decision making. *Journal of Management, 26*, 705–732.
Freeman, J., & Hannan, M. T. (1983). Niche width and the dynamics of organizational populations. *American Journal of Sociology, 88*, 1115–1145.
Giddens, A. (1984). *The constitution of society: Outline of the theory of structuration.* Oxford, UK: Polity.
Hannan, M. T., & Freeman, J. (1977). The population ecology of organizations. *American Journal of Sociology, 82*, 929–964.
Hannan, M. T., & Freeman, J. (1984). Structural inertia and organizational change. *American Sociological Review, 49*, 149–164.
Heath, C., & Sitkin, S. B. (2001). Big-B versus Big-O: What is organizational about organizational behavior? *Journal of Organizational Behavior, 22*, 43–58.
Levitt, B., & Nass, C. (1989). The lid on the garbage can: Institutional constraints on decision-making in the technical core of college-text publishers. *Administrative Science Quarterly, 34*, 190–207.
Lewin, A. Y., Long, C. P., & Carroll, T. N. (1999). The co-evolution of new organizational forms. *Organization Science, 10*, 535–550.
March, J. G. (1991). Exploration and exploitation in organizational learning. *Organizational Science, 2*, 71–87.
March, J. G., & Simon, H. A. (1958). *Organizations.* New York: Wiley.
McKelvey, B. (1982). *Organizational systematics.* Berkeley: University of California Press.
Meyer, J. W., & Rowan, B. (1977). Institutionalized organizations: Formal structure as myth and ceremony. *American Journal of Sociology, 83*, 340–636.
Mizruchi, M. S., & Fein, L. C. (1999). The social construction of organizational knowledge: A study of the uses of coercive, mimetic, and normative isomorphism. *Administrative Science Quarterly, 44*, 653–683.
Powell, W. W. (1991). Expanding the scope of institutional analysis. In W. W. Powell & P. J. DiMaggio (Eds.), *The new institutionalism in organizational analysis* (pp. 183–203). Chicago: University of Chicago Press.
Rousseau, D. M., & Fried, Y. (2001). Location, location, location: Contextualizing organizational research. *Journal of Organizational Behavior, 22*, 1–13.
Simonton, D. K. (1999). Creativity as blind variation and selective retention: Is the creative process Darwinian? *Psychological Inquiry, 10*, 309–328.
Staw, B. M. (1995). Why no one really wants creativity. In C. M. Ford & D. A. Gioia (Eds.), *Creative action in organizations: Ivory tower visions & real world voices* (pp. 161–166). Thousand Oaks, CA: Sage.
Stinchcomb, A. L. (1965). Social structure and organizations. In J. G. March (Ed.), *Handbook of organizations* (pp. 142–193). Chicago: Rand McNally.
Utterback, J. M. (1994). *Mastering the dynamics of innovation.* Cambridge, MA: Harvard Business School Press.
Weick, K. E. (1979). *The social psychology of organizing.* Reading, MA: Addison-Wesley.
Woodman, R., Sawyer, J., & Griffin, R. (1993). Toward a theory of organizational creativity. *Academy of Management Review, 18*(2), 293–321.

Chapter 15

Management: Synchronizing Different Kinds of Creativity

Min Basadur
McMaster University DeGroote School of Business

INTRODUCTION

How do people think, work, and act creatively in diverse domains? Is creativity a general attribute or do different kinds of creativity apply in different domains? These are the main themes of this book. This chapter suggests that not only are there different kinds of creativity, but also that there are different kinds of creativity within the domain of management. This is because there is a need for different kinds of creativity within various kinds of work and jobs in organizations. "Applied creativity" may be viewed as a process with multiple stages or phases. Different kinds of creativity are associated with the various phases or stages of the process. Within organizations, different kinds of work favor specific kinds of creativity, which must be synchronized to achieve innovative results for profitability and competitive edge. What does this process of applied creativity involve?

DIFFERENT APPROACHES TO CREATIVITY

Studying and discussing creativity can be difficult and complex, both because no single, agreed-on definition of this quality exists and because researchers have taken many different approaches to studying it. Under the *identification* approach, Guilford (1967) and MacKinnon (1962, 1977) developed cognitive, aptitude, and personality tests to identify relatively more or less creative people. Others have studied *organizational factors* that are likely to inhibit or nurture creative performance (e.g., goals, incentives, and freedom from time pressure; Baker, Winkofsky, Langmeyer, & Sweeney, 1976). A third approach involves *deliberate improvement*: Can we train people and make them "more creative" or better able to use their innate creativity (Basadur, Runco, & Vega, 2000; Parnes, Noller, & Biondi, 1977)?

Researchers have begun to organize the study of creativity into the four "Ps": product, press (environmental factors), person, and process (Murdock & Puccio, 1994). For example, some researchers (e.g., O'Quin & Besemer, 1989) study creative products: What makes a more or less creative product, from a car to a story? Jackson and Messick (1964) identified four criteria to measure the creativity of a product. Besides being unusual, they said, the new product must be appropriate. The product must also be transformative: Does it make us think about the world in a different way? And it must convey "condensation": Does this product feel fresh every time you use or encounter it? Researchers studying "press" have examined environmental factors that can induce creativity in organizations (Amabile & Gryskiewicz, 1989). Others study personal characteristics related to creativity. For example, Kirton (1976) differentiated between people with more "adaptive" styles of creativity and people with more "innovative" styles of creativity, and Myers (1962) addressed the relationship between personality and creative behavior.

THE PROCESS APPROACH TO APPLIED CREATIVITY

Still others focus on modeling creativity as a process with steps, phases, or stages. Inherent in this approach is the idea that people may follow a process to increase creative performance and to communicate more efficiently with others in creative teamwork. Taking the process approach, Kabanoff and Rossiter (1994) defined applied creativity as "occurring in a real-world, industrial, organizational or social context; pertaining to the finding or solving of complex problems; and having an actual behavioral creative product (or plan) as the final result" (p. 283). They said that applied creativity is vital in several fields, including science (inventive research and development), business (new product innovation and management), government (administrative planning for more heterogeneous and globalizing societies), and the arts (cultural and aesthetic developments). In fact, organizations in any industry may benefit from applied creativity. (Certainly, applying creativity to increase profitability is far more satisfying than the alternative route of cutting costs and paying the attendant penalty in unemployment.)

COGNITIVE PROCESS MODELS

Several other researchers have written about cognitive models of the process of creative thinking and problem solving, all involving a sequential flow through specific stages, phases, or steps. Kabanoff and Rossiter (1994) reviewed the growth of cognitive models of multistage creative thinking and problem-solving processes, beginning with Wallas' (1926) four main stages: preparation, incubation, illumination, and verification. Parnes et al. (1977) identified five steps: fact finding, problem finding, idea finding, solution finding, and acceptance finding. To that model, Isaksen and Treffinger's (1985) model added an extra step called "mess finding." Amabile (1988) also identified five stages: presentation, preparation, generation, validation, and assessment. Basadur, Graen, and Green's (1982) model of applied creativity is a circular, three-phase process of finding good problems, solving them, and implementing good solutions (Basadur, 1992). All of these models represent a sequential flow through specific stages, phases, or steps. Figure 15.1 shows a three-phase circular model of creative activity in an organization that continuously cycles through problem finding, problem solving, and solution implementing phases (see Basadur, 1992, 1997).

PROBLEM FINDING

Problem finding means continuously and deliberately discovering and formulating new and useful problems to be solved. Most researchers recognize that creativity requires more than the generation of a variety of ideas in response to a cue, and often does not begin with or depend on "given information." Guilford (1950) stressed the importance of "sensitivity to problems" in creativity and related it to our everyday notion of curiosity. Wakefield (1991) contrasted one type of thinking—"single open" problems, whose definition is *closed* but whose solution is *open*—with another type of thinking involving "double open" problems, or first formulating a previously undefined problem and then generating alternative solutions. Others have emphasized that discovering and defining new important problems to solve (problem finding) and implementing new solutions (solution implementation) is as important as or even more important than creating the new solutions (problem solving; Ackoff, 1979; Getzels, 1975; Leavitt, 1975; Levitt, 1963; Livingston, 1971; Mackworth, 1965; Simon, 1960). Basadur (1979) and Basadur et al. (1982) provided empirical evidence that attitudes, behaviors, and skills associated with problem finding were distinctly different from those associated with problem solving, and

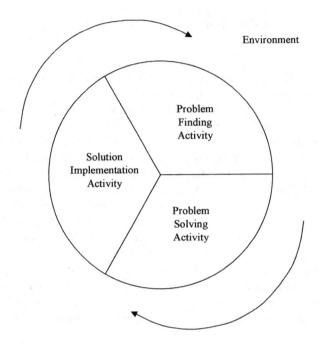

FIG. 15.1. Creativity activity in an organization.

that such attitudes, behaviors, and skills can be successfully learned in appropriate training.

Kabanoff and Rossiter (1994) cited problem finding as one of the most vital and difficult frontiers for creativity researchers—a "messy" concept that is hard to define and use. Problem finding is a crucial element of creativity, especially real-world creativity in applied settings. Basadur, Ellspermann, and Evans (1994) identified two separate components of problem-finding activity. The first component is problem generation, which involves discovering new problems for subsequent definition. This is similar to what Simon (1977) called "opportunistic surveillance." Edwin Land attributed his invention of the Polaroid camera to his unexpected finding of a problem (how to obtain instantaneous pictures), not its subsequent solution (Callahan, 1972). The second component involves formulating a previously discovered but undefined problem. This second component is called *problem formulation* (or conceptualization, or definition). Land further stated that "if you can state a problem, it can be solved" (Callahan, 1972, p. 46), and Dewey suggested that a problem well stated is half-solved. Albert Einstein is reputed to have said that, given an hour to solve a problem to save the world, he would devote 55 minutes to defining the problem, and only 5 minutes to solving it.

SOLUTION IMPLEMENTATION

As for *solution implementation,* Thomas Edison said that genius is 1% inspiration and 99% perspiration. Similarly, Alex Osborn said that a fair idea put into practice is better than a good idea kept on the polishing wheel. The world is full of people who have great ideas but are unable to take them through to completion. How can an artist claim to have been creative without yet having drawn the picture? Indeed, an entire industry has emerged that consists of small consulting companies with one function: to help larger organizations put ideas into practice and move projects through to completion. Many researchers, including Leavitt (1975) and Basadur et al. (1982), have identified the process of overcoming resistance to change and procrastination as an important part of creative thinking.

MORE THAN JUST GENERATING IDEAS

These viewpoints contrast sharply with research that confines creative thinking merely to generating ideas to presented problems using techniques such as "brainstorming." Such research dominated the literature from the 1950s into the 1980s (see review by Basadur, 1994). Practitioners who employ such limited conceptions of creative thinking seldom attain practical results (Sternberg, O'Hara, & Lubart, 1997). More recent literature contains more complete conceptions of applied creativity (Basadur, 1995; Kabanoff & Rossiter, 1994; Rickards, 1994). Such complete models include not only multiple stages (beyond simply solving presented problems) but other important individual, group, and organizational variables affecting creative performance such as motivation, cohesiveness, environment, linkage to goals, and specific skills, behaviors, and attitudes.

FOUR DISTINCT STAGES

Basadur and Gelade (2002) provided a theory of applied creativity consisting of four stages: generating, conceptualizing, optimizing, and implementing. In each of these stages, people gain and use knowledge and understanding in varying ways, as illustrated in Fig. 15.2. Each quadrant in Fig. 15.2 corresponds to a specific stage of the creative process. The first two quadrants represent the components of problem finding: generation and conceptualization. The third and fourth quadrants represent problem solving (optimization) and solution implementation as the final two stages of the creative process.

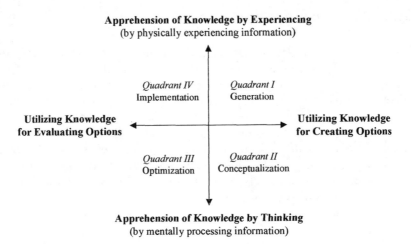

FIG. 15.2. Four combinations of different methods of gaining and using understanding.

Quadrant I

The first quadrant gets the creative process rolling. Here, creative activity includes gaining knowledge and understanding by physical contact with and involvement in real-world activities and utilizing this knowledge to create new problems, challenges, opportunities, and projects that might be worth defining and solving. Understanding is derived from what is experienced, including emotions and feelings of self and others through empathy. New possibilities are imagined from what is experienced. Quadrant I activity thus consists of sensing, seeking, or anticipating problems and opportunities; this is called *generation*.

An outcome of this stage is a problem worthy of investigation but not yet clearly defined or understood. In a *Life* magazine cover story (Callahan, 1972), Edwin Land explained his invention of the Polaroid camera. Having snapped the last exposure on his film, he suggested to his 3-year-old daughter that they take the film for processing so that they could see the pictures in about a week's time. Her frustrated response was: Why do I have to wait a week to see my picture? Like a flashbulb going off in his mind, her simple question sparked a challenge that had never occurred to him: How can one make a device that yields instantaneous pictures? Within about an hour, he had formulated several directions toward a solution. And within about 4 years, he had commercialized a product that has changed our lives. Looking back, the then-chair of Polaroid said the most important part of the process was not finding the solution itself (the camera), but instead finding the problem: how to get instantaneous pictures. Had Land not experienced the chance encounter, he might never have created the problem to be solved. He demonstrated the generation stage of the creative process: initiating problems to be solved instead of waiting for the problems to be provided.

At Japan's electronics giant Toshiba, most engineers and scientists beginning their careers in research and development start off in the sales department (Basadur, 1992). This apparently backward approach is designed to teach them the process of problem finding. Because these people will spend their working lives creating products to solve customers' problems, what better start could they have than to learn firsthand about those customers' needs, habits, and problems—both visible and hidden? A major auto parts supplier, Nippondenso, trains and encourages employees from Day 1 to find problems and to be discontented with their jobs. Employees write down their discontents and post them for other workers to read. Here and at many other Japanese companies, this is actually the start of the creative process called the *employee suggestion system*. The entire suggestion system hinges on problem finding.

Quadrant II

The second quadrant, conceptualizing, keeps the creative process going. Creative activity in this quadrant involves gaining knowledge and understanding mentally, working in the abstract, analyzing, pondering, and theorizing about the information received to create a sound conceptualization or model of the problem domain. Understanding is gained not by direct experience but instead by detached, abstract thought. What is understood through rational, systematic analysis is turned into new insights that help define problems and create theoretical models and ideas to explain things. Quadrant II activity consists of turning a problem recognized in Quadrant I into a well-understood problem definition and some fledgling solution ideas and, thus, is called *conceptualization.*

For example, a Procter & Gamble product development team formed at short notice once asked me to help them respond to a competitor's new product. Colgate's green-striped Irish Spring soap had been the first striped soap bar introduced to North America. With its aggressive advertising campaign emphasizing "refreshment," Colgate's new product was finding ready customer acceptance. Procter & Gamble worked by the rule that if a team or person were the second entrant into a new market, it had to demonstrate a product's competitive advantage before it could carry out a market test. When asked what was going wrong, the team members said they had been unable to produce a green-striped bar that worked better than Irish Spring in a consumer preference blind test. The team had experimented with several green-striped bars, all of which had merely equaled

Irish Spring in blind testing. It became evident that the team had chosen to define its problem as: How might we make a green-striped bar that consumers will prefer over Irish Spring?

During a creative problem-solving meeting, one of the important activities was to develop alternative ways to define the challenge. The flash of inspiration came from an answer to a question posed from a consumer's point of view: We want to make a bar that makes people feel more refreshed. This led to the new conceptualized challenge: How might we better connote refreshment in a soap bar? This less restrictive conceptualization, which included no mention of green stripes, provided more room for creative solutions. The team broke this new problem into a conceptualization with three separate components—How might we better connote refreshment in appearance, shape, and odor?—and then focused their imaginations on ideas. Beginning with the product's appearance, the team members visualized scenes, images, and situations that suggested refreshment. One pictured himself at the sea coast. Another imagined sitting on a beach and looking at a blue sky and white clouds. Later, when the team evaluated its many ideas, these two ideas were selected and combined. The result was the concept of a blue-and-white swirled bar with a unique odor and shape. The concept later achieved market success under the brand name Coast. By leaping prematurely into solutions, the team had wasted almost 6 months before coming up with a superior conceptualization.

Quadrant III

The third quadrant moves the creative process further. Creative activity in this quadrant involves gaining knowledge and understanding mentally by working in the abstract—thoroughly analyzing a defined problem and utilizing this knowledge to develop and evaluate ideas and options and create an optimal, practical solution. What is understood through rational, systematic, and orderly analysis is used to mentally evaluate situations and options to convert abstract ideas into practical solutions and plans. Quadrant III activity is called *optimization*. At this point, a good solution to an important, well-defined problem exists but has not yet been implemented. For example, the newly defined concept of a refreshment bar in the previous example still had to be converted into a practical solution. The team's engineers created and evaluated several optional versions of the new appearance, odor, and shape. The options were evaluated on several criteria including cost, feasibility, and time to implement. A final optimal prototype was chosen and successfully tested with consumers, showing an exploitable competitive advantage over its competitor.

Quadrant IV

The fourth quadrant completes the creative process. Apprehension in this quadrant involves gaining knowledge and understanding by physical contact and involvement in the real world. Utilization consists of employing evaluation to convert this knowledge into implemented solutions that work, accomplish valuable results, and are accepted by others. What is experienced and felt is used to evaluate. Creative activity in this quadrant consists of gaining experience with new solutions, evaluating the outcomes, and making adjustments to successfully implement them. Thus, this stage is called *implementation*. For example, in the refreshment bar example, the team was still not finished. Before the new soap formula could be sold, a patent problem in the machinery design had to be overcome. There were already no fewer than six worldwide patents restricting how blue-and-white soap pastes could be blended. The team had to find a machine design in order to manufacture the new product without infringing on anybody else's technique. The team assembled diverse points of view in a special group of engineers, technicians, lawyers, and even a few people who were unfamiliar with this technology. Sketches and prototypes of the patented processes were displayed and examined until a breakthrough insight emerged. The equipment was adjusted and rebuilt repeatedly until the new product was produced satisfactorily for delivery for purchase. A full cycle of the creative process was now complete.

APPLIED CREATIVITY AS CIRCULAR AND NEVERENDING

Gordon (1956, 1971) recognized that apprehension (learning) and utilization (for inventing) represent two different modes of thinking. Invention was characterized as a mental process of breaking old connections, or making the familiar strange (similar to generation and conceptualization), whereas learning was characterized as a mental process of making new connections or making the strange familiar (similar to optimization and implementation). These separate processes of knowledge application (for inventing) and knowledge acquisition (learning) flow continuously into one another in sequence. Field research by Carlsson, Keane, and Martin (1976) supported Gordon's approach by showing that the research and development process in organizations follows a continuous, circular flow of creating new knowledge to replace old knowledge.

Based on extensive field research and practical experience within business organizations (Basadur, 1974, 1979, 1981, 1983) consistent with Gordon's theory and Carlsson, Keane, and Martin's empirical evidence, we can understand the creative process as an ongoing cycle. Here, the different stages of the creative process are arranged in a circle, recognizing that new problems and new opportunities arise as new problems are sought, discovered, and defined, and as new solutions are subsequently developed, optimized, and implemented. For example, the automobile's invention provided not only a new solution to an old problem (improving transportation) but created many brand-new problems (e.g., pollution, energy, and accidents). This circular process, which emphasizes continuous creativity beginning with problem finding, reflects Mott's (1972) research that showed that effective organizations continually and intentionally scan the external environment to anticipate new opportunities and problems, and to proactively change their routines and find new products and methods to implement, thus leapfrogging their competitors. Each implemented solution leads to new, useful problems to be discovered. This concept, called *adaptability*, may be represented as a continuous four-stage process of creativity, as shown in Fig. 15.3.

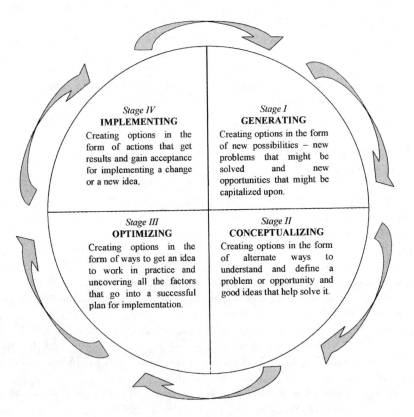

FIG. 15.3. The four stages of the creative process.

DIFFERENT STAGES AND DIFFERENT KINDS OF CREATIVITY

If we consider creativity as a multistage synchronized process, then might people differentially favor or prefer various stages of the process requiring different aspects of creativity? And might those differences be reflected in people's occupations, with certain kinds of jobs favoring certain parts of the process: generation, conceptualization, optimization, implementation? Furthermore, do people draw on different kinds of creativity as they advance through an organization, particularly into higher management ranks? There is evidence to suggest an affirmative answer—that creativity differs in kind, both among job types and within organization levels.

To determine individuals' relative preferences for each of the four stages, an instrument called the *Creative Problem Solving Profile (CPSP) inventory* has been developed (Basadur & Gelade, 2002). By returning to those quadrants of Fig. 15.2, individual preferences for each of the four stages of the creative process can be established by considering differences in how people both gain (apprehension) and use (utilization) knowledge. Again, the first quadrant combines gaining knowledge through experience with using knowledge for creating options. Quadrant I activity corresponds to generation, and yields a problem worthy of investigation but not yet clearly defined or understood. The second quadrant combines gaining knowledge by mental processing with using knowledge for creating options. Quadrant II activity consists of turning a problem from Quadrant I into a well-understood problem definition and some fledgling solution ideas, and is called *conceptualization*. The third quadrant combines gaining knowledge by mental processing with using such knowledge for evaluating options. This stage, called *optimization*, yields a good solution to an important, well-defined problem. The fourth quadrant combines gaining knowledge by experiencing with using such knowledge for evaluating options. In this stage, called *implementation*, an untried solution is put into practice. Plotting the scores obtained from the CPSP inventory and connecting them yields an irregular shape or profile, as in Fig. 15.4. As the figure shows, dominant quadrants are identified that describe an individual style or profile of the creative process.

In a creative organization, everyone is responsible for doing at least one of the four stages defined by Fig. 15.3. Some people initiate new things. Some are responsible for understanding and defining new initiatives and planning. Some produce practical solutions to new problems and initiatives. Others are responsible for finishing things off—taking action to implement new solutions. If the four-stage process of creativity outlined previously adequately represents the creative process, it would be expected that teams with a heterogeneous mix of preferred creative process styles (Fig. 15.3) would significantly outperform teams with a homogeneous mix of creative process styles

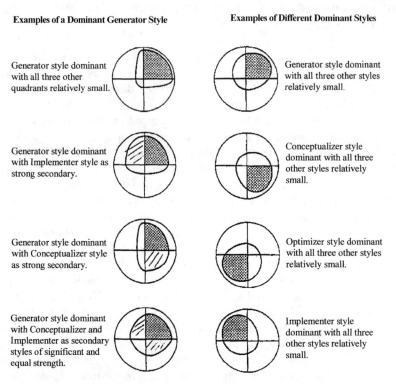

FIG. 15.4. Examples of different creative problem-solving profiles.

in innovative work, because in the former case all stages of the process are readily available within the team. One could also predict that members of homogeneous teams would experience more satisfaction working with their teammates because they are interacting with like-minded people. These predictions have been verified (Basadur & Head, 2001).

In addition, an individual's preference for a certain stage of the creative process should be predicted by the main ways in which that individual gains and uses understanding, as depicted in Fig. 15.2. The combination of ways in which individuals gain and use knowledge should also lead them toward certain fields of endeavor, or occupations.

KINDS OF CREATIVITY AND OCCUPATIONS

Perhaps the most influential career development theory in occupational psychology is Holland's (1985) theory of vocational personalities and work environments. According to this theory, people and work environments can be meaningfully classified into different types and people search for [work] environments that will allow them to exercise their skills and abilities, express their attitudes and values, and take on agreeable problems and roles. The occupation that people will find most satisfactory, and the one in which they will be the most successful, is the one that maximizes the congruence between the demands of the work environment and their vocational personality. Therefore, we might expect to find certain occupations to be disproportionately populated by individuals with a matching creative problem-solving style.

Occupations that require people to initiate change, recognize opportunities and new possibilities, start projects, and work with people in unstructured situations might thus be expected to contain a relatively high proportion of generator (Quadrant I dominant) individuals. Typical occupations here would be the artistic and academic professions, training and teaching, and marketing. Similarly, fields such as strategic planning and research and development—in which defining problems, understanding situations, and creating direction and strategy are important—might be expected to contain a relatively high proportion of conceptualizers (Quadrant II dominant). Quadrant II activity would likely typify fields such as market research, organization development, strategic planning, R&D scientist, university professor/researcher, and senior systems consultant. Quadrant III (optimizer) activities involve solving problems with precision and evaluating and optimizing products and procedures. This should be characteristic of fields such as engineering/engineering design, information technology (IT) systems development, finance, and accounting. Quadrant IV (implementer) fields would likely emphasize shorter-term implementation work, such as sales, manufacturing production, secretarial or administrative support, and project management.

Empirical research bears out these predictions. The CPSP styles associated with different occupations are most clearly seen in Table 15.1. In the first column of Table 15.1, the occupations are ranked (in descending order) by the percentage of generators in each. Thus, the occupation with the highest proportion of generators is schoolteacher, and the occupation with the next highest proportion is academic, followed by artistic. In the second column, occupations are ranked by the percentage of conceptualizers. The occupations that contain the highest proportion of conceptualizers are organization development, strategic planning, and market research. In the last two columns, occupations are ranked by the percentages of optimizers and implementers, respectively. Inspection of these two columns shows that the occupations that contain the most optimizers include engineering, finance, and IT systems developer, and the occupations that contain the most implementers include IT operations, customer relations, secretarial/administrative support, project manager, sales, and purchasing. Certain oc-

TABLE 15.1
Ranking of Occupations by Percentages of CPSP Styles

Rank	Generators	Conceptualizers	Optimizers	Implementers
1	Schoolteacher	Organization Development	Engineering/Engineering Design	Information Technology Operations
2	Academic	Strategic Planning	Manufacturing Engineering	Customer Relations
3	Artistic	Market Research	Finance	Secretarial/Administrative Support
4	Nonprofit/University Administrative	Design	Information Technology Systems Developer	Project Manager
5	Training	Research and Development	Information Technology Programmer/Analyst	Sales
6	Marketing	Artistic	Accounting	Purchasing
7	Design	Product Development	Strategic Planning	Manufacturing Production
8	Health Management Executive	Information Technology Senior Consultant	Technical Customer Support	Logistics

Note. Occupations ranked 1 contain the highest percentages of the relevant style.

cupations appear in more than one column because they rank highly in more than one quadrant.

These results generally support the idea that an individual's occupation matches his or her preferred creative problem-solving style. Perhaps individuals with certain CPSP styles are attracted to the kinds of jobs that emphasize their innate preferences, or perhaps an individual's natural preferences are modified by exposure to work experiences that reward types of cognitive activity appropriate to the job. These occupational differences are also consistent with the dynamic flow of the four-stage creative process. Typically in an organization, ideas for new products to meet emerging customer needs and problems originate in the marketing department, which contains a high proportion of generators. Market research and design departments then articulate the product more clearly, and assess its market potential. These occupations contain a high proportion of conceptualizers. Next, engineers develop prototypes for field testing with consumers and establish optimal specifications. Engineering occupations contain a high proportion of optimizers. Finally, the production department manufactures the product for logistics to distribute and sales to sell. These three occupations contain a high proportion of implementers.

KINDS OF CREATIVITY AND ORGANIZATIONAL LEVELS

A similar relationship might be found between dominant CPSP style and organizational level. Increasing levels of responsibility are defined as non-management, first-line supervision, middle management, and upper management. As individuals assume increasing levels of responsibility in an organization, the less important it is to implement day-to-day operational tasks and the more important it is to create vision and policy, to think strategically about the future, to conceptualize the "big picture," and to define problems and goals for others to solve and achieve. These activities are characteristic of Stage II of the creative process, depicted in Fig. 15.3. According to this logic, one might expect to find a higher proportion of people preferring Stage II activity (conceptualizers) at higher organizational levels than at lower levels. One might further predict that a higher proportion of conceptualizers would be found among highly specialized technical and professional workers—including economists, scientists, and planners—who are employed by their organizations primarily to *think* rather than to execute.

Empirical research bears out these predictions. The CPSP styles associated with different organizational levels are shown in Table 15.2. For each level, Table 15.2 reports the percentage of individuals preferring each CPSP quadrant or process stage.

TABLE 15.2
Percentage of Individuals Preferring Each
CPSP Quadrant, by Organizational Level

		Percentage Preferring			
Organizational Level	n	Generation	Conceptualization	Optimization	Implementation
Nonmanager	449	19.4	16.9	22.3	41.4
Supervisor/Team Leader	1,073	19.9	17.3	21.8	40.9
Middle Manager	843	19.5	24.4	22.3	33.8
Upper Manager	357	17.9	35.9	17.4	28.9
Technical/Professional	1,061	22.8	30.2	23.3	23.8

Note. n = base size.

As predicted, the percentage preferring conceptualization increases and the percentage preferring implementation decreases with increasing levels of strategic thinking responsibility. The percentages preferring generation and optimization, on the other hand, are relatively stable across organizational level. At the nonmanagement and supervisor/team leader levels, there is a very large gap between preference for implementation (much higher) and preference for conceptualization (much lower). At the upper manager level, this gap is significantly reduced, with preference for conceptualization becoming slightly higher than preference for implementation. This indicates that as a person rises through the ranks, he or she develops an increasingly higher level of preference for conceptualization at the expense of preference for implementation.

WHERE ARE THE GENERATORS?

One particular creative thinking style bears greater consideration by organizations. The distribution of respondents in this study by preferred creative process stage was: generator, 20.1%; conceptualizer, 26.2%; optimizer, 21.7%; and implementer, 32.0%. Interestingly, individuals preferring the generator style were predominantly found in nonindustrial occupations. Few business or industrial occupations in this study had a high proportion of generators. This finding is perhaps the most provocative for business and industry, whose most perplexing challenge today is how to be more innovative in the face of accelerating change. Indeed, many leading management consultants exhort corporations to "begin their revolutions"—to expand their thinking and do things differently. Improving current methods and procedures is no longer sufficient, these consultants say. Instead, they advocate deliberate change and advise corporations to explore new markets rather than defend old ones. The new rule seems to be "If it ain't broke, break it anyway." Although many corporations consider this an appealing strategy, they also find it difficult to implement. Perhaps one reason for this difficulty is the lack of employees with a preference for the generator style of thinking. If indeed organizational success depends so critically on deliberate change, and if Holland's theory of vocational choice is correct, why are employees with generator characteristics apparently underrepresented in business organizations? Perhaps many companies have yet to learn how to retain and motivate individuals who prefer the generator style. Generators are the furthest away from the work that is visibly measurable. In contrast to people in sales and manufacturing, for example, generators do not produce tangible and measurable results such as sales completed or goods produced. Rather, they initiate work that others carry forward and complete. Maybe organizations find it more difficult to recognize their contributions and reward the kind of work they do.

SUMMARY

Gone are the days when a company could assign "creative work" to a select group of people, say, in the marketing or research and development departments. Today, much more complex challenges posed by globalization of competition and technological advancement make it imperative for organizations to solve problems and capitalize on opportunities, and that requires the creativity of all the organization's members, across multiple disciplines. No longer can the creative process be seen as a "relay race," with one department handing off pieces of a problem to the next. Rather than wait for others to "do their job first," each department must be involved from the beginning throughout the stages of the creative process. By blending different kinds of knowledge and various kinds of creativity, the entire organization implements new solutions to newly discovered, well-defined problems and opportunities, both more rapidly and more successfully.

The research reported here supports this point of view. Recognizing the need for different kinds of creativity within various kinds of work and jobs in organizations has been the main theme of this chapter. Creativity has been portrayed as a multistage process, and moreover as a process with an "applied" focus. Managers and other organizational leaders must recognize, nurture, reward, and synchronize the different kinds of creativity associated with the various stages of the creative process. Evidence has been provided that within organizations, different kinds of domains of work favor different kinds of creativity. These different kinds of creativity are equally valuable and must be synchronized effectively to produce a continuous supply of innovative results. Different parts of organizations tend to prefer different stages of the creative process, and hence they contribute differently to the creative process. Thus, in the world of organizational managing, rather than thinking of management as a single "domain," it should be realized that there are many different domains within the management of organizational work. Perhaps even more important, the different domains require different kinds of creativity.

REFERENCES

Ackoff, R. L. (1979). The future of operational research is past. *Journal of Operational Research Society, 30,* 93–104.

Amabile, T. M. (1988). A model of creativity and innovation. In B. M. Staw & L. L. Cummings (Eds.), *Research in organizational behavior* (Vol. 10, pp. 123–167). Greenwich, CT: JAI.

Amabile, T. M., & Gryskiewicz, N. D. (1989). The creative environment scales: Work environment inventory. *Creativity Research Journal, 2,* 231–253.

Baker, N. R., Winkofsky, E., Langmeyer, L., & Sweeney, D. J. (1976). *Idea generation: A procrustean bed of variables, hypotheses and implications.* Cincinnati: College of Business Administration, University of Cincinnati.

Basadur, M. S. (1974, July–September). Think or sink. *The Deliberate Methods Change Bulletin,* p. 2.

Basadur, M. S. (1979). *Training in creative problem solving: Effects on deferred judgment and problem finding and solving in an industrial research organization.* Unpublished doctoral dissertation, University of Cincinnati, OH.

Basadur, M. S. (1981). Training in creative problem solving and measuring improvement. *Engineering Digest, 27*(3), 59–61.

Basadur, M. S. (1983). Employee involvement creative problem-solving workshop. In *Ford education and training catalog* (p. 115). Dearborn, MI: Ford Education and Personnel Research Department.

Basadur, M. S. (1992). Managing creativity: A Japanese model. *Academy of Management Executive, 6*(2), 29–42.

Basadur, M. S. (1994). Managing the creative process in organizations. In M. J. Runco (Ed.), *Problem finding, problem solving, and creativity* (pp. 237–268). New York: Ablex.

Basadur, M. S. (1995). *The power of innovation.* London: Pitman.

Basadur, M. S. (1997). Organizational development interventions for enhancing creativity in the workplace. *Journal of Creative Behavior, 31*(1), 59–72.

Basadur, M. S., Ellspermann, S. J., & Evans, G. W. (1994). A new methodology for formulating ill-structured problems. *OMEGA: The International Journal of Management Science, 22*(6), 627–645.

Basadur, M. S., & Gelade, G. (2002). Knowing and thinking: A new theory of creativity. *Management of Innovation and New Technology Research Centre Working Paper No. 105.* Hamilton, Ontario: McMaster University.

Basadur, M. S., Graen, G. B., & Green, S. G. (1982). Training in creative problem solving: Effects on ideation and problem finding in an applied research organization. *Organizational Behavior and Human Performance, 30,* 41–70.

Basadur, M. S., & Head, M. (2001). Team performance and satisfaction: A link to cognitive style within a process framework. *Journal of Creative Behavior, 35,* 1–22.

Basadur, M. S., Runco, M. A., & Vega, L. A. (2000). Understanding how creative thinking skills, attitudes and behaviors work together: A causal process model. *Journal of Creative Behavior, 34*(2), 77–100.

Callahan, S. (1972, October). Dr. Land's magic camera. *Life, 27,* 46.

Carlsson, B., Keane, P., & Martin, J. B. (1976, Spring). R&D organization as learning systems. *Sloan Management Review, 17*(1), 1–15.
Getzels, J. W. (1975). Problem finding and the inventiveness of solutions. *The Journal of Creative Behavior, 9*(1), 12–18.
Gordon, W. J. J. (1956). Operational approach to creativity. *Harvard Business Review, 9*(1).
Gordon, W. J. J. (1971). *The metaphorical way.* Cambridge, MA: Porpoise.
Guilford, J. P. (1950). Creativity. *American Psychologist, 5,* 444–454.
Guilford, J. P. (1967). *The nature of human intelligence.* New York: McGraw-Hill.
Holland, J. L. (1985). *Making of vocational choices: A theory of vocational personalities and work environments* (2nd ed.). Englewood Cliffs, NJ: Prentice-Hall.
Isaksen, G. S., & Treffinger, D. J. (1985). *Creative problem solving: The basic course.* Buffalo, NY: Bearly.
Jackson, P. W., & Messick, S. (1964). *The person, the product and the response: Conceptual problems in the assessment of creativity.* Princeton, NJ: Educational Testing Service.
Kabanoff, B., & Rossiter, J. R. (1994). Recent developments in applied creativity. *International Review of Industrial and Organizational Psychology, 9,* 283–324.
Kirton, M. J. (1976). Adaptors and innovators: A description and measure. *Journal of Applied Psychology, 61,* 622–629.
Leavitt, H. J. (1975). Beyond the analytic manager. *California Management Review, 17*(3), 5–12.
Levitt, T. (1963). Creativity is not enough. *Harvard Business Review, 41,* 72–83.
Livingston, J. S. (1971). Myth of the well-educated manager. *Harvard Business Review, 48,* 79–89.
MacKinnon, D. W. (1962). The nature and nurture of the creative talent. *American Psychologist, 17,* 484–495.
MacKinnon, D. W. (1977). Foreword. In S. Parnes, A. Noller, & A. Biondi (Eds.), *Guide to creative action* (p. xiii). New York: Scribner's.
Mackworth, N. H. (1965). Originality. *The American Psychologist, 20,* 51.
Mott, P. E. (1972). *The characteristics of effective organizations.* New York: Harper & Row.
Murdock, M. C., & Puccio, G. J. (1994). A contextual organizer for conducting creativity research. In S. G. Isaksen, M. C. Murdock, R. L. Firestien, & D. J. Treffinger (Eds.), *Nurturing and developing creativity: The emergence of a discipline* (pp. 249–280). Norwood, NJ: Ablex.
Myers, I. B. (1962). *Myers-Briggs type indicator manual.* Princeton, NJ: Educational Testing Service.
O'Quin, K., & Besemer, S. P. (1989). The development, reliability and validity of the Revised Creative Product Semantic Scale. *Creativity Research Journal, 2,* 268–279.
Parnes, S. J., Noller, R. B., & Biondi, A. M. (1977). *Guide to creative action.* New York: Scribner's.
Rickards, T. R. (1994). Creativity from a business school perspective: Past, present, and future. In S. G. Isaksen, M. C. Murdock, R. L. Firestien, & D. J. Treffinger (Eds.), *Nurturing and developing creativity: The emergence of a discipline* (pp. 155–176). Norwood, NJ: Ablex.
Simon, H. A. (1960). *The new science of management decision.* Englewood Cliffs, NJ: Prentice-Hall.
Simon, H. A. (1977). *The new science of management decision.* Englewood Cliffs, NJ: Prentice-Hall.
Sternberg, R. J., O'Hara, L. A., & Lubart, T. I. (1997). Creativity as investment. *California Management Review, 40*(1), 8–21.
Wakefield, J. F. (1991). The outlook for creativity tests. *Journal of Creative Behavior, 25,* 184–193.
Wallas, G. (1926). *The art of thought.* New York: Harcourt Brace.

Chapter 16

Creativity in Teaching: Essential Knowledge, Skills, and Dispositions[1]

Don Ambrose
Rider University

Creative teaching is a highly complex endeavor that requiring a broad array of skills and dispositions. Contextual pressures on educators largely prescribe the most effective pedagogical work processes. The immediate classroom context demands exceptional planning and managerial skills, facilitative leadership, flexibility, pattern perception, and intuitive capacities. The larger, societal context often pressures teachers to confine their practice to insular, one-sided perspectives on teaching and learning. Nonreflective compliance with dogmatic philosophies or ideologies and insular practices erodes the professional decision making that underpins instructional creativity. The most creative teachers preserve their professionalism by finding artful ways to keep their students creative, even in confining conditions. In so doing, they turn their own careers into long-term, creative experimental journeys.

There is growing interest in the extent to which creative thought and action emerge from the specific demands and limitations imposed by domains of human activity (Amabile, 1983; Baer, 1993, 1998; Diakidoy & Constantinou, 2001; Gardner, 1993a; Ruscio, Whitney, & Amabile, 1998). Broadly defined, a domain is a specific area of knowledge that requires a specific set of skills (Baer, 1999b). The perspective taken in this chapter is

---
[1]Don Ambrose, Graduate Department, School of Education and Human Services, College of Liberal Arts Education and Sciences, Rider University, 2083 Lawrenceville Road, Lawrenceville, NJ 08648-3099. Electronic mail address is ambrose@rider.edu

that teaching is a broad domain encompassing a body of professional knowledge and a variety of domain-relevant skills and dispositions.

Some domains require complex but narrowly confined cognitive processes. For example, in their explorations of the subatomic realm, theoretical physicists have relied on exceptional facility with logical mathematical formalism and varying degrees of visual thought capacities, with the latter depending on the eras in which they worked (Miller, 1989, 1996; Omnès, 1999). However, most have little use for philosophical proclivities or political acumen, except as the latter applies to promotion of their work in the field. In contrast, some other domains demand a broader variety of skills and dispositions.

Creative teaching demands exceptional breadth of skills and entails the implicit invitation to develop many of these skills to very high levels of proficiency. Some of this breadth derives from the multifaceted nature of teachers' work and the diverse professional roles they fulfill. A typical teacher is responsible for short- and long-range planning; diagnosis of students' developmental levels and learning differences; motivation; discipline; counseling; strategic implementation of diverse, complex instructional strategies; public-relations initiatives; and artful problem solving. An effective teacher handles all of this while mastering, to the extent possible, the most salient knowledge within one or more academic disciplines.

Further complexity arises from the diversity of teachers' roles in school systems. Elementary teachers typically serve as subject matter generalists and focus more on the needs of 25 or 30 children. Of necessity, most secondary teachers focus more on subject matter and somewhat less on the specific needs of the 130 students who confront them in clusters each day. Moreover, the ways in which a specific teacher handles all of these tasks is influenced by the philosophical orientation of his or her school or district.

In short, the diverse natures of teachers' roles create many subdomains within the larger domain of teaching. These complex, multiple dimensions of teaching make much room for creative growth on the part of adventurous educators while simultaneously posing barriers to innovation. More research into teachers' creativity is needed to guide such exploration (Rejskind, 2000).

CONTEXTS FOR TEACHING: AN OVERVIEW

In order to understand the knowledge, skills, and dispositions required in the domain of teaching, we need to appreciate the contextual influences on teachers' work, from the immediate context of the classroom to the large-scale context of society. Doyle (1986) delineated six properties that make classrooms highly complex and demanding environments. Most of these properties are relevant to the emergence or suppression of teacher creativity. The properties of multidimensionality and simultaneity require teachers to juggle many different interpersonal, instructional, and managerial tasks and problems at the same time. The properties of immediacy and unpredictability demand that teachers handle many of these tasks and problems on the spot, with little or no warning. The principle of publicness pertains to the fishbowl visibility of actions in the classroom. For the teacher, this implies constant scrutiny of one's work by students, most of whom report their impressions to parents. In addition to these complexity-generating properties, teachers also must diagnose and address the needs of many youthful but highly complex minds with their attendant cognitive, affective, and physiological subsystems.

A comparison of professional roles can illustrate the complex demands of the classroom context. Lawyers must employ complex diagnostic cognitive processes, but they are able to minimize multidimensionality and simultaneity by dealing with one client and one set of targeted issues at a time. Movement of clients through private offices also enables lawyers to avoid publicness, except when they enter the courtroom.

At the larger contextual level of the school and district, there is one phenomenon that partially counters the publicness of the teachers' role in the classroom. Schools are loosely coupled systems in which employees often can ignore or idiosyncratically interpret managerial directives (Weick, 1982). Consequently, it is difficult for administrators to micromanage a teacher's work, except in times of crisis when loosely coupled organizations suddenly cohere tightly around a specific problem response.

Whether or not crises prevail, the managerial dimensions of schools and school systems can provide widely varying contexts for creative work. Research in the field of organizational development shows that some organizations, schools included, are plagued by myopic, coercive management and affective climates dominated by a combination of anger, fear, frustration, and premature criticism. These organizations promote excessively conformist ritual while suppressing creative collaboration. Other systems—guided by visionary, facilitative leadership—promote affective climates of excitement, pride, and purpose that nurture creative teamwork. They tend to produce a healthy balance of creative idea generation and critical refinement of new ideas (Ambrose, 1995). Consequently, the specific school or district environment can play a large role in providing or denying latitude for teacher creativity.

The macroscale community and societal levels also exert considerable pressure that supports, suppresses, or shapes teacher creativity. In society, there is no shortage of pressure groups that want educators to move sharply in one direction or another, and thus curriculum innovation bandwagons tend to come and go regularly. Many large-scale undertakings fail due to insufficient tangible support for change processes (Fullan, 1991). However, some initiatives persist and take extreme forms because they are fueled by vociferous, reactionary battles among political, ideological, or philosophical pressure groups. For example, the wild pendulum swings in the reading wars between proponents of phonetic and whole-language approaches exert strong pressure for teachers to conform strictly to one approach or the other when a blending of the two would foment optimal instruction (Flippo, 1999).

Some societal pressures become so powerful that they threaten to destroy much of the educator's professional autonomy and the teacher creativity that ensues from it. For example, critics of public education have managed to undermine public confidence in the system to the extent that sweeping reform measures are emerging at state and national levels. Many of these measures entail standards and accountability systems that narrow and fragment the curriculum, thereby making it much less conducive to teacher creativity (Bracey, 2002; Brady, 2000; Dart, 2001; Eisner, 2002).

Baer (1999a) delineated insightful ways that teacher creativity can coexist with standards, but without sufficient knowledge of these possibilities for creative harmonization many teachers are likely to succumb to deprofessionalization. The heavy emphasis on external measurement for accountability is likely to magnify extrinsic motivation in teaching while undermining intrinsic motivation. Much creativity research points to the necessity of intrinsic motivation for creative work (Amabile, 1983, 2001; Hennessey & Amabile, 1988; Joussemet & Koestner, 1999; Ruscio et al., 1998), and teachers' work should be no exception. Although some extrinsic motivation can be used judiciously to promote skill building helpful to creative work over the long term, the narrowly conceived, high-stakes accountability measures that accompany many of today's reform initiatives represent blunt instruments capable of rupturing teaching innovations.

Many of these pressures on teacher creativity arise from philosophical conflicts between essentialist and progessivist-constructivist pressure groups in society. Based primarily on the work of William Bagley (1941), essentialism promotes reduction of learning to rigorous transmission of a core collection of essential knowledge and skills. Constructivism, which is rooted in the thinking of John Dewey (1902, 1938), promotes students' self-construction of knowledge through exploratory, discovery processes.

Furthermore, this conflict and others like it in education and related fields are embedded in dogmatic adherence to opposing root-metaphorical worldviews, which are deeply ingrained, tacit philosophical assumptions about the world (Ambrose, 1996, 1998a, 1998b, 2000, 2003; Cohen & Ambrose, 1993; Gillespie, 1992). For example, phonetic approaches to reading—which encourage teachers to break language into component, somewhat decontextualized building blocks—are rooted in the reductive, machinelike tenets of the mechanistic worldview. In contrast, whole-language approaches—which encourage holistic integration of language processes through immersion in a literacy-rich context—are rooted in the holistic, integrative tenets of the organicist worldview and the context-sensitive, novelty magnifying tenets of the contextualist worldview (Ambrose, 2003). Similar reductionist–holistic battles rage in the field of mathematics education (Wilson, 2002). To some extent, it is this dogmatic entrapment within tacit worldviews that makes paradigm wars in education such powerful forces for suppression or support of teacher creativity.

In summary, today's contexts for education present daunting obstacles that discourage teacher creativity yet provide some opportunities for innovation. Doyle's (1986) properties of the classroom environment and the inherent complexity of students' cognitive, affective, and physiological subsystems are too intimidating for many teachers who cope by restrictively oversimplifying their roles and the roles of students, thereby avoiding the risks of creative exploration. On the plus side, constant immersion in complexity can develop the quick-response, problem-solving skills of teachers who have the ability and willingness to embrace ambiguity.

Contextual pressures can vary considerably at the school and district levels, ranging from visionary, supportive organizational climates for innovation to confining, suppressive environments. The latter can be ameliorated somewhat by the phenomenon of loose coupling. At the large-scale societal levels, highly prescriptive, mandated reforms and raucous conflicts between influential pressure groups with opposing philosophies force many teachers to become reactive technocrats, mindlessly and mechanically implementing the latest top-down curricular initiative. But for teachers with creative inclinations, the dynamic tension between polarized positions represents interesting opportunities for dialectical thinking, which can lead to creative synthesis of opposing views. Dialectical processes are particularly conducive to creative thinking (Ambrose, 2003; Bohm, 1994; Sternberg, 1999, 2001; Yan & Arlin, 1999). More specific domain-relevant skills and dispositions for creative teaching are explored in the next section.

SKILLS AND DISPOSITIONS PREVALENT IN THE TEACHING PROFESSION

A conjectural comparison of a noncreative teacher with a creative teacher can foster understanding of the domain-relevant skills and dispositions necessary for instructional creativity. Of course, there are no absolutely noncreative or perfectly creative teachers. However, the descriptors that follow, which are derived largely from the contextual examination in the preceding section, set the stage for deeper analysis of teacher creativity.

Behaviors and Dispositions That Work Against Teacher Creativity

Student creativity is an important creative product of teachers' work, so, to some extent, we can discern whether or not teaching is creative or noncreative by observing its effects on students and classroom dynamics. Suppression of student creativity occurs when the teacher sees knowledge, learning processes, and students themselves in oversimplified, reified terms. Specific behaviors and dispositions of noncreative teachers include the following:

Oversimplifying Curriculum and Instruction and Leeching It of Creative Opportunity. They react to reform mandates and philosophical conflicts by mechanically and inflexibly implementing canned programs and by employing a few overused instructional strategies. Consequently, rote learning prevails.

Viewing Knowledge as a Set of Discrete, Separable Elements. They break academic content into decontextualized information bits that fit into well-bounded, tightly confined disciplinary containers. These bits are taught piece by piece, often in linear sequence, with no intent to synthesize concepts or to make creative interdisciplinary connections.

Basing Assessment on the Lowest Levels of Cognition. Their assessments emphasize tests of students' learning that shake out grades based on superficial content regurgitation. There is little thought about ways in which assessments could convey the relevance of learning while providing formative guidance for students and extending creative thinking.

Undervaluing Student Creativity. Many teachers dislike student characteristics that are associated with creativity (Dawson, D'Andrea, Affinito, & Westby, 1999; Scott, 1999; Westby & Dawson, 1995). Students who crave room for divergent thinking and novelty generate some nonconformity, especially in classrooms devoid of processes conducive to creative thinking and intrinsic motivation. This runs counter to the noncreative teacher's desire for simplicity and excessive order.

Ignoring Students' Individual Differences. They impose a one-size-fits-all curriculum, solely attributing the frustrations and failures of special-needs students to poor motivation or intransigence. Students with learning disabilities must sink or swim with little help. Students of high potential or exceptional talent must cope in an environment that imposes a low, impermeable conceptual ceiling.

Relying Heavily on Extrinsic Motivation. A curriculum sanitized of higher-order thinking removes much opportunity for students to develop intrinsic motivation. Thus, noncreative teachers depend heavily on extrinsic motivation. Fear of disorder and confusion prevails, so they base most or all of their motivation systems for students' work and behavior on clear-cut behavioristic reinforcement principles. The emphasis is on grades, sticker charts, and punishments derived from top-down imposition of rules.

Avoiding Reflection and Falling Prey to Dogmatic Insularity. They nonreflectively employ habitual processes from day to day, and their inflexible instructional plans replicate intact from year to year. When things don't go well they externalize blame, thereby avoiding responsibility for creative problem solving. In addition, their lack of reflective capacities inclines them to take dogmatic stands on pedagogical issues without thinking through the deeper philosophical reasons for paradigm shifts in academic disciplines and the ideological polarization that separates societal pressure groups.

Behaviors and Dispositions Consistent With Teacher Creativity

Noncreative teaching seriously limits the effectiveness of instruction. It also predisposes teachers to unwittingly or even willingly succumb to the deprofessionalization demanded by many of today's reform measures. Fortunately, there are educators who are more motivated and imaginative about their professional roles, and are much more resistant to deprofessionalization. Creative teachers exhibit the following, contrasting set of characteristics, which serve as the framework for analysis of the domain-relevant skills and dispositions for teacher creativity:

Employing Coherent but Flexible Instructional Planning. Expert, creative teachers use their plans as general outlines to be fleshed out as instruction progresses (Ornstein, 1995). They leave flexibility in their plans to make room for creative improvisation, which emerges from students' responses and needs (Borko & Livingston, 1989). Some of this improvisation takes the form of creative problem finding and problem solving within the context of planned lessons (Moore, 1993).

Placing High Value on Student Creativity and Establishing an Inquiry-Based Learning Atmosphere. As much as possible, they employ problem-based learning, which establishes interesting questions and discrepant events as focal points for student investigation (Gordon, Rogers, Comfort, Gavula, & McGee, 2001; Pithers & Soden, 2000; Stepien & Gallagher, 1993). Problem-based learning makes the classroom environment conducive to students' problem solving, open-ended inquiry, and especially problem finding, which is an important aspect of creative thinking (Moore, 1993; Runco & Chand, 1995; Runco & Nemiro, 1994). Where time constraints prevail, and where the nature of the curriculum is less conducive to discovery, the creative teacher artfully blends rote learning of basic skills and concepts with creative discovery learning for the sake of efficiency. However, the prevailing climate in his or her class conveys the importance of student-centered inquiry.

Actively Exploring, Adapting, and Applying a Wide Variety of Instructional Models and Strategies. Creativity scholars recommend fostering a creative climate in the classroom that will support students' creative thinking (Fasko, 2001; Feldhusen & Treffinger, 1980). Fortunately, teachers have access to instructional models and strategies that can establish much of that climate. Educational researchers have discovered and refined a collection of highly effective, step-by-step instructional processes that have emerged from excellent teachers' classrooms (for overviews, see Eggen & Kauchak, 2001; Joyce & Weil, 1996). For example, the integrative model enables students to generate their own questions about a topic, carry out research to answer the most pertinent of these questions, map their findings onto a large integrative matrix, discover patterns in the matrix, and then develop generalizations about the topic based on the patterns. The model engages students in problem finding and creative connection making among other higher-order thinking processes. Other models promote concept discovery, concept formation, dialectical synthesis of polarized positions, metaphorical analysis, creative mnemonic generation for content mastery, inquiry learning, and various versions of cooperative learning processes.

In addition to these models, educators have access to a wide variety of strategies that are specifically designed to generate creative thinking. Strategies and programs that elicit processes such as creative problem solving, creative association, invention, creative imagery, and various forms of divergent thinking as well as general advice for enhancing creativity in the classroom are available in some excellent creativity sources (e.g., Baer, 1997; Davis, 1998; Piirto, 1998; Starko, 1995; Sternberg & Williams, 1996; Treffinger, Isaksen, & Dorval, 1994).

Creative teachers think about instructional models and creative instructional strategies as being analogous to diverse tools in a pedagogical toolbox. They think divergently about the potential applications of these tools in their classrooms, experiment with the most promising applications, and critique the results to set the stage for more effective future experimentation.

Synthesizing and Integrating Curriculum and Assessment. Contrary to the common practices of fragmenting and overcompartmentalizing content by discipline, creative educators—particularly those at the elementary levels—

find ways to build bridges between disciplines (Jacobs, 1989). Most often this involves thematic curriculum integration in which a theme such as European ocean-going exploration (in this case drawn from the social studies curriculum) serves as an integrative magnet for interdisciplinary thinking. Students tie in the science curriculum by studying the rudimentary physics of buoyancy and wind power applicable to English sailing vessels, or the science behind outbreaks of scurvy on those ships. They connect with mathematics by graphing the distances covered in major explorations or by calculating the time it would take to reach the Guinea coast from Lisbon in a Portuguese caravel. They hook the language arts curriculum to the theme by carrying out biographical readings on famous explorers.

Curriculum integration presents teachers and students with another set of dynamic tensions that begs resolution. Exploring a theme through multiple disciplinary lenses spins the mind off into creative, divergent trajectories in which many diverse science, mathematics, literature, art, and history concepts can come into play. However, the theme also encourages creative connection making of these concepts. Teachers and their students must cope with the initial ambiguity posed by this dynamic tension while searching for connective patterns that will resolve it.

Creativity scholars recommend that teachers involve students in real-world challenges to promote creative thinking (Treffinger, Isaksen, & Firestein, 1983). Consistent with this advice, creative teachers also integrate assessment tightly with instruction while connecting it to the real world. They generate authentic assessments that approximate real-world tasks relevant to the skills or knowledge under study (Keating, Diaz-Greenberg, Baldwin, & Thousand, 1998; Newmann, Secada, & Wehlage, 1995). They ensure that these assessments closely mirror the instructional objectives and processes from which they emerge while providing helpful feedback to guide students' future growth. Authentic assessment helps both students and teachers conceive of education as a seamless whole as opposed to a series of disconnected events.

Exercising Efficient, Facilitative Leadership That Shapes Routines, the Classroom Environment, and Student Behavior. The mile-wide, inch-deep curriculum typically imposed on American schools poses a barrier to deep, substantive learning (Dempster, 1993). This, combined with the necessity of keeping 30 captive, distractible minds engaged in productive pursuits all day long, magnifies the need for efficient yet flexible leadership. Creative teachers efficiently manage the routines and physical environment of the classroom to make it conducive to learning while simultaneously exercising facilitative leadership in the management of students' behavior. These aspects of teachers' work are particularly demanding of creative skills and dispositions. Classroom management is a highly complex and difficult endeavor that consumes much attention from novices and veterans alike. Teachers must plan for efficient space and traffic patterns in the classroom, establish clear expectations for task completion, and develop systems for problem solving when something inevitably goes awry.

Effective classroom management requires skillful foresight, constant vigilance, consistency over time, and strong congruence of word and action (Charles, 1996; Jones & Jones, 1998). It also demands exquisitely nuanced, on-the-spot, intuitive pattern perception in the interpretation of classroom processes, students' moods, and emerging trouble spots (Kounin, 1970).

Fortunately, the intrinsic motivation that derives from insightful planning, creative instructional strategies, and authentic assessment minimizes behavior problems in the classroom, thereby diminishing the need for extrinsic reward and punishment. But even the most experienced, proficient classroom managers can confront a few persistent, niggling problems that waste valuable time, and the occasional intractable problem that seriously undermines instruction.

The best, expert teachers keep these difficulties to a minimum because they are particularly adept at creative, facilitative leadership. According to scholars in the field of organizational development (Kanter, 1989; Senge, 1990), facilitative leaders enhance employee effectiveness and satisfaction. They support creativity in their organizations by recognizing the importance of front-line personnel—those who create the products and deliver the services at the lowest levels of the hierarchy—and by helping them develop a sense of ownership and engagement in the system. They empower front-liners and enhance their intrinsic motivation by sharing decision-making power and by providing for some individual autonomy within the parameters of a collaboratively developed mission. Without giving way to anarchy, they open the channels of communication so that all can have at least some of their concerns heard, and they make room for some democratic decision making.

Interestingly, the most effective teachers tend to establish similar dynamics in their management of classrooms. They encourage ownership of classroom processes and rules by providing choice, where possible, in assignments and by engaging students in the development of rules for behavior. They encourage open communication and collaboration by holding nonhierarchical problem-solving meetings when necessary to adjust classroom dynamics or the rules themselves (Glasser, 1969; Nelson, Lott, & Glenn, 1993). Of course, the teacher retains much of the responsibility and decision making, but to the extent possible, empowers his or her "front-line personnel."

Diagnosing and Addressing Students' Special Needs. In virtually every classroom, some students are difficult to serve because their cognitive, emotional, or physical needs diverge markedly from the norm. Increasing recognition of these needs has spawned large, complex subfields such as special education and gifted education within the larger field of general education (for overviews, see Hallahan & Kauffman, 1997; Heller, Mönks, Sternberg, & Subotnik, 2000). Interest also is growing in special needs deriving from diverse cultural backgrounds (Gay, 2000). As if this isn't complex enough, teachers also feel pressure to address student diversity in cognitive styles, learning styles, and multiple forms of intelligence (see Dunn & Dunn, 1987; Gardner, 1983, 1993b; Gregorc, 1982; Martinsen, 1995; McCarthy, 1990; O'Hara & Sternberg, 1999; Sternberg, 1994; Sternberg & Lubart, 1991; Sternberg & Zhang, 2000).

A trend toward inclusion of special-needs children in regular classrooms, as opposed to their removal for special programming elsewhere, substantially elevates the complexity of teachers' work while presenting yet another opportunity for creative problem solving. Today's teachers can expect to assume responsibility for students' special learning needs that emerge from a daunting array of disabilities and strengths (Hallahan & Kauffman, 1997). Just a few examples from this array highlight the complexity of this dimension of teachers' work. Students diagnosed with attention deficit hyperactivity disorder have very short attention spans and are excessively impulsive. Those with emotional disturbances exhibit age-inappropriate behaviors and initiate classroom conflicts. Students with orthopedic handicaps, chronic illnesses, or hearing and visual problems may need special equipment or adaptations in the arrangements of classroom space, materials, or processes. The gifted and talented need opportunities to explore concepts above or beyond the grade-level curriculum. On top of all this, many otherwise capable students have learning disabilities of various forms and complexities that prevent them from effectively processing information in reading, writing, or computational tasks.

Creative teachers are perceptive enough to recognize the debilitating effects a mismatch between instruction and these special needs can have on students' functioning, and on their long-term life chances. This requires good measures of sensitivity and empathy, because recognition of special needs brings, in turn, the often-unpalatable recognition of one's own considerable responsibility as an educator. It also requires high levels of diagnostic skill based on exceptional pattern perception because each student's particular blend of special strengths and weaknesses often is not clearly evident. Finally, it requires superior organizational skill and diligence in order to plan and manage a variety of curriculum modifications and differentiation plans (Tomlinson, 1996).

Striving for Intrinsic Motivation and Using Extrinsic Motivation Sparingly. As previously mentioned, students' intrinsic motivation is a natural by-product of creative teachers' approaches to planning, instruction, classroom management, and assessment. The intrigue of discovery learning and diverse instructional strategies, the democratic flavor of front-line empowerment, and recognition of individual differences are compelling motivators for most students.

Although enjoying the benefits of these natural motivators, creative teachers still are vigilant about enhancing intrinsic motivation in their classrooms because they recognize that the schools in which they work are the artifacts of the 19th-century industrial factory model of organization (Levin, 1994). No matter how creative the personnel may be, there is a residue of assembly-line drudgery in the design of the grade-level system and in the buildings themselves. The residue is particularly strong when reactionary school reform initiatives erode teacher professionalism. Consequently, extrinsic motivation is necessary at least some of the time in virtually any classroom, but creative teachers keep it to a minimum.

Maintaining an Open Mind to Avoid Dogmatic Insularity. Whereas noncreative teachers are threatened by complex philosophical conflicts over pedagogy and seek to escape their angst by aligning themselves with one or the other insular position, creative teachers see opportunity in conflict. They recognize the remote possibility that one side may be absolutely right and the other completely wrong, but are more likely to suspect that both perspectives can contribute to instructional improvement even if one shows more promise than the other. Consistent with the strength of dialectical thinking (Ambrose, 2003; Bohm, 1994; Sternberg, 1999; Yan & Arlin, 1999), they search for a creative synthesis, borrowing the best elements of opposing positions to create a more promising approach to instruction. This penchant for dialectical thinking enables them to avoid narrow-minded insularity and dogmatism.

Summary of Domain-Relevant Skills and Dispositions for Teacher Creativity

Some larger patterns emerge from this analysis of teachers' behaviors and dispositions. Creative teachers tend to be calculated risk takers who tolerate ambiguity and embrace complexity. They engage in pedagogical experimentation throughout their careers, and develop impressive organizational skills to manage the complexity of the classroom and to enhance the efficacy of their experimentation. In addition, much of their creative success derives from refined intuition and strong empathic capacities.

More specifically, creative teachers' willingness to (a) devise flexible plans while reflecting deeply on the success of those plans and making appropriate revisions, (b) experiment with a wide variety of complex instructional strategies, (c) seek interdisciplinary connections, (d) address the complex special needs of students, (e) value students' creative inquiry, and (f) relinquish some managerial control all reduce the ability to predict and control processes and outcomes in classrooms. Willingness to give up prediction and control in a complex classroom environment requires exceptional levels of both risk-taking propensity and tolerance of ambiguity, especially in an increasingly conformist climate.

However, creative teachers take fewer foolish risks and more calculated ones. Consequently, they develop their organizational skills to impressive levels. When planning creative classroom processes, they anticipate problems and revise their coherent yet flexible plans accordingly. Successful problem anticipation requires strong intuitive capacities. Intuition—which entails the ability to guide decision making on the basis of nebulous, subjective impressions—can lead to either great insight or serious mistakes (Myers, 2002). Creative teachers seem to know this and are able to generate more useful insights while making use of their mistakes as learning experiences.

All of these creative abilities and propensities combined produce an experimental mindset that promotes long-term, classroom-based research. Creative teachers bent on instructional improvement tend to engage in action research, which involves them in systematic but largely informal research in their own classrooms as opposed to relying solely on the formal research of educational scholars (Cochrane-Smith & Lytle, 1993; Keating et al., 1998). Much of this research takes the form of long-term creative problem solving in which resolution of one classroom problem leads to a neverending series of experimental inquiries and refinements.

Finally, all of this risk taking, planning, experimentation, and problem solving requires a great deal of intrinsic motivation on the part of the teacher. Creativity can be its own intrinsic reward, but many teachers rely on an additional boost—their ability to empathize with children. Teachers who can appreciate students' diverse, complex needs while recognizing the intellectual and affective suffocation that occurs in confining, noncreative classrooms find strong reasons for commitment to long-range instructional improvement.

CONCLUSION

Teaching is a highly complex profession because it has multiple dimensions pertaining to the dynamics of brain-mind systems, social relationships, organizational systems, and sociopolitical, economic, and ethical pressures from the larger society. Professionals who are willing to explore the intricacies of their work find that they peel away familiar surface layers to reveal even more complexity beneath. For the adventurous, these deeper discoveries represent compelling invitations for long-term creative development of self and students. In contrast, educators who cannot tolerate ambiguity tend to strip away complexity from their classroom systems, thereby avoiding opportunities for creative growth.

Becoming a creative teacher requires a career-long commitment to reflective experimentation and skill building. Those unwilling or unable to engage in such exploration remain at a low level of professional development, not much beyond that of a novice. According to expert–novice research, novices in a domain focus on superficial detail while inflexibly and inefficiently applying algorithmic rules to problems that require much more nuanced judgment. In contrast, experts see broad patterns and underlying structures in problems while generating their own flexible heuristics for problem solution (Carter, Doyle, & Riney, 1995; Pelletier & Shore, 2003).

Teachers who embark on the path of creative career exploration experience small successes and failures as they haltingly move beyond algorithmic application of prescribed instructional models and creative thinking processes. As they progress, however, they enjoy increasing automaticity of domain-relevant skills and deeper, more expansive perception of the subtleties in pedagogical obstacles and opportunities. Their intensely interesting engagement with more and more complex patterns and problems builds long-term intrinsic motivation and the strong sense of life-long, creative purpose that Gruber (1989) contended is characteristic of highly creative people. It is this persistent and growing motivation that enables the best educators to amass the highly complex and extensive collection of domain-relevant skills and dispositions necessary for success in this most challenging profession.

REFERENCES

Amabile, T. M. (1983). *The social psychology of creativity*. New York: Springer-Verlag.
Amabile, T. M. (2001). Beyond talent: John Irving and the passionate craft of creativity. *American Psychologist, 56*, 333–336.
Ambrose, D. (1995). Creatively intelligent post-industrial organizations and intellectually impaired bureaucracies. *Journal of Creative Behavior, 29*, 1–15.
Ambrose, D. (1996). Unifying theories of creativity: Metaphorical thought and the unification process. *New Ideas in Psychology, 14*, 257–267.
Ambrose, D. (1998a). Comprehensiveness of conceptual foundations for gifted education: A world-view analysis. *Journal for the Education of the Gifted, 21*, 452–470.
Ambrose, D. (1998b). A model for clarification and expansion of conceptual foundations. *Gifted Child Quarterly, 42*, 77–86.
Ambrose, D. (2000). World-view entrapment: Moral-ethical implications for gifted education. *Journal for the Education of the Gifted, 23*, 159–186.
Ambrose, D. (2003). Theoretic scope, dynamic tensions, and dialectical processes: A model for discovery of creative intelligence. In D. Ambrose, L. M. Cohen, & A. J. Tannenbaum

(Eds.), *Creative intelligence: Toward theoretic integration* (pp. 325–345). Cresskill, NJ: Hampton.
Baer, J. (1993). *Divergent thinking and creativity: A domain-specific approach.* Hillsdale, NJ: Lawrence Erlbaum Associates.
Baer, J. (1997). *Creative teachers: Creative students.* Needham Heights, MA: Allyn & Bacon.
Baer, J. (1998). The case for domain specificity of creativity. *Creativity Research Journal, 11,* 173–177.
Baer, J. (1999a). Creativity in a climate of standards. *Focus on Education, 43,* 16–21.
Baer, J. (1999b). Domains of creativity. In M. A. Runco & S. R. Pritzker (Eds.), *Encyclopedia of creativity* (pp. 591–596). New York: Academic Press.
Bagley, W. C. (1941). The case for essentialism in education. *National Education Association Journal, 30,* 202–220.
Bohm, D. (1994). *Thought as a system.* London: Routledge.
Borko, H., & Livingston, C. (1989). Cognition and improvisation: Differences in mathematics instruction by expert and novice teachers. *American Educational Research Journal, 26,* 473–498.
Bracey, G. W. (2002). *The war against America's public schools: Privatizing schools, commercializing education.* Boston: Allyn & Bacon.
Brady, M. (2000). The standards juggernaut. *Phi Delta Kappan, 81,* 649–651.
Carter, K., Doyle, W., & Riney, M. (1995). Expert-novice differences in teaching. In A. C. Ornstein (Ed.), *Teaching: Theory into practice* (pp. 259–272). Needham Heights, MA: Allyn & Bacon.
Charles, C. M. (1996). *Building classroom discipline* (5th ed.). New York: Longman.
Cochrane-Smith, M., & Lytle, S. L. (1993). *Inside outside: Teacher research and knowledge.* New York: Teachers College Press.
Cohen, L. M., & Ambrose, D. (1993). Theories and practice for differentiated education for the gifted and talented. In K. A. Heller, F. J. Mönks, & A. H. Passow (Eds.), *International handbook of research and development of giftedness and talent* (pp. 339–363). Oxford, UK: Pergamon.
Dart, L. (2001). Literacy and the lost world of the imagination. *Educational Research, 43,* 63–77.
Davis, G. A. (1998). *Creativity is forever* (4th ed.). Dubuque, IA: Kendall Hunt.
Dawson, V. L., D'Andrea, T., Affinito, R., & Westby, E. L. (1999). Predicting creative behavior: A reexamination of the divergence between traditional and teacher-defined concepts of creativity. *Creativity Research Journal, 12,* 57–66.
Dempster, F. N. (1993). Exposing our students to less should help them learn more. *Phi Delta Kappan, 74,* 432–437.
Dewey, J. (1902). *The child and the curriculum.* Chicago: University of Chicago Press.
Dewey, J. (1938). *Experience and education.* New York: Macmillan.
Diakidoy, I.-A. N., & Constantinou, C. P. (2001). Creativity in physics: Response fluency and task specificity. *Creativity Research Journal, 13,* 401–410.
Doyle, W. (1986). Classroom organization and management. In M. C. Wittrock (Ed.), *Handbook of research on teaching* (3rd ed., pp. 392–431). New York: Macmillan.
Dunn, K., & Dunn, R. (1987). Dispelling outmoded myths about student learning. *Educational Leadership, 44*(6), 55–62.
Eggen, P. D., & Kauchak, D. P. (2001). *Strategies for teachers: Teaching content and thinking skills* (4th ed.). Boston: Allyn & Bacon.
Eisner, E. W. (2002). *The educational imagination.* Upper Saddle River, NJ: Merrill Prentice Hall.
Fasko, D. (2001). Education and creativity. *Creativity Research Journal, 13,* 317–327.
Feldhusen, J. F., & Treffinger, D. J. (1980). *Creative thinking and problem solving in gifted education.* Dubuque, IA: Kendall/Hunt.

Flippo, R. F. (1999). Redefining the reading wars: The war against reading researchers. *Educational Leadership, 57*(2), 38–41.
Fullan, M. G. (1991). *The new meaning of educational change.* New York: Teachers College Press.
Gardner, H. (1983). *Frames of mind: The theory of multiple intelligences.* New York: Basic Books.
Gardner, H. (1993a). *Creating minds.* New York: HarperCollins.
Gardner, H. (1993b). *Multiple intelligences: The theory in practice.* New York: Basic Books.
Gay, G. (2000). *Culturally responsive teaching: Theory, research, and practice.* New York: Teachers College Press.
Gillespie, D. (1992). *The mind's we: Contextualism in cognitive psychology.* Carbondale: Southern Illinois University Press.
Glasser, W. (1969). *Schools without failure.* New York: Harper & Row.
Gordon, P. R., Rogers, A. M., Comfort, M., Gavula, N., & McGee, B. P. (2001). A taste of problem-based learning increases achievement of urban minority middle-school students. *Educational Horizons, 79,* 171–175.
Gregorc, A. (1982). *An adult's guide to style.* New York: Gabriel Systems.
Gruber, H. E. (1989). The evolving systems approach to creative work. In D. B. Wallace & H. E. Gruber (Eds.), *Creative people at work* (pp. 3–24). New York: Oxford University Press.
Hallahan, D., & Kauffman, J. (1997). *Exceptional children* (7th ed.). Needham Heights, MA: Allyn & Bacon.
Heller, K. A., Mönks, F. J., Sternberg, R. J., & Subotnik, R. (Eds.). (2000). *International handbook of giftedness and talent* (2nd ed.). Oxford, UK: Pergamon.
Hennessey, B. A., & Amabile, T. M. (1988). The conditions of creativity. In R. J. Sternberg (Ed.), *The nature of creativity: Contemporary psychological perspectives* (pp. 11–38). New York: Cambridge University Press.
Jacobs, H. H. (1989). *Interdisciplinary curriculum: Design and implementation.* Alexandria, VA: ASCD.
Jones, V. F., & Jones, L. S. (1998). *Comprehensive classroom management.* Needham Heights, MA: Allyn & Bacon.
Joussemet, M., & Koestner, R. (1999). Effect of expected rewards on children's creativity. *Creativity Research Journal, 12,* 231–239.
Joyce, B., & Weil, M. (1996). *Models of teaching* (5th ed.). Needham Heights, MA: Allyn & Bacon.
Kanter, R. M. (1989). *When giants learn to dance.* New York: Simon & Schuster.
Keating, J., Diaz-Greenberg, R., Baldwin, M., & Thousand, J. (1998). A collaborative action research model for teacher preparation programs. *Journal of Teacher Education, 49,* 381–390.
Kounin, J. S. (1970). *Discipline and group management in classrooms.* New York: Holt, Rinehart & Winston.
Levin, B. (1994). Improving educational productivity: Putting learners at the center. *Phi Delta Kappan, 75,* 758–760.
Martinsen, O. (1995). Cognitive styles and experience in solving insight problems: Replication and extension. *Creativity Research Journal, 8,* 291–298.
McCarthy, B. (1990). Using the 4MAT system to bring learning styles to schools. *Educational Leadership, 48*(2), 31–37.
Miller, A. I. (1989). Imagery and intuition in creative scientific thinking: Albert Einstein's invention of the special theory of relativity. In D. B. Wallace & H. E. Gruber (Eds.), *Creative people at work* (pp. 171–188). New York: Oxford University Press.
Miller, A. I. (1996). *Insights of genius: Imagery and creativity in science and art.* New York: Springer-Verlag.

Moore, M. T. (1993). Implications of problem finding on teaching and learning. In S. G. Isaksen, M. C. Murdock, R. L. Firestien, & D. J. Treffinger (Eds.), *Nurturing and developing creativity: The emergence of a discipline* (pp. 51–69). Norwood, NJ: Ablex.

Myers, D. G. (2002). *Intuition: Its powers and perils.* New Haven, CT: Yale University Press.

Nelson, J. L., Lott, L., & Glenn, H. (1993). *Positive discipline in the classroom.* Rocklin, CA: Prima.

Newmann, F. M., Secada, W. G., & Wehlage, G. G. (1995). *A guide to authentic instruction and assessment: Vision, standards and scoring.* Madison: Wisconsin Center for Education Research.

O'Hara, L. A., & Sternberg, R. J. (1999). Learning styles. In M. A. Runco & S. R. Pritzker (Eds.), *Encyclopedia of creativity* (Vol. 2, pp. 147–153). New York: Academic Press.

Omnès, R. (1999). *Quantum philosophy: Understanding and interpreting contemporary science* (A. Sangalli, Trans.). Princeton, NJ: Princeton University Press.

Ornstein, A. C. (1995). Beyond effective teaching. *Peabody Journal of Education, 70,* 2–3.

Pelletier, S., & Shore, B. M. (2003). The gifted learner, the novice, and the expert: Sharpening emerging views of giftedness. In D. Ambrose, L. M. Cohen, & A. J. Tannenbaum (Eds.), *Creative intelligence: Toward theoretic integration* (pp. 237–281). Cresskill, NJ: Hampton.

Piirto, J. (1998). *Understanding those who create* (2nd ed.). Tempe, AZ: Gifted Psychology Press.

Pithers, R. T., & Soden, R. (2000). Critical thinking in education: A review. *Educational Research, 42,* 237–249.

Rejskind, F. G. (2000). TAG teachers: Only the creative need apply. *Roeper Review, 22,* 153–157.

Runco, M. A., & Chand, I. (1995). Cognition and creativity. *Educational Psychology Review, 7,* 243–267.

Runco, M. A., & Nemiro, J. (1994). Problem finding, creativity, and giftedness. *Roeper Review, 16,* 235–241.

Ruscio, J., Whitney, D. M., & Amabile, T. M. (1998). Looking inside the fishbowl of creativity: Verbal and behavioral predictors of creative performance. *Creativity Research Journal, 11,* 243–263.

Scott, C. L. (1999). Teachers' biases toward creative children. *Creativity Research Journal, 12,* 321–337.

Senge, P. M. (1990). *The fifth discipline: The art and practice of the learning organization.* New York: Doubleday.

Starko, A. J. (1995). *Creativity in the classroom: Schools of curious delight.* New York: Longman.

Stepien, W., & Gallagher, S. (1993). Problem-based learning: As authentic as it gets. *Educational Leadership, 50,* 25–28.

Sternberg, R. J. (1994). Allowing for thinking styles. *Educational Leadership, 52,* 36–40.

Sternberg, R. J. (1999). A dialectical basis for understanding the study of cognition. In R. J. Sternberg (Ed.), *The nature of cognition* (pp. 51–78). Cambridge, MA: MIT Press.

Sternberg, R. J. (2001). What is the common thread of creativity? Its dialectical relation to intelligence and wisdom. *American Psychologist, 56,* 360–362.

Sternberg, R. J., & Lubart, T. L. (1991). Creating creative minds. *Phi Delta Kappan, 72,* 608–614.

Sternberg, R. J., & Williams, W. M. (1996). *How to develop student creativity.* Alexandria, VA: ASCD.

Sternberg, R. J., & Zhang, L.-F. (2000). *Perspectives on cognitive, learning, and thinking styles.* Mahwah, NJ: Lawrence Erlbaum Associates.

Tomlinson, C. A. (1996). Good teaching for one and all: Does gifted education have an instructional identity? *Journal for the Education of the Gifted, 20,* 155–174.

Treffinger, D. J., Isaksen, S. G., & Dorval, K. B. (1994). *Creative problem solving: An introduction* (Rev. ed.). Sarasota, FL: Center for Creative Learning.

Treffinger, D. J., Isaksen, S. G., & Firestien, R. L. (1983). Theoretical perspectives on creative learning and its facilitation. *Creativity Research Journal, 17,* 9–17.

Weick, K. E. (1982). Administering education in loosely coupled schools. *Phi Delta Kappan, 63,* 673–676.
Westby, E. L., & Dawson, V. L. (1995). Creativity: Asset or burden in the classroom. *Creativity Research Journal, 8,* 1–10.
Wilson, S. M. (2002). *California dreaming: Reforming mathematics education.* New Haven, CT: Yale University Press.
Yan, B., & Arlin, P. (1999). Dialectical thinking: Implications for creative thinking. In M. A. Runco & S. R. Pritzker (Eds.), *Encyclopedia of creativity* (Vol. 1, pp. 547–552). New York: Academic Press.

Chapter 17

The Domain Generality Versus Specificity Debate: How Should It Be Posed?[1]

Robert J. Sternberg
Yale University

For any set of mental representations or processes, one can ask whether the representations are domain specific or domain general. But most representations are neither wholly domain specific nor wholly domain general (Sternberg, 1989). In this chapter, I argue that the construal of a dichotomy between domain generality and domain specificity is overstated. Although my remarks are oriented toward the study of creativity, they would apply as well to other psychological phenomena.

A SPATIAL-REPRESENTATIONAL MODEL OF DOMAINS AND THEIR ELEMENTS

In discussing domains, Tourangeau and Sternberg (1981, 1982; see also Sternberg, Tourangeau, & Nigro, 1979) argued, as had many before them (e.g., Rumelhart & Abrahamson, 1973; Shepard, 1969), that elements of a domain can be viewed as being represented in a multidimensional space.

---

[1] Preparation of this chapter was supported by Grant REC-9979843 from the National Science Foundation and by a government grant under the Javits Act Program (Grant No. R206R00001) as administered by the Office of Educational Research and Improvement, U.S. Department of Education. Grantees undertaking such projects are encouraged to express freely their professional judgment. This chapter, therefore, does not necessarily represent the positions or the policies of any of the funding agencies.

We extended this argument, however, and suggested that the domains themselves could be represented in a multidimensional space, whereby some domains (e.g., names of cats and names of dogs) would be closer to each other in Euclidean distance than would be other domains (e.g., names of cats and names of countries of the world). On this view, domains are no different than the elements in the domains. Just as the elements are relationally situated with respect to each other in a domain space, so are the domains in a hyperdomain space, and these hyperdomains could be mapped to even higher-order domains.

If this view holds, then we need to reexamine exactly what domain generality versus domain specificity means. For example, suppose that we consider five domains: personality psychology, social psychology, anthropology, geology, and art. Is each of these really a domain? It is not clear, because exactly what a domain is has never been defined very well. But let's say, for the sake of argument, that they are domains, because the argument I am about to make could be made for any set of similar items. In the spatial model, personality psychology presumably would be closer to social psychology than in anthropology, closer to anthropology than in geology, and perhaps closer to geology than to art (depending always on exactly how the domains are defined). If we were to ask whether someone's creativity extends across domains, then we would probably observe some gradient. The personality psychologist likely would be more creative in social psychology than in anthropology, in anthropology than in geology, and in geology than in art. This gradient might not apply for every individual, but might plausibly apply on average. Even if it did not hold in these particular instances, one could find gradients of a similar nature that would hold.

The question of domain generality versus domain specificity, then, becomes one of the function of decay of creativity as one moves from one domain to another. On average, the farther away two domains are in the multidimensional space of domains, the less creative one would expect an individual to be. Even someone as extraordinarily creative and diversified as Leonardo da Vinci would presumably have some decay function of creativity, however shallow it might be. For most of us, the decay function across Euclidean distances in the multidimensional space of domains presumably would be much steeper.

If we assume that there is some kind of (perhaps exponential) decay function across Euclidean distances in the multidimensional space, then we are stating that creativity is not domain general or domain specific, but instead is something in between. However, as psychologists, we must ask an additional question: Why do we get that particular decay function?

In answering this question, we realize that the question of domain generality versus specificity is even more complex than it appears in the spatial metaphor. The additional complexity pertains to the distinction between content and the mental representations that store it, and processes.

REPRESENTATION AND PROCESS

The distinction between the mental representations of content and mental processes can be illustrated with regard to two theories of intelligence—Gardner's (1983, 1999) and my own (Sternberg, 1997, 1999). When Gardner wrote of multiple intelligences, he was really writing of the application of thinking to content domains, such as the linguistic, logical-mathematical, musical, and spatial. His argument was that each of these domains is characterized by a separate symbol system, which mentally represents the content in a domain. However, the evidence suggests that his domains do not hold together, either psychometrically or in everyday life.

For example, Thurstone (1938) found verbal comprehension and verbal fluency to be two distinct psychometric factors. Modern hierarchical psychometric theories based on large databases, notably Carroll's (1993), similarly distinguish between verbal comprehension and fluency. To be a good reader is not necessarily to be a good writer, and vice versa. Similarly, spatial ability is multidimensional (Lohman, 2000): People are not simply strong spatially or not. For example, spatial rotation and spatial location memory are relatively distinct abilities; men, on average, excel over women on the first, and women, on average, excel over men on the second (Silverman & Eals, 1992). What appears to be a domain, therefore, on the surface level may not hold up as a domain (e.g., that underlying Gardner's "linguistic intelligence" on a deeper level). The reason is that a domain is probably better defined as a combination of mental representations and processes rather than solely in terms of the mental representations (i.e., symbol systems).

Even within a set of processes operating on a set of mental representations, there is lack of homogeneity. Consider reading, which is perhaps a gold standard for verbal-comprehension ability. There is a large difference between lower-order word recognition processes and higher-order reading comprehension (see essays in Sternberg & Spear-Swerling, 1999). Someone could be quite strong in decoding words, yet not be a good higher-order comprehender. Decoding is necessary but not sufficient for comprehension. Thus, even within a narrower ability, such as verbal comprehension, it is not clear that there is uniformity. Scores on a typical reading-comprehension test usually will represent a mixed measurement of some set of not-so-well-defined skills. There is no single "domain" operating here, at least from the standpoint of processes and the individual differences they produce.

The theory of successful intelligence (Sternberg, 1997, 1999) is complementary to Gardner's theory of multiple intelligences in that it specifies processes that can operate across domains. It distinguishes analytical, creative, and practical processing, and at least some evidence suggests that these domains are relatively (although not wholly) distinct psychometrically (Sternberg, 1999, 2003). Thus, one might be strong in analyzing a poem (linguistic domain), but not necessarily equally strong in writing a poem (also the linguistic domain). Indeed, the people who analyze poems often are not the same people who write them, anymore than outstanding music critics are necessarily outstanding musical performers. Indeed, quite the contrary: Many people who become music critics do so because their performance in music was anything but outstanding and they needed to look elsewhere for incorporating music into their careers.

Hence, a multidimensional space of content domains or of the mental representations that act on them would be insufficient to characterize the domain generality versus specificity of creativity, because it does not take into account the processes that act on these representations. People are not "creative" in the linguistic domain or not creative. Their creativity is likely to vary across the myriad processes that perfuse these domains. Guilford (1982) might even have argued that there is a third element that would need to be taken into account in a complete theory of domain generality versus specificity—namely, products—although I believe the evidence for a psychological separation of products from contents and processes was never strong.

IDENTIFYING THE STRUCTURES AND CONTENTS OF THE MULTIDIMENSIONAL REPRESENTATIONS

Even if we were to agree that separate multidimensional spaces would need to be constructed to characterize the mental representations and processes that underlie domain-based performance, we would still be left with the question of how we would go about identifying the structures and contents of the multidimensional representations. There are several alternative ways in which this identification might take place. I do not claim to know at this point which is best, or even if any would be satisfactory.

Mental Representations

Ratings. A traditional way of identifying the structure of a multidimensional psychological space has been to ask people to rate all possible pairs of items (usually assuming reflexivity, symmetry, and the triangle inequality; Shepard, 1969) and then to scale the ratings using nonmetric multidimensional scaling. Alternative but related methods include sorting of items into piles and rating triplets rather than pairs (for most similar and least similar pairs of elements within each triplet). There are three obvious problems with these methods. The first is how one decides what elements to rate. This decision is important, because the structure that emerges can be nothing more than a transformation of the input. The second problem is that people's implicit theories as to the relations of elements in a domain, or of domains to each other, may not well represent the actual relations in terms of their performance. The third problem is that some of the assumptions, such as symmetry, do not always hold up, as Tversky and Gati (1978) showed when participants were asked to rate both how similar a country such as North Korea was to China and how similar China was to North Korea. North Korea seemed, to many people, to be more similar to China than China did to North Korea.

Priming. A second option is to use some kind of priming or response-time task and then to use the reaction times or error rates as input to the multidimensional scaling algorithm. The data resulting from such procedures may be different from those resulting from implicit-theory-based ratings; however, the data resulting from different such procedures also may differ among themselves. For example, the concepts of "fish" and "chicken" may seem more alike if one is thinking in terms of airline or conference meal offerings than if one is thinking about reproductive methods.

ARE THERE UNIQUE MENTAL REPRESENTATIONS?

These considerations lead us to an even greater conundrum than we have faced before. The problem is whether there even are unique representations, not only between people, but even within people, or whether representations will depend on the demand characteristics of particular situations. Because mental representations can be elicited only through tasks, we are left with the biases that one particular task or another present in terms of the mental representations they yield.

We could, of course, use multiple dependent measures in order to "average out" over error. However, such averaging would assume that the differences we obtain are due to error. They might, in fact, be real differences.

Consider an example: How do we represent information about illnesses? The functional representation is likely to differ as a function of the question we are asked. For example, if we are asked about the effectiveness of antibiotics in treating a particular illness, we might use a taxonomic representation that distinguishes bacterial from viral illnesses. Antibiotics can be effective against bacterial but not viral illnesses, so this particular representation of information potentially will be very helpful to us. If, however, we are asked about symptoms, we may think in terms of clusters of illnesses that cause similar symptoms, such as respiratory diseases, gastric diseases, skin diseases, and so forth. If we are asked about whether people with the illness can survive it, we might use yet a different representation, separating chronic from acute illnesses. There may be some "meta-representation" that underlies all of these different representations, but whether it exists is unclear, and how we would know what it is seems even less clear, given that we can infer mental representations only through performance on tasks. And even if were to infer this meta-representation, we would still have difficulty separating representations from the processes that act on them.

Some people might wish to wash their hands of the problem by using a different form of representation for domains, the processes that operate in domains, or both. I have used a spatial form of representation, but for illustrative purposes only. Precisely the same problems would arise with any other form of representation, such as a set-theoretic one. We would still need a way of characterizing domain similarity (perhaps in terms of overlap among set elements), and we might find that measures obtained for other representations also would differ as a function of task. In other words, the conundrum results not as a function of the particular form of representation I have chosen, but rather as a result of the problem we have posed when we consider domain generality and domain specificity. We really have no good way of specifying what the domains are, whether they are the same across persons, whether they are the same across tasks, whether they are the same across cultures. And, of course, the same problems arise for the processes that operate on mental representations within domains. In other words, the domain generality versus specificity problem is a false dichotomy. It is conceptually vacuous because it fails to address the numerous problems underlying even what it *means*.

THE PROBLEM OF KNOWLEDGE

One of the reasons it is so difficult to test the domain specificity of creativity is that, by consensus, serious real-world creativity requires a substantial knowledge base (see essays in Sternberg, 1999), but few people have substantial knowledge bases across domains, for whatever they may be. In the times of Leonardo da Vinci, perhaps it was more plausible to assume that a very learned person could become knowledgeable in several domains. Today, it is extremely difficult. The knowledge explosion has created conditions in which it is even difficult to master one complex domain. If one wishes to make world-class contributions that go beyond where things are, one needs to know where things are, and often learning where they are can take many years of study.

If one looks at an experimental situation designed to test domain specificity, including our own (Lubart & Sternberg, 1995), one finds that the problems used are inevitably fairly simple ones. Torrance (1974) used extremely simple problems that require only a minimum of knowledge to solve. The advantage is that one can measure creativity across domains. The disadvantage is that one is measuring creativity across domains (in Torrance's case, verbal and nonverbal) using only highly impoverished knowledge bases, which is not typical of the way creativity occurs in the real world, or at least the world of world-class creative contributions. Although the kinds of tasks used by Lubart and Sternberg (1995)—such as writing short stories, designing advertisements, and making artworks—are more knowledge dependent, they are still quite content lean. Participants never could be taught in an experimental context the knowledge they would need to engage in serious creative endeavors.

CONCLUSION: THE NEED TO REDEFINE THE PROBLEM

If the traditional definition of the problem of domain generality versus domain specificity is not productive, might there be an alternative one that is more productive? I suggest that there is. We cannot talk about domain specificity until we have a theory of domains. In the absence of such a theory, we stand on very shaky ground when we try to analyze the domain generality versus specificity of any psychological construct. In all likelihood, we will find that within a domain, things are neither wholly domain general nor wholly domain specific. When we have defined the domains, we will then have a basis for deciding how domain general or domain specific skills, including creativity, truly are.

REFERENCES

Carroll, J. B. (1993). *Human cognitive abilities: A survey of factor-analytic studies.* New York: Cambridge University Press.
Gardner, H. (1983). *Frames of mind: The theory of multiple intelligences.* New York: Basic Books.
Gardner, H. (1999). Multiple approaches to understanding. In C. M. Reigeluth (Ed.), *Instructional-design theories and models: A new paradigm of instructional theory, Vol. II* (pp. 69–89). Mahwah, NJ: Lawrence Erlbaum Associates.
Guilford, J. P. (1982). Is some creative thinking irrational? *Journal of Creative Behavior, 16,* 151–154.
Lohman, D. F. (2000). Complex information processing and intelligence. In R. J. Sternberg (Ed.), *Handbook of intelligence* (pp. 285–340). New York: Cambridge University Press.

Lubart, T. I., & Sternberg, R. J. (1995). An investment approach to creativity: Theory and data. In S. M. Smith, T. B. Ward, & R. A. Finke (Eds.), *The creative cognition approach* (pp. 269–302). Cambridge, MA: MIT Press.

Rumelhart, D. E., & Abrahamson, A. A. (1973). A model for analogical reasoning. *Cognitive Psychology, 5*, 1–28.

Shepard, R. N. (1969). The analysis of proximities: Multidimensional scaling with an unknown distance function. *Psychometrika, 27*, 125–140.

Silverman, I., & Eals, M. (1992). The hunter-gatherer theory of spatial sex differences: Proximate factors mediating the female advantage in recall of object arrays. *Ethology and Sociobiology, 15*, 95–105.

Sternberg, R. J. (1989). Domain-generality versus domain-specificity: The life and impending death of a false dichotomy. *Merrill-Palmer Quarterly, 35*, 115–130.

Sternberg, R. J. (1997). *Successful intelligence.* New York: Plume.

Sternberg, R. J. (1999). The theory of successful intelligence. *Review of General Psychology, 3*, 292–316.

Sternberg, R. J. (2003). Construct validity of the theory of successful intelligence. In R. J. Sternberg, J. Lautrey, & T. I. Lubart (Eds.), *Models of intelligence for the new millennium* (pp. 55–80). Washington, DC: American Psychological Association.

Sternberg, R. J., & Spear-Swerling, L. (Eds.). (1999). *Perspectives on learning disabilities: Biological, cognitive, contextual.* Boulder, CO: Westview.

Sternberg, R. J., Tourangeau, R., & Nigro, G. (1979). Metaphor, induction, and social policy: The convergence of macroscopic and microscopic views. In A. Ortony (Ed.), *Metaphor and thought* (pp. 325–353). New York: Cambridge University Press.

Thurstone, L. L. (1938). *Primary mental abilities.* Chicago: University of Chicago Press.

Torrance, E. P. (1974). *Torrance tests of creative thinking.* Lexington, MA: Personnel Press.

Tourangeau, R., & Sternberg, R. J. (1981). Aptness in metaphor. *Cognitive Psychology, 13*, 27–55.

Tourangeau, R., & Sternberg, R. J. (1982). Understanding and appreciating metaphors. *Cognition, 11*, 203–244.

Tversky, A., & Gati, I. (1978). Studies of similarity. In E. Rosch & B. Lloyd (Eds.), *Cognition and categorization* (pp. 79–98). Hillsdale, NJ: Lawrence Erlbaum Associates.

Chapter 18

The (Relatively) Generalist View of Creativity

Jonathan A. Plucker
Indiana University

I appreciate the opportunity to respond to the preceding chapters. The authors covered a very wide breadth of creative activity, and all of the material is thought-provoking. My purpose in this chapter is to provide a succinct analysis of these domain-specific perspectives, and to do so using a domain-general conceptualization of creativity.

However, this leads to a problem: I do not consider myself to be a creativity generalist! But neither am I a domain specifist. My perspective, described briefly in the next section, is one that attempts to stake out the middle ground in this complex debate. From a specifist perspective, which has gained immensely in popularity over the past decade, one wonders why general assessments of creativity are associated with only limited evidence of predictive validity. At the same time, generalists point to the theoretical and methodological weaknesses of domain-specific positions (and weaknesses of related perspectives on cognition in context and situated cognition).

THE MIDDLE GROUND?

In an attempt to address these issues, Ronald Beghetto and I recently proposed a hybrid conceptualization suggesting that creativity is predominantly domain general but appears to be domain specific when applied to real-world tasks (Plucker & Beghetto, in press). This position is based on the following definition: Creativity is the interplay between ability and process by which an individual or group produces an outcome or product that is both novel and useful as defined within some social context (Plucker, Beghetto, & Dow, in press).

Based on this definition, many components of creativity are arguably domain neutral or general, but the need for people to specialize as they age and the role of social context give the strong appearance of domain specificity. However, this distinction is not practically important, because the middle-ground position suggests that it is more important to describe *how* people have chosen to be creative or are viewed by others to be creative as opposed to whether they should be labeled creative within or across specific domains. Furthermore, the hybrid position emphasizes the role of flexible thinking (a general cognitive skill) in order to promote transfer of knowledge to problems in different areas (a domain-specific attribute). Finally, and perhaps most supportive of the traditional generalist perspective, people already use too little of their creativity, so why further discourage them from applying it to life's problems by burdening them with domain specificity?

DEFINITIONS ARE IMPORTANT

A major difficulty in the study of creativity is that authors and researchers often define the construct very differently from one another (Plucker et al., in press). Hence, an important step of any comparison of viewpoints on creativity is to investigate how the authors define their terms. I reviewed each chapter of this volume carefully to identify the authors' definitions of creativity. Unfortunately, only four chapters contained explicit definitions of creativity. To summarize three of them: Zimmerman (chap. 4) used Clark et al.'s definition of creativity as "unconventional behavior"; Basadur (chap. 15) relied on Kabanoff and Rossiter's (1994) definition of applied creativity as "occurring in a real-world, industrial, organizational, or social context; pertaining to the finding or solving of complex problems; and having an actual behavioral creative product (or plan) as the final result"; and Averill (chap. 13) noted that creativity is generally novel, effective, and authentic with specific contexts. Although I found it difficult to identify a specific definition in the chapter on engineering, Cropley and Cropley (chap. 10) essentially explored how engineers can and should define creativity (and provided a particularly interesting exploration, at that).

This is not to say that the other chapters did not contain a definition of creativity: With only one or two exceptions, authors provided implicit definitions of creativity in their chapters. But it is worth noting that providing explicit definitions of the main construct of interest would make analysis of ideas about creativity much easier. After all, researchers would generally avoid an analysis of the nature of intelligence if the construct were not carefully defined by participants in the debate.

WHAT CAN WE LEARN ABOUT DOMAIN SPECIFICITY–GENERALITY FROM THESE CHAPTERS?

Given the breadth and depth of material covered in this volume, a chapter-by-chapter review struck me as being unwieldy and probably not very helpful. As an alternative, I reviewed each chapter in an attempt to identify reasons why specificity or generality are important to the conceptualization and enhancement of creativity in each given domain. This chapter concludes with a reflection on the hybrid perspective described earlier.

Specificity Is Important

Identifying domain-specific arguments was much more difficult than I anticipated. A majority of authors first introduced general theories and conceptualizations of creativity, and then provided examples of the unique (and often not very unique) ways that general theories apply to creativity in a specific domain. For example, Piirto (chap. 1) described relevant personality characteristics and Wallas' well-known model of creative process (i.e., preparation, incubation, illumination, verification), and then provided a comprehensive analysis of how this material applies to creativity among poets.

Another common theme among the chapters was the introduction of a domain-specific perspective that could easily be used to describe creativity in other areas: Perry's (chap. 2) analysis of key aspects of fiction writers' creative process (i.e., have a reason to write, think like a writer, loosen up, focus in, balance among opposites) was similar to other authors' emphasis on preparation, motivation, having relevant technical skills, task commitment, and cognitive processes. Likewise, Sawyer's (chap. 3) differentiation between most forms of creativity as products versus acting as creative process is very interesting, but a case can be made that his three stages of acting (i.e., preparation, rehearsal, performance) mirror the stages of Wallas' model.

At the same time, several authors introduced complexities into the notion of domain-specific creativity that I had never previously considered. Most notably, both Perry and Simonton (chap. 8) discussed general influences that work across domains, but they also noted specific differences in the nature and application of creativity *within* specific domains: Perry explored differences in the self-reported metaphor usage among poets and writers, and Simonton addressed differences in creativity within various subdomains of psychology. This point is worthy of further investigation, because it has considerable potential to impact how we conceptualize creativity within increasingly complex and differentiated fields.

Several authors proposed that differences in creativity among domains largely result from differences in questions that are asked across those domains. Saunders and Thagard (chap. 9) discussed differences in creativity in engineering versus the natural sciences as a matter of being interested in different questions. In the same vein, Basadur described a general model of creativity and noted that the different requirements of different jobs (even within a single domain) and individuals' creative preferences lead to different forms of creativity. The same theme was apparent in the analyses of creativity and leadership by Mumford, Strange, Scott, and Gaddis (chap. 12) and creativity and teaching by Ambrose (chap. 16). This perspective appears to imply that creative processes are similar across domains, but these processes may be used differently in each domain, leading to observations of domain specificity.

Generality Is Important

Discussion of concepts that apply to all forms of creative endeavor was also common. Nearly every chapter contained significant discussion of general factors related to creativity. For example, the concept of flow or high levels of task commitment and intrinsic motivation was discussed in several chapters, most notably by Piirto and Perry in their analyses of poets and fiction writers, respectively. Many authors drew connections between their domain of interest and related domains (i.e., multidomain concepts as opposed to domain-general factors). Saunders and Thagard noted that "Creative problem solving about computers requires all the cognitive processes that go into scientific research, including means-ends reasoning with rules, hypothesis formation, and generation of new concepts."

Several authors provided an interesting, unexpected wrinkle: Perhaps domain-specific creative activities can be beneficial to creativity in all other domains. Zimmerman noted that developing talent in artistic creativity takes considerable time and effort, but there is a domain-general value to using art to help one take multiple perspectives, be open to change, and so on that can be used in other domains. Sawyer implied a comparable benefit to the study of improvisation through acting. This makes a great deal of sense, but I wonder how to best achieve this transfer to other domains—guided practice, scaffolding, perhaps even a "creative apprenticeship"? In my mind, this problem of transfer remains the single biggest barrier to generalizing domain-specific skills and attitudes to creative activities in other domains.

RETURNING TO THE HYBRID POSITION

As noted previously, it became increasingly difficult to distill aspects of creativity that were truly domain specific as I worked through the chapters. In essence, many authors made a case that creativity is heavily influenced by domain general (or at least multidomain) traits, processes, and influences, and descriptions of proposed domain-specific processes appeared very similar to domain general theories such as those proposed by Wallas, Torrance, and Guilford, among many others.

Indeed, most authors provided evidence in support of the hybrid position described earlier. Creative psychologists appear to have many traits in common with creators in other domains, especially productivity, expertise, motivation, and independence, although differences may exist in the creativity of psychologists across specialty areas within the domain (as Simonton noted). Furthermore, Milgram and Livne (chap. 11) proposed that general creative thinking ability is a necessary but not sufficient condition for domain-specific creativity, a major tenet of the hybrid position.

Cropley and Cropley offered a perspective on creativity in engineering that was product focused, with criteria of relevance and effectiveness, novelty, elegance, and generalizability. This conceptualization is highly compatible with the definition I offered at the beginning of the chapter, with elegance and generalizability a result of the social context mentioned in my definition. Leman (chap. 6), in his analysis of musical creativity, provided an especially insightful analysis of the influence of social context on creativity.

Feist's (chap. 7) ideas may offer the greatest challenge to the hybrid view, as he theorized that creativity in the physical sciences has developed—in an evolutionary sense—distinct from other domains of human endeavor. However, as I read that chapter, I kept returning to the notion that just because people end up at different places doesn't mean that they don't use comparable means to arrive there. Not identical means, for certain, but why not common means? One can go the airport and choose from several different flights: No two flight experiences are identical, although most are very similar in practical ways (e.g., engines, seats too close together). Yet these similar travel strategies have the potential to help you arrive at an almost unlimited number of destinations. Thus, physics may have developed in a different epistemological direction than did the fine arts, but that does not necessarily mean that domain-general aspects of creativity are without value in each of these domains. Perhaps this is an example of the long-term effects of social context on creativity in a particular domain.

MOVING AHEAD

Of course, all of this discussion is not truly about generality versus specificity. Rather, it is a debate about how to best foster creativity across a wide range of domains. Taken collectively, the contributions in this volume appear to make the case that context matters to a point, but perhaps not as much as many creativity scholars would like to believe. In other words, focusing enhancement efforts solely on domain-specific strategies will be difficult—if not impossible—and probably not very effective. As several authors noted in their chapters, creators are not a homogeneous group. The field, and society in general, will be much better off if we focus on identifying the ways in which enhanceable aspects of creativity are domain general and domain specific within each context of interest (and define our terms more explicitly!).

REFERENCES

Kabanoff, B., & Rossiter, J. R. (1994). Recent developments in applied creativity. *International Review of Industrial and Organizational Psychology, 9*, 283–324.

Plucker, J. A., & Beghetto, R. A. (2004). Why creativity is domain general, why it looks domain specific, and why the distinction does not matter. In R. J. Sternberg, E. L. Grigorenko, & J. L. Singer (Eds.), *Who's creative?* (pp. 153–167). Washington, DC: American Psychological Association.

Plucker, J. A., Beghetto, R. A., & Dow, G. T. (2004). Why isn't creativity more important to educational psychologists? Potential, pitfalls, and future directions in creativity research. *Educational Psychologist, 39*, 83–96.

Chapter 19

Whence Creativity? Overlapping and Dual-Aspect Skills and Traits

John Baer
Rider University

James C. Kaufman
California State University at San Bernardino

In some ways, the design of this book may have encouraged the idea of domain specificity by asking each author to focus on a specific domain. Nonetheless, almost all the experts noted connections of various kinds between the personality traits or skills important to creative people in their domain and the traits or skills necessary for creativity in other domains. At the same time, almost all the contributors also pointed to differences between domains in the kinds of cognitive processes, specific content knowledge, personality traits, or ways of working that lead to creative performance. Many noted that even within the domain about which they were writing there was more than one constellation of skills and/or traits that could lead to success in that domain (e.g., Simonton, chap. 8; Saunders & Thagard, chap. 9; Mumford, Strange, Scott, & Gaddis, chap. 12; Basadur, chap. 15).

Many of the contributors made specific reference to an arts/science distinction in the personality traits, skills, or working styles of creative people (e.g., Cropley & Cropley, chap. 10; Simonton, chap. 8; Zimmerman, chap. 4; Feist, chap. 7). This seemed to be a kind of first pass at distinguishing domain-specific and general, domain-transcending factors influencing creative performance. The authors of at least two of the chapters (Milgram & Livne, chap. 11; Piirto, chap. 1) cast this distinction in a way that fits nicely with Amabile's (1983, 1996) componential framework, which includes general creativity-relevant skills and domain-specific skills as separate classes of skills that influence creative performance (in addition to a third component, task motivation, discussed later in this chap.).

Most of the contributors, however, did not classify the skills or traits important in their domain in a way that neatly separated domain-specific and general creativity-relevant skills or traits. Instead, they tended to choose metaphors, like *overlap* (Averill, chap. 13), in describing how creativity in their domain is more similar to that in some domains than that in others (e.g., Saunders & Thagard's connection between creativity in computer science and in the natural sciences, Ambrose's reference to philosophical conflicts that affect "education and related fields," or Mumford et al.'s recognition of the different "emphasis placed on certain skills" in different domains). In some cases, authors identified factors that, although they might have had some relevance in other domains, were especially important in one particular domain (e.g., Ford & Sullivan's comment in chap. 14 that "the tensions between novelty and ascribed value present challenges that are unique, or at least substantially more salient, in business domains" than in other task domains, and their argument that novelty "is not always good ... [which] is true in all task domains, but we believe it is especially true in organizational settings").

This model[1] (which is perhaps too fancy a word for what is at heart a rather loosely defined concept) might be called an "overlapping skills model" (or, to add just a bit more precision, perhaps a "varying gradient of generalizability model") because it acknowledges that:

- Some skills or traits may be important in many domains (e.g., Simonton's intelligence and motivation; Piirto's risk taking, self-discipline, motivation, sense of naiveté, unconventionality, and tolerance for ambiguity; Milgram & Livne's ideational fluency and intelligence).
- Other skills or traits are shared by a limited set of domains (e.g., Mumford et al.'s connection between dramatic skills and certain kinds of leadership creativity; or the personality attributes that Piirto found common to both poets and fiction writers, such as ambition/envy, concern with philosophical matters, frankness often expressed in political or social activism, psychopathology, depression, empathy, and a sense of humor).
- Some personality attributes and skills are quite domain specific (e.g., in chap. 16, Ambrose's "establishing an inquiry-based learning atmosphere" and "applying a wide variety of instructional models and strategies"; Simonton's reference to "domain-specific expertise" and the 10-year rule [Ericsson, 1996], which suggested that to be creative in any domain, novices must first "spend many hours everyday for a full dec-

---

[1]In the chapter following this one (chap. 20) we have tried to put this idea together with the results of some recent research we have been conducting to build a comprehensive theory of creative abilities (the "amusement park theory of creativity").

ade before they can attain world-class competence in a given achievement domain"; Piirto's comment that "not only engineers and novelists, but also poets and prose writers work differently").

This admittedly vague model would include Amabile's componential framework as a possibility but does not commit itself to clear lines of any kind that separate different classes of skills or traits. What does seem clear is that the experts polled in this volume believe that there are varying degrees of overlap in the extent to which diverse individual attributes contribute to creativity in different domains.

The goal of this book was to consider how creators in various domains do their work. We believe that this volume's most important contribution is in the details each author has given us about what kinds of underlying abilities or attributes lead to creative performance in each of the domains discussed. We assert that the fact that many of these authors referred to some rather general creativity-relevant skills or dispositions, however, deserves special notice, and it is to those commonalities that we now turn.

Motivation is a word that came up in almost every chapter in some form, sometimes with special reference to the importance of intrinsic motivation, other times just to the importance of being motivated to do the hard work of creativity. As Saunders and Thagard wrote in the final sentence of their chapter, "Creativity requires caring about a problem sufficiently to work on it intensely. . . ." It may not be quite as important as Woody Allen suggested when he said that "90% of success is showing up,"[2] but one does need to "show up" if one hopes to be creative; that is, one must be sufficiently motivated to do or produce *something* in order to be creative (and, as Simonton reminded us, the more "somethings" one produces, the more likely it is that some of those things will be creative). Based on the experts' varied comments, it is not clear whether it matters if the motivation is intrinsic, extrinsic, or even the product of "laziness, impatience, and hubris" (Wall, 1996, p. xiii, as cited by Saunders & Thagard).

Thus, motivation seems to be a general, domain-transcending factor in creativity *par excellence*—on par, perhaps, with intelligence (which is also mentioned by several contributors). But is it the same kind of construct as intelligence? In the case of intelligence, the evidence is quite strong that

---

[2]A Google search to help us track down the origin of this quote was unsuccessful. There were, however, more than 100 references to this quote (all crediting Woody Allen) in places like *Forbes* magazine, several "favorite quotes" web pages, and quite a few online syllabi. Interestingly, the exact percentage given varied from a low of 50% to a fairly common 95% (and included some rather surprisingly specific percentages like 88% and 83.1%). There was also variation in what the 90% explained: success, genius, or life. We don't think the exact percentage, or even its exact source, matter a great deal in the context of this chapter, however, so we decided to include it without a proper citation.

there is some general g factor and perhaps many more domain-specific skills that some, such as Gardner (1983), have also called intelligences. When we speak of intelligence, however, we are generally speaking of g, which (whatever it is) has been shown psychometrically to be related to a vast range of abilities in almost every imaginable domain (Gottfredson, 1997; Jensen, 1998; Neisser et al., 1996).

Is there a parallel to g in the case of motivation? Is there something in the construct "motivation" that we can measure—or, at this point, even conceive of—that we have reason to believe is applicable across domains the way intelligence has been shown to be? Or, when we speak of motivation, are we not perhaps referring to a diverse group of motivations that vary, within the same person, from domain to domain (and often from task to task within a domain, and even from moment to moment on the same task)? Does it make sense to suggest that Einstein's motivation to understand the physical universe could have equally well been directed (in the sense of spurring him to work with equal intensity) toward the problem of deciphering the nature of DNA, or toward the task of writing sonnets (Kaufman & Baer, 2004)? Motivation, as Amabile (1983, 1996) showed us, varies even within subjects working on the same task but under different environmental constraints. And we all experience different levels of motivation as we approach different tasks that are in no way commensurable or transferable from task to task. (Wouldn't it be convenient if we could simply direct our motivations so easily? It would mark the end of procrastination. Not feeling much like doing your taxes today? Simply take your motivation for playing video games and apply it to filling out those 1040s.)

Our point is that although in one sense it may make sense to group some attributes (like motivation) together, those traits may not be general traits in the same way that g is a general trait. Yes, motivation is important in any domain that one considers, but it is at least possible (if not probable) that it must be the right *kind* of motivation for the task at hand—motivation to dance for dancing creativity, motivation to solve a certain kind of problem for engineering creativity, and so on. Labeling all these diverse motivations as "motivation" is conceptually helpful (and allows us to see commonalities among motivations, e.g., the importance of intrinsic motivation in creative performance). However, that doesn't make motivation a general attribute in the way that intelligence has been shown to be. In terms of an individual's ability to be creative, motivation may be *very* domain specific (and this is perhaps especially true of eminent creators, who must devote so much of their time to work in a single domain).

So much of what can, at one level, be called general, may be (when looked at more closely) very domain linked. Motivation thus presents two very different faces—one general and one domain specific—and many other creativity-relevant skills and traits may also have this dual aspect. Intrinsic motivation in physical science may be like intrinsic motivation in leadership or intrinsic motivation in teaching only in a very rarified sense, and it may be impossible to take intrinsic motivation in writing poetry and transfer it in any meaningful way to engineering, psychology, or dance. By using the same word to describe these different motivational experiences we point out their commonality, which is very real; however, motivation may be a general attribute only in an analytic sense, not in a productive or applied sense. It's rather like saying one needs skill, or one needs knowledge, to do something. Yes, this is certainly true, but it also begs the question of exactly *what* skill or knowledge is necessary. Skills and knowledge are, for the most part, fairly specific: One's knowledge of computer languages may be essential to creativity in computer science, but isn't likely to have much of an impact on how creative a photographer one may become (or even how creative a physical scientist one may become). One's skill in expressing emotions is unlikely to help one solve challenging mathematics problems.

Skills and knowledge are required in every domain for creative performance, but most of that requisite knowledge and skill are very domain linked and not terribly useful in other domains. Calling skill or knowledge a *general* creativity-relevant factor in creative performance, therefore, would be in one sense true, but it could also be very misleading. At an abstract level, skill and knowledge are important for creativity in all domains, but the relevant skills and knowledge are often very domain specific. Recognition of this dual aspect of creativity-relevant variables—one analytical, the other functional or practical—may help us better understand creativity and allow more insightful interpretations of research regarding domain specificity.

The importance of this distinction in what we mean when we say that a trait or skill is a general, domain-transcending trait or skill may be true of some other commonalities, such as divergent thinking, imagination, flow, insight, or even tolerance of ambiguity or self-discipline (all of which were mentioned by contributors to this volume, and by many others before them, as being general creativity-relevant skills or traits). These, too, may be general skills or traits in the sense that they have been shown to influence creative performance in many domains, but at the same time they may in fact be very domain specific in terms of the actual skills in question. These skills and traits might not be things one can actually apply in different domains but may instead be (as we have suggested motivation and most kinds of knowledge may be) domain linked, so that when one leaves one domain to act in a different domain, one is likely to leave behind those skills and traits also (or at least they may be of little value in the new domain). Is being tolerant of ambiguity when searching for a solution to a computer problem the same as being tolerant of ambiguity when searching for a metaphor for a poem, or the same as being tolerant of ambiguity when developing a psychological theory? It may be, but we have no evidence on which to base such an opinion, and the same is true of many of the other traits and skills common to creativity across domains, such as self-discipline, flow, imagination, or insight (areas ripe for enterprising researchers to explore).

One area in which significant work has been done in this regard is in the area of divergent thinking, where there is a growing body of evidence that divergent-thinking skills are domain specific in the sense that they do not transfer from one task domain to another (Baer, 1991, 1993, 1994, 1996, 2003; Diakidoy & Constantinou, 2001, 2002; Han, 2000, 2003; Han & Marvin, 2002; Mumford, Marks, Connelly, Zaccaro, & Johnson, 1998; Scott, 1997; Stokes, 2001). In the area of motivation, Ruscio, Whitney, and Amabile (1998) showed that different kinds of motivation lead to creativity in different domains.

We are suggesting that there is a need to deconstruct general creativity-relevant skills and traits to avoid the possibility that we are grouping things that, although similar in one sense, are very dissimilar in another, equally important sense. Such a critical reappraisal may help explain confusing and sometimes conflicting research results. For example, there is much dispute about the nature of the connection between divergent thinking and creativity (Baer, 1993, 1998; Crockenberg, 1972; Hocevar, 1981; Plucker, 1998; Plucker & Renzulli, 1999). Perhaps the reason that some researchers find significant correlations between divergent thinking test scores and actual creative performance while others find no relationship between the two is due to confusion about two different meanings of divergent thinking. If we think of divergent thinking as a variety of different skills applicable in different domains, then scores on divergent thinking tests may or may not correlate with creative performance, depending on which domain is being examined and the nature of the divergent thinking test itself. If both the creative performance task and the divergent thinking test happen to focus on the same domain, they will be correlated; but if the task and the test come from very different domains, they may not be correlated at all, or they may have a very minor correlation. At the same time, it may be true that divergent thinking *of some kind* is an important contributor to creativity in virtually all domains, and in that sense divergent thinking could fairly be thought of as a general factor relevant to creative performance in all domains.

Divergent thinking represents two very different (although of course related) ideas—it has a dual aspect. It's rather like saying fruit is good for one's health, which is true, but if the particular nutrient one needs from fruit is vitamin C, then it matters *which* fruit one eats. Eating both apples and oranges both may contribute to one's health, but they contribute to different aspects of one's health, and thus eating fruit is a factor both generally related to health and at the same time related only in ways very specific to the particular fruit in question. In the same way, it may be that skills like divergent thinking and traits like motivation may be both general creativity-relevant skills or traits in a very abstract sense and (at the same time) very domain-specific skills or traits at the functional or practical level.

We hope that this volume provides insight into what it means to be creative in the many domains discussed, and that it may also lead to more careful thought and research to help clarify what it means when we say that some skills and traits are generally important to creative performance in all domains.

REFERENCES

Amabile, T. M. (1983). *The social psychology of creativity*. New York: Springer-Verlag.

Amabile, T. M. (1996). *Creativity in context: Update to the social psychology of creativity*. Boulder, CO: Westview.

Baer, J. (1991). Generality of creativity across performance domains. *Creativity Research Journal, 4*, 23–39.

Baer, J. (1993). *Creativity and divergent thinking: A task-specific approach*. Hillsdale, NJ: Lawrence Erlbaum Associates.

Baer, J. (1994). Divergent thinking is not a general trait: A multi-domain training experiment. *Creativity Research Journal, 7*, 35–46.

Baer, J. (1996). The effects of task-specific divergent-thinking training. *Journal of Creative Behavior, 30*, 183–187.

Baer, J. (1998). The case for domain specificity in creativity. *Creativity Research Journal, 11*, 173–177.

Baer, J. (2003). Evaluative thinking, creativity, and task specificity: Separating wheat from chaff is not the same as finding needles in haystacks. In M. A. Runco (Ed.), *Critical creative processes* (pp. 129–151). Cresskill, NJ: Hampton.

Crockenberg, S. B. (1972). Creativity tests: A boon or boondoggle for education? *Review of Educational Research, 42*, 27–45.

Diakidoy, I. A., & Constantinou, C. P. (2001). Creativity in physics: Response fluency and task specificity. *Creativity Research Journal, 13*, 401–410.

Diakidoy, I. A., & Constantinou, C. P. (2002). Domain specificity in creativity testing: A comparison of performance on a general divergent-thinking test and a parallel, content-specific test. *Journal of Creative Behavior, 36*, 41–61.

Ericsson, K. A. (1996). The acquisition of expert performance: An introduction to some of the issues. In K. A. Ericsson (Ed.), *The road to expert performance: Empirical evidence from the arts and sciences, sports, and games* (pp. 1–50). Mahwah, NJ: Lawrence Erlbaum Associates.

Gardner, H. (1983). *Frames of mind: The theory of multiple intelligences*. New York: Basic Books.

Gottfredson, L. S. (1997). Mainstream science on intelligence: An editorial with 52 signatories, history, and bibliography. *Intelligence, 24*(1), 13–23.

Han, K. S. (2000). Varieties of creativity: Investigating the domain-specificity of creativity in young children. *Dissertation Abstracts International Section A: Humanities and Social Sciences, 61*, 1796.

Han, K. S. (2003). Domain-specificity of creativity in young children: How quantitative and qualitative data support it. *Journal of Creative Behavior, 37*, 117–142.

Han, K. S., & Marvin, C. (2002). Multiple creativeness? Investigating domain-specificity of creativity in young children. *Gifted Child Quarterly, 46,* 98–109.

Hocevar, D. (1981). Measurement of creativity: Review and critique. *Journal of Personality Assessment, 45,* 450–464.

Jensen, A. R. (1998). *The g factor: The science of mental ability.* Westport, CT: Praeger.

Kaufman, J. C., & Baer, J. (2004). Hawking's haiku, Madonna's math: Why it's hard to be creative in every room of the house. In R. J. Sternberg, E. L. Grigorenko, & J. L. Singer (Eds.), *Creativity: From potential to realization* (pp. 3–19). Washington, DC: American Psychological Association.

Mumford, M. D., Marks, M. A., Connelly, M. S., Zaccaro, S. J., & Johnson, T. F. (1998). Domain based scoring of divergent thinking tests: Validation evidence in an occupational sample. *Creativity Research Journal, 11,* 151–164.

Neisser, U., Boodoo, G., Bouchard, T. J., Boykin, A. W., Brody, N., Ceci, S. J., Halpern, D. F., Loehlin, J. C., Perloff, R., Sternberg, R. J., & Urbina, S. (1996). Intelligence: Knowns and unknowns. *American Psychologist, 51,* 77–101.

Plucker, J. A. (1998). Beware of simple conclusions: The case for the content generality of creativity. *Creativity Research Journal, 11,* 179–182.

Plucker, J. A., & Renzulli, J. S. (1999). Psychometric approaches to the study of human creativity. In R. J. Sternberg (Ed.), *Handbook of creativity* (pp. 35–61). New York: Cambridge University Press.

Ruscio, J., Whitney, D. M., & Amabile, T. M. (1998). Looking inside the fishbowl of creativity: Verbal and behavioral predictors of creative performance. *Creativity Research Journal, 11,* 243–263.

Scott, T. E. (1997). The role of domain-specific knowledge in divergent thinking. *Dissertation Abstracts International: Section B: The Sciences & Engineering, 57,* 7256.

Stokes, P. D. (2001). Variations on Guilford's creative abilities. *Creativity Research Journal, 13,* 277–283.

Wall, L. (1996). *Programming Perl* (2nd ed.). Sebastopol, CA: O'Reilly.

Chapter 20

The Amusement Park Theory of Creativity

James C. Kaufman
California State University at San Bernardino

John Baer
Rider University

The amusement park theory of creativity grew out of the "overlapping skills" or "varying gradient of generalizability" model discussed in the previous chapter. That rather vague initial model was, in turn, a response to the many ideas of the contributors to this volume. We have linked these ideas to data we have been collecting for 2 years about how people conceptualize creativity to create the amusement park theory of creativity. Although our data set is not yet complete—we eventually hope to factor analyze the responses of more than 2,000 subjects from a wide range of fields—what it has revealed thus far dovetails nicely with the combined ideas of experts writing about creativity in diverse domains. Our theory has been nourished from the ideas presented by the contributors to this volume, and we therefore thought it proper to present it for the first time here, although it is incomplete in some respects, as a kind of coda to the book. Because it remains a work in progress, this chapter is something of a promissory note for an evolving theory that we hope will become a useful addition to creativity theory.

Although any sizable amusement park could do the metaphorical work we need for our model, we have chosen one such park—Disney World—as our example, because it is perhaps the amusement park most familiar to the greatest number of people. Its size is also a plus, both because this makes it easy to conceptualize the different levels of the theory and because it is commensurate with the rather large scope of the theory. For readers unfamiliar with Disney World, however, we believe that it will be an easy matter to translate the Disney examples we have used to ones from other amusement parks.

INITIAL REQUIREMENTS ("You must be this high to ride")

Initial requirements include things that are necessary (but not sufficient) for any type of creative production—notably intelligence, motivation, and suitable environments. And just as the height requirements of the "You must be this high to ride" signs at different rides may vary depending on the nature of the ride, so too do the specific degrees of intelligence, motivation, and suitable environments needed to succeed in different areas of creative endeavor vary. Nonetheless, each of these factors is, in some measure, a prerequisite to creative achievement in any domain. Let us explain what we mean by each.

Intelligence

Some basic level of intelligence is needed to be creative. Most studies find a solid (if low) correlation between creativity and intelligence that extends to about a 120 IQ (Getzels & Jackson, 1962; Renzulli, 1986; Sternberg & O'Hara, 1999; Winner, 1996).[1] This doesn't mean that someone must be smart to be creative, but rather that someone with a very low level of intelligence is very unlikely to demonstrate creativity.[2] Some areas require a higher level of intelligence[3] than others, such as mathematical theory versus art. This is not meant to suggest that artists are never intellectual geniuses, or that all creative mathematicians have higher IQs than all creative artists. However, a higher minimal level of intelligence is required to make creative achievements in mathematics than in art.

Motivation

It is important to note at the outset that when we say *motivation* in this particular context, we are *not* referring to the distinction between intrinsic and extrinsic motivation, but rather to the simple necessity of being highly motivated one way or another. If someone is not motivated to do something—*anything*—for any reason, then this person will not create anything in the first place. A fish that gets away may be long talked about by the fisherman,

---

[1] Once a person's IQ reaches approximately 120, the chances are small that any further advances in IQ will increase. It most likely will not hurt, and may help. But in extreme cases, Simonton (1994) hypothesized, a very high-IQ individual may not be able to communicate his or her ideas (creative or otherwise) in an effective manner to other people. Indeed, Hollingworth (1942) found several instances of this inability of high-IQ individuals to function well in their environment. This lack of communication may result in their ideas never being implemented, regardless of how brilliant these ideas may be.

[2] There are some exceptions, as in autistic children who create celebrated paintings.

[3] Intelligence as traditionally defined, either as g or as crystallized-fluid intelligence.

but a writer who never picks up the pen (or types at the keyboard) is not going to be a creative writer.

We should alert the reader that motivation makes more than one appearance in this theory. Motivation is a varying and multidimensional attribute;[4] unlike intelligence, it can change (and does change) greatly from day to day (even from moment to moment) and also from task to task (as discussed later in this chap.). When we speak of motivation as an initial requirement, we mean motivation in the most general sense. One must first have the desire to do *some*thing; to this general initial level of motivation to do something, one's motivation to do some (specific) thing can then be added.

Environment

Environments are important in both the past and present tenses. A person who grows up in a culture or in a family in which creative thoughts or actions are not encouraged (or are even punished) will have a harder time being creative. Similarly, a person living or working in an environment that is supportive of original thought is more likely to be creative than is a person in an environment that discourages such thought. Being creative is a very different thing to a woman living in Saudi Arabia or Pakistan as compared to a woman living in California or France. And no matter the country, a child growing up in an abusive household may have a more difficult time expressing novel ideas than may a child growing up in a nurturing family.

As with motivation, we are referring to environment here in a very general way. There are also more specific environmental influences to be found at other levels of the model, such as a family that invites study or inquiry in one area, such as music, but not in another, such as engineering; or an environment that contains the tools and materials necessary to one kind of creativity but not another (e.g., if one has an abundance of sports equipment but not any musical instruments, one's environment is more conducive to athletic creativity that to musical creativity).

GENERAL THEMATIC AREAS ("Which theme park shall we go to—the Magic Kingdom, EPCOT, Disney-MGM Studios, or the Animal Kingdom?")

Once at Disney World, you must decide which of the four theme parks you want to go to, because the rides and other attractions one can find in each of the theme parks are very different. To take the elevator up (and down)

---

[4]Motivation also presents a dual aspect in which it may be understood as a general trait in an analytic sense but as a wide range of different domain-specific abilities in an applied sense. See chapter 19 in this volume ("Whence Creativity? Overlapping and Dual-Aspect Skills and Traits") for a more thorough explanation of motivation's dual aspect.

the Tower of Terror, it's no use going to the Magic Kingdom, EPCOT, or the Animal Kingdom—you need to go to Disney-MGM Studios to find the Tower of Terror.

Similarly, every field of creative endeavor is part of a large general thematic area, all of whose component fields share an underlying unity. Our large-scale factor analysis is not complete, but early results have identified at least three very large general thematic areas: creativity in empathy/communication (creativity in the areas of interpersonal relationships, communication, solving personal problems, and writing); "hands-on" creativity (art, crafts, and bodily/physical creativity); and math/science creativity (creativity in math or science; Kaufman & Baer, in press). We find it interesting that these map rather closely to the three factors that Amabile (1989; reported in Ruscio, Whitney, & Amabile, 1998) found for student motivation: writing, art, and problem solving. Provided that an individual has the requisite levels of intelligence and motivation and is in a suitable environment—that he or she has met the initial requirements for any kind of creative activity—then we need next consider in which of these general thematic areas that person is engaged to see if he or she has the necessary skills and traits associated with creativity in that arena.

Some basic differences have emerged at the level of general thematic areas. For example, some skills—such as math or verbal skills—are essential for creative performance in one general thematic area, but not in another. Emotional intelligence, although it may be of some use in all three general thematic areas, may play a larger role in creativity in the area of empathy/communication than in the math/science area.

DOMAINS ("Okay, we're at the Magic Kingdom. Do we want to go to Fantasyland, Adventureland, Liberty Square, Frontierland, Mickey's Toontown Fair, or Tomorrowland?")

Within the Magic Kingdom there are several large sections, each with its own personality and set of related rides and other attractions. Similarly, within each of the general thematic areas there are several more narrowly defined creativity domains. The domain you choose at this point may well have its own specific profile. Let's compare, for example, a creative poet and a creative journalist. Both would fall in the general thematic area of empathy/communication and, indeed, there will likely be many similarities (e.g., both are likely to have strong verbal abilities). However, early research has shown differences in practitioners of these closely related fields (Kaufman, 2002).

For example, based on this research, a journalist may have a different thinking style than a poet may have—a journalist may prefer a more executive thinking style (in which one prefers to follow directions, to carry out orders, and to work under a great deal of structure; see Sternberg, 1997) or a more paradigmatic thinking style (in which one prefers to think in a more logical or scientific manner; see Bruner, 1986). A poet may prefer to think in a more legislative thinking style (in which one prefers to create things and to be self-directed; see Sternberg, 1997) or a more narrative thinking style (in which one prefers to think of possibilities and what "may be"; see Bruner, 1986).

The *type* of motivation is more important at this level—perhaps the poet does his or her most creative writing when working with an intrinsic motivation, whereas the journalist may put forward his or her best and most creative work under a deadline (and perhaps when angling for an above-the-fold story). Also, one's motivation to write may be quite strong for one kind of writing but at the same time weak for another.

Knowledge plays a large role here. Although psychology, sociology, criminal justice, and political science may require many skills in the general thematic area of empathy/communication, the knowledge bases for these four social science subjects are strikingly different, with only modest overlap, as are the knowledge bases that are foundational for work in the life sciences, chemistry, and physics, even though all will require skill in the math/science general thematic area.

Some personality traits may also be particularly useful in some domains (i.e., conscientiousness[5] for scientists) but of negligible importance (or possibly even harmful) in others (i.e., conscientiousness for artists). Similarly, some traits may prove to be related to creative performance in one domain in only a minor way, but at the same time be overwhelmingly important in another (i.e., although openness to experience is of some importance for mathematicians, it is *essential* for artists; see Feist, 1999). Environment also is a component here. As an example, some creative acts require a particular *kind* of nurturing background. A child who wants to play the violin (or take up horseback riding) may be out of luck if his or her family cannot afford lessons. If that child's sibling has an interest in poetry—which requires less of a financial investment to get started—then poverty may be less of an obstacle for him or her. If one is working for Exxon, the working environment may be more conducive to creativity in the domain of geology than in the domain of pure math.

---

[5]Conscientiousness is a mix of organization, persistence, accuracy, discipline, and integrity (Kyllonen, Walters, & Kaufman, 2002).

SPECIFIC TASKS, OR MICRODOMAINS ("This is Tomorrowland—now where is Space Mountain?")

All the rides in Tomorrowland may have something to do with the future, but there is still a big difference between Space Mountain and Buzz Lightyear's Space Ranger Spin. Similarly, even within a domain, although there are many commonalities among all the tasks that are part of that domain, there are still big differences in what one needs to know, and what one needs to know how to do, in order to be creative when undertaking different tasks in that domain.

It's rather like the transition from undergraduate to graduate education. Everyone in a graduate program in psychology may be preparing for a career as a psychologist, but future clinical psychologists, social psychologists, and cognitive psychologists take few of the same courses. Similarly, studying fruit flies intensively for 5 years may help one develop creative theories in one of biology's microdomains but be of little use in another; and practicing on a 12-string guitar may help one perform creatively in some microdomains of the music world but not others. Microdomain-specific motivation may also come into play as well: A poet may love to write haiku but have little interest in writing epic poetry or sonnets.

STRANGE CONNECTIONS: ERRORS IN THE MODEL
("The 3D show *Honey I Shrunk the Audience* at EPCOT was fun, so let's try the Animal Kingdom's 3D show *It's Tough to Be a Bug!*")

This nested hierarchy of microdomains grouped within domains grouped within general thematic areas is tidy, but it is also necessarily incomplete. Just as there are important similarities among the very differently themed roller coasters located in different theme parks, there may occasionally be connections among domains and microdomains in different general thematic areas that will surprise us. In studies with elementary and middle school children, for example, Baer (1993) found relatively small and generally statistically insignificant correlations among the creativity ratings given to different kinds of creative products (including poems, collages, mathematical word problems, equations, and stories), but there was a surprisingly consistent (but as yet unexplained) correlation between creativity in writing poetry and creativity in the microdomain of producing interesting mathematical word problems. This may point to an as-yet undiscovered linkage between these tasks, even though they come from different general thematic areas. Also, there may be what might be called odd-lot connections. For example, if Bill is multitalented but is motivated to do things that will impress Jane—and *only* things that will impress Jane—then the resulting mixed category of creative pursuits in which Bill might become engaged are related (although perhaps only for Bill, unless Jane has other similarly single-minded suitors).

We recognize that the hierarchy that makes up the amusement park theory of creativity is not all-inclusive, but we hope it is *mostly* inclusive, enough that it can provide a broad conceptual framework that will help us better understand creative abilities and guide future research into their nature. We also recognize that the distinctions between levels are fuzzy and that even as the theory is fleshed out these boundaries will in all likelihood remain somewhat fuzzy. Stage theories in developmental psychology tend to describe development in ways that suggest greater discontinuities than we actually observe in child development, in order that we might see patterns in what is otherwise an undifferentiated collection of discrete observations. In a similar way, we hope that the amusement park theory of creativity will allow creativity researchers a clearer vision of the skills, traits, and attributes necessary for creative performance in diverse fields.

REFERENCES

Amabile, T. M. (1989). *The student interest and experience questionnaire.* Unpublished instrument, Brandeis University.

Baer, J. (1993). *Divergent thinking and creativity: A task-specific approach.* Hillsdale, NJ: Lawrence Erlbaum Associates.

Bruner, J. (1986). *Actual minds, possible worlds.* Cambridge, MA: Harvard University Press.

Feist, G. J. (1999). The influence of personality on artistic and scientific creativity. In R. J. Sternberg (Ed.), *Handbook of human creativity* (pp. 273–296). New York: Cambridge University Press.

Getzels, J. W., & Jackson, P. W. (1962). *Creativity and intelligence.* New York: Wiley.

Hollingworth, L. S. (1942). *Children above 180 IQ Stanford-Binet; origin and development.* Yonkers-on-Hudson, NY: World Book.

Kaufman, J. C. (2002). Narrative and paradigmatic thinking styles in creative writing and journalism students. *Journal of Creative Behavior, 36*(3), 201–220.

Kaufman, J. C., & Baer, J. (in press). Sure, I'm creative—but not in math!: Self-reported creativity in diverse domains. *Empirical Studies of the Arts.*

Kyllonen, P. C., Walters, A. M., & Kaufman, J. C. (2002). *Non-cognitive constructs in graduate education: A review and some applications* (graduate record examination). Princeton, NJ: Educational Testing Service.

Renzulli, J. S. (1986). The three-ring conception of giftedness: A developmental model for creativity productivity. In R. J. Sternberg & J. E. Davidson (Eds.), *Conceptions of giftedness* (pp. 53–92). New York: Cambridge University Press.

Ruscio, J., Whitney, D. M., & Amabile, T. M. (1998). Looking inside the fishbowl of creativity: Verbal and behavioral predictors of creative performance. *Creativity Research Journal, 11,* 243–263.

Simonton, D. K. (1994). *Greatness*. New York: Guilford.
Sternberg, R. J. (1997). *Thinking styles*. New York: Cambridge University Press.
Sternberg, R. J., & O'Hara, L. A. (1999). Creativity and intelligence. In R. J. Sternberg (Ed.), *Handbook of creativity* (pp. 251–272). New York: Cambridge University Press.
Winner, E. (1996). *Gifted children: Myths and realities*. New York: Basic Books.

Author Index

A

Abelson, R. P., *211*
Abra, J., 206
Abrahamson, A. A., *299*
Ackoff, R. L., 263
Adamson, G., *63*
Adcock, G. L., 130
Adderholdt-Elliot, M., 5
Adhikurya, R. F., *215*
Affinito, R., *286*
Agor, W. H., 214
Aguirre, G. K., *129*
Ahluwalia, J., *133*
Albert, M. L., *129, 132*, 143
Albert, R. S., 142, 172, *188, 201*
Aldrich, H. E., *253, 255*
Alexander, R. C., *163*
Allen, B., *63*
Allende, I., 11
Alsop, D. C., *129*
Alter, J., 42, 88
Altman, W., *182*
Amabile, T. M., xiii, 3, 24, 27, 29, 65, *91,* 172, 175, 189, 201, 250, *262,* 263, 281, 284, 313, 316, *318,* 324
Ambrose, D., 283, 284, 285, 292

Ambrose, D. C., *188, 201*
Ames, C., 107
Anastasi, A., *144*
Anderson, J. R., *xiii, 201*
Anderson, P., *253, 254, 255*
Anderson, R. E., *197, 199*
Andreason, N., 8
Andrews, F. M., *209*
Andrews, J., *73*
Arad, R., *196*
Arfib, D., 117
Arieti, S., 229
Arlin, P., *285, 292*
Arnheim, R., 231, 232
Arthur, N. B., *209*
Atkinson, G., *31*
Averill, J. R., 229, *231,* 234, 235, 237, *238,* 239
Avolio, B. J., *209, 217*

B

Bachelor, P., *188*
Baer, J., xiii, xiv, 188, 189, 281, 284, 288, 318, 326
Baillargèon, R., 132

Bagley, W. C., 284
Baker, N. R., 262
Baldwin, M., 289, 293
Bandura, A., 5
Barker, A., 110
Barlow, C. M., 209
Barnett, W. P., 251
Baron, R. R., 216
Bar-On, R., 236
Baron-Cohen, S., 133
Barron, A., 27, 87
Barron, F., 3, 5, 6, 27, 62, 87, 188
Barron, F. X., 141
Basadur, M. S., 182, 209, 262, 263, 264, 265, 266, 269, 271, 272
Bass, B. M., 206, 209, 217
Bates, B., 50
Bateson, M. C., 88
Batki, A., 133
Battier, M., 119
Baughman, W. A., 64, 207, 208
Bayer, A. E., 143
Beane, W. E., 141
Beals, M., 94
Bedell, B. T., 236
Behymer, C. E., 142
Belgrad, D., 44
Bell, D., 109
Bell, M. S., 37
Benbow, C. P., 3
Bentler, P. M., 197
Berger, D. E., 208
Berger, R. M., 212, 214
Berry, C., 145
Besemer, S. P., 175, 262
Binford, L. R., 125
Biondi, A. M., 262, 263
Black, W. C., 197, 199
Blackburn, R. T., 142
Blades, M., 128
Blakelock, E., 142
Blaut, J., 128
Bliss, W. D., 144
Block, J., 5
Blom, L. A., 87
Bloom, 3
Bloom, B., 69
Bluedorn, A. C., 213
Boes, J. O., 208
Bogartz, R. S., 132
Bohm, D., 285, 292
Bold, A., 11

Bollen, K. A., 197, 199
Bolton, P., 133
Boodoo, G., 316
Boring, E. G., 144
Boring, M. D., 144
Borko, H., 287
Borland, J. H., 63
Born, G., 112
Bouchard, T. J., 316
Boucouvalas, M., 83
Bowers, J., xiii
Bowman, E. D., 214
Boykin, A. W., 316
Bracey, G. W., 284
Bradley, K. K., 88
Brady, M., 284
Brand, A. G., 33
Brands, H. W., 205
Bray, D. W., 207, 212
Brems, C., 147
Brenneman, L., 124
Brennan, M. A., 88
Brody, N., 316
Brook, P., 46, 50–51
Brooks, F. P., 156
Brown, N., 71, 196, 197
Broyles, S. J., 30
Bruner, J., 325
Bruner, J. S., 173
Bryden, M. P., 128
Buch, E., 105
Burghardt, M. D., 171, 172
Burton, D., 47
Busse, T. V., 142
Byrne, B. M., 197
Byrne, R. W., 124, 127

C

Caf, B., 88
Call, J., 127
Callahan, C., 61, 64
Callahan, S., 264, 266
Campbell, D. P., 145
Campbell, D. T., 52, 246, 247
Campbell, R. S., 207, 212
Camurri, A., 119, 120
Canter, A., 8
Cardinal, L. B., 209
Carey, S., 125, 131

AUTHOR INDEX

Carlsson, B., 269
Carroll, J. B., 301
Carroll, T. N., 246
Carruth, H., 17
Carruthers, P., 134
Carter, K., 294
Caruso, D. R., 236, 237
Castrogiovani, G. T., 211
Cattell, J. M., 145
Cattell, R. B., 3, 143, 145
Caudle, F. M., 47
Ceci, S. J., 316
Chambers, J. A., 145
Chamrad, D. L., 63
Chand, I., 208, 288
Chaplin, L. T., 87
Charles, C. M., 290
Charness, N., 133
Childs, R. A., 207
Chon, K. K., 231
Christensen, C. M., 251, 253, 254, 256, 257
Christensen, P. R., 210, 212, 214
Christiaans, H. H. C. M., 189
Chusmir, K., 207, 212
Clapham, M. M., 171, 182, 183
Clark, G., 60, 63, 64, 72
Clark, R. D., 144
Clark, W. R., 130
Clarke, G., 35
Clemente, F., 142
Clifford, P. I., 172
Clubley, 133
Coan, R. W., 146, 147
Cobb, P., xiii
Cochrane-Smith, M., 293
Cohen, H. F., 110
Cohen, L. A., 188, 201
Cohen, L. M., 284
Cohen, M., 86
Cohen, S. J., 86
Cole, D., 50
Collins, A. M., xiii
Comfort, M., 287
Condon, W. S., 46
Conger, J. A., 209
Connellan, J., 133
Connelly, M. S., 64, 205, 206, 207, 208, 210, 212, 218, 318
Constantinou, C. P., 281, 318
Conti, R., xiii, 201
Conway, J. B., 147
Cook, S. A., 154

Coon, H., xiii, 201
Cooper, C., 182
Cooper, E. E., 129
Copeland, R., 86
Corno, L., 5
Costa, P. T., 5
Costanza, D. P., 208
Cote, R., 65
Court, J. H., 197
Cox, C., 141
Cranberg, L. D., 129, 132
Crandall, R., 142
Crane, D., 144
Crockenberg, S. B., 318
Croft, D., 159, 165
Cronbach, L. J., 139, 146
Cropley, A. J., 171, 173, 175, 177, 178, 183
Cropley, D. H., 175, 183
Cross, J. A., 70
Crozier, R. A., 209
Csikszentmihalyi, M. M., 2, 3, 15, 23, 24, 25–26, 43, 51, 53, 62, 64, 65, 68, 70, 71, 73, 75, 82, 84, 87–88, 172, 208, 240, 246

D

D'Andrea, T., 286
Dabrowski, K., 3
Damanpour, F., 206
Damasio, A. R., 108, 225
Dansereau, F., 206, 217
Dart, L., 284
Davidson, J., 3, 31
Davidson, J. E., 84, 188, 201
Davidson, I., 125
Davidson, R. J., 31
Davis, G. A., 288
Davis, S. N., 188
Dawson, V. L., 286
Day, G. S., 254
Day, M., 60, 66
Dean, J. S., 211
Deci, E. L., 29
Decroupet, P., 6, 114
Deephouse, D. L., 255
Dekker, D. L., 171, 172
Delbanco, N., 44
Dempster, F. N., 289
Dennis, E. S., 130

Dennis, W., 142
De Poli, G., *120*
Deselles, M. C., *214*
Desmond, J. C., *85*, *87*, 89
D'Esposito, M., *129*
Detre, J. A., *129*
Detweiler, J. B., *236*
Dewey, J., 3, 284
Dewhurst, H. D., *217*
DeYoe, E. A., 129
Diakidoy, I. A., *318*
Diakidoy, I. -A. N., D. HH *281*
Diderot, D., 51
Diamond, M., 87
Diana, M., *207*
Diaz de Chumaceiro, C. L., 114
Diaz-Greenberg, R., *289*, *293*
Diepold, J. H., Jr., 89
Dimaggio, P. J., *252*, *255*
Doares, L., *207*
Doerner, D., *212*, *213*
Donald, M., 127
Dorval, K. B., *288*
Dougherty, D., *211*
Dowd, I., 90
Doyle, *211*
Doyle, W., 282, 285, *294*
Drazin, R., *210*, *211*, *253*
Drevdahl, J. E., *143*
Dudek, S. Z., *65*
Dunbar, K., 157
Dunham, L., *209*
Dunn, K., *291*
Dunn, R., *291*
Dunn, R. E., 89–90

E

Eals, M., *128*, *301*
Easteal, S., 130
Eddy, M. H., 90, 98
Edelmann, R. J., *50*, *52*
Efland, A., *73*
Efran, J. S., *139*
Eggen, P. D., *288*
Eiduson, B. T., *145*
Eisenberger, R., *206*, 214, *217*
Eisenman, R., 144
Eisner, E. W., 284
Ekman, P., 49
Elguea, S., *128*

Ellis, J., 205, 210
Ellis, J. H., 162
Ellison, R. L., *145*
Ellspermann, S. J., *264*
Elsbach, K. D., *256*
Epel, N., 28
Epstein, R., *129*
Ericsson, K. A., 141
Erkut, C., *119*
Evans, G. W., 264
Eysenck, H. J., 32

F

Farris, G. F., 208
Fasko, D., *288*
Fave, A. D., 23
Fein, D., *132*, *133*
Fein, L. C., *251*, *252*
Feist, G. J., 134, 142, 143, 144, 218, *325*
Feist, J., 62, 67, 70
Feldhusen, J. F., 61, *63*, *217*, *288*
Feldman, D. H., *2*, 62, 65, *66*, 70, *73*, 188, 189
Fichman, M., *250*
Figart, D. M., *233*
Finke, R. A., 93
Finkelstein, S., 213
Fiol, C. M., *255*
Firestein, R. L., *289*
Fleishman, E. A., *206*, *207*
Flippo, R. F., 284
Florida, R., 240, 241
Fodor, J. A., 124
Foley, J., 130
Ford, C. M., 246, 247, 248, 250, *255*
Fraas, J., *3*
Fragaszy, D., *128*
Franklin, E., 90
Freedman, K., *73*
Freeman, J., *250*, *251*
Freeman, R. E., *209*
Frenkel, K. A., 154
Freud, S., 2
Frick, J. W., *212*
Fried, Y., *249*, *257*
Frosch, W. A., 105
Fullan, M. G., 284

G

Gaddis, B. P., *211*, 216
Gaffney, E., *13*
Gagné, F., 63
Galanter, E., *211*
Gallagher, J. J., 73
Gallagher, S., *287*
Gallagher, T., 14, 15
Gallucci, P., *147*
Galton, F., 141, 145
Garaigordobil-Landazabal, M., 88
Gardner, H., xiv, *2*, 43, 62, 63, 65, 67, 68, 70, 73, 84, 88, 89, 125, 140, 188, 189, 201, 281, 291, 301, 316
Gardner, M., 153
Garner, A., *182*
Garey, M., *154*
Gati, I., *303*
Gaulin, S. J. C., 128
Gavula, N., *287*
Gawain, T. H., 182
Gay, G., 291
Gelade, G., *265*, 271
Gelman, R., 124
Germer, C. K., 139
Gesell, A., *131*
Geslin, Y., 113
Getz, I., *225, 226, 227, 228*
Getzels, J. F., *208*
Getzels, J. W., 62, *65, 68*, 263, *322*
Ghiselin, B., 15, 87
Giddens, A., 246
Gilbert, J. A., *207, 210, 215, 218*
Gillespie, D., 284
Gilmore, M., 31
Gioia, D. A., *246, 255*
Gist, M. E., *141*
Glanz, I., 197
Glasser, W., 290
Glenn, H., *290*
Glisky, M. L., *31*
Glück, L., 15
Gluskinos, U. M., 182
Gluksberg, S., 226
Glynn, M. A., 210, 213, *253*
Godlovitch, S., 46
Goertzel, M. G., *145*
Goertzel, T. G., *145*
Goertzel, V., *145*
Goldsmith, L., *66,* 68, *70, 73*
Goldstine, H., 154, 155, 157
Goleman, D., 32, 36
Golomb, C., 66, 68, 69
Goodall, J., 127
Goodyer, I., *133*
Gopnik, A., 125, 130
Gordon, P. R., *287*
Gordon, W. J., 172
Gordon, W. J. J., 266
Gorman, M. E., *134*
Gottfredson, L. S., 316
Graen, G. B., *182, 263,* 265
Grant, D. C., *207, 212*
Graves, R., 10
Green, J., 88
Green, S. G., *263,* 265
Greenlaw, M. J., *63, 73*
Greeno, J. G., *xiii*
Greer, W. D., *60*
Gregorc, A., 291
Griffin, R., *249, 250*
Griffiths, R., 111
Gruber, H. E., xiv, 62, *66, 71*, 188, 206, 294
Grudin, R., 177
Grunstein, M., *130*
Gryskiewicz, N. D., *262*
Guerin, B., 51
Guilford, J. P., 52, 169, 187, 188, *210, 212, 214,* 261, 263, 302
Gunther, R. E., 254
Gustafson, S. B., *214*
Gutbezahl, J., *235*
Guttman, L., 192, *206*

H

Habegger, A., 6
Hackman, J. R., *206*
Hadamard, J., 52, 163
Hafez, O. M., 48
Hafner, K., 157
Hahn, D. W., *231*
Hair, J. F., Jr., *197, 199*
Hakstain, A. R., *207, 212*
Hall, D. E., *142*
Hallahan, D., *290, 291*
Halpern, D. F., *316*
Hamilton, J. A., 28, 32
Hamman, M., 114
Hammond, J., *50, 52*

Hammond, K. J., 211
Han, K. S., 318
Hannan, M. T., *250*
Hanstein, P., 88
Harding, F. D., *206, 218*
Hardy, B. F., *211*
Harpster, L., 29
Harrington, D. M., *141, 188*
Harrington-Lueker, xiv
Harrison, J., 18
Harrison, P. L., *63*
Hase, K., *141*
Hashimoto, S., *119*
Hawkins, A., 87
Hawkins, E., 87
Hayes-Roth, B., *212, 213*
Hayes-Roth, F., *212,* 213
H'Doubler, M. N., 86, 89
Head, M., *272*
Heath, C., *246, 257*
Heffron, J., 24
Heinz, D., 1, 10
Heller, K. A., *291*
Helmholtz, H. V., 110
Helmreich, R. L., *141,* 145
Hennessey, B. A., 27, 29, *91, 284*
Hequet, M., 171
Herman, V., 47
Heth, C., 85
Higgins, J. M., 171, 173
Highwater, J., 87
Hiipakka, J., *119*
Hill, K. G., *29*
Hillman, J., 6
Hiltzik, M. A., 158, 161, 162
Hirsch, E. D., Jr., xiii, 13
Hitt, M. A., *215*
Hobsbawn, E., 106, 109
Hocevar, D., *188,* 318
Hochschild, A. R., 232, 233
Hodges, A., 154, 162
Hodges, J., 9
Hogan, J., 17
Holland, J. L., 272
Hollingworth, L. S., 322
Holyoak, K. J., *157*
Hong, E., *191*
Hoover, S. M., *61, 63*
Hopper, R., 47
Horenstein, M. N., 171, 172
Horowitz, F. D., *188, 201*
Hoskisson, R. E., *215*

Hosmer, R., 18
House, R. J., *209*
Houts, A., 134
Howell, J. M., *209*
Hoyle, R. H., *199*
Hubel, D. H., *123*
Huenemann, L. F., 85
Huisman, D., 158
Humphrey, D., 87
Hung, S. S., *142*
Hunsaker, S. L., *61, 64*
Hurwitz, A., 63, *66*
Huttley, G. A., 130

I

Inhelder, B., *131*
Isaksen, G. S., *263, 279, 288, 289*
Isen, A. M., 164, 225
Isenberg, D. J., 214
Issacharoff, M., 47

J

Jackson, P. W., *175, 262, 322*
Jacobs, H. H., 289
Jacobs, T. D., *206*
Jacobsen, C., *209*
James, P., 64–65, 72, 143
James, W., 143, 235
Jamison, K. R., 8
Jaques, E., 207, 213
Jay, G., 67
Jefferson, G., *48*
Jenkins, R., 205
Jenkins-Friedman, R., *5*
Jensen, A. R., 316
Jermilin, L. S., 130
Jimerson, J. B., 54
Johnson, D., *154*
Johnson, J. A., *139*
Johnson, J. F., *207*
Johnson, K., *15*
Johnson, M. E., *147*
Johnson, R. A., *215*
Johnson, T. F., *212, 318*
Johnson-Laird, P. N., xiv
Jones, L. S., *290*
Jones, V. F., *290*
Joussemet, M., *284*

AUTHOR INDEX

Joyce, B., *288*
Joyner, W., 31
Jung, C. G., 2, 6

K

Kabanoff, B., *262, 263, 264, 265, 308*
Kacmar, K. M., *216*
Kahai, S. S., *209, 217*
Kahn, R. L., *206*
Kanfer, R., *5*
Kanter, R. M., 290
Kanwisher, N., *129*
Kanungo, R. S., *209*
Karjalainen, M., *119*
Karmiloff-Smith, A., xiv, 124, 125, 130
Kassinger, J. P., *212*
Katz, D., *206*
Kauchak, D. P., *288*
Kaufman, A. S., 63
Kaufman, J. C., xiv, 189, 324, *325*
Kaufmann, G., 214
Kauffman, J., *291*
Kay, A. C., 158
Kazanjian, R. K., *210, 213, 253*
Kealiinohomoku, J., 97
Keane, P., *269*
Keating, J., *289, 293*
Keller, R. T., 216
Kenny, M., 232
Kenworthy, A., *253*, 255
Kerr, W. A., *145*
Kettner, N. W., *210*
Kevles, B., 10
Keysar, B., *226*
Khatena, J., *52*, 63, 64
Kihlstrom, J. F., *31*
Kimble, G. A., 139, 146–147
King, L. A., *30*
Kirkpatrick, S., *209*
Kirton, M. J., *262*
Kizer, C., 10
Knobloch, E., 107, 118
Koberg, E., *207, 212*
Koestner, R., *284*
Kogan, N., *188*, 189
Kolodny, S., 33
Komaki, J. C., 214
Konijn, E. A., 49, 51
Koreck, K. G., *209*
Kounin, J. S., 290

Krainitzki, H., *130*
Kramer, R. M., *256*
Kreemer, C., 86
Kremen, A. M., *5*
Krings, M., *130*
Kroflic, B., *88*
Kuder, G. F., 196
Kuhl, P. K., 125
Kuhn, L., 213
Kuhn, R. L., *213*
Kuhn, T., 115
Kuhn, T. S., 240
Kuipers, B., *212*
Kulp, M., *63*
Kyllonen, P. C., *325F*

L

Laing, D., 106, 109
Lang, R. J., *52*
Langer, E. J., 33
Langer, S. K., 3, 87
Langmeyer, L., *262*
Laurson, M., *119*
Leavitt, H. J., *263*, 264
Lee, C., *141*
Leman, M., *120*
Lehman, H. C., 113, 146
Leonard, L., 11
Leong, F. T. L., *147*
Levertov, D., 14
Levin, B., 292
Levine, P., 18
Levinthal, D. A., *250*
Levitt, B., *253*
Levitt, T., 263
Levy, R. I., 226
Levy, S., 156
Lewin, A. Y., *246*
Livingston, C., *287*
Livingston, J. S., 263
Livne, N. L., *192*, 196, *197*, 199
Livne, O. E., *192, 196, 197*
Locke, E. A., *141, 209*
Loeb, R. C., 67
Loehlin, J. C., *316*
Lohman, D. F., 301
Long, C. P., *246*
Long, C. R., *235*
Long, J. S., *197, 199*
Lotka, A. J., 142

Lott, L., *290*
Louis, M., 87
Lowe, K. B., *209*
Lowenfeld, V., 60
Lubart, T. I., xiv, *5, 8, 16, 59, 61, 64, 72–73, 143*, 206, 207, *209, 225, 226, 227, 228, 265, 305*
Lubart, T. L., *291*
Luca, M., *63*
Lucker, G. W., *141*
Ludwig, A. M., 144, 145
Lutz, C., 234
Lyon, M., 157
Lytle, S. L., *293*

M

MacAdamn, A., 10
Maccoby, M., 210
MacDonald, B., *129*
MacIntosh, M. K., *174*
MacKinnon, D., 5
MacKinnon, D. W., 261
Mackintosh, A. R., 163
Mackler, B., *52*
Mackworth, N. H., 263
Maier, M., *177, 209*
Maier, N. R. F., *209*
Mansfield, R. S., *142*
Maranto, C. L., *142, 145*
March, J. G., 248
Marcus, S., *50*
Marks, M. A., *64, 206, 207, 208, 210, 212, 218, 318*
Marshall-Mies, J. C., *207*
Martin, *133*
Martin, J. A., *207*
Martin, J. B., *269*
Martindale, C., *143*, 226, 240
Martinez-Pons, M., *5*
Martino, G., *65*
Martinsen, O., 291
Marvin, C., *318*
Masi, J. V., 182
Massimini, F., *23*, 32
Matsumoto, D., 234
Matsuzawa, T., 127
Mathews, G., *236*
Matthews, K. A., *141*
Mayer, J. D., *236*, 237
McCarthy, B., 291
McCaulley, M., *3*, 5, *9*
McClure, M., 11
McConkey, K. M., *31*
McCrae, R. R., *5*, 30, 235
McGee, B. P., *287*
McGee, M. C., *207*
McGraw, M., 131
McGrew, W., 127
McIntosh, M. E., *63, 73*
McKelvey, B., 250
McKinney, M. L., 125, *126, 127, 128*
McPherson, G. E., 64
McRay, E. P., *209*
Mead, G., 133
Mednick, S. A., 226
Meltzoff, A. N., 125
Merrifield, P. R., *212*
Merrill, J., 17
Messick, S., *175, 262*
Mestrovic, S. G., 233
Meyer, J. W., *252, 255*
Michael, W. B., *188*
Milbrath, C., 66
Miles, J., 17
Milford, N., 6
Milgram, N. A., 196
Milgram, R. M., 189, 190, 191, 192, *196–197, 211*, 200
Miller, A. I., 178, 282
Miller, G. A., *211*
Mills, H., 18
Mintzberg, H., 213, 214
Mithen, S., 124, 127, 125, 128, 134
Mizruchi, M. S., *251, 252*
Mobley, M. I., *207*
Moertl, P., *216*
Moesel, D. D., *215*
Mönks, F. J., *291*
Montuori, A., *27*, 87
Moore, M. T., *287*, 288
More, T. A., *235*
Morgan, C., *29, 237, 238*
Morrell, D., 28
Morris, E., 205
Morris, J., 81, 83
Moskowitz, A. J., *212*
Mossholder, K. W., *217*
Mott, P. E., 270
Moulin, L., 133, 145
Moyers, B., 8, 16

AUTHOR INDEX

Mumford, M. D., *64, 70,* 71, *205,* 206, *207, 208, 209, 210, 211, 212,* 213, *214,* 215, *216, 217, 218, 318*
Murdock, M. C., *262*
Murmann, J. P., *209*
Murray, R. L., 86
Myers, C. R., 143
Myers, D. G., 292
Myers, I., *3,* 5, *9*
Myers, I. B., 262

N

Nadel, L., *128*
Nagrin, D., 87, 93
Nass, C., 253
Neacsu, G., 50
Neisser, U., *316*
Nelson, J. L., *290*
Nemiro, J., 47, 48, 49, 50, *71, 288*
Nettle, D., 8
Newmann, F. M., *289*
Nigro, G., *299*
Nobel, W., *125*
Noice, H., 48, 49, 214, 217
Noice, T., *48, 49*
Noller, R. B., 262, *263*

O

Ohta, S., *129*
Ogston, W. D., *46*
Okuda, S. M., *208*
Olken, H., 182
O'Brien, M., *188, 201*
O'Hara, L. A., *265,* 291, 322
O'Keefe, J., *129*
Omnès, R., 282
O'Neill, D. V., 88
O'Quin, K., *175, 262*
O'Reilly, *207*
Ornstein, A. C., *287*
Ornstein, R., 32
Ortony, A., 226
Osburn, H. K., *211, 213*
Osgood, C. E., 227
Over, R., 143, 147
Overton, W. F., *139*

P

Pääbo, S., *130*
Paine, S., 66
Pankove, E., *188*
Panter, A. T., *199*
Paradiso, J., 119
Pariser, D., 66, *71,* 74
Parker, J. D. A., *236*
Parker, J. P., 63
Parker, S. T., 125, *126, 127, 128*
Parkerson, J., *144*
Parkhurst, H. B., 65
Parkinson, B., 237
Parloff, M. B., 130
Parnes, S. J., *262, 263*
Patalano, A. L., *211*
Paulenich, C., *15*
Peacock, M., 10
Peacock, W. J., 130
Peat, F. D., 73, 75
Pelletier, S., *294*
Pelz, D. C., *209*
Perez-Fernandez, J. I., 88
Perloff, R., *316*
Perry, S. K., 24
Peterson, N. G., *207*
Piaget, J., *131*
Pichevin, A., 106
Piechowski, M. M., 3
Piirto, J., xiv, 1, 2, 3, 4, 5, 6, 7, 8, 18, *288*
Pinker, S., 125
Pithers, R. T., *287*
Platz, A., 142
Pleiss, M. K., *217*
Plimpton, G., 1, 6, 24
Plucker, J. A., xiii, *188,* 189, 318
Poffenberger, A. T., 145
Policastro, E., 214
Post, F., 144, 145
Powell, W. W., *252, 255,* 257
Pred, R. S., *141*
Prescott, F. C., 14
Prescott, J. B., *174*
Press, C., 88
Press, D. Z., *129*
Preston-Dunlop, V., 86
Pribram, K. H., *211*
Pritzker, S. R., *82*
Puccio, G. J., *262*

Q

Quantance, M. K., 214
Quinn, J. B., 211, *213*

R

Rabkin, L., *196–197*
Rasher, S. P., 141, *144*
Raskin, E. A., 142, 144, 145
Rathunde, K., *3, 26–27*
Raymond, E. S., 156
Raven, J., *197*
Raven, J. C., *197*
Raven, J. C. M. S. C., 197
Reber, D. S., 214
Rechtin, E., *177*
Reciniello, S., 48
Reder, L. M., *xiii, 201*
Redmond, M. R., *208*
Reiter-Palmon, R., *207, 208, 210, 218*
Rejskind, F. G., 282
Renzulli, J. S., 3, 5, *63, 188,* 318, 322
Resnick, L. B., *xiii*
Rhoades, L., *217*
Ricchetti, M., *119*
Rice, G. A., 144
Richards, R., 235
Richardson, M. W., *196*
Richert, E. S., 72
Rickards, T. R., *265*
Rimland, B., *132, 133*
Riney, M., *294*
Risset, J. C., 108, 119
Roberts, R. D., *236, 237*
Robertson, A., 68
Robinson, N. M., *63*
Roche, S. M., *31*
Rodgers, R. C., *142, 145*
Rodgers, E. W., *215*
Roe, A., 141, 145, 172
Roen, D. H., *34*
Rogers, A. M., *287*
Roland, C., 71
Rosen, A. C., *129*
Rosenbloom, G., *196–197*
Rossiter, J. R., *262, 263, 264, 265, 308*
Rossman, J., 172
Rostan, S. M., *66, 71, 208*
Rothenberg, A., 12, 52

Rothman, L. P., *31*
Rousseau, D. M., *249, 257*
Rousseau, J. J., 105
Rovai, E., *142*
Rowan, B., *252, 255*
Rubinstein, M. F., 182
Rugg, H., 3
Rumelhart, D. E., *299*
Runco, M. A., xiv, 71, *82,* 188, 189, 208, *209, 201, 262, 288*
Ruscio, J., 281, 274, 318, 324
Rushton, J. P., 142
Russ, S. W., 27
Russell, J. A., 234
Rutherford, M., *133*
Ryan, R. M., 29
Ryba, K. A., *52*

S

Sabbe, H., 106
Sacks, H., *48*
Salovey, P., *236*
Sansone, C., 29
Santayana, G., 3
Saum, K., 11
Savage-Rumbaugh, S. E., 128
Sawyer, J., *250*
Sawyer, R. K., 41, 43, 44, 46, 48, 53, 54
Scahill, V., *133*
Scaldaferri, N., 110
Scandura, T., 182
Schaefer, C. E., *144*
Schank, R. C., *211*
Schaub, H., *212, 213*
Scheflen, A. E., 46
Schegloff, E., *48*
Schilling, T. H., 132
Schlesinger, J., 8
Schmitz, R. W., *130*
Schoemaker, P. J. H., *254*
Schoonhoven, C. B., *211*
Schubert, D. S. P., 63, *144*
Schubert, H. J. P., *144*
Schultz, R. A., *211, 213*
Schuster, D. H., 182
Schwartz, G. E., *31*
Schwenk, C. R., *209*
Scott, C. L., 286
Scott, G. M., *211, 216*

AUTHOR INDEX

Scott, T. E., 318
Scratchley, L. S., *207, 212*
Seburn, M., *235*
Secada, W. G., *289*
See, C., 27
Seifert, C. M., *211*
Senge, P. M., 290
Sergent, J., 129
Seymour, M., 11
Shamir, B., *209*
Shanock, *206*
Sharfman, M. P., *211*
Sharma, A., 209
Shasha, D., 155, 157, 159, 160
Sheldrake, R., 94, 95
Shepard, R. N., *299,* 302
Shinskey, J. L., *132*
Shontz, F. C., *52*
Shore, B. M., *294*
Short, L., *133*
Silverman, I., *128, 301*
Silverman, L. K., 3, 5
Simon, H. A., *xiii, 201, 248,* 263, 264
Simon, J., *13*
Simonton, D. K., xiv, 24, 52, 105, 133, 134, 139, 140, 141, 142, 143, 144, 145, 146, 147, 214, 246
Simpson, L., 19
Sitarenios, G., *236*
Sitkin, S. B., *246, 257*
Sivasubamaniam, N., *209*
Skinner, *133*
Slater, R., 157, 162, 163
Sloan, K. D., *69*
Smalley, D., 116
Smart, J. C., 143
Smith, A., 125, *133*
Smith, D. K., *163*
Smith, S. I., 13, 93
Snider, J. G., 227
Snowden, S., *128*
Snyder, B., 182
Soden, R., *287*
Sortore, M. R., *70*
Sosik, J. M., *209, 217*
Sosniak, L. A., *69*
Spearman, C., 196, 197
Spear-Swerling, L., *301*
Spelke, E., *125,* 131, *132*
Spence, J. T., *141*
Spencer, C., *128*
Sperber, D., 124

Stariha, W. E., *170*
Starko, A. J., 71, 288
Startwell, C., 232
Staw, B. M., 247
Stea, D., *128*
Steinberg, R. J., *233*
Steiner, C. J., 172
Stephens, J., *128*
Stepien, W., *287*
Sternberg, R. J., *xiv,* 3, *5, 8, 16,* 24, *59, 61,* 62, 63, 64, 65, 71, 72–73, *84, 143,* 170, 178, *188, 201, 226, 265,* 285, 288, 291, 292, 299, 301, 302, 304, 305, 316, 322, 325
Stewart, J. A., 142
Stinchcomb, A. L., 250
Stokes, P. D., 68, 318
Stone, A., *130*
Stone, V., *133*
Stoneking, M., *130*
Storr, A., 18
Stott, C., *133*
Strange, J. M., *209, 210,* 211, *216*
Strouse, J., 205
Strykowski, B. F., *142*
Stucky, N., 47, 48
Stuhr, P., 73
Stumpf, C., 110
Subotnik, R., *291*
Suedfeld, P., 141
Sulloway, F. J., 144
Supinski, E. P., *208*
Suzuki, K., *119*
Sweeney, D. J., *262*
Sweet, J. D., 85
Swentzell, R., *85*

T

Tabor, J. N., 118
Tancig, S., *88*
Tan, A., 26
Tannenbaum, A., 3
Tannenbaum, A. J., *188*
Tatham, R. L., *197,* 199
Tataryn, D. J., *31*
Tartar, B. J., *63*
Taylor, A., *145,* 175
Taylor, C. W., 82, 145
Taylor, M. S., *141*

Teach, R. J., 208
Tellegen, A., 31
Terman, L. M., 145
Terry, W. S., 145
Thackray, J., 171
Thagard, P., 157, 159, 164, 165
Thalbourne, M. A., 9
Thomas, K., 71
Thomas-Knowles, C., 235
Thompson, H., 131
Thor, 215
Thorne, A., 130
Thousand, J., 289, 293
Threlfall, K. V., 207, 208, 210, 218
Thurstone, L. L., 301
Tipton, J., 11
Tobias, B. A., 31
Tollefson, N., 5
Tolonen, T., 119
Tomlinson, C. A., 291
Torrance, E. P., 52, 63–64, 305
Tourangeau, R., 226, 299
Treffinger, D. J., 63, 70, 263, 288, 289
Trocca, R., 119
Tushman, M. L., 207, 209, 253, 254, 255
Tversky, A., 303

U

Uhlman, C. E., 207
Urbina, S., 316
Utterback, J. M., 254

V

Välimäki, V., 119
VanDoorn, J., 211, 215, 216, 217
Van Zelst, R. H., 145
Veitl, A., 113
Vega, L. A., 209, 262
Vernon, D., 63
Vernon, P. E., 63
Visalberghi, E., 128
Volpe, G., 119, 120
Voyer, D., 128
Voyer, S., 128

W

Wagner, M. E., 144

Wakefield, D., 13
Wakefield, J. F., 64, 263
Walberg, H. J., 141, 142, 144, 170
Waldman, A., 10
Walker, L. M., 30
Wall, L., 156, 315
Wallace, D. B., 206
Wallach, M. A., 187, 188, 189
Wallas, G., 82, 263
Walters, A. L., 82, 84
Walters, A. M., 325
Walton, R. E., 206
Wanderley, M., 119
Ward, T. B., 93
Warren, D., 85
Wasserman, S., 132
Watts, A., 98
Wehlage, G. G., 289
Weil, M., 288
Weick, K. E., 246, 247, 283
Weir, C., 29
Weisberg, R. W., 157, 188
West, S. S., 144
Westby, E. L., 286
Whalen, S., 3
Wheeler, D. A., 156
Wheelwright, S., 133
Whitney, D. M., 281, 284, 318, 324
Wiesel, T. N., 123
Wilber, K., 84, 88
Willey, R. L., 34
Williams, W. M., 71, 288
Wilson, B., 68, 69
Wilson, G., 42, 51, 52
Wilson, M., 68, 69
Wilson, S. M., 285
Winkofsky, E., 262
Winner, E., xiv, 63, 65–66, 322
Wispé, L. G., 141, 144, 145
Wojan, T. J., 129
Woodman, R., 250
Woods, D. R., 11, 182

X, Y

Xiao, 211, 212
Yammarino, F. J., 206, 217
Yan, B., 285, 292
Yeats, W. B., 18
Yukl, 206, 207, 211

Z

Zaccaro, S. J., *206, 207, 208, 210, 212, 215, 218, 318*
Zachar, P., *147*
Zeidner, M., *236*
Zhang, L.-F., *291*
Zimmerman, B. J., *5*
Zimmerman, E., *63,* 64, 66, 68, 69, 71, 72, 73, 74
Zölzer, U., 117, 119
Zuckerman, H., 145

Subject Index

C

Convergent thinking, 71, 169–170, 187, 188
Creative problem solving, 9, 70, 72, 73, 143, 156–159, 171, 182, 183, 206–209, 213, 214, 216, 218, 219, 263–264, 268, 310
Creative process, 8–9, 16, 41, 43, 93, 103, 172, 309
  acting, 41, 47, 48–49
  dance, 87
  dreams, 17
  imagination, 14
  inspiration, 9–10
Creative thinking, 64, 71, 74, 159–163, 188, 189, 190, 199, 201, 205–208, 210, 211, 263, 265, 276
Creativity, xiv, 8, 32, 41, 43, 59, 61–62, 63–64, 65, 73, 75, 82, 85, 98, 103, 104, 107, 108, 110, 120–121, 134, 140–141, 143–144, 159–160, 169–170, 172–173, 178, 182, 183, 187–189, 206, 211, 218, 225, 231, 238, 246, 248, 255, 256, 261–262, 263, 271, 277–278, 284, 302, 307–310, 311, 315, 321. *See also* Domains

amusement park theory, 321–327
  domains, 324
  environment, 323
  errors in, 326
  general thematic areas, 323–324
  initial requirements, 322–323
  intelligence, 322
  microdomains, 326
  motivation, 322–323
casual mode, 161–164, 165
functional creativity, 174, 175–182
  aesthetic creativity, 181
  four dimensions, 175–177
  latent functional creativity, 180–182
intense mode, 160–161, 163, 165

D

Divergent thinking, 71, 170, 182, 187, 188–196, 207, 212, 218, 318–319
Domains, 1–19, 23–39, 41–55, 59–75, 81–98, 103–121, 123–135, 139–147, 153–166, 169–184, 187–201, 205–219, 225–241, 245–258, 261–278, 281–294, 299–305, 324

343

Domains *(cont.)*
  acting, 41–55
    anxiety and flow, 51–52
    cognitive process, 52–54
    emotion, 49–51
    group interaction, 54–55
    improvisation, 42, 44, 45–46
    literary fallacy, 42
    personality, 52
    psychology of, 48–54
    scripted acting, 42, 44, 46–48
    stages of creative process, 48–49
  business, 245–258
    creative action, 245
    organizational contexts, 255–257
    selective retention process, 249–255
  computer science, 153–166
    analogies in, 156–159
    comparison with natural science, 164–166
    creativity in, 159–160
      casual mode, 161–164
      intense mode, 160–161
    problems in, 154–156
  dance, 81–98
    culture and creativity, 84–85
    dance improvisation, 92–95
    dance making, 95–97
    dance performance, 89–92
    overview, 83–84
    research, 86–89
  engineering, 169–184
    case study, 178–180
    creative products, 171–175
    fostering creativity in engineers, 182–184
    functional creativity, 175–182
      aesthetic creativity, 181
      four dimensions, 175–177
      latent functional creativity, 180–182
  emotional expression, 225–241
    criteria for creativity, 231–234
    emotional feelings as mediators, 226–228
    emotional syndromes, 228–231
    empirical evidence, 234–238
    generality, 238–240
    implicit theories of emotion, 229–230
    specificity, 238–240
    three models of metaphor formation, 226–227
  fiction, 8, 23–39

    benefits of writing in flow, 23–24
    keys to flow entry, 26–34
      key 1, 26–27
      key 2, 30–32
      key 3, 32
      key 4, 32–33
      key 5, 33–34
    techniques for, 34–38
  leadership, 205–219
    actions, 211–215
    direction, 206–211
    reactions, 215–217
  management, 261–278
    applied creativity, 261, 269–270
    approaches to creativity, 261–262
    cognitive process models, 263
    creativity and occupations, 272–275
    creativity: stages and types, 271–272
    four stages, 265–269
    generators, 276–277
    organizational levels, 275–276
    problem finding, 263–264
    process approach, 262
    solution implementation, 265
  mathematics, 187–201
    ability types and ability levels, 197–199
    general and domain-specific abilities, 192–197
    Milgram 4 × 4 model of the structure of giftedness, 190–192, 197, 198–199
  music, 103–121
    musical creation, 108–113
    musical creativity research, 113–120
    rationalist view, 104, 107–108, 121
    romantic view, 104–107, 121
  physical sciences, 123–135
    developmental evidence, 130–133
    early and automatic expression, 131–132
    evolutionary evidence, 125–130
    comparative, 126–128
    cross-cultural universality, 128
    fossil, 129
    genetic, 129
    neuroscience, 129
    physical creativity, 133–135
    physical knowledge, 124
    precocious talent-giftedness, 132–133
    technical intelligence, 124
  poets, 1–19. *See also* Piirto Pyramid of Talent Development, 3–8
    core attitudes, 3

SUBJECT INDEX

creative process, 8–9
  dreams, 17
  fasting, 15
  flow, 15
  imagination, 14
  improvisation, 16
  inspiration, 9–10
  inspiration of the muse, 10
  inspiration of nature, 11
  inspiration of novel surroundings, 12
  inspiration through substances, 11
  inspiration by works of art and music, 13
  meditation, 15
  quest for silence, 9
  rituals, 9
  solitude, 18
  talent, 5–6
psychology, 139–147
  distinguished scientists, 144–145
  eminent achievers, 140–142, 146
    illustrious psychologists, 145–147
    correlational, 146
    experimental, 146
  intelligence, 141–142
  outstanding creators, 142–144
teaching, 281–294
  overview, 282–285
  skills and dispositions, 285–293
visual arts, 59–75
  art talent development, 70–72
  art teachers, 70–72
  case studies, 68–70
  creative acts of adults, 67–68
  creative acts of children and art students, 64–66
  diversity, 72–74
  gender issues, 66–67
  global issues, 72–74
  IQ, creativity, and achievement tests, 63–64
  postmodern, 72–74
Domain generality, 43, 83, 188–196, 200, 238–240, 299–305, 307–312, 313
  hybrid conceptualization, 307
  multidimensional representations, 302–304
  representation and process, 301–302
  spatial representational model, 299–301

Domain specificity, xiv, 43, 83, 124, 125, 130, 141, 188–189, 196, 199, 200, 238–240, 299–305, 307–312, 313
  amusement park theory, 321–327
  hybrid conceptualization, 307

F

Flow, 9, 15, 23–34, 26–39, 84, 310
  acting, 51–52
  benefits of writing in flow, 23–24
  group flow, 54
  keys to flow entry, 26–34
    key 1, 26–27
    key 2, 30–32
    key 3, 32
    key 4, 32–33
    key 5, 33–34
  music, 36
  techniques for, 34–38

G

Gifted, 61–62, 63, 132–133, 141, 188, 190–192

I

Inspiration, 9–10, 24, 33–34
  dreams, 17
Intelligence, 5, 61, 62, 63–64, 141–142, 146, 160, 169–170, 172, 196–198, 239, 315–316, 322
  IQ and achievement tests, 63–64, 141, 200
  intelligence-creativity, 187, 239
  emotional intelligence, 236–237
  multiple intelligence, 43, 301
  successful intelligence, 302

M

Motivation, 3, 146, 160, 315–319, 322–323, 325
  extrinsic, 29, 284
  intrinsic, 26, 29, 284, 290, 291
  in writing, 27, 28

O, P

Oceanic consciousness. *See* Flow
Personality, 3–5, 52, 67, 70, 235, 325
   big five personality, 5, 235
   personality traits, 133, 144–145, 239, 313, 314
     in actors, 52
     in arts, 66–67, 74
     in writers, 30–32
     in physical sciences, 133–135
Piirto Pyramid of Talent Development, 3–8
   aspect of talent in domains, 5
   cognitive aspect, 5
   emotional aspect, 3
   The Thorn: The Notion of a "Calling," 6
   the five suns, 7
     sun of chance, 4, 7–8
     sun of community and culture, 4, 7
     sun of gender, 4, 8
     sun of home, 4, 7
     sun of school, 4, 7
   genetic aspect, 3

S, T

Skills, 313–319
Talent, 5–6, 61–62, 65–66, 70–72, 74, 123–133, 134, 188
   talent development, 70
     Piirto Pyramid of Talent Development, 3–8

V

Visitation of the muse. *See* Flow